Eric Tyson's Keys to Personal Financial Success

- **Take charge of your finances.** Procrastinating is detrimental to your long-term financial health. Don't wait for a crisis or major life event to get your act together. Read this book and start implementing a plan now!

- **Don't buy consumer items (cars, clothing, vacations, and so on) that lose value over time on credit.** Use debt only to make investments in things that gain value, such as real estate, a business, or an education.

- **Use credit cards only for convenience, not for carrying debt.** If you have a tendency to run up credit-card debt, then get rid of your cards and use only cash, checks, and debit cards.

- **Live within your means and don't try to keep up with your co-workers, neighbors, and peers.** Many who engage in conspicuous consumption are borrowing against their future; some end up bankrupt.

- **Save and invest at least 5 to 10 percent of your income.** Preferably, invest through a retirement savings account to reduce your taxes and ensure your future financial independence.

- **Understand and use your employee benefits.** If you're self-employed, find the best investment and insurance options available to you and use them.

- **Research before you buy.** Never purchase a financial product or service on the basis of an advertisement or salesperson's solicitation.

- **Avoid financial products that carry high commissions and expenses.** Companies that sell their products through aggressive sales techniques generally have the worst financial products and the highest fees and commissions.

- **Don't purchase any financial product that you don't understand.** Ask questions and compare what you're being offered to what you can get from the best sources, which I recommend in this book.

- **Invest the majority of your long-term money in ownership vehicles that have appreciation potential, such as stocks, real estate, and your own business.** When you invest in bonds or bank accounts, you're simply lending your money to others, and the return you earn probably won't keep you ahead of inflation and taxes.

- **Avoid making emotionally based financial decisions.** For example, investors who panic and sell their stock holdings after a major market correction miss a buying opportunity. Be especially careful in making important financial decisions after a major life change, such as a divorce, job loss, or death in your family.

- ✔ **Make investing decisions based upon your needs and the long-term fundamentals of what you're buying.** Ignore the predictive advice offered by financial prognosticators — nobody has a working crystal ball. Don't make knee-jerk decisions based on news headlines.

- ✔ **Own your home.** In the long run, owning is more cost-effective than renting, unless you have a terrific rent-control deal. But don't buy until you can stay put for a number of years.

- ✔ **Purchase broad insurance coverage to protect against financial catastrophes.** Eliminate insurance for small potential losses.

- ✔ **If you're married, make time to discuss joint goals, issues, and concerns.** Be accepting of your partner's money personality; learn to compromise and manage as a team.

- ✔ **Prepare for life changes.** The better you are at living within your means and anticipating life changes, the better off you will be financially and emotionally.

- ✔ **Read publications that have high quality standards and that aren't afraid to take a stand and recommend what's in your best interests.** Avoid those that base their content on the hottest financial headlines or the whims of advertisers.

- ✔ **Prioritize your financial goals and start working toward them.** Be patient. Focus on your accomplishments and learn from your mistakes.

- ✔ **Hire yourself first.** You are the best financial person that you can hire. If you need help making a major decision, hire conflict-free advisors who charge a fee for their time. Work in partnership with advisors — don't abdicate control.

- ✔ **Invest in yourself and others.** Invest in your education, your health, and your relationships with family and friends. Having a lot of money isn't worth much if you don't have your health and people with whom to share your life. Give your time and money to causes that better our society and world.

Praise for Eric Tyson

"Eric Tyson is doing something important — namely, helping people at all income levels to take control of their financial futures. This book is a natural outgrowth of Tyson's vision that he has nurtured for years. Like Henry Ford, he wants to make something that was previously accessible only to the wealthy accessible to middle-income Americans."

> — James C. Collins, coauthor of the national bestsellers
> *Built to Last* and *Good to Great*

"*Personal Finance For Dummies* is the perfect book for people who feel guilty about inadequately managing their money but are intimidated by all of the publications out there. It's a painless way to learn how to take control."

> — Karen Tofte, producer, National Public Radio's
> *Sound Money*

"Eric Tyson . . . seems the perfect writer for a . . .*For Dummies* book. He doesn't tell you what to do or consider doing without explaining the why's and how's — and the booby traps to avoid — in plain English. . . . It will lead you through the thickets of your own finances as painlessly as I can imagine."

> — *Chicago Tribune*

"This book provides easy-to-understand personal financial information and advice for those without great wealth or knowledge in this area. Practitioners like Eric Tyson, who care about the well-being of middle-income people, are rare in today's society."

> — Joel Hyatt, founder of Hyatt Legal Services, one of
> the nation's largest general-practice personal legal
> service firms

"Worth getting. Scores of all-purpose money-management books reach bookstores every year, but only once every couple of years does a standout personal finance primer come along. *Personal Finance For Dummies,* by financial counselor and columnist Eric Tyson, provides detailed, action-oriented advice on everyday financial questions. . . . Tyson's style is readable and unintimidating."

> — Kristin Davis, *Kiplinger's Personal Finance* magazine

"This is a great book. It's understandable. Other financial books are too technical and this one really is different."

> — Business Radio Network

More Bestselling For Dummies Titles by Eric Tyson

Investing For Dummies®

A Wall Street Journal bestseller, this book walks you through how to build wealth in stocks, real estate, and small business as well as other investments. Also check out the recently released *Investing in Your 20s and 30s For Dummies*.

Mutual Funds For Dummies®

This best-selling guide is now updated to include current fund and portfolio recommendations. Using the practical tips and techniques, you'll design a mutual fund investment plan suited to your income, lifestyle, and risk preferences.

Personal Finance in Your 20s For Dummies®

This hands-on, friendly guide provides you with the targeted financial advice you need to establish firm financial footing in your 20s and to secure your finances for years to come. When it comes to protecting your financial future, starting sooner rather than later is the smartest thing you can do.

Home Buying For Dummies®

America's #1 real-estate book includes coverage of online resources in addition to sound financial advice from Eric Tyson and frontline real-estate insights from industry veteran Ray Brown. Also available from America's best-selling real-estate team of Tyson and Brown — *House Selling For Dummies* and *Mortgages For Dummies*.

Real Estate Investing For Dummies®

Real estate is a proven wealth-building investment, but many people don't know how to go about making and managing rental property investments. Real-estate and property management expert Robert Griswold and Eric Tyson cover the gamut of property investment options, strategies, and techniques.

Personal Finance FOR DUMMIES®
A Wiley Brand
8th Edition

by Eric Tyson, MBA

Personal Finance For Dummies®, 8th Edition

Published by
John Wiley & Sons, Inc.
111 River St.
Hoboken, NJ 07030-5774
www.wiley.com

Published by John Wiley & Sons, Inc., Hoboken, New Jersey

Published simultaneously in Canada

For general information on our other products and services, please contact our Customer Care Department within the U.S. at 877-762-2974, outside the U.S. at 317-572-3993, or fax 317-572-4002. For technical support, please visit www.wiley.com/techsupport.

Wiley publishes in a variety of print and electronic formats and by print-on-demand. Some material included with standard print versions of this book may not be included in e-books or in print-on-demand. If this book refers to media such as a CD or DVD that is not included in the version you purchased, you may download this material at http://booksupport.wiley.com. For more information about Wiley products, visit www.wiley.com.

Library of Congress Control Number: 2015956233

ISBN 978-1-119-11429-1 (pbk); ISBN 978-1-119-11417-8 (ebk); ISBN 978-1-119-11413-0 (ebk)

Manufactured in the United States of America

10 9 8 7

Contents at a Glance

Table of Contents

Part III: Building Wealth through Investing................. 143

Chapter 8: Considering Important Investment Concepts............145

Introduction

You're probably not a personal finance expert, for good reason. Historically, Personal Finance 101 hasn't been offered in our schools — not in high school, college, or even graduate programs. Thankfully, a small but growing number of schools have begun offering personal-finance-type courses; some even use *Personal Finance For Dummies* as a textbook.

However, even if you got some financial education and acquired some financial knowledge over the years, you're likely a busy person who doesn't have enough hours in the day to get everything done. Thus, you want to know how to diagnose your financial situation efficiently (and painlessly) to determine what you should do next. Unfortunately, after figuring out which financial strategies make sense for you, choosing specific financial products in the marketplace is often overwhelming. You have literally thousands of investment, insurance, and loan options to choose from. Talk about information overload!

To further complicate matters, you probably hear about most products through advertising that can be misleading, if not downright false. Of course, some ethical and outstanding firms advertise, but so do those that are more interested in converting your hard-earned income and savings into their short-term profits. And they may not be here tomorrow when you need them.

Perhaps you've ventured online and been attracted to the promise of "free" advice. Unfortunately, discerning the expertise and background (and even identity) of those behind various blogs and websites is nearly impossible. And, as I discuss in this book, conflicts of interest (many of which aren't disclosed) abound online.

Despite the development of new media and new financial products and services, folks keep making the same common financial mistakes — procrastinating and lack of planning, wasteful spending, falling prey to financial salespeople and pitches, failing to do sufficient research before making important financial decisions, and so on. This book can keep you from falling into the same traps and get you going on the best paths.

As unfair as it may seem, numerous pitfalls await you when you seek help for your financial problems. The world is filled with biased and bad financial advice. As a former practicing financial counselor and now as a writer, I constantly see and hear about the consequences of poor advice. All too often, financial advice ignores the big picture and focuses narrowly on investing. Because money is not an end in itself but a part of your whole life, this book helps connect your financial goals and challenges to the rest of your life. You need a broad understanding of personal finance that includes all areas of your financial life: spending, taxes, saving and investing, insurance, and planning for major goals like education, buying a home, and retirement.

Even if you understand the financial basics, thinking about your finances in a holistic way can be difficult. Sometimes you're too close to the situation to be objective. Your finances may reflect the history of your life more than they reflect a comprehensive plan for your future.

You want to know the best places to go for your circumstances, so this book contains specific, tried-and-proven recommendations. I also suggest where to turn next if you need more information and help.

About This Book

You selected wisely in picking up a copy of *Personal Finance For Dummies,* 8th Edition! Over two million copies of prior editions of this book are in print, and as you can see from the quotes in the front of this edition, readers and reviewers alike have been pleased. This book also previously earned the prestigious Benjamin Franklin Award for best book of the year in business.

However, I never rest on my laurels. So the book you hold in your hands reflects more hard work and brings you the freshest material for addressing your personal financial quandaries. Here are some of the updates I've made to the book:

- Updated coverage of the best ways to get the most for your spending

- Expanded information regarding smart ways to minimize the cost of and eliminate consumer debt, use credit, and qualify for the best loan terms, as well as how to improve your credit scores

- Coverage of new and revised tax laws, pending and likely future tax law changes, and how to best take advantage of them

- The latest information on government assistance programs, Social Security, and Medicare and what it means in terms of how you should prepare for and live in retirement

- Updated investment recommendations for exchange-traded funds, mutual funds, real estate, and more

- Revised recommendations for where to get the best insurance deals and info on how government mandated health insurance has changed coverage options and costs

- Expanded and updated coverage of how to use and make sense of the news and financial resources (especially online resources)

Aside from being packed with updated information, another great feature of this book is that you can read it from cover to cover if you want, or you can read each chapter and part without having to read what comes before. Handy cross-references direct you to other places in the book for more details on a particular subject. If you like, you can skip the sidebars (shaded boxes) and text marked with the Technical Stuff icon; that info is interesting but nonessential.

Foolish Assumptions

In writing this book, I made some assumptions about you, dear reader:

- ✔ You want expert advice about important financial topics (such as paying off and reducing the cost of debt, planning for major goals, making wise investments), and you want answers quickly.

- ✔ You want a crash course in personal finance and are looking for a book you can read cover-to-cover to help solidify major financial concepts and get you thinking about your finances in a more comprehensive way.

This book is basic enough to help novices get their arms around thorny financial issues. But it challenges advanced readers as well to think about their finances in a new way and identify areas for improvement.

Icons Used in This Book

The icons in this book help you find particular kinds of information that may be useful to you.

This target flags strategy recommendations for making the most of your money.

This icon highlights the best financial products in the areas of investments, insurance, and so on. These products can help you implement my strategy recommendations.

This icon points out information that you'll definitely want to remember.

This icon marks things to avoid and points out common mistakes people make when managing their finances.

This icon alerts you to scams and scoundrels who prey on the unsuspecting.

This icon tells you when you should consider doing some additional research. I explain what to look for and what to look out for.

This nerdy-looking guy appears beside discussions that aren't critical if you just want to understand basic concepts and get answers to your financial questions. You can safely ignore these paragraphs, but reading them can help deepen and enhance your personal financial knowledge.

Beyond the Book

In addition to the material in the print or e-book you're reading right now, this product also comes with some access-anywhere goodies on the web. Check out these features:

- ✔ **Cheat Sheet (`www.dummies.com/cheatsheet/personalfinance`):** Check out a list of pointers that can help you think about the role of money in your life and start achieving your financial goals.

- ✔ **Dummies.com articles (`www.dummies.com/extras/personal finance`):** You can also find relevant online articles that supplement each part in this book with additional tips and techniques. Read helpful articles that explain how to keep your wits during uncertain investing times, how to make sure the insurance company you use is financially stable, and more.

Where to Go from Here

This book is organized so you can go wherever you want to find complete information. Want advice on investing strategies, for example? Go to Part III for that. You can check out the table of contents to find broad categories of information and a chapter-by-chapter rundown of what this book offers, or you can look up a specific topic in the index.

If you're not sure where you want to go, you may want to start at the beginning with Part I. It gives you all the basic info you need to assess your financial situation and points to places where you can find more detailed information for improving it.

Part I

Getting Started with Personal Finance

In this part . . .

- ✔ Understand your financial literacy.
- ✔ Assess your current personal financial health.
- ✔ Determine where your money is going.
- ✔ Set and accomplish personal and financial goals.

Chapter 1

Improving Your Financial Literacy

In This Chapter

▶ Looking at what your parents and others taught you about money

▶ Questioning reliability and objectivity

▶ Overcoming real and imagined barriers to financial success

*I*n recent years, a continuing stream of studies has indicated that Americans are by and large financially illiterate. The vast majority of survey respondents have "failing" scores — meaning that they answered less than 60 percent of the questions correctly.

I know from my many years of work previously as a personal financial counselor and teacher and now as a writer that many folks do indeed have significant gaps in their personal financial knowledge. Though more folks have greater access today to more information than in prior generations, the financial world has grown more complicated, and there are more choices, and pitfalls, than ever before.

Unfortunately, most Americans don't know how to manage their personal finances because they were never taught how to do so. Their parents may have avoided discussing money in front of them, and most high schools and colleges lack courses that teach this vital, lifelong-needed skill.

Some people are fortunate enough to learn the financial keys to success at home, from knowledgeable friends, and from the best expert-written books like this one. Others either never discover important personal finance concepts, or they learn them the hard way — by making lots of costly mistakes. People who lack knowledge make more mistakes, and the more financial errors you commit, the more money passes through your hands and out of your life. In addition to the enormous financial costs, you experience the emotional toll of not feeling in control of your finances. Increased stress and anxiety go hand in hand with not mastering your money.

This chapter examines where people learn about finances and helps you decide whether your current knowledge is helping you or holding you back. You can find out how to improve your financial literacy and take responsibility for your finances, putting you in charge and reducing your anxiety about money. After all, you have more important things to worry about, like what's for dinner.

Talking Money at Home

I was fortunate — my parents taught me a lot of things that have been invaluable throughout my life, and among those things were sound principles for earning, spending, and saving money. My parents had to know how to do these things, because they were raising a family of three children on (usually) one modest income. They knew the importance of making the most of what you have and of passing that vital skill on to your kids.

However, my parents' financial knowledge did have some gaps. I observed firsthand the struggles my late father endured handling some retirement money after being laid off from a job when I was in middle school. In subsequent years, this situation propelled me to learn about investing to help myself, my family, and others.

In many families money is a taboo subject — parents don't level with their kids about the limitations, realities, and details of their budgets. Some parents I talk with believe that dealing with money is an adult issue and that children should be insulated from it so they can enjoy being kids. In many families, kids hear about money *only* when disagreements and financial crises bubble to the surface. Thus begins the harmful cycle of children having negative associations with money and financial management.

In other cases, parents with the best of intentions pass on their bad money-management habits. You may have learned from a parent, for example, to buy things to cheer yourself up. Or you may have witnessed a family member maniacally chasing get-rich-quick business and investment ideas. Now I'm not saying that you shouldn't listen to your parents. But in the area of personal finance, as in any other area, poor family advice and modeling can be problematic.

Think about where your parents learned about money management and then consider whether they had the time, energy, or inclination to research choices before making their decisions. For example, if they didn't do enough research or had faulty information, your parents may mistakenly have thought that banks were the best places for investing money or that buying stocks was like going to Las Vegas. (You can find the best places to invest your money in Part III of this book.)

In still other cases, the parents have the right approach, but the kids do the opposite out of rebellion. For example, if your parents spent money carefully and thoughtfully and often made you feel denied, you may tend to do the opposite, buying yourself gifts the moment any extra money comes your way.

Although you can't change what the educational system and your parents did or didn't teach you about personal finances, you now have the ability to find out what you need to know to manage your finances.

If you have children of your own, don't underestimate their potential or send them out into the world without the skills they need to be productive and happy adults. Buy them some good financial books when they head off to college or begin their first job.

Personal finance at school

In schools, the main problem with personal finance education is the lack of classes, not that kids already know the information or that the skills are too complex for children to understand.

Nancy Donovan teaches personal finance to her fifth-grade math class as a way to illustrate how math can be used in the real world. "Students choose a career, find jobs, and figure out what their taxes and take-home paychecks will be. They also have to rent apartments and figure out a monthly budget," says Donovan. "Students like it, and parents have commented to me how surprised they are by how much financial knowledge their kids can handle." Donovan also has her students invest $10,000 (play money) and then track their investments' performance.

Urging schools to teach the basics of personal finance is just common sense. Children need to be taught how to manage a household budget, the importance of saving money for future goals, and the consequences of overspending. Unfortunately, few schools offer classes like Donovan's. In most cases, the financial basics aren't taught at all.

In the minority of schools that do offer a course remotely related to personal finance, the class is typically in economics (and an elective at that). "Archaic theory is being taught, and it doesn't do anything for the students as far as preparing them for the real world," says one high school principal I know. Having taken more than my fair share of economics courses in college, I understand the principal's concerns.

Some people argue that teaching children financial basics is the parents' job. However, this well-meant sentiment is what we're relying on now, and for all too many, it isn't working. In some families, financial illiteracy is passed on from generation to generation.

Education takes place in the home, on the streets, and in the schools. Therefore, schools must bear some responsibility for teaching this skill. However, if you're raising children, remember that no one cares as much as you do or has as much ability to teach the important life skill of personal money management.

Identifying Unreliable Sources of Information

Most folks know that they're not financial geniuses. So they set out to take control of their money matters by reading about personal finance or consulting a financial advisor.

But reading and seeking advice to find out how to manage your money can be dangerous if you're a novice. Misinformation can come from popular and seemingly reliable information sources, as I explain in the following sections. (Because the pitfalls are numerous and the challenges significant when choosing an advisor, I devote Chapter 18 to the financial planning business and tell you what you need to know to avoid being duped and disappointed.)

Understanding the dangers of free financial content online

In addition to being able to quickly access what we want, the other major attraction of the Internet is the abundance of seemingly free websites providing piles of free content. Appearances, however, can be greatly deceiving.

While there are exceptions to any rule, the fact of the matter is that the vast majority of websites purporting to provide a seemingly never-ending array of "free" content are rife with conflicts of interest and quality problems due to the following:

✔ **Advertising:** Any publication that accepts advertising has a potential conflict of interest because it may not want to publish articles that would upset its advertisers. Such a mindset, however, can stand in the way of telling consumers the unvarnished truth about various products and services. For example, auto leasing companies aren't very interested in advertising someplace that publishes articles highlighting the negatives of leasing. (Check out the section "Publishers pandering to advertisers" later in this chapter for more on the power of advertising to influence the financial information you encounter online, on TV, and elsewhere.)

✔ **Advertorials:** Too many website owners are unwilling or unable to pay real writers for quality content and instead publish articles that are written and provided by advertisers. These pieces of "content" are known as *advertorials* and, in the worst cases, aren't even clearly labeled as advertisements, which is precisely what they are.

✔ **Affiliate relationships:** Many companies now pay "referral fees" to websites that bring in new customers. Here's how that practice causes major conflicts of interest. On a financial website, you read a glowing review of a particular financial product or service. And the site provides a helpful link to the website of the provider of that product or service. Unbeknownst to you, when you click on that link and buy something, the seller kicks money back to the "affiliate" who reeled you in. At a minimum, such relationships should be clearly disclosed and detailed in any review.

✔ **Insufficient editorial oversight:** At most established, quality print publications, there are usually several layers of editors who oversee the publication and all of its articles. This structure helps ensure the accuracy of what gets into print (although bias, such as political bias, isn't necessarily controlled). Unfortunately, the shoestring budget on which many websites operate precludes these quality control checks and balances. Thus, sites operated by non-experts proffering advice place you at great risk.

✔ **Lack of accountability:** In part because of a lack of editorial oversight, there's also often a lack of accountability for advice given online. This situation is especially problematic on the numerous sites that are run without disclosure of who is actually in charge of the site and/or who is writing the articles. Although such anonymity may be helpful to the site and its content providers, it's certainly not in your best interests because it prevents you from checking out the background, qualifications, and track record of the providers.

Recognizing fake financial gurus

Before you take financial advice from anyone, examine her background, including professional work experience and education credentials. This is true whether you're getting advice from an advisor, writer, talk show host, or TV financial reporter.

If you can't easily find such information, that's usually a red flag. People with something to hide or a lack of something redeeming to say about themselves usually don't promote their background.

Of course, just because someone seems to have a relatively impressive-sounding background doesn't mean that she has your best interests in mind or has honestly presented her qualifications. *Forbes* magazine journalist

William P. Barrett presented a sobering review of financial author Suze Orman's stated credentials and qualifications:

> "Besides books and other royalties, Orman's earned income has come mainly from selling insurance — which gets much more attention in her book than do stocks or bonds. . . . The jacket of her video says she has '18 years of experience at major Wall Street institutions.' In fact, she has 7."

When the *Forbes* piece came out, Orman's publicist tried to discredit it and made it sound as if the magazine had falsely criticized Orman. In response, the *San Francisco Chronicle,* which is the nearest major newspaper to Orman's hometown, picked up on the *Forbes* piece and ran a story of its own — written by Mark Veverka in his "Street Smarts" column — which substantiated the *Forbes* story.

Veverka went through the *Forbes* piece point by point and gave Orman's company and the public relations firm numerous opportunities to provide information contrary to the piece, but they did not. Here's some of what Veverka recounts from his contact with them:

> "If you want your side told, you have to return reporters' telephone calls. But alas, no callback.

> ". . . Orman's publicist said a written response to the *Forbes* piece and the 'Street Smarts' column would be sent by facsimile to the *Chronicle*. . . . However, no fax was ever sent. They blew me off. Twice.

> "In what was becoming an extraordinary effort to be fair, I placed more telephone calls over several days to Orman Financial and the publicist, asking for either an interview with Orman or an official response. If Orman didn't fudge about her years on Wall Street or didn't let her commodity-trading adviser license lapse, surely we could straighten all of this out, right?

> "Still, no answer. Nada . . . I called yet again. Finally, literally on deadline, a woman who identified herself as Orman's 'consultant' called me to talk 'off the record' about the column. What she ended up doing was bashing the *Forbes* piece and my column but not for publication. More importantly, she offered no official retort to allegations made by veteran *Forbes* writer William Barrett. I have to say, it was an incredibly unprofessional attempt at spinning. And I've been spun by the worst of them."

You can't always accept stated credentials and qualifications at face value, because some people lie (witness the billions lost to hedge fund Ponzi-scheme-man Bernie Madoff). You can't sniff out liars by the way they look, their resume, their gender, or their age. You can, however, increase your chances of being tipped off by being skeptical (and by regularly reading the "Guru Watch" section of my website at www.erictyson.com).

You can see a number of hucksters for what they are by using common sense in reviewing some of their outrageous claims. Some sources of advice, such as Wade Cook's investment seminars, lure you in by promising outrageous returns. The stock market has generated average annual returns of about 9 to 10 percent over the long term. However, Cook, a former taxi driver, promoted his seminars as an "alive, hands-on, do the deals, two-day intense course in making huge returns in the stock market. If you aren't getting 20 percent per month, or 300-percent annualized returns on your investments, you need to be there." (I guess I do, as does every investment manager and individual investor I know!)

Cook's get-rich-quick seminars, which cost more than $6,000, were so successful at attracting people that his company went public in the late 1990s and generated annual revenues of more than $100 million. Cook's "techniques" included trading in and out of stocks and options after short holding periods of weeks, days, or even hours. His trading strategies can best be described as techniques that are based upon technical analysis — that is, charting a stock's price movements and volume history, and then making predictions based on those charts.

The perils of following an approach that advocates short-term trading with the allure of high profits are numerous:

- ✔ You'll rack up enormous brokerage commissions.

- ✔ On occasions where your short-term trades produce a profit, you'll pay high ordinary income tax rates rather than the far lower capital gains rate for investments held more than 12 months.

- ✔ You won't make big profits — quite the reverse. If you stick with this approach, you'll underperform the market averages.

- ✔ You'll make yourself a nervous wreck. This type of trading is gambling, not investing. Get sucked up in it, and you'll lose more than money — you may also lose the love and respect of your family and friends.

If Cook's followers were able to indeed earn the 300 percent annual returns his seminars claimed to help you achieve, any investor starting with just $10,000 would vault to the top of the list of the world's wealthiest people (ahead of Bill Gates and Warren Buffett) in just 11 years!

How some gurus become popular

You may be wondering how Wade Cook became so popular despite the obvious flaws in his advice (see the section "Recognizing fake financial gurus" for the goods on Cook). He promoted his seminars through infomercials and other advertising, including radio ads on respected news stations. The high stock market returns of the 1990s brought greed back into fashion. (My experience has been that you see more of this greed near market tops.)

The attorneys general of numerous states sued Cook's company and sought millions of dollars in consumer refunds. The suits alleged that the company lied about its investment track record (not a big surprise — this company claimed that you'd make 300 percent per year in stocks!).

Cook's company settled the blizzard of state and Federal Trade Commission (FTC) lawsuits against his firm by agreeing to accurately disclose its trading record in future promotions and give refunds to customers who were misled by past inflated return claims. (That didn't stop Cook, however, from getting into more legal hot water — and serving a seven-year prison term for failing to pay millions in personal income taxes.)

According to a news report by *Bloomberg News,* Cook's firm disclosed that it lost a whopping 89 percent of its own money trading during one year in which the stock market fared well. As Deb Bortner, director of the Washington State Securities Division and president of the North American Securities Administrators Association, observed, "Either Wade is unable to follow his own system, which he claims is simple to follow, or the system doesn't work."

Don't assume that someone with something to sell, who is getting good press and running lots of ads, will take care of you. That "guru" may just be good at press relations and self-promotion. Certainly, talk shows and the media at large can and do provide useful information on a variety of topics, but bad eggs sometimes turn up. These bad eggs may not always smell bad up-front. In fact, they may hoodwink people for years before finally being exposed. Please review Part V for the details on resources you can trust and those that could cause you to go bust!

Publishers pandering to advertisers

Thousands of publications and media outlets — newspapers, magazines, websites, blogs, radio, TV, and so on — dole out personal financial advice and perspectives. Although some of these "service providers" collect revenue from subscribers, virtually all are dependent — in some cases, fully dependent (especially the Internet, radio, and TV) — on advertising dollars. Although advertising is a necessary part of capitalism, advertisers can taint and, in some cases, dictate the content of what you read, listen to, and view.

Be sure to consider how dependent a publication or media outlet is on advertising. I find that "free" publications, websites/blogs, radio, and TV are the ones that most often create conflicts of interest by pandering to advertisers. (All derive all their revenue from advertising.)

Much of what's on the Internet is advertiser-driven as well. Many of the investing sites on the Internet offer advice about individual stocks. Interestingly, such sites derive much of their revenue from online brokerage firms seeking to recruit customers who are foolish enough to believe that selecting their own stocks is the best way to invest. (See Part III for more information about your investment options.)

As you read various publications, watch TV, or listen to the radio, note how consumer-oriented these media are. Do you get the feeling that they're looking out for your interests? For example, if lots of auto manufacturers advertise, does the media outlet ever tell you how to save money when shopping for a car or the importance of buying a car within your means? Or are they primarily creating an advertiser-friendly broadcast or publication?

Jumping over Real and Imaginary Hurdles to Financial Success

Perhaps you know that you should live within your means, buy and hold sound investments for the long term, and secure proper insurance coverage; however, you can't bring yourself to do these things. Everyone knows how difficult it is to break habits that have been practiced for many years. The temptation to spend money lurks everywhere you turn. Ads show attractive and popular people enjoying the fruits of their labors — a new car, an exotic vacation, and a lavish home.

Maybe you felt deprived by your tightwad parents as a youngster, or maybe you're bored with life and you like the adventure of buying new things. If only you could hit it big on one or two investments, you think, you could get rich quick and do what you really want with your life. As for disasters and catastrophes, well, those things happen to other people, not to you. Besides, you'll probably have advance warning of pending problems, so you can prepare accordingly, right?

Your emotions and temptations can get the better of you. Certainly, part of successfully managing your finances involves coming to terms with your shortcomings and the consequences of your behaviors. If you don't, you may end up enslaved to a dead-end job so you can keep feeding your spending addiction. Or you may spend more time with your investments than you do with your family and friends. Or unexpected events may leave you reeling financially; disasters and catastrophes can happen to anyone at any time.

Discovering what (or who) is holding you back

A variety of personal and emotional hurdles can get in the way of making the best financial moves. As I discuss earlier in this chapter, a lack of financial knowledge (which stems from a lack of personal financial education) can stand in the way of making good decisions.

But I've seen some people caught in the psychological trap of blaming something else for their financial problems. For example, some people believe that adult problems can be traced back to childhood and how they were raised.

I don't want to disregard the negative impact particular backgrounds can have on some people's tendency to make the wrong choices during their lives. Exploring your personal history can certainly yield clues to what makes you tick. That said, adults make choices and engage in behaviors that affect themselves as well as others. They shouldn't blame their parents for their own inability to plan for their financial futures, live within their means, and make sound investments.

Some people also tend to blame their financial shortcomings on not earning more income. Such people believe that if only they earned more, their financial (and personal) problems would melt away. My experience working and speaking with people from diverse economic backgrounds has taught me that achieving financial success — and more importantly, personal happiness — has virtually nothing to do with how much income a person makes but rather with what she makes of what she has. I know financially wealthy people who are emotionally poor even though they have all the material goods they want. Likewise, I know people who are quite happy, content, and emotionally wealthy even though they're struggling financially.

Americans — even those who have not had an "easy" life — ought to be able to come up with numerous things to be happy about and grateful for: a family who loves them; friends who laugh at their stupid jokes; the freedom to catch a movie or play or to read a good book; or a great singing voice, a good sense of humor, or a full head of hair.

Developing good financial habits

After you understand the basic concepts and know where to buy the best financial products when you need them, you'll soon see that managing personal finances well is not much more difficult than other things you do regularly, like tying your shoelaces and getting to work each day.

Regardless of your income, you can make your dollars stretch farther if you practice good financial habits and avoid mistakes. In fact, the lower your income, the more important it is that you make the most of your income and savings (because you don't have the luxury of falling back on your next big paycheck to bail you out).

More and more industries are subject to global competition, so you need to be on your financial toes now more than ever. Job security is waning; layoffs and retraining for new jobs are increasing. Putting in 30 years for one company and retiring with the gold watch and lifetime pension are becoming as rare as never having problems with your computer.

Speaking of company pensions, odds are increasing that you work for an employer that has you save toward your own retirement instead of providing a pension for you. Not only do you need to save the money, you must also decide how to invest it. Chapter 11 can help you get a handle on investing in retirement accounts.

Personal finance involves much more than managing and investing money. It also includes making all the pieces of your financial life fit together; it means lifting yourself out of financial illiteracy. Like planning a vacation, managing your personal finances means forming a plan for making the best use of your limited time and dollars.

Intelligent personal financial strategies have little to do with your gender, ethnicity, or marital status. All people need to manage their finances wisely. Some aspects of financial management become more or less important at different points in your life, but for the most part, the principles remain the same for everyone.

Knowing the right answers isn't enough. You have to practice good financial habits just as you practice other good habits, such as brushing your teeth or eating a healthy diet and getting some exercise. Don't be overwhelmed. As you read this book, make a short list of your financial marching orders and then start working away. Throughout this book, I highlight ways you can overcome temptations and keep control of your money rather than let your emotions and money rule you. (I discuss common financial problems in Chapter 2.)

What you do with your money is a quite personal and confidential matter. In this book, I try to provide guidance that can keep you in sound financial health. You don't have to take it all — pick what works best for you and understand the pros and cons of your options. But from this day forward, please don't make the easily avoidable mistakes or overlook the sound strategies that I discuss throughout this book.

Throughout your journey, I hope to challenge and even change the way you think about money and about making important personal financial decisions — and sometimes even about the meaning of life. No, I'm not a philosopher, but I do know that money — for better but more often for worse — is connected to many other parts of our lives.

Chapter 2

Measuring Your Financial Health

*H*ow financially healthy are you? When was the last time you reviewed your overall financial situation, including analyzing your spending, savings, future goals, and insurance? If you're like most people, either you've never done this exercise or you did so too long ago.

This chapter guides you through a *financial physical* to help you detect problems with your current financial health. But don't dwell on your "problems." View them for what they are — opportunities to improve your financial situation. In fact, the more areas you can identify that stand to benefit from improvement, the greater the potential you may have to build real wealth and accomplish your financial and personal goals.

Avoiding Common Money Mistakes

Financial problems, like many medical problems, are best detected early (clean living doesn't hurt, either). Here are the common personal financial problems I've seen in my work as a financial counselor:

✔ **Not planning:** Most of us procrastinate. That's why we have deadlines (like April 15) — and deadline extensions (need another six months to get that tax return done?). Unfortunately, you may have no explicit deadlines with your personal finances. You can allow your credit-card debt to accumulate, or you can leave your savings sitting in lousy investments for years. You can pay higher taxes, leave gaps in your retirement and insurance coverage, and overpay for financial products. Of course, planning your finances isn't as much fun as planning a vacation, but doing the former can help you take more of the latter. See Chapter 4 for details on setting financial goals.

✓ **Overspending:** Simple arithmetic helps you determine that savings is the difference between what you earn and what you spend (assuming that you're not spending more than you're earning!). To increase your savings, you either have to work more, increase your earning power through education or job advancement, get to know a wealthy family who wants to leave its fortune to you, or spend less. For most people, especially over the short-term, the thrifty approach is the key to building savings and wealth. (Check out Chapter 3 for a primer on figuring out where your money goes; Chapter 6 gives advice for reducing your spending.)

✓ **Buying with consumer credit:** Even with the benefit of today's low interest rates, carrying a balance month-to-month on your credit card or buying a car on credit means that even more of your future earnings are going to be earmarked for debt repayment. Buying on credit encourages you to spend more than you can really afford. Chapter 5 discusses debt and credit problems.

✓ **Delaying saving for retirement:** Most folks say that they want to retire by their mid-60s or sooner. But to accomplish this goal, they need to save a reasonable chunk (around 10 percent) of their incomes starting sooner rather than later. The longer you wait to start saving for retirement, the harder reaching your goal will be. And you'll pay much more in taxes to boot if you don't take advantage of the tax benefits of investing through particular retirement accounts. For information on planning for retirement, see Chapters 4 and 11.

✓ **Falling prey to financial sales pitches:** Steer clear of people who pressure you to make decisions, promise you high investment returns, and lack the proper training and experience to help you. Great deals that can't wait for a little reflection or a second opinion are often disasters waiting to happen. A sucker may be born every minute, but a slick salesperson is pitching something every second! For important investment concepts and what kinds of investments to avoid, turn to Chapter 8.

✓ **Not doing your homework:** To get the best deal, shop around, read reviews, and get advice from objective third parties. You also need to check references and track records so you don't hire incompetent, self-serving, or fraudulent financial advisors. (For more on hiring financial planners, see Chapter 18.) But with all the different financial products available, making informed financial decisions has become an over-whelming task. I do a lot of the homework for you with the recommendations in this book. I also explain what additional research you need to do and how to do it.

✔ **Making decisions based on emotion:** You're most vulnerable to making the wrong moves financially after a major life change (a job loss or divorce, for example) or when you feel pressure. Maybe your investments plunged in value. Or perhaps a recent divorce has you fearing that you won't be able to afford to retire when you planned, so you pour thousands of dollars into some newfangled financial product. Take your time and keep your emotions out of the picture. In Chapter 21, I discuss how to approach major life changes and determine what changes you may need to make to your financial picture.

✔ **Not separating the wheat from the chaff:** In any field in which you're not an expert, you run the danger of following the advice of someone you think is an expert but really isn't. This book shows you how to separate the financial fluff from the financial facts. (Flip to Chapter 19 for information on how to evaluate financial advice online and Chapter 20 for how to evaluate financial coverage in the mass media.) You are the person who is best able to manage your personal finances. Educate and trust yourself!

✔ **Exposing yourself to catastrophic risk:** You're vulnerable if you and your family don't have insurance to pay for financially devastating losses. People without a savings reserve and a support network can end up homeless. Many people lack sufficient insurance coverage to replace their income. Don't wait for a tragedy to strike to find out whether you have the right insurance coverage. Check out Part IV for more on insurance.

✔ **Focusing too much on money:** Placing too much emphasis on making and saving money can warp your perspective on what's important in life. Money is not the first — or even second — priority in happy people's lives. Your health, relationships with family and friends, career satisfaction, and fulfilling interests are more significant.

Money problems can be fixed over time with changes in your behavior. That's what the rest of this book is all about.

Determining Your Financial Net Worth

Your financial net worth is an important barometer of your monetary health. Your net worth indicates your capacity to accomplish major financial goals, such as buying a home, retiring, and withstanding unexpected expenses or loss of income.

Your *net worth* is your financial assets minus your financial liabilities:

Financial Assets – Financial Liabilities = Net Worth

The following sections explain how to determine those numbers.

Adding up your financial assets

A *financial asset* is real money or an investment you can convert into your favorite currency that you can use to buy things now or in the future. Financial assets generally include the money you have in bank accounts, stocks, bonds, mutual funds, and exchange-traded funds (see Part III, which deals with investments). Money that you have in retirement accounts (including those with your employer) and the value of any businesses or real estate that you own are also counted.

I generally recommend that you exclude your personal residence when figuring your financial assets. Include your home only if you expect to sell it someday or otherwise live off the money you now have tied up in it (perhaps by taking out a reverse mortgage, which I discuss in Chapter 14). If you plan on eventually tapping into the *equity* (the difference between the market value and any debt owed on the property), add that portion of the equity that you expect to use to your list of assets.

Assets can also include your future expected Social Security benefits and pension payments (if your employer has such a plan). These assets are usually quoted in dollars per month rather than as a lump sum value. In Table 2-1, I explain how to account for these monthly benefits when tallying your financial assets.

Consumer items — such as your car, clothing, stereo, and so forth — do *not* count as financial assets. I know that adding these things to your assets makes your assets *look* larger (and some financial software and publications encourage you to list these items as assets), but you can't live off them unless you sell them.

Subtracting your financial liabilities

To arrive at your financial net worth, you must subtract your *financial liabilities* from your assets. Liabilities include loans and debts outstanding, such as credit-card and auto-loan debts. When figuring your liabilities, include money you borrowed from family and friends — unless you're not expected to pay it back!

Include mortgage debt on your home as a liability *only* if you include the value of your home in your asset list. Be sure to also include debt owed on other real estate — no matter what (because you count the value of investment real estate as an asset).

Crunching your numbers

Table 2-1 provides a place for you to figure your financial assets. Go ahead and write in the spaces provided, unless you plan to lend this book to someone and don't want to put your money situation on display. *Note:* See Table 4-1 in Chapter 4 to estimate your Social Security benefits.

Table 2-1	Your Financial Assets
Account	*Value*
Savings and investment accounts (including retirement accounts):	
Example: Bank savings account	$5,000
_____	$_____
_____	$_____
_____	$_____
_____	$_____
_____	$_____
_____	$_____
Subtotal =	$_____
Benefits earned that pay a monthly retirement income:	
Employer's pensions	$_____ / month
Social Security	$_____ / month
	$\times 240^{*}$
Subtotal =	$_____
Total Financial Assets (add the two subtotals) =	$_____

*To convert benefits that will be paid to you monthly into a total dollar amount, and for purposes of simplification, assume that you will spend 20 years in retirement. Inflation may reduce the value of your employer's pension if it doesn't contain a cost-of-living increase each year in the same way that Social Security does. Don't sweat this now — you can take care of that concern in the section on retirement planning in Chapter 4.

Now comes the potentially depressing part — figuring out your debts and loans in Table 2-2.

Table 2-2	Your Financial Liabilities
Loan	*Balance*
Example: Gouge 'Em Bank Credit Card	$4,000
_____	$_____
_____	$_____
_____	$_____
_____	$_____
_____	$_____
_____	$_____
Total Financial Liabilities =	$_____

Now you can subtract your liabilities from your assets to figure your net worth in Table 2-3.

Table 2-3	Your Net Worth
Find	*Write It Here*
Total Financial Assets (from Table 2-1)	$_____
Total Financial Liabilities (from Table 2-2)	– $_____
Net Worth =	$_____

Interpreting your net worth results

Your net worth is important and useful only to you and your unique situation and goals. What seems like a lot of money to a person with a simple lifestyle may seem like a pittance to a person with high expectations and a desire for an opulent lifestyle.

In Chapter 4, you can crunch numbers to determine your financial status more precisely for goals such as retirement planning. I also discuss saving toward other important goals in that chapter. In the meantime, if your net worth (excluding expected monthly retirement benefits such as those from Social Security and pensions) is negative or less than half your annual income, take notice. If you're in your 20s and you're just starting to work, a low net worth is less concerning and not unusual. Focus on turning this number positive over the next several years. However, if you're in your 30s or older, consider this a wake-up call to aggressively address your financial situation.

Getting rid of your debts — the highest-interest rate ones first — is the most important thing. Then you want to build a safety reserve equal to three to six months of living expenses. Your overall plan should involve getting out of debt (Chapter 5), reducing your spending (Chapter 6), and developing tax-wise ways to save and invest your future earnings (Part III).

Examining Your Credit Score and Reports

You may not know it (or care), but you probably have a personal credit report and a credit score. Lenders examine your credit report and score before granting you a loan or credit line. This section highlights what you need to know about your credit score and reports, including how to obtain them and how to improve them.

Understanding what your credit data includes and means

A _credit report_ contains information such as

- **Personal identifying information:** Includes your name, address, Social Security number, and so on

- **Record of credit accounts:** Details when each account was opened, the latest balance, your payment history, and so on

- **Bankruptcy filings:** Indicates whether you've filed bankruptcy in recent years

- **Inquiries:** Lists who has pulled your credit report because you applied for credit

Your _credit score,_ which is not the same as your credit report, is a three-digit score based on the report. Lenders use your credit score as a predictor of your likelihood of defaulting on repaying your borrowings. As such, your credit score has a major impact on whether a lender is willing to extend you a particular loan and at what interest rate.

FICO, developed by Fair Isaac and Company, is the leading credit score in the industry. FICO scores range from a low of 300 to a high of 850. Most scores fall in the 600s and 700s. As with college entrance examinations, higher scores are better. (In recent years, the major credit bureaus — Equifax,

Experian, and TransUnion — have developed their own credit scoring systems, but many lenders still use FICO the most.)

The higher your credit score, the lower your predicted likelihood of defaulting on a loan (see Figure 2-1). The "rate of credit delinquency" refers to the percentage of consumers who will become 90 days late or later in repaying a creditor within the next two years. As you can see in the chart, consumers with low credit scores have dramatically higher rates of falling behind on their loans. Thus, low credit scorers are considered much riskier borrowers, and fewer lenders are willing to offer them a given loan; those who do offer loans charge relatively high interest rates.

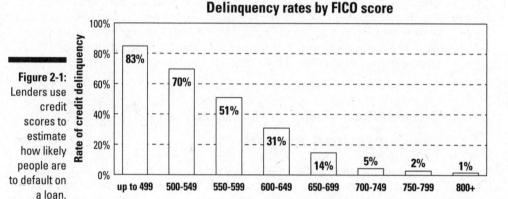

Figure 2-1:
Lenders use credit scores to estimate how likely people are to default on a loan.

The median FICO score is around 720. You generally qualify for the best lending rates if your credit score is in the mid-700s or higher.

Obtaining your credit reports and score

Given the importance of your personal credit report, you may be pleased to know that federal law entitles you to receive a free copy of your credit report annually from each of the three credit bureaus (Equifax, Experian, and TransUnion).

If you visit www.annualcreditreport.com, you can view and print copies of your credit report information from each of the three credit agencies online (alternatively, call 877-322-8228 to have your reports mailed to you). After entering some personal data at the website, check the box indicating that you want to obtain all three credit reports, because each report may have slightly different information. You'll then be directed to one of the three bureaus, and after you finish verifying that you are who you claim to be at that site, you can easily navigate back to www.annualcreditreport.com so you can continue to the next agency's site.

When you receive your reports, the best first step is to examine them for possible mistakes (see the upcoming section "Getting credit report errors corrected" to find out how to fix problems in your reports). In the past, I found minor errors on two of the three reports. It took me several minutes to correct one of the errors (by submitting a request to that credit reporting agency's website), and it took about half an hour to get the other mistake fixed (a small doctor's bill was erroneously listed as unpaid and in collections).

You may be surprised to find that your credit reports do *not* include your credit score. The reason for this is quite simple: The 2003 law mandating that the three credit agencies provide a free credit report annually to each U.S. citizen who requests a copy did not mandate that they provide the credit score. Thus, if you want to obtain your credit score, it's going to cost you.

You can request your credit score from Fair Isaac, but you'll get charged $19.95 for every request (that can set you back nearly $60 to see your FICO score for all three credit bureaus). Save your money. If you want to purchase your credit score, you can often do so for less by ordering it from the individual credit bureaus when you obtain your credit report(s) via www.annualcreditreport.com — Equifax, for example, charges just $7.95 to obtain your current credit score.

If you do spring for your current credit score, be clear about what you're buying. You may not realize that you're agreeing to some sort of ongoing credit monitoring service for, say, $50 to $100+ per year, an expenditure I don't generally feel is worthwhile.

Improving your credit reports and score

Instead of simply throwing money into buying your credit scores or paying for some ongoing monitoring service to which you may not give much attention, take an interest in improving your credit standing and score. Working to boost your credit rating is especially worthwhile if you know that your credit report contains detrimental information.

Here are the most important actions that you can take to boost your attractiveness to lenders:

- ✔ **Get all three of your credit reports, and be sure each is accurate.** Correct errors (as I explain in the next section) and be especially sure to get accounts removed if they aren't yours and they show late payments or are in collection.

- ✔ **Ask to have any late or missed payments that are more than seven years old removed.** Ditto for a bankruptcy that occurred more than ten years ago.

- ✔ **Pay all your bills on time.** To ensure on-time payments, sign up for automatic bill payment, a service that most companies (like phone and utility providers) offer.

- ✔ **Be loyal if it doesn't cost you.** The older your open loan accounts are, the better your credit rating will be. Closing old accounts and opening a bunch of new ones generally lowers your credit score. But don't be loyal if it costs you! For example, if you can refinance your mortgage and save some money, by all means do so. The same logic applies if you're carrying credit-card debt at a high interest rate and want to transfer that balance to a lower-rate card. If your current credit-card provider refuses to match a lower rate you find elsewhere, move your balance and save yourself some money (see Chapter 5 for details).

- ✔ **Limit your debt and debt accounts.** The more loans, especially consumer loans, that you hold and the higher the balances, the lower your credit score will be.

- ✔ **Work to pay down consumer revolving debt (such as credit-card debt).** Turn to Chapters 5 and 6 for suggestions.

Getting credit report errors corrected

If you obtain your credit report and find a blemish on it that you don't recognize as being your mistake or fault, do *not* assume that the information is correct. Credit reporting bureaus and the creditors who report credit information to these bureaus often make errors.

You hope and expect that, if a credit bureau has negative and incorrect information in your credit report and you bring the mistake to their attention, they will graciously and expeditiously fix the error. If you believe that, you're the world's greatest optimist; perhaps you also think you won't have to wait in line at the Department of Motor Vehicles or the post office!

You're going to have to fill out a form on a website, make some phone calls, or write a letter or two to fix the problems on your credit report. Here's how to correct most errors that aren't your fault:

- ✔ **If the credit problem is someone else's:** A surprising number of personal credit report glitches are the result of someone else's negative information getting on your credit report. If the bad information on your report is completely foreign-looking to you, contact the credit bureau (by phone or online) and explain that you need more information because you don't recognize the creditor.

- ✔ **If the creditor made a mistake:** Creditors make mistakes, too. You need to write or call the creditor to get it to correct the erroneous information that it sent to the credit bureau. Phoning first usually works best. (The credit bureau should be able to tell you how to reach the creditor if you don't know how.) If necessary, follow up with a letter.

Whether you speak with a credit bureau or an actual lender, make note of your conversations. If representatives say that they can fix the problem, get their names, email addresses, and phone extensions, and follow up with them if they don't deliver as promised. If you're ensnared in bureaucratic red tape, escalate the situation by speaking with a department manager. By law, bureaus are required to respond to a request to fix a credit error within 30 days — hold the bureau accountable!

Telling your side of the story

With a minor credit infraction, some lenders may simply ask for an explanation. Years ago, I had a credit report blemish that was the result of being away for several weeks and missing the payment due date for a couple of small bills. When my proposed mortgage lender saw my late payments, the lender asked for a simple written explanation.

You and a creditor may not see eye to eye on a problem, and the creditor may refuse to budge. If that's the case, credit bureaus are required by law to allow you to add a 100-word explanation to your credit file.

Sidestepping "credit repair" firms

Online and in newspapers and magazines, you may see ads for credit repair companies that claim to fix your credit report problems. In the worst cases I've seen, these firms charge outrageous amounts of money and don't come close to fulfilling their marketing hype.

If you have legitimate glitches on your credit report, credit repair firms can't make the glitches disappear. Hope springs eternal, however — some people would like to believe that their credit problems can be fixed.

If your problems are fixable, you can fix them yourself; you don't need to pay a credit repair company big bucks to do it.

Knowing the Difference between Bad Debt and Good Debt

Why do you borrow money? Usually, you borrow money because you don't have enough to buy something you want or need — like a college education. A four-year college education can easily cost $100,000, $150,000, $200,000, or more. Not too many people have that kind of spare cash. So borrowing money to finance part of that cost enables you to buy the education.

How about a new car? A trip to your friendly local car dealer shows you that a new set of wheels will set you back $20,000+. Although more people may have the money to pay for that than, say, the college education, what if you don't? Should you finance the car the way you finance the education?

The auto dealers and bankers who are eager to make you an auto loan say that you deserve and can afford to drive a nice, new car, and they tell you to borrow away (or lease, which I don't love either — please see Chapter 6). I say, "No! No! No!" Why do I disagree with the auto dealers and lenders? For starters, I'm not trying to sell you a car or loan from which I derive a profit! More importantly, there's a *big* difference between borrowing for something that represents a long-term investment and borrowing for short-term consumption.

If you spend, say, $1,500 on a vacation, the money is gone. Poof! You may have fond memories and photos, but you have nothing of financial value to show for it. "But," you say, "vacations replenish my soul and make me more productive when I return . . . the vacation more than pays for itself!"

I'm not saying that you shouldn't take a vacation. By all means, take one, two, three, or as many as you can afford yearly. But the point is to *take what you can afford.* If you have to borrow money in the form of an outstanding balance on your credit card for many months in order to take the vacation, then you *can't afford* it.

Consuming your way to bad debt

I coined the term *bad debt* to refer to debt incurred for consumption, because such debt is harmful to your long-term financial health. (I used this term back in the early 1990s when the first edition of this book was published, and I'm flattered that others have since used the same terminology.)

You'll be able to take many more vacations during your lifetime if you save the cash in advance. If you get into the habit of borrowing and paying all the associated interest for vacations, cars, clothing, and other consumer items, you'll spend more of your future income paying back the debt and interest, leaving you with less money for your other goals.

The relatively high interest rates that banks and other lenders charge for bad (consumer) debt is one of the reasons you're less able to save money when using such debt. Not only does money borrowed through credit cards, auto loans, and other types of consumer loans carry a relatively high interest rate, but it also isn't tax-deductible.

I'm not saying that you should never borrow money and that all debt is bad. Good debt, such as that used to buy real estate and small businesses, is generally available at lower interest rates than bad debt and is usually tax-deductible. If well managed, these investments may also increase in value. Borrowing to pay for educational expenses can also make sense. Education is generally a good long-term investment because it can increase your earning potential. And student loan interest is tax-deductible, subject to certain limitations (see Chapter 7).

Recognizing bad debt overload

Calculating how much debt you have relative to your annual income is a useful way to size up your debt load. Ignore, for now, good debt — the loans you may owe on real estate, a business, an education, and so on (I get to that in the next section). I'm focusing on bad debt, the higher-interest debt used to buy items that depreciate in value.

To calculate your bad debt danger ratio, divide your bad debt by your annual income. For example, suppose you earn $40,000 per year. Between your credit cards and an auto loan, you have $20,000 of debt. In this case, your bad debt represents 50 percent of your annual income.

$$\frac{\text{bad debt}}{\text{annual income}} = \text{bad debt danger ratio}$$

The financially healthy amount of bad debt is zero. While enjoying the convenience of credit cards, *never* buy anything with your card that you can't afford to pay off in full when the bill comes at the end of the month. Not everyone agrees with me. One major U.S. credit-card company says — in its "educational" materials, which it "donates" to schools to teach students about supposedly sound financial management — that carrying consumer debt amounting to 10 to 20 percent of your annual income is just fine.

When your bad debt danger ratio starts to push beyond 25 percent, it can spell real trouble. Such high levels of high-interest consumer debt on credit cards and auto loans grow like cancer. The growth of the debt can snowball and get out of control unless something significant intervenes. If you have consumer debt beyond 25 percent of your annual income, see Chapter 5 to find out how to get out of debt.

How much good debt is acceptable? The answer varies. The key question is: Are you able to save sufficiently to accomplish your goals? In the "Analyzing Your Savings" section later in this chapter, I help you figure out how much you're actually saving, and in Chapter 4, I help you determine how much you need to save to accomplish your goals. (See Chapter 14 to find out how much mortgage debt is appropriate to take on when buying a home.)

Borrow money only for investments (good debt) — for purchasing things that retain and hopefully increase in value over the long term, such as an education, real estate, or your own business. Don't borrow money for consumption (bad debt) — for spending on things that decrease in value and eventually become financially worthless, such as cars, clothing, vacations, and so on.

The lure of easy credit

Many years ago, I worked as a management consultant and did a lot of work with companies in the financial services industry, including some of the major credit-card companies. Their game then, as it is now, was to push cards into the hands of as many people as possible who have a tendency and propensity to carry debt month to month at high interest rates. Their direct marketing campaigns are quite effective. Ditto for the auto manufacturers who successfully entice many people who can't really afford to spend $20,000, $30,000, $40,000, or more on a brand-new car to buy new autos financed with an auto loan or lease.

And just as alcohol and cigarette makers target young people with their advertising,

credit-card companies are recruiting and grooming the next generation of overspenders on college campuses. Unbelievably, our highest institutions of learning receive large fees from credit-card companies for allowing them to promote their cards on campuses!

As widely available as credit is today, so, too, are suggestions for how to spend it. We're bombarded with ads 24/7 on radio, TV, websites, cellphones, PDAs, the sides of buses and trains and the tops of taxicabs, people's clothing, and cars. You couldn't go a day without being exposed to advertising if you wanted to — you're surrounded!

Assessing good debt: Can you get too much?

As with good food, you can get too much of a good thing, including good debt! When you incur debt for investment purposes — to buy real estate, for small business, even your education — you hope to see a positive return on your invested dollars.

But some real-estate investments don't work out. Some small businesses crash and burn, and some educational degrees and programs don't help in the way that some people hope they will.

There's no magic formula for determining when you have too much "good debt." In extreme cases, I've seen entrepreneurs, for example, borrow up to their eyeballs to get a business off the ground. Sometimes this works, and they end up financially rewarded, but in most cases, it doesn't.

Here are three important questions to ponder and discuss with your loved ones about the seemingly "good debt" you're taking on:

✔ Are you and your loved ones able to sleep well at night and function well during the day, free from great worry about how you're going to meet next month's expenses?

✔ Are the likely rewards worth the risk that the borrowing entails?

✔ Are you and your loved ones financially able to save what you'd like to work toward your goals (see Chapter 4)?

If you answer "no" to these questions, see the debt-reduction strategies in Chapter 5 for more information.

Playing the credit-card float

Given what I have to say about the vagaries of consumer debt, you may think that I'm always against using credit cards. Actually, I have credit cards, and I use them — but I pay my balance in full each month. Besides the convenience credit cards offer me — in not having to carry around other forms of payment such as extra cash and checks — I receive another benefit: I have free use of the bank's money until the time the bill is due. (Some cards offer other benefits, such as frequent flyer miles, and I have one of those types of cards too. Also, purchases made on credit cards may be contested if the sellers of products or services don't stand behind what they sell.)

When you charge on a credit card that *does not* have an outstanding balance carried over from the prior month, you typically have several weeks (known as the *grace period*) from the date of the charge to the time when you must pay your bill. This is called *playing the float*. Had you paid for this purchase by cash or check, you would have had to shell out the money sooner.

If you have difficulty saving money and plastic tends to break your budget, forget the float game. You're better off not using credit cards. The same applies to those who pay their bills in full but spend more because it's so easy to do so with a piece of plastic. (For information on alternatives to using credit cards, see Chapter 5.)

Analyzing Your Savings

How much money have you actually saved in the past year? By that I mean the amount of new money you've added to your nest egg, stash, or whatever you like to call it.

Most people don't know or have only a vague idea of the rate at which they're saving money. The answer may sober, terrify, or pleasantly surprise you. In order to calculate your savings over the past year, you need to calculate your net worth as of today *and* as of one year ago.

The amount you actually saved over the past year is equal to the change in your net worth over the past year — in other words, your net worth today minus your net worth from one year ago. I know it may be a pain to find statements showing what your investments were worth a year ago, but bear with me: It's a useful exercise.

If you own your home, ignore this in the calculations. (However, you can consider the extra payments you make to pay off your mortgage principal faster as new savings.) And don't include personal property and consumer goods, such as your car, computer, clothing, and so on, with your assets. (See the earlier section "Determining Your Financial Net Worth" if you need more help with this task.)

When you have your net worth figures from both years, plug them into Step 1 of Table 2-4. If you're anticipating the exercise and are already subtracting your net worth of a year ago from what it is today in order to determine your rate of savings, your instincts are correct, but the exercise isn't quite that simple. You need to do a few more calculations in Step 2 of Table 2-4. Why? Well, counting the appreciation of the investments you've owned over the past year as savings wouldn't be fair. Suppose you bought 100 shares of a stock a year ago at $17 per share, and now the value is at $34 per share.

Your investment increased in value by $1,700 during the past year. Although you'd be the envy of your friends at the next party if you casually mentioned your investments, the $1,700 of increased value is not really savings. Instead, it represents appreciation on your investments, so you must remove this appreciation from the calculations. (Just so you know, I'm not unfairly penalizing you for your shrewd investments — you also get to add back the decline in value of your less-successful investments.)

Table 2-4		Your Savings Rate over the Past Year	
Step 1: Figuring your savings			
Today		*One Year Ago*	
Savings & investments	$_____	Savings & investments	$_____
– Loans & debts	$_____	– Loans & debts	$_____
= Net worth today	$_____	= Net worth 1 year ago	$_____
Step 2: Correcting for changes in value of investments you owned during the year			
Net worth today			$_____
– Net worth 1 year ago			$_____
– Appreciation of investments (over past year)			$_____
+ Depreciation of investments (over past year)			$_____
= Savings rate			$_____

If all this calculating gives you a headache, you get stuck, or you just hate crunching numbers, try the intuitive, seat-of-the-pants approach: Save a regular portion of your monthly income. You can save it in a separate savings or retirement account.

How much do you save in a typical month? Get out the statements for accounts you contribute to or save money in monthly. It doesn't matter if you're saving money in a retirement account that you can't access — money is money.

Note: If you save, say, $200 per month for a few months, and then you spend it all on auto repairs, you're not really saving. If you contributed $5,000 to an individual retirement account (IRA), for example, but you depleted money that you had from long ago (in other words, money that wasn't saved during the past year), don't count the $5,000 IRA contribution as new savings.

Save at least 5 to 10 percent of your annual income for longer-term financial goals such as retirement (Chapter 4 helps you to fine-tune your savings goals). If you're not saving that much, be sure to read Chapter 6 to find out how to reduce your spending and increase your savings.

Evaluating Your Investment Knowledge

Congratulations! If you've stuck with me from the beginning of this chapter, you've completed the hardest part of your financial physical. The physical is much easier from here!

Regardless of how much or how little money you have invested in banks, mutual funds, or other types of accounts, you want to invest your money in the wisest way possible. Knowing the rights and wrongs of investing is vital to your long-term financial well-being. Few people have so much extra money that they can afford major or frequent investing mistakes.

Answering "yes" or "no" to the following questions can help you determine how much time you need to spend with my Investing Crash Course in Part III, which focuses on investing. *Note:* The more "no" answers you reluctantly scribble, the more you need to find out about investing, and the faster you should turn to Part III.

_____ Do you understand the investments you currently hold?

_____ Is the money that you'd need to tap in the event of a short-term emergency in an investment where the principal does not fluctuate in value?

_____ Do you know what marginal income-tax bracket (combined federal and state) you're in, and do you factor that in when choosing investments?

_____ For money outside of retirement accounts, do you understand how these investments produce income and gains and whether these types of investments make the most sense from the standpoint of your tax situation?

_____ Do you have your money in different, diversified investments that aren't dependent on one or a few securities or one type of investment (that is, bonds, stocks, real estate, and so on)?

_____ Is the money that you're going to need for a major expenditure in the next few years invested in conservative investments rather than in riskier investments such as stocks or pork bellies?

_____ Is the money that you have earmarked for longer-term purposes (more than five years) invested to produce returns that are likely to stay ahead of inflation?

_____ If you currently invest in or plan to invest in individual stocks, do you understand how to evaluate a stock, including reviewing the company's balance sheet, income statement, competitive position, price-earnings ratio versus its peer group, and so on?

_____ If you work with a financial advisor, do you understand what that person is recommending that you do, are you comfortable with those actions and that advisor, and is that person compensated in a way that minimizes potential conflicts of interest in the strategies and investments he recommends?

Making and saving money are not guarantees of financial success; rather, they're prerequisites. If you don't know how to choose sound investments that meet your needs, you'll likely end up throwing money away, which leads to the same end result as never having earned and saved it in the first place. Worse still, you won't be able to derive any enjoyment from spending the lost money on things that you perhaps need or want. Turn to Part III to discover the best ways to invest; otherwise, you may wind up spinning your wheels working and saving.

Assessing Your Insurance Savvy

In this section, you have to deal with the prickly subject of protecting your assets and yourself with _insurance_. The following questions help you get started. Answer "yes" or "no" for each question.

_____ Do you understand the individual coverages, protection types, and amounts of each insurance policy you have?

_____ Does your current insurance protection make sense given your current financial situation (as opposed to your situation when you bought the policies)?

_____ If you wouldn't be able to make it financially without your income, do you have adequate long-term disability insurance coverage?

_____ If you have family members who are dependent on your continued income, do you have adequate life insurance coverage to replace your income if you die?

_____ Do you know when it makes sense to buy insurance through discount brokers, fee-for-service advisors, and companies that sell directly to the public (bypassing agents) and when it doesn't?

_____ Do you carry enough liability insurance on your home, car (including umbrella/excess liability), and business to protect all your assets?

_____ Have you recently (in the last year or two) shopped around for the best price on your insurance policies?

_____ Do you know whether your insurance companies have good track records when it comes to paying claims and keeping customers satisfied?

That wasn't so bad, was it? If you answered "no" more than once or twice, don't feel bad — nine out of ten people make significant mistakes when buying insurance. Find your insurance salvation in Part IV. If you answered "yes" to all the preceding questions, you can spare yourself from reading Part IV, but bear in mind that many people need as much help in this area as they do in other aspects of personal finance.

Chapter 3

Managing Where Your Money Goes

In This Chapter

▶ Understanding why people overspend

▶ Assessing your spending

▶ Tracking your expenses via "free" websites

As a financial counselor, I've worked with people who have small incomes, people who have six-figure and even seven-figure incomes, and everyone in between. At every income level, people fall into one of the following three categories:

✔ People who spend more than they earn (accumulating debt)

✔ People who spend all that they earn (saving nothing)

✔ People who save 2, 5, 10, or even 20 percent (or more!)

I've seen $40,000 earners who save 20 percent of their income ($8,000), $80,000 earners who save just 5 percent ($4,000), and people earning well into six figures annually who save nothing or accumulate debt.

Suppose that you currently earn $50,000 per year and spend all of it. You may wonder, "How can I save money?" Good question! Rather than knock yourself out at a second job, you may want to try living below your income — in other words, spending less than you earn. Consider that for every discontented person earning and spending $50,000 per year, someone else is out there making do on $45,000.

A great many people live on less than you make. If you spend as they do, you can save and invest the difference. In this chapter, I examine why people overspend and help you look at your own spending habits. When you know where your money goes, you can find ways to spend less and save more (see Chapter 6) so that someday, you, too, can live richly and achieve your life's goals.

Examining Overspending

If you're like most people, you must live within your means to accomplish your financial goals. Doing so requires spending less than you earn and then investing your savings intelligently (unless you plan on winning the lottery or receiving a large inheritance). To put yourself in a position that allows you to start saving, take a close look at your spending habits.

Many folks earn just enough to make ends meet. And some can't even do that; they simply spend more than they make. The result of such spending habits is, of course, an accumulation of debt.

Most of the influences in society encourage you to spend. Think about it: More often than not, you're referred to as a *consumer* in the media and in the hallowed halls of U.S. government. You're not referred to as a person, a citizen, or a human being. This section looks at some of the adversaries you're up against as you attempt to control your spending.

Having access to credit

As you probably already know, spending money is easy. Thanks to innovations like ATMs, credit cards, PayPal, and so on, your money is always available, 24/7.

Sometimes it may seem as though lenders are trying to give away money by making credit so easily available. But this free money is a dangerous illusion. Credit is most perilous when you make consumption purchases you can't afford in the first place. When it comes to consumer debt (credit cards, auto loans, and the like), lenders aren't giving away anything except the misfortune of getting in over your head, racking up high interest charges, and delaying your progress toward your financial and personal goals.

Misusing credit cards

The modern-day bank credit card was invented by Bank of America near the end of the baby boom. The credit industry has been generally growing along with the boomers ever since.

If you pay your bill in full every month, credit cards offer a convenient way to buy things with an interest-free, short-term loan. But if you carry your debt over from month to month at high interest rates, credit cards encourage you to live beyond your means. Credit cards make it easy and tempting to spend money that you don't have.

You'll never pay off your credit-card debt if you keep charging on your card and make only the minimum monthly payments. Interest continues to pile up on your outstanding debt. Paying only the minimum monthly payment can lead to your carrying high-interest debt on your card for decades (not just months or years)!

Some credit cards are now trying to sell cardholders "insurance" at a cost of 10-plus percent annually to pay the minimum payments due on credit-card balances for those months that the debtor is unable to pay because of some life transition event (such as a job layoff). One such card normally charges a 13 percent annual interest rate on credit-card balances, so with the insurance charges, the annual interest rate is upward of 25 percent!

If you have a knack for charging up a storm and spending more than you should with those little pieces of plastic, only one solution exists: Get rid of your credit cards. Put scissors to the plastic. Go cold turkey. You can function without them. (See Chapter 5 for details on how to live without credit cards.)

Taking out car loans

Walking onto a car lot and going home with a new car that you could never afford if you had to pay cash is easy. The dealer gets you thinking in terms of monthly payments that sound small when compared to what that four-wheeler is *really* gonna cost you. Auto loans are easy for just about anyone to get (except maybe a recently paroled felon).

Suppose you're tired of driving around in your old clunker. The car is battle-scarred and boring, and you don't like being seen in it. Plus, the car is likely to need more repairs in the months ahead and perhaps doesn't have all the safety features of newer models. So off you go to your friendly local car dealer.

You start looking around at all the shiny, new cars, and then — like the feeling you experience when spotting a water fountain on a scorching hot day — there it is: your new car. It's sleek and clean, and has air conditioning, an amazing stereo, a rearview camera, Bluetooth, and heated seats. Before you can read the fine print on the sticker page on the side window, the sales-person moseys on up next to you. He gets you talking about how nice the car is, the weather, or anything but the sticker price of that car.

"How can this guy afford to spend time with me without knowing if I can afford this thing?" you think. After a test drive and more talk about the car, the weather, and your love life (or lack thereof) comes your moment of truth. The salesperson, it seems, doesn't care about how much money you have. Whether you have lots of money or very little doesn't matter. The car is only $399 a month!

"That price isn't bad," you think. Heck, you were expecting to hear that the car would cost you at least 25 grand. Before you know it, the dealer runs a credit report on you and has you sign a few papers, and minutes later you're driving home with your new car.

The dealer wants you to think in terms of monthly payments because the cost *sounds* so cheap: $399 for a car. But, of course, that's $399 per month for many, many months. You're gonna be payin' forever — after all, you just bought a car that cost a huge chunk of your yearly take-home income.

But it gets worse. What does the total sticker price come to when interest charges are added in? (Even if interest charges are low, you may still be buying a car with a sticker price you can't afford.) And what about the cost of insurance, registration, and maintenance over the seven or so years that you'll probably own the car? Now you're probably up to more than a year's worth of your income. Ouch! (See Chapter 6 for information on how to spend what you can afford on a car.)

Bending to outside influences and agendas

You go out with some friends to dinner, a sporting event, or a show. Try to remember the last time one of you said, "Let's go someplace (or do something) less costly. I can't afford to spend this much." On the one hand, you don't want to be a stick in the mud. But on the other hand, some of your friends may have more money than you do — and the ones who don't may be running up debt fast.

Some people just have to see the latest hit movie, wear the latest designer clothes, or get the newest smartphone or tablet. They don't want to feel left out or behind the times.

When was the last time you heard someone say that she decided to forgo a purchase because she was saving for retirement or a home purchase? It doesn't happen often, does it? Just dealing with the here-and-now and forgetting your long-term needs and goals is tempting. This mindset leads people to toil away for too many years in jobs they dislike.

Living for today has its virtues: Tomorrow *may* not come. But odds are good that it will. Will you still feel the same way about today's spending decisions tomorrow? Or will you feel guilty that you again failed to stick to your goals?

Your spending habits should be driven by *your* desires and plans, not those of others. If you haven't set any goals yet, you may not know how much you should be saving. Chapter 4 helps you kick-start the planning and saving process.

Spending to feel good

Life is full of stress, obligations, and demands. "I work hard," you may say, "and darn it, I deserve to indulge!" Especially after your boss took the credit for your last great idea or blamed you for her last major screwup. So you buy something expensive or go to a fancy restaurant. Feel better? You won't when the bill arrives. And the more you spend, the less you save, and the longer you'll be stuck working for jerks like your boss!

Just as people can become addicted to alcohol, tobacco, television, and the Internet, some people also become addicted to the high they get from spending. Researchers can identify a number of psychological causes for a spending addiction, with some relating to how your parents handled money and spending. (And you thought you'd identified all the problems you can blame on Mom and Dad!)

If your spending and debt problems are chronic, or even if you'd simply like to be a better consumer and saver, see Chapter 5 for more information.

Analyzing Your Spending

Brushing your teeth, eating a diverse diet including plenty of fruits and vegetables, and exercising regularly are good habits. Spending less than you earn and saving enough to meet your future financial objectives are the financial equivalents of these habits.

Despite relatively high incomes compared with the rest of the world, some Americans have a hard time saving a good percentage of their incomes. Why? Often it's because they spend too much — sometimes far more than necessary.

The first step to saving more of the income that you work so hard for is to figure out where that income typically gets spent. The spending analysis in the next section helps you determine where your cash is flowing. Do the spending analysis if any of the following apply to you:

- ✔ You aren't saving enough money to meet your financial goals. (If you're not sure whether this is the case, please see Chapter 4.)

- ✔ You feel as though your spending is out of control, or you don't really know where all your income goes.

- ✔ You're anticipating a significant life change (for example, marriage, leaving your job to start a business, having children, retiring, and so on).

If you're already a good saver, you may not need to complete the spending analysis. After you save enough to accomplish your goals, I don't see as much value in continually tracking your spending. You've already established the good habit — saving. Tracking exactly where you spend your money month after month is *not* the good habit. (You may still benefit from perusing my smarter spending recommendations in Chapter 6.)

The immediate goal of a spending analysis is to figure out where you typically spend your money. The long-range goal is to establish a good habit: maintaining a regular, automatic savings routine.

Notice the first four letters in the word *analysis.* Knowing where your money is going each month is useful, and making changes in your spending behavior and cutting out the fat so you can save more money and meet your financial goals is terrific. However, you may make yourself and those around you miserable if you're anal about documenting precisely where you spend every single dollar and cent.

Saving what you need to achieve your goals is what matters most.

Tracking spending the "low-tech" way

Analyzing your spending is a little bit like being a detective. Your goal is to reconstruct the spending. You probably have some major clues at your fingertips or somewhere on the desk or computer where you handle your finances.

Unless you keep meticulous records that detail every dollar you spend, you won't have perfect information. Don't sweat it! A number of sources can enable you to detail where you've been spending your money. To get started, get out/access your

- ✔ Recent pay stubs
- ✔ Tax returns
- ✔ Online banking/bill payment record
- ✔ Log of checks paid and monthly debit card transactions
- ✔ Credit and charge card bills

Ideally, you want to assemble the information needed to track 12 months of spending. But if your spending patterns don't fluctuate greatly from month to month (or you won't complete the exercise if it means compiling a year's worth of data), you can reduce your data gathering to one six-month period, or to every second or third month for the past year. If you take a major vacation or spend a large amount on gifts during certain months of the year, make sure that you include these months in your analysis. Also account for insurance or other financial payments that you may choose not to pay monthly and instead pay quarterly, semiannually, or annually.

Purchases made with cash are the hardest to track because they don't leave a paper trail. Over the course of a week or perhaps even a month, you *could* keep a record of everything you buy with cash. Tracking cash can be an enlightening exercise, but it can also be tedious. (See the section "Tracking your spending on 'free' websites and apps" later in this chapter.) If you lack the time and patience, you can try *estimating.* Think about a typical week or month — how often do you buy things with cash? For example, if you eat lunch out four days a week, paying around $8 per meal, that's about $130 a month. You may also want to try adding up all the cash withdrawals from your checking account statement and then working backward to try to remember where you spent the cash.

Separate your expenditures into as many useful and detailed categories as possible. Table 3-1 gives you a suggested format; you can tailor it to fit your needs. Remember, if you lump too much of your spending into broad, meaningless categories like "Other," you'll end up right back where you started — wondering where all the money went. (**Note:** When completing the tax section in Table 3-1, report the total tax you paid for the year as tabulated on your annual income tax return — and take the total Social Security and Medicare taxes paid from your end-of-year pay stub — rather than the tax withheld or paid during the year.)

Table 3-1	Detailing Your Spending	
Category	*Monthly Average ($)*	*Percent of Total Gross Income (%)*
Taxes, taxes, taxes (income)		_____
FICA (Social Security & Medicare)	_____	
Federal	_____	
State and local	_____	
The roof over your head		_____
Rent	_____	
Mortgage	_____	
Property taxes	_____	
Gas/electric/oil	_____	

(continued)

Table 3-1 *(continued)*

Category	Monthly Average ($)	Percent of Total Gross Income (%)
Water/garbage	_____	
Phones	_____	
Cable TV & Internet	_____	
Gardener/housekeeper	_____	
Furniture/appliances	_____	
Maintenance/repairs	_____	
Food, glorious food		_____
Supermarket	_____	
Restaurants and takeout	_____	
Getting around		_____
Gasoline	_____	
Maintenance/repairs	_____	
State registration fees	_____	
Tolls and parking	_____	
Bus or subway fares	_____	
Style		_____
Clothing	_____	
Shoes	_____	
Jewelry (watches, earrings)	_____	
Dry cleaning	_____	
Debt repayments (excluding mortgage)		_____
Credit/charge cards	_____	
Auto loans	_____	
Student loans	_____	
Other	_____	
Fun stuff		_____
Entertainment (movies, concerts)	_____	
Vacation and travel	_____	
Gifts	_____	
Hobbies	_____	

Category	Monthly Average ($)	Percent of Total Gross Income (%)
Subscriptions/memberships		
Pets		
Other		
Personal care		
Haircuts		
Health club or gym		
Makeup		
Other		
Personal business		
Accountant/attorney/financial advisor		
Other		
Health care		
Physicians and hospitals		
Drugs		
Dental and vision		
Therapy		
Insurance		
Homeowner's/renter's		
Auto		
Health		
Life		
Disability		
Long-term care		
Umbrella liability		
Educational expenses		
Tuition		
Books		
Supplies		
Housing costs (room & board)		
Children		
Day care		
Toys		

(continued)

Table 3-1 *(continued)*

Category	Monthly Average ($)	Percent of Total Gross Income (%)
Activities	_____	
Child support	_____	
Charitable donations	_____	_____
Other		_____
_____	_____	
_____	_____	
_____	_____	

Tracking your spending on "free" websites and apps

Software programs and websites can assist you with paying bills and tracking your spending. The main advantage of using software or websites is that you can continually track your spending as long as you keep entering the information. Software packages and websites can even help speed up the check-writing process (after you figure out how to use them, which isn't always an easy thing to do).

But you don't need a computer and fancy software to pay your bills and figure out where you're spending money. Many people I know stop entering data after a few months. If tracking your spending is what you're after, you need to enter information from the bills you pay by check and the expenses you pay by credit card and cash. Like home exercise equipment and exotic kitchen appliances, such software often ends up in the consumer graveyard.

Plenty of folks have trouble saving money and reducing their spending. Thus, it's no surprise that in the increasingly crowded universe of free websites, plenty are devoted to supposedly helping you to reduce your spending.

More of these sites keep springing up, but among those you may have heard of and stumbled upon are Budget Tracker, Geezeo, Mint, and Yodlee. I've kicked the tires and checked out these sites, and frankly, I have mixed-to-negative feelings about them. The biggest problem that I have with these "free" sites is that they're loaded with advertising and/or have *affiliate relationships* with companies. This simply means that the site gets paid if you click on a link to one of their recommended service providers and buy what they are selling.

This compensation, of course, creates an enormous conflict of interest and thoroughly taints any recommendation made by "free" sites that profit from affiliate referrals. For starters, they have no incentive or reason to recommend companies that won't pay them an affiliate fee. And, there's little — if any — screening of companies for quality, service levels, and other criteria important to you as a consumer.

Also, be forewarned that after registering you as a site user, the first thing most of these sites want you to do is connect directly to your financial institutions (banks, brokerages, investment companies) and download your investment account and spending data. If your intuition tells you this may not be a good idea, trust your instincts. Yes, there are security concerns, but those pale in comparison to privacy concerns and apprehension about the endless pitching to you of products and services.

Another problem I have with these websites is the incredibly simplistic calculators that they have. One that purports to help with retirement planning doesn't allow users to choose a retirement age younger than 62 and has no provisions for part-time work. When it asks about your assets, it makes no distinction between equity in your home and financial assets (stocks, bonds, mutual funds, and so on). Finally, these sites generally offer no phone support, so if you encounter a problem using them, you're relegated to ping-ponging emails in the hope of getting your questions answered.

I noticed over time that many "free" financial websites were singing the praises of the software "You Need A Budget" (YNAB). I test-drove the product (which is like a slimmed-down version of Quicken) and found it to be a decent, but not exceptional, product. My research uncovered the fact that the makers of YNAB pay a whopping 35 percent commission to website affiliates who pitch to users and direct them to buy the product. The owner of a website promoting YNAB pockets about $21 of the software's sales price ($60) for each customer it refers who buys a copy. Does that taint a site's recommendation of YNAB? Of course it does.

Paper, pencil, and a calculator can work just fine for tracking your spending. For those who want to use technology to track bill payments and expenses, I recommend the best software packages and discuss websites and apps in detail in Chapter 19.

Don't waste time on financial administration

Tom is the model of financial organization. His financial documents are neatly organized into color-coded folders. Every month, he reviews all his spending information on his computer. He even carries a notebook to detail his cash spending so that every penny is accounted for. Tom also balances his checkbook "to make sure that everything is in order." He can't remember the last time his bank made a mistake, but he knows someone who once found a $50 error.

If you spend seven hours per month balancing your checkbook and detailing all your spending (as Tom does), you may be wasting about two weeks' worth of time per year — the equivalent of two-thirds of your vacation time if you take three weeks annually.

Suppose that, every other year, you're "lucky" enough to find a $100 error the bank made in its favor. If you spend just three hours per month tracking your spending and balancing your checkbook to discover this glitch, you're spending 72 hours over two years to find a $100 mistake. Your hourly pay: a wafer-thin $1.39 per hour. (***Note:*** If you make significant-sized deposits or withdrawals, make sure you capture them on your statement.)

To add insult to injury, you may not have the desire and energy to do the more important stuff after working a full week and doing all your financial and other chores. Your big personal financial picture — establishing goals, choosing wise investments, securing proper insurance coverage — may continue to be shoved to the back burner. As a result, you may lose thousands of dollars annually. Over the course of your adult life, this amount can translate into tens or even hundreds of thousands of lost dollars.

Tom, for example, doesn't know how much he should be saving to meet his retirement goals. He doesn't review his employer's benefit materials, so he doesn't understand his insurance and retirement plan options. He knows that he pays a lot in taxes, but he isn't sure how to reduce his taxes.

You want to make the most of your money. Unless you truly enjoy dealing with dollars and cents, you need to prioritize the money activities you work on. Time is limited, and life is short. Working harder on financial administration doesn't earn you bonus points. The more time you spend dealing with your personal finances, the less time you have available to gab with friends, watch a good movie, read a good novel, and do other things you really enjoy.

Don't get me wrong — nothing is inherently wrong with balancing your checkbook. In fact, if you regularly bounce checks because you don't know how low your balance is, the exercise may save you a lot in returned check fees. However, if you keep enough money in your checking account so you don't have to worry about the balance reaching $0 or if you have overdraft protection, balancing your checkbook is probably a waste of time, even if your hourly wages aren't lofty. I haven't balanced mine in years (but please don't tell my bank — it might start making some "mistakes" and siphoning money out).

If you're busy, consider ways to reduce the amount of time you spend on mundane financial tasks like bill paying. Many companies, for example, allow you to pay your monthly bills electronically via your bank checking account or your credit card. (Don't use this option unless you pay your credit-card bill in full each month.) The fewer bills you have to pay, the fewer separate checks and envelopes you must process each month. That translates into more free time and fewer paper cuts!

Chapter 4

Establishing and Achieving Goals

. . . .

In This Chapter

▶ Defining what matters most to you

▶ Setting and prioritizing your financial goals

▶ Saving for unexpected expenses, a real-estate purchase, a small business, or educational needs

▶ Estimating what you need for retirement and making up for lost time

. . . .

*I*n my work as a financial counselor, I always asked new clients what their short- and long-term personal and financial goals were. Most people reported that reflecting on this question was incredibly valuable, because they hadn't considered it for a long time — if ever.

In this chapter, I help you dream about what you want to get out of life. Although my expertise is in personal finance, I wouldn't be doing my job if I didn't get you to consider your nonfinancial goals and how money fits into the rest of your life goals. So before I jump into how to establish and save toward common financial goals, I discuss how to think about making and saving money, as well as how to best fit your financial goals into the rest of your life.

Creating Your Own Definition of Wealth

Peruse any major financial magazine, newspaper, or website, and you'll quickly see our culture's obsession with financial wealth. The more money financial executives, movie stars, or professional athletes have, the more publicity and attention they seem to get. In fact, many publications go as far as ranking those people who earn the most or have amassed the greatest wealth!

I can tell you from my decades of working as a personal financial advisor and writer and interacting with folks from varied backgrounds that there's surprisingly little correlation between financial wealth and emotional wealth. That's why in your pursuit of financial wealth and security, you should always remember the emotional side. The following sections can help you gain some perspective.

Acknowledging what money can't buy

Recall the handful of best moments in your life. Odds are these times don't include the time you bought a car or found a designer sweater that you liked. The old saying is true: The most enjoyable and precious things of value in your life can't be bought.

The following statement should go without saying, but I must say it, because too many people act as if it isn't so: Money can't buy happiness. It's tempting to think that if you could only make 20 percent more or twice as much money, you'd be happier because you'd have more money to travel, eat out, and buy that new car you've been eyeing, right? Not so. A great deal of thoughtful research suggests that little relationship exists between money and happiness.

"Wealth is like health: Although its absence can breed misery, having it is no guarantee of happiness," says psychology professor Dr. David G. Myers, who has written and researched happiness across cultures for decades. Despite myriad technological gadgets and communication devices, cheap air travel, microwaves, personal computers, voice mail, smartphones, and all the other stuff that's supposed to make life easier and more enjoyable, Americans aren't any happier than they were five decades ago, according to research conducted by the National Opinion Research Center. These results occur even though incomes, after being adjusted for inflation, have more than doubled during that time.

Managing the balancing act

Believe it or not, some people save too much. In my counseling practice, I saw plenty of people who fell into that category. If making and saving money are good things, then the more the better, right? Well, take the admittedly extreme case of Anne Scheiber, who, on a modest income, started saving at a young age, allowing her money to compound in wealth-building investments such as stocks over many years. As a result, she was able to amass $20 million before she passed away at the age of 101.

Scheiber lived in a cramped studio apartment and never used her investments. She didn't even use the interest or dividends — she lived solely on her Social Security benefits and a small pension from her employer. Scheiber was extreme in her frugality and obsessed with her savings. As reported by James Glassman in *The Washington Post,* "She had few friends . . . she was an unhappy person, totally consumed by her securities accounts and her money." Most people, myself included, wouldn't choose to live and save the way that Scheiber did.

Even those who are saving for an ultimate goal can become consumed by their saving habits. I see some people pursuing higher-paying jobs and pinching pennies in order to retire early. But sometimes they make too many personal sacrifices today while chasing after some vision of their expected lives tomorrow. Others get consumed by work and then don't understand why their family and friends feel neglected — or don't even notice that they do.

Another problem with seeking to amass wealth is that tomorrow may not come. Even if all goes according to plan, will you know how to be happy when you're not working if you spend your entire life making money? More important, who will be around to share your leisure time? One of the costs of an intense career is time spent away from friends and family. You may realize your goal of retiring early, but you may be putting off too much living today in expectation of living tomorrow. As Charles D'Orleans said in 1465, "It's very well to be thrifty, but don't amass a hoard of regrets."

Of course, at the other extreme are spendthrifts who live only for today. A friend of mine once said, "I'm not into delayed gratification." "Shop 'til you drop" seems to be the motto of this personality type. "Why save when I might not be here tomorrow?" reasons this type of person.

The danger of this approach is that tomorrow may come after all, and most people don't want to spend all their tomorrows working for a living. The earlier neglect of saving, however, may make it necessary for you to work when you're much older. And if for some reason you can't work and you have little money to live on, much less live enjoyably, the situation can be tragic. The only difference between a person without any savings or access to credit and some homeless people is a few months of unemployment.

Making and saving money are like eating food. If you don't eat enough, you may suffer. If you eat too much, the overage may go to waste or make you overweight. The right amount, perhaps with some extra to spare, affords you a healthy, balanced, peaceful existence. Money should be treated with respect and acknowledged for what it is — a means to an end and a precious resource that shouldn't be thoughtlessly squandered and wasted.

As Dr. David Myers, whom I introduce earlier in this chapter, says, "Satisfaction isn't so much getting what you want as wanting what you have. There are two ways to be rich: One is to have great wealth; the other is to have few wants."

Find ways to make the most of the money that does pass through your hands, and never lose sight of all that is far more important than money.

Prioritizing Your Savings Goals

Most people I know have financial goals. The rest of this chapter discusses the most common financial goals and how to work toward them. See whether any of the following reflect your ambitions:

- **Owning your home:** Renting and dealing with landlords can be a financial and emotional drag, so most folks want to buy into the American dream and own some real estate — the most basic of which is your own home. (Despite the slide in property prices in the late 2000s, real estate has a solid track record as a long-term investment. As this book goes to press, the median U.S. home price in late 2015 has exceeded its previous peak achieved in 2006.)

- **Making major purchases:** Most folks need to plan ahead for major purchases such as a car, living room furniture, vacations, and so on.

- **Retiring:** No, retiring doesn't imply sitting on a rocking chair watching the world go by while hoping that some long-lost friend, your son's or daughter's family, or the neighborhood dog comes by to visit. *Retiring* is a catchall term for discontinuing full-time work or perhaps not even working for pay at all.

- **Educating the kids:** All those diaper changes, late-night feedings, and trips to the zoo aren't enough to get Junior out of your house and into the real world as a productive, self-sufficient adult. You may want to help your children get a college education. Unfortunately, that can cost a truckload of dough.

- **Owning your own business:** Many employees want to take on the challenges and rewards that come with being the boss. The primary reason that most people continue just to dream is that they lack the money to leave their primary job. Although many businesses don't require gobs of start-up cash, almost all require that you withstand a substantial reduction in your income during the early years.

Because everyone is different, you can have goals (other than those in the preceding list) that are unique to your own situation. Accomplishing such goals almost always requires saving money. As one of my favorite Chinese proverbs says, "Do not wait until you are thirsty to dig a well," so don't wait to save money until you're ready to accomplish a personal or financial goal!

Knowing what's most important to you

Unless you earn really big bucks or have a large family inheritance to fall back on, your personal and financial desires will probably outstrip your resources. Thus, you must prioritize your goals.

One of the biggest mistakes I see people make is rushing into a financial decision without considering what's really important to them. Because many people get caught up in the responsibilities of their daily lives, they often don't have time for reflection.

As a result of my experience counseling and teaching people about better personal financial management, I can tell you that the folks who accomplish their goals aren't necessarily smarter or higher-income earners than those who don't. People who identify their goals and then work toward them, which often requires changing some habits, are the ones who accomplish their goals.

Valuing retirement accounts

Where possible, try to save and invest in accounts that offer you a tax advantage, which is precisely what retirement accounts do. These accounts — known by such enlightening acronyms and names as 401(k), 403(b), SEP-IRAs, Keoghs, and so on — offer tax breaks to people of all economic means. Consider the following advantages to investing in retirement accounts:

✔ **Contributions are usually tax-deductible.** By putting money in a retirement account, not only do you plan wisely for your future, but you also get an immediate financial reward: lower taxes, which means more money available for saving and investing. Retirement account contributions generally aren't taxed at either the federal or state income tax level until withdrawal (but they're still subject to Social Security and Medicare taxes when earned). If you're paying, say, 35 percent between federal and state taxes (see Chapter 7 to determine your tax bracket), a $5,000 contribution to a retirement account lowers your taxes by $1,750.

✔ **In some company retirement accounts, companies match a portion of your own contributions.** Thus, in addition to tax breaks, you get free extra money courtesy of your employer!

✔ **Returns on your investment compound over time without taxation.**
After you put money into a retirement account, any interest, dividends, and appreciation add to your account without being taxed. Of course, there's no such thing as a free lunch — these accounts don't allow for complete tax avoidance. Yet you can get a really great lunch at a discount: You get to defer taxes on all the accumulating gains and profits until you withdraw the money down the road. Thus, more money is working for you over a longer period of time. (The Roth IRA that I discuss in Chapter 11 offers no upfront tax breaks but does allow future tax-free withdrawal of investment earnings.)

The tax rates on stock dividends and *long-term capital gains* (investments held more than one year) are lower than the tax rates levied on ordinary income (such as that earned through working). This fact makes some people think that investing through retirement accounts may not be worthwhile because all investment earnings are taxed at the relatively high ordinary income tax rates when money is withdrawn from retirement accounts. I'll cut to the chase: The vast majority of people are better off contributing to retirement accounts (please see Chapter 7 for more details).

Dealing with competing goals

Unless you enjoy paying higher taxes, why would you save money outside of retirement accounts, which shelter your money from taxation? The reason is that some financial goals are not easily achieved by saving in retirement accounts. Also, retirement accounts have caps on the amount you can contribute annually.

If you're accumulating money for a down payment on a home or to start or buy a business, for example, you'll probably need to save that money outside of a retirement account. Why? Because if you withdraw funds from retirement accounts before age 59½ and you're not retired, not only do you have to pay income taxes on the withdrawals, but you also generally have to pay *early withdrawal penalties* of 10 percent of the withdrawn amount in federal tax plus whatever your state charges. (See the sidebar "Avoiding retirement account early withdrawal penalties" for exceptions to this rule.)

Because you're constrained by your financial resources, you need to prioritize your goals. Before funding your retirement accounts and racking up those tax breaks, read on to consider your other goals.

Avoiding retirement account early withdrawal penalties

You can find ways to avoid the early withdrawal penalties that the tax authorities normally apply. Suppose you read this book at a young age, develop sound financial habits early, and save enough to retire before age 59½. In this case, you can take money out of your retirement account without triggering penalties (which are normally 10 percent of the amount withdrawn for federal income tax plus whatever your state levies). Of course, you will still owe income tax on your withdrawals.

The IRS allows you to withdraw money before 59½ if you do so in equal, annual installments based on your life expectancy. (You generally must do such distributions for at least five years or until age 59½, whichever is later.) The IRS (this is slightly chilling) even has a little table that allows you to look up your life expectancy.

You can now also make penalty-free withdrawals from individual retirement accounts for a first-time home purchase (up to $10,000) or qualifying higher educational expenses for you, your spouse, your children, or your grandchildren. The other conditions under which you can make penalty-free early withdrawals from retirement accounts are not as enjoyable: If you have major medical expenses (exceeding 7.5 percent of your income; 10 percent if you're under age 65) or a disability, you may be exempt from the penalties under certain conditions. (You will still owe ordinary income tax on withdrawals.)

If you get into a financial pinch while you're still employed, be aware that some company retirement plans allow you to borrow against your balance. This tactic is like loaning money to yourself — the interest payments go back into your account.

If you lose your job and withdraw retirement account money simply because you need it to live on, the penalties do apply. However, if you're not working and you're earning so little income that you need to tap your retirement account, you surely fall into a low tax bracket. The lower income taxes you pay (when compared to the taxes you would have paid on that money had you not sheltered it in a retirement account in the first place) should make up for most or all of the penalty.

Building Emergency Reserves

Because you don't know what the future holds, preparing for the unexpected is financially wise. Even if you're the lucky sort who sometimes finds $5 bills on street corners, you can't control the sometimes chaotic world in which we live.

Conventional wisdom says that you should have approximately six months of living expenses put away for an emergency. This particular amount may or may not be right for you, because it depends, of course, on how expensive the emergency is. Why six months, anyway? And where should you put it?

How much of an emergency stash you need depends on your situation. I recommend saving the following emergency amounts under differing circumstances (in Chapter 12, I recommend preferred places to invest this money):

- ✔ **Three months' living expenses:** Choose this option if you have other accounts, such as a 401(k), or family members and close friends whom you can tap for a short-term loan. This minimalist approach makes sense when you're trying to maximize investments elsewhere (for example, in retirement accounts) or you have stable sources of income (employment or otherwise).

- ✔ **Six months' living expenses:** This amount is appropriate if you don't have other places to turn for a loan or you have some instability in your employment situation or source of income.

- ✔ **Up to one year's living expenses:** Set aside this much if your income fluctuates wildly from year to year or if your profession involves a high risk of job loss, finding another job could take you a long time, and you don't have other places to turn for a loan.

In the event that your only current source of emergency funds is a high-interest credit card, first save at least three months' worth of living expenses in an accessible account before funding a retirement account or saving for other goals.

Saving to Buy a Home or Business

When you're starting out financially, deciding whether to save money to buy a home or to put money into a retirement account presents a dilemma. In the long run, owning your own home is generally a wise financial move. On the other hand, saving sooner for retirement makes achieving your goals easier.

Presuming both goals are important to you, save toward both buying a home *and* for retirement. If you're eager to own a home, you can throw all your savings toward achieving that goal and temporarily put your retirement savings on hold. Save for both purposes simultaneously if you're not in a rush.

You may be able to have the best of both worlds if you work for an employer that allows borrowing against retirement account balances. You can save money in the retirement account and then borrow against it for the down payment of a home. Be extra careful, though. Retirement account loans typically must be paid back within a set number of years (check with your employer) or immediately if you quit or lose your job. As I mention earlier in this chapter, you're also allowed to make penalty-free withdrawals of up to $10,000 from individual retirement accounts toward a first-time home purchase.

When saving money for starting or buying a business, most people encounter the same dilemma they face when deciding to save to buy a house: If you fund your retirement accounts to the exclusion of earmarking money for your small-business dreams, your entrepreneurial aspirations may never become a reality. Generally, I advocate hedging your bets by saving money in your tax-sheltered retirement accounts as well as toward your business venture. As I discuss in Part III, an investment in your own small business can produce great rewards, so you may feel comfortable focusing your savings on your own business.

Funding Kids' Educational Expenses

Wanting to provide for your children's future is perfectly natural, but doing so before you've saved adequately toward your own goals can be a major financial mistake. The college financial-aid system effectively penalizes you for saving money outside of retirement accounts and penalizes you even more if the money's invested in the child's name.

This concept may sound selfish, but you need to take care of *your* future first. Take advantage of saving through your tax-sheltered retirement accounts before you set aside money in custodial savings accounts for your kids. This practice isn't selfish: Do you really want to have to leech off your kids when you're old and frail because you didn't save any money for yourself? (See Chapter 13 for a complete explanation of how to save for educational expenses.)

Saving for Big Purchases

If you want to buy a car, a canoe, and a plane ticket to Thailand, do not, I repeat, do not buy such things with *consumer credit* (that is, carry debt month-to-month to finance the purchase on a credit card or auto loan). As I explain in Chapter 5, cars, boats, vacations, and the like are consumer items, not wealth-building investments, such as real estate or small businesses. A car begins to depreciate the moment you drive it off the sales lot. A plane ticket is worthless the moment you arrive back home. (I know your memories will be priceless, but they won't pay the bills.)

Don't deny yourself gratification; just learn how to delay it. Get into the habit of saving for your larger consumer purchases to avoid paying for them over time with high-interest consumer credit. When saving up for a consumer purchase such as a car, a money-market account or short-term bond fund (see Chapter 12) is a good place to store your short-term savings.

Paying for high-interest consumer debt can cripple your ability not only to save for long-term goals but also to make major purchases in the future. Interest on consumer debt is exorbitantly expensive — upwards of 20 percent on credit cards. When contemplating the purchase of a consumer item on credit, add up the total interest you'd end up paying on your debt and call it the price of instant gratification.

Preparing for Retirement

Many people toil away at work, dreaming about a future in which they can stop the daily commute and grind; get out from under that daily deluge of voice mails, emails, and other never-ending technological intrusions; and do what they want, when they want. People often assume that this magical day will arrive when they retire or win the lottery — whichever comes first.

I've never cared much for the term *retire,* which seems to imply idleness or the end of usefulness to society. But if retirement means not having to work at a job (especially one you don't enjoy) and having financial flexibility and independence, then I'm all for it.

Many folks aspire to retire sooner rather than later. But this idea has some obvious problems. First, you set yourself up for disappointment. If you want to retire by your mid-60s (when Social Security kicks in), you need to save enough money to support yourself for 20 to 30 years, maybe longer. Two to three decades is a long time to live off your savings. You're going to need a good-sized chunk of money — more than most people realize.

The earlier you hope to retire, the more money you need to set aside and the sooner you have to start saving — unless you plan to work part-time in retirement to earn more income! See Chapter 11 for more details about how to save for retirement.

Many of the people I speak to say that they do want to retire, and most say "the sooner, the better." Yet more than half of Americans between the ages of 18 and 34, and a quarter of those ages 35 to 54, have not begun to save for retirement. When I asked one of my middle-aged counseling clients, who had saved little for retirement, when he would like to retire, he deadpanned, "Sometime before I die." If you're in this group (and even if you're not), determine where you stand financially regarding retirement. If you're like most working people, you need to increase your savings rate for retirement.

Don't neglect nonfinancial preparations for retirement

Investing your money is just one (and not even the most important) aspect of preparing for your retirement. In order to enjoy the lifestyle that your retirement savings will provide you, you need to invest energy into other areas of your life as well:

✔ Few things are more important than your health. Without your health, enjoying the good things in life can be hard. Unfortunately, many people aren't motivated to care about their health until *after* they discover problems. By then, it may be too late.

Although exercising regularly, eating a balanced and nutritious diet, driving safely, and avoiding substance abuse can't guarantee you a healthful future, these good habits go a long way toward preventing many of the most common causes of death and debilitating disease. Regular medical exams also are important in detecting problems early.

✔ In addition to your physical health, be sure to invest in your psychological health. People live longer and have happier and ... when they have a circle of ... friends around them for support.

Un... ... many people become more isol... ... regular contact with business asso... ... and family members as they grow older.

Happy retirees tend to stay active, getting involved in volunteer organizations and new social circles. They may travel to see old friends or younger relatives who may be too busy to visit them.

Treat retirement life like a bubbly, inviting hot tub set at 102 degrees. You want to ease yourself in nice and slow; jumping in hastily can take most of the pleasantness out of the experience. Abruptly leaving your job without a plan for spending all that free time is an invitation to boredom and depression. Everyone needs a sense of purpose and a sense of routine. Establishing hobbies, volunteer work, or a sideline business while gradually cutting back your regular work schedule can be a terrific way to ease into retirement.

Figuring out what you need for retirement

If you hope to someday reduce the time you spend working or cease working altogether, you'll need sufficient savings to support yourself. Many people — particularly young people and those who don't work well with numbers — underestimate the amount of money needed to retire. To figure out how much you should save per month to achieve your retirement goals, you need to crunch a few numbers. (Don't worry — this number-crunching is usually easier than doing your taxes.)

Luckily for you, you don't have to start cold. Studies show how people typically spend money before and during retirement. Most people need about 70 to 80 percent of their pre-retirement income throughout retirement to maintain their standard of living. For example, if your household earns $50,000 per year before retirement, you're likely to need $35,000 to $40,000 (70 to 80 percent of $50,000) per year during retirement to live the way you're accustomed to living. The 70 to 80 percent is an average. Some people may need more simply because they have more time on their hands to spend their money. Others adjust their standard of living and live on less.

So how do you figure out what you're going to need? The following three profiles provide a rough estimate of the percentage of your pre-retirement income you're going to need during retirement. Pick the one that most accurately describes your situation. If you fall between two descriptions, pick a percentage in between those two.

To maintain your standard of living in retirement, you may need about

✔ **65 percent of your pre-retirement income if you**

- Save a large amount (15 percent or more) of your annual earnings
- Are a high-income earner
- Will own your home free of debt by the time you retire
- Do not anticipate leading a lifestyle in retirement that reflects your current high income

If you're an especially high-income earner who lives well beneath your means, you may be able to do just fine with even less than 65 percent. Pick an annual dollar amount or percentage of your current income that will allow the kind of retirement lifestyle you desire.

✔ **75 percent of your pre-retirement income if you**

- Save a reasonable amount (5 to 14 percent) of your annual earnings
- Will still have some mortgage debt or a modest rent to pay by the time you retire
- Anticipate having a standard of living in retirement that's comparable to what you have today

✔ **85 percent of your pre-retirement income if you**

- Save little or none of your annual earnings (less than 5 percent)
- Will have a relatively significant mortgage payment or sizeable rent to pay in retirement
- Anticipate wanting or needing to maintain your current lifestyle throughout retirement

Of course, you can use a more precise approach to figure out how much you need per year in retirement. Be forewarned, though, that using a more-personalized method is far more time-consuming, and because you're making projections into an uncertain future, it may not be any more accurate than the simple method I explain here. If you're data-oriented, you may feel comfortable tackling this method: Figure out where you're spending your money today (worksheets are available in Chapter 3) and then work up some projections for your expected spending needs in retirement (the information in Chapter 19 may help you as well).

Understanding retirement building blocks

Did you play with Lego blocks or Tinkertoys when you were a child? You start by building a foundation on the ground, and then you build up. Before you know it, you're creating bridges, castles, and animal figures. Although preparing financially for retirement isn't exactly like playing with blocks, the concept is the same: You need a basic foundation so your necessary retirement reserves can grow.

If you've been working steadily, you may already have a good foundation, even if you haven't been actively saving toward retirement. In the pages ahead, I walk you through the probable components of your future retirement income and show you how to figure how much you should be saving to reach particular retirement goals.

Counting on Social Security

According to polls, about half of American adults under the age of 35, and more than a third of those between the ages of 35 and 49, think that Social Security benefits will not be available by the time they retire.

Contrary to widespread skepticism, Social Security should be available when you retire, no matter how old you are today. In fact, Social Security is one of the sacred cow political programs. Imagine what would happen to the group of politicians who voted to greatly curtail benefits! (Congress may make some reductions in benefits, probably for the highest income earners, at some point due to the federal debt problems.)

If you think that you can never retire because you don't have any money saved, I'm happy to inform you that you're probably wrong. You likely have some Social Security. But Social Security generally isn't enough to live on comfortably.

Social Security is intended to provide you with a subsistence level of retirement income for the basic necessities: food, shelter, and clothing. Social Security is not intended to be your sole source of income. Some of the elderly are quite dependent upon Social Security: It's the only source of income for 21 percent of the elderly, and about two out of three Social Security recipients derive at least half of their total retirement income from their Social Security retirement check. Few working people can maintain their current lifestyles into retirement without supplementing Social Security with personal savings and company retirement plans.

How much work makes me eligible?

To be eligible to collect Social Security benefits, you need to have worked a minimum number of calendar quarters. If you were born after 1928, you need 40 quarters of work credits to qualify for Social Security retirement benefits.

If, for some reason, you work only the first half of a year or only during the summer months, don't despair. You don't need to work part of every quarter to get a quarter's credit. You get credits based on the income you earn during the year. As of this writing, you get the full four quarters credited to your account if you earn $4,880 or more ($1,220 per credit) in a year. To get 40 quarters of coverage, you basically need to work (at least portions of) ten years.

To get credits, your income must be reported and you must pay taxes on it (including Social Security tax). In other words, you and those you employ encounter problems when you neglect to declare income or you pay people under the table: You may be cheating yourself, or others, out of valuable benefits.

How much will I get from Social Security?

The average monthly benefit Social Security pays out to retirees is about $1,328. The higher your employment earnings have been on average, the more you can expect to receive. If you're married and one of you doesn't work for pay, the nonworking spouse collects 50 percent of what the working spouse collects. Working spouses are eligible for either individual benefits or half of their spouse's benefits — whichever amount is greater.

To get a more precise handle on your Social Security benefits, visit the Social Security Administration (SSA) website at www.ssa.gov or call the SSA at 800-772-1213 and ask for Form 7004, which allows you to receive a record of your reported earnings and an estimate of your Social Security benefits. Check your earnings record, because occasional errors do arise and — surprise — they usually aren't in your favor.

More Social Security details

When the Social Security system was created in the 1930s, its designers underestimated how long people would live in retirement. Thanks to scientific advances and improved medical care, life expectancies have risen substantially since that time. As a result, many recent retirees get back far more than they paid into the system.

The age at which you can start collecting full benefits has increased, and it may increase again. In the "good old days" (prior to changes made in Social Security regulations in 1983), you could collect full Social Security payments at age 65, assuming you were eligible. Under current rules, if you were born before 1938, you're still eligible to collect full Social Security benefits at age 65. If you were born after 1959, you have to wait until age 67 for full benefits. If you were born between 1938 and 1959, full benefits are payable to you at age 66 (plus or minus some number of months, depending on the year you were born).

These regulations may seem unfair, but they're necessary for updating the system to fit with the realities of increased longevity, large federal budget deficits, and aging baby boomers. Without changes, the Social Security system could collapse, because it would be fed by a relatively small number of workers while supporting large numbers of retirees.

In addition to paying for retirement-income checks for retirees, a portion of your Social Security taxes also help fund disability insurance for you, survivor income insurance for your financial dependents, and Medicare (the health insurance program for retirees).

The amount of Social Security benefits you receive in retirement depends on your average earnings during your working years. Don't worry about the fact that you probably earned a lot less many years ago. The Social Security benefits calculations increase your older earnings to account for the lower cost of living and wages in prior years.

Planning your personal savings/investment strategy

Money you're saving toward retirement can include money under the mattress as well as money in a retirement account such as an individual retirement account (IRA), 401(k), or similar plan (see Chapter 11). You may also earmark investments in nonretirement accounts for your retirement.

Equity (the difference between the market value less any mortgage balances owed) in rental or investment real estate can be counted toward your retirement as well. Deciding whether to include the equity in your primary residence (your home) is trickier. If you don't want to count on using this money in retirement, don't include it when you tally your stash.

You may want to count a portion of your home equity in your total assets for retirement. Some people sell their homes when they retire and move to a lower-cost area, move closer to family, or downsize to a more manageable-size home. And increasing numbers of older retirees are tapping their homes' equity through reverse mortgages (see Chapter 14 for information on mortgages).

Making the most of pensions

Pension plans are a benefit offered by some employers — mostly larger organizations and government agencies. Even if your current employer doesn't offer a pension, you may have earned pension benefits through a previous job.

The plans I'm referring to are known as *defined-benefit plans*. With these plans, you qualify for a monthly benefit amount to be paid to you in retirement based on your years of service for a specific employer.

Although each company's plan differs, all plans calculate and pay benefits based on a formula. A typical formula may credit you with 1.5 percent of your salary for each year of service (full-time employment). For example, if you work ten years, you earn a monthly retirement benefit worth 15 percent of your monthly salary.

Pension benefits can be quite valuable. In the better plans, employers put away the equivalent of 5 to 10 percent of your salary to pay your future pension. This money is in addition to your salary — you never see it in your paycheck, and it isn't taxed. The employer puts this money away in an account for your retirement.

To qualify for pension benefits, you don't have to stay with an employer long enough to receive the 25-year gold watch. Under current government regulations, employees must be fully *vested* (entitled to receive full benefits based on years of service upon reaching retirement age) after five years of full-time service.

Defined-benefit pension plans are becoming rarer for two major reasons:

✔ They're costly for employers to fund and maintain. Many employees don't understand how these plans work and why they're so valuable, so companies don't get mileage out of their pension expenditures — employees don't see the money, so they don't appreciate the company's generosity.

✔ Most of the new jobs being generated in the U.S. economy are with smaller companies that typically don't offer these types of plans.

More employers offer plans like 401(k)s, in which employees elect to save money out of their own paychecks. Known as *defined-contribution plans,* these plans allow you to save toward your retirement at your own expense rather than at your employer's expense. (To encourage participation in defined-contribution plans, some employers "match" a portion of their employees' contributions.) More of the burden and responsibility of investing for retirement falls on your shoulders with 401(k) and similar plans, so understanding how these plans work is important. Most people are ill-equipped to know how much to save and how to invest the money. The retirement planning worksheet in the next section can help you get started with figuring out the amount you need to save. (Part III shows you how to invest.)

Crunching numbers for your retirement

Now that you've toured the components of your future retirement income, take a shot at tallying where you stand in terms of retirement preparations. Don't be afraid to do this exercise — it's not difficult, and you may find that you're not in such bad shape. I even explain how to catch up if you find that you're behind in saving for retirement.

Note: The following worksheet (Table 4-1) and the Growth Multiplier (Table 4-2) assume that you're going to retire at age 66 and that your investments will produce an annual rate of return that is 4 percent higher than the rate of inflation. (For example, if inflation averages 3 percent, this table assumes that you will earn 7 percent per year on your investments.)

Table 4-1	Retirement Planning Worksheet
Retirement Income or Needs	*Amount*
1. Annual retirement income needed in today's dollars (see earlier in this chapter)	$ _____ / year
2. Annual Social Security	– $ _____ / year
3. Annual pension benefits (ask your benefits department); multiply by 60% if your pension won't increase with inflation during retirement	– $ _____ / year
4. Annual retirement income needed from personal savings (subtract lines 2 and 3 from line 1)	= $ _____ / year
5. Savings needed to retire at age 66 (multiply line 4 by 15)	$ _____
6. Value of current retirement savings	$ _____
7. Value of current retirement savings at retirement (multiply line 6 by Growth Multiplier in Table 4-2)	$ _____
8. Amount you still need to save (line 5 minus line 7)	$ _____
9. Amount you need to save per month (multiply line 8 by Savings Factor in Table 4-2)	$ _____ / month

To get a more precise handle on where you stand in terms of retirement planning (especially if you'd like to retire earlier than your mid-60s), call T. Rowe Price at 800-638-5660 and ask for the company's retirement planning booklets. You can also turn to Chapter 19, where I recommend retirement planning software and websites that can ease your number-crunching burdens.

Table 4-2	Growth Multiplier	
Your Current Age	*Growth Multiplier*	*Savings Factor*
26	4.8	0.001
28	4.4	0.001
30	4.1	0.001
32	3.8	0.001
34	3.5	0.001
36	3.2	0.001
38	3.0	0.002
40	2.8	0.002
42	2.6	0.002
44	2.4	0.002
46	2.2	0.003
48	2.0	0.003
50	1.9	0.004
52	1.7	0.005
54	1.6	0.006
56	1.5	0.007
58	1.4	0.009
60	1.3	0.013
62	1.2	0.020
64	1.1	0.041

Making up for lost time

If the amount you need to save per month to reach your retirement goals seems daunting, all is not lost. Remember: Winners never quit, and quitters never win. Here are my top recommendations for making up for lost time:

✔ **Question your spending.** You have two ways to boost your savings: Earn more money or cut your spending (or do both). Most people don't spend their money nearly as thoughtfully as they earn it. See Chapter 6 for suggestions and strategies for reducing your spending.

✔ **Be more realistic about your retirement age.** If you extend the age at which you plan to retire, you get a double benefit: You earn and save money for more years, and you spend your nest egg over fewer years. Of course, if your job is making you crazy, this option may not be too appealing. Try to find work that makes you happy, and consider working, at least part-time, during your "early" retirement years.

✔ **Use your home equity.** The prospect of tapping the cash in your home can be troubling. After getting together the down payment, you probably worked for many years to pay off that sucker. You're delighted not to have to mail a mortgage payment to the bank anymore. But what's the use of owning a house free of mortgage debt when you lack sufficient retirement reserves? All the money that's tied up in the house can be used to help increase your standard of living in retirement.

You have a number of ways to tap your home's equity. You can sell your home and either move to a lower-cost property or rent an apartment. Current tax laws allow you to realize up to $250,000 in tax-free profit from the sale of your house ($500,000 if you're married). Another option is a *reverse mortgage,* in which you get a monthly income check as you build a loan balance against the value of your home. The loan is paid when your home is finally sold. (See Chapter 14 for more information about reverse mortgages.)

✔ **Get your investments growing.** The faster the rate at which your money grows and compounds, the less you need to save each year to reach your goals. (Make sure, however, that you're not reckless; don't take huge risks in the hopes of big returns.) Earning just a few extra percentage points per year on your investments can dramatically slash the amount you need to save. The younger you are, the more powerful the effect of compounding interest. For example, if you're in your mid-30s and your investments appreciate 6 percent per year (rather than 4 percent) faster than the rate of inflation, the amount you need to save each month to reach your retirement goals drops by about 40 percent! (See Part III for more on investing.)

✔ **Turn a hobby into supplemental retirement income.** Even if you earn a living in the same career over many decades, you have skills that are portable and can be put to profitable use. Pick something you enjoy and are good at, develop a business plan, and get smart about how to market your services and wares (check out the latest edition of *Small Business For Dummies* from Wiley, which I co-wrote with veteran entrepreneur Jim Schell). Remember, as people get busier, more specialized services are created to support their hectic lives. A demand for quality, homemade goods of all varieties also exists. Be creative! You never know — you may wind up profiled in a business publication!

✔ **Invest to gain tax-free and other free money.** By investing in a tax-wise fashion, you can boost the effective rate of return on your investments without taking on additional risk.

In addition to the tax benefits you gain from funding most types of retirement accounts in this chapter (see the earlier section "Valuing retirement accounts"), some employers offer free matching money. Also, the government now offers tax credits (see Chapter 7) for low- and moderate-income earners who use retirement accounts.

As for money outside of tax-sheltered retirement accounts, if you're in a relatively high tax bracket, you may earn more by investing in tax-free investments and other vehicles that minimize highly taxed distributions.

✔ **Think about inheritances.** Although you should never count on an inheritance to support your retirement, you may inherit money someday. If you want to see what impact an inheritance has on your retirement calculations, add a conservative estimate of the amount you expect to inherit to your current total savings in Table 4-1.

Part II
Spending Less, Saving More

5 Ways to Cut Your Spending on Credit Cards

- **Reduce your credit limit.** Keep a lid on your credit card's *credit limit* (the maximum balance allowed on your card). Call your credit card service's toll-free phone number and lower your credit limit to a level you're comfortable with.

- **Replace your credit card with a charge card.** A *charge card* requires you to pay your balance in full each billing period. You have no credit line or interest charges.

- **Never buy anything on credit that depreciates in value.** Meals out, cars, clothing, and shoes all depreciate in value. Don't buy these things on credit. (It's fine to charge such purchases on a card if you pay the balance in full each month.)

- **Think in terms of total cost.** Everything sounds cheaper in terms of monthly payments. Take a calculator along, if necessary, to tally up the sticker price, interest charges, and upkeep. The total cost will scare you.

- **Limit what you can spend.** Go shopping with a small amount of cash and no plastic or checks. That way, you can spend only what little cash you have with you.

How you feel about money has an impact on how good you are at managing money and making financial decisions. You have to balance your financial goals with your other life goals. For more on this concept, check out the free article at www.dummies.com/extras/personalfinance.

In this part . . .

- ✔ Find out how to cope with and reduce debt.
- ✔ Review strategies for reducing your spending.
- ✔ Understand how to slash your taxes.

Chapter 5

Dealing with Debt

. . . .

In This Chapter

▶ Using your savings to lower your debt

▶ Getting out of debt when you don't have savings

▶ Understanding the pros and cons of filing bankruptcy

▶ Halting your spending and staying out of debt

. . . .

Accumulating *bad debt* (consumer debt) by buying things like new living room furniture or a new car that you really can't afford is like living on a diet of sugar and caffeine: a quick fix with little nutritional value. Borrowing on your credit card to afford an extravagant vacation is detrimental to your long-term financial health.

When you use debt for investing in your future, I call it *good debt* (see Chapter 2). Borrowing money to pay for an education, to buy real estate, or to invest in a small business is like eating fruits and vegetables for their vitamins. That's not to say that you can't get yourself into trouble when using good debt. Just as you can gorge yourself on too much good food, you can develop financial indigestion from too much good debt.

In this chapter, I mainly help you battle the pervasive problem of consumer debt. Getting rid of your bad debts may be even more difficult than giving up the junk foods you love. But in the long run, you'll be glad you did; you'll be financially healthier and emotionally happier. And after you get rid of your high-cost consumer debts, make sure you practice the best way to avoid future credit problems: *Don't borrow with bad debt.*

Before you decide which debt reduction strategies make sense for you, you must first consider your overall financial situation (see Chapter 2) and assess your alternatives. (I discuss strategies for reducing your current spending — which help you free up more cash to pay down your debts — in the next chapter.)

Using Savings to Reduce Your Consumer Debt

Many people build a mental brick wall between their savings and investment accounts and their consumer debt accounts. By failing to view their finances holistically, they simply fall into the habit of looking at these accounts individually. The thought of putting a door in that big brick wall doesn't occur to them. This section helps you see how your savings can be used to lower your consumer debt.

Understanding how you gain

If you have the savings to pay off consumer debt, like high-interest credit-card and auto loans, consider doing so. (Make sure you pay off the loans with the highest interest rates first.) Sure, you diminish your savings, but you also reduce your debts. Although your savings and investments may be earning decent returns, the interest you're paying on your consumer debts is likely higher.

Paying off consumer loans on a credit card at, say, 12 percent is like finding an investment with a guaranteed return of 12 percent — *tax-free*. You would actually need to find an investment that yielded even more — around 18 percent — to net 12 percent after paying taxes on those investment returns in order to justify not paying off your 12 percent loans. The higher your tax bracket (see Chapter 7), the higher the return you need on your investments to justify keeping high-interest consumer debt.

Even if you think that you're an investing genius and you can earn more on your investments, swallow your ego and pay down your consumer debts anyway. In order to chase that higher potential return from investments, you need to take substantial risk. You *may* earn more investing in that hot stock tip or that bargain real estate, but you probably won't.

If you use your savings to pay down consumer debts, be careful to leave yourself enough of an emergency cushion. (In Chapter 4, I tell you how to determine what size emergency reserve you should have.) You want to be in a position to withstand an unexpected large expense or temporary loss of income. On the other hand, if you use savings to pay down credit-card debt, you can run your credit-card balances back up in a financial pinch (unless your card gets canceled), or you can turn to a family member or wealthy friend for a low-interest loan.

Finding the funds to pay down consumer debts

Have you ever reached into the pocket of an old winter parka and found a rolled-up $20 bill you forgot you had? Stumbling across some forgotten funds is always a pleasant experience. But before you root through all your closets in search of stray cash to help you pay down that nagging credit-card debt, check out some of these financial jacket pockets you may have overlooked:

- **Borrow against your cash value life insurance policy.** If a life insurance agent ever lured you into buying a policy, she probably sold you a cash value policy because it pays high commissions to insurance agents. Or perhaps your parents bought one of these policies for you when you were a child. Borrow against the cash value to pay down your debts. (*Note:* You may want to consider discontinuing your cash value policy altogether and simply withdraw the cash balance — see Chapter 16 for details.)

- **Sell investments held outside of retirement accounts.** Maybe you have some shares of stock or a Treasury bond gathering dust in your safety deposit box. Consider cashing in these investments to pay down your consumer loans. Just be sure to consider the tax consequences of selling these investments. If possible, sell only those investments that won't generate a big tax bill.

- **Tap the equity in your home.** If you're a homeowner, you may be able to tap in to your home's *equity,* which is the difference between the property's market value and the outstanding loan balance. You can generally borrow against real estate at a lower interest rate and get a tax deduction. However, you must take care to ensure that you don't overborrow on your home and risk losing it to foreclosure.

- **Borrow against your employer's retirement account.** Check with your employer's benefits department to see whether you can borrow against your retirement account balance. The interest rate is usually reasonable. Be careful, though — if you leave or lose your job, you may have to repay the loan within 60 days. Also recognize that you'll miss out on investment returns on the money borrowed.

- **Lean on family.** They know you, love you, realize your shortcomings, and probably won't be as cold-hearted as some bankers. Money borrowed from family members can have strings attached, of course. Treating the obligation seriously is important. To avoid misunderstandings, write up a simple agreement listing the terms and conditions of the loan. Unless your family members are the worst bankers I know, you'll probably get a fair interest rate, and your family will have the satisfaction of helping you out. Just don't forget to pay them back.

Decreasing Debt When You Lack Savings

If you lack savings to throw at your consumer debts, not surprisingly, you have some work to do. If you're currently spending all your income (and more!), you need to figure out how you can decrease your spending (see Chapter 6 for lots of great ideas) and/or increase your income. In the meantime, you need to slow the growth of your debt.

Reducing your credit card's interest rate

Different credit cards charge different interest rates. So why pay 14, 16, or 18 percent (or more) when you can pay less? The credit-card business is highly competitive. Until you get your debt paid off, slow the growth of your debt by reducing the interest rate you're paying. Here are sound ways to do that:

- ✔ **Apply for a lower-rate credit card.** If you're earning a decent income, you're not too burdened with debt, and you have a clean credit record, qualifying for lower-rate cards is relatively painless. Some persistence (and cleanup work) may be required if you have income and debt problems or nicks in your credit report. After you're approved for a new, lower-interest-rate card, you can simply transfer your outstanding balance from your higher-rate card.

   CreditCards.com's website (www.creditcards.com) carries information on low-interest-rate and no-annual-fee cards (among others, including secured cards).

- ✔ **Call the bank(s) that issued your current high-interest-rate credit card(s) and say that you want to cancel your card(s) because you found a competitor that offers no annual fee and a lower interest rate.** Your bank may choose to match the terms of the "competitor" rather than lose you as a customer. But be careful with this strategy and consider just paying off or transferring the balance. Canceling the credit card, especially if it's one you've had for a number of years, may lower your credit score.

- ✔ **While you're paying down your credit-card balance(s), stop making new charges on cards that have outstanding balances.** Many people don't realize that interest starts to accumulate *immediately* when they carry a balance. *You have no grace period* — the 20 or so days you normally have to pay your balance in full without incurring interest charges — if you carry a credit-card balance from month to month.

Understanding all credit-card terms and conditions

Avoid getting lured into applying for a credit card that hypes an extremely low interest rate. One such card advertised a 1.9 percent rate, but you had to dig into the fine print for the rest of the story.

First, any card that offers such a low interest rate will honor that rate only for a short period of time — in this case, six months. After six months, the interest rate skyrocketed to nearly 15 percent.

But wait, there's more: Make just one late payment or exceed your credit limit, and the company raises your interest rate to 19.8 percent (or even 24 percent, 29 percent, or more) and slaps you with a $25 fee — $35 thereafter. If you want a cash advance on your card, you get socked with a fee equal to 3 percent of the amount advanced. (Some banks have even advertised 0 percent interest rates — although that rate generally has applied only to balances transferred from another card, and such cards have been subject to all of the other vagaries discussed in this section.)

I'm not saying that everyone should avoid this type of card. Such a card may make sense for you if you want to transfer an outstanding balance and then pay off that balance within a matter of months and cancel the card to avoid getting socked with the card's high fees.

If you hunt around for a low-interest-rate credit card, be sure to check out all the terms and conditions. Start by reviewing the uniform rates and terms disclosure, which details the myriad fees and conditions (especially how much your interest rate can increase for missed or late payments). Also, be sure you understand how the future interest rate is determined on cards that charge variable interest rates.

Cutting up your credit cards

If you have a tendency to live beyond your means by buying on credit, get rid of the culprit — the credit card. To kick the habit, a smoker needs to toss *all* the cigarettes, and an alcoholic needs to get rid of *all* the booze. Cut up *all* your credit cards and call the card issuers to cancel your accounts. And when you buy consumer items such as cars and furniture, do not apply for E-Z credit.

The world worked fine back in the years B.C. (Before Credit). Think about it: Just a couple generations ago, credit cards didn't even exist. People paid with cash and checks — imagine that! You *can* function without buying anything on a credit card. In certain cases, you may need a card as collateral — such as when renting a car. When you bring back the rental car, however, you can pay with cash or a check. Leave the card at home in the back of your sock drawer or freezer, and pull (or thaw) it out only for the occasional car rental.

If you can trust yourself, keep a separate credit card *only* for new purchases that you know you can absolutely pay in full each month. No one needs three, five, or ten credit cards! You can live with one (and actually none), given the wide acceptance of most cards.

Retailers such as department stores and gas stations just love to issue cards. Not only do these cards charge outrageously high interest rates, but they're also not widely accepted like Visa and MasterCard. Virtually all retailers accept Visa and MasterCard. More credit lines mean more temptation to spend what you can't afford.

If you decide to keep one widely accepted credit card instead of getting rid of them all, be careful. You may be tempted to let debt accumulate and roll over for a month or two, starting up the whole horrible process of running up your consumer debt again. Rather than keeping one credit card, consider getting a debit card.

Discovering debit cards: The best of both worlds

Credit cards are the main reason today's consumers are buying more than they can afford. So logic says that one way you can keep your spending in check is to stop using your credit cards. But in a society that's used to the widely accepted Visa and MasterCard plastic for purchases, changing habits is hard. And you may be legitimately concerned that carrying your checkbook or cash can be a hassle or can be costly if you're mugged.

Debit cards truly offer the best of both worlds. The beauty of the debit card is that it offers you the convenience of making purchases with a piece of plastic without the temptation or ability to run up credit-card debt. Debit cards keep you from spending money you don't have and help you live within your means.

A *debit card* looks just like a credit card with either the Visa or MasterCard logo. The big difference between debit cards and credit cards is that, as with checks, debit card purchase amounts are deducted electronically from your checking account within days. (Bank ATM cards are also debit cards; however, if they lack a Visa or MasterCard logo, they're accepted by far fewer merchants.)

If you switch to a debit card and you keep your checking account balance low and don't ordinarily balance your checkbook, you may need to start balancing it. Otherwise, you may face charges for overdrawing your account.

Here are some other differences between debit and credit cards:

- ✔ If you pay your credit-card bill in full and on time each month, your credit card gives you free use of the money you owe until it's time to pay the bill. Debit cards take the money out of your checking account almost immediately.

- ✔ Credit cards make it easier for you to dispute charges for problematic merchandise through the issuing bank. Most banks allow you to dispute charges for up to 60 days after purchase and will credit the disputed amount to your account pending resolution. Most debit cards offer a much shorter window, typically less than one week, for making disputes.

Because moving your checking account can be a hassle, see whether your current bank offers Visa or MasterCard debit cards. If your bank doesn't offer one, shop among the major banks in your area, which are likely to offer the cards. Because such cards come with checking accounts, make sure you do some comparison shopping among the different account features and fees.

A number of investment firms offer Visa or MasterCard debit cards with their asset management accounts. Not only can these investment firm "checking accounts" help you break the credit-card overspending habit, but they may also get you thinking about saving and investing your money. One drawback of these accounts is that most of them require fairly hefty minimum initial investment amounts — typically $5,000 to $10,000. Among brokerages with competitive investment offerings and prices are TD Ameritrade (phone 800-934-4448; website www.tdameritrade.com), Vanguard (phone 800-992-8327; website www.vanguard.com), and T. Rowe Price (phone 800-537-1936; website www.troweprice.com).

What if your debit card is lost or stolen?

Personal credit cards and debit cards offer you similar so-called "zero liability" if someone illegally uses your card. If your debit card is lost or stolen and someone makes fraudulent charges on your debit card, you simply sign statements with your bank stating that the charges aren't yours. You'll be reimbursed typically in a matter of days. (You should report your card as lost or stolen as soon as you notice it is missing.)

However, cards designated and listed as business (commercial) cards may not have the same zero liability as consumer cards. Generally speaking, banks view businesses as riskier and more prone to internal fraud. Suppose, for example, that your business issued debit cards to its employees and one of them gave it to a friend to use and then said the card was lost and those purchases were fraudulent.

Therefore, I recommend getting a separate consumer debit card for your small business (simply keep your name, not the business's, on the account) or use a bank that offers the same protections on their business debit cards as on their consumer debit cards. Otherwise, you could get socked with a hefty bill that you don't deserve.

Turning to Credit Counseling Agencies

Prior to the passage of the 2005 bankruptcy laws discussed later in this chapter, each year hundreds of thousands of debt-burdened consumers sought "counseling" from credit counseling service offices. Now, more than a million people annually get the required counseling. Unfortunately, some people find that the service doesn't always work the way it's pitched.

Beware biased advice at credit counseling agencies

Leona Davis, whose family racked up significant debt due largely to unexpected medical expenses and a reduction in her income, found herself in trouble with too much debt. So she turned to one of the large, nationally promoted credit counseling services, which she heard about through its advertising and marketing materials.

The credit counseling agency Davis went to markets itself as a "nonprofit community service." Davis, like many others I know, found that the "service" was not objective. After her experience, Davis feels that a more appropriate name for the organization she worked with would be the Credit Card Collection Agency.

Unbeknownst to Davis and most of the other people who use supposed credit counseling agencies is the fact that the vast majority of their funding comes from the fees that creditors pay them. Most credit counseling agencies collect fees on a commission basis — just as collection agencies do! Their strategy is to place those who come in for help on their "debt management program." Under this program, counselees like Davis agree to pay a certain amount per month to the agency, which in turn parcels out the money to the various creditors.

Because of Davis's tremendous outstanding consumer debt (it exceeded her annual income), her repayment plan was doomed to failure. Davis managed to make 10 months' worth of payments, largely because she raided a retirement account for $28,000. Had Davis filed bankruptcy (which she ultimately needed to do), she would've been able to keep her retirement money. But Davis's counselor never discussed the bankruptcy option. "I received no counseling," says Davis. "Real counselors take the time to understand your situation and offer options. I was offered one solution: a forced payment plan."

Others who have consulted various credit counseling agencies, including one of my research assistants who, undercover, visited an office to seek advice, confirm that some agencies use a cookie-cutter approach to dealing with debt. Such agencies typically recommend that debtors go on a repayment plan that has the consumer pay, say, 3 percent of each outstanding loan balance to the agency, which in turn pays the money to creditors.

Unable to keep up with the enormous monthly payments, Davis finally turned to an attorney and filed for bankruptcy — but not before she had unnecessarily lost thousands of dollars because of the biased recommendations.

Although credit counseling agencies' promotional materials and counselors aren't shy about highlighting the drawbacks to bankruptcy, counselors are reluctant to discuss the negative impact of signing up for a debt payment plan. Davis's counselor never told her that restructuring her credit-card payments would tarnish her credit reports and scores. The counselor my researcher met with also neglected to mention this important fact. When asked, the counselor was evasive about the debt "management" program's impact on his credit report.

If you're considering bankruptcy or are otherwise unable to meet your current debt obligations, first be sure to read the rest of this chapter. Second, interview any counseling agency you may be considering working with. Remember that you're the customer and you should do your homework first and be in control. Don't allow anyone or any agency to make you feel that they're in a position of power simply because of your financial troubles.

Ask questions and avoid debt management programs

Probably the most important question to ask a counseling agency is whether it offers *debt management programs* (DMPs), whereby you're put on a repayment plan with your creditors and the agency gets a monthly fee for handling the payments. You do *not* want to work with an agency offering DMPs because of conflicts of interest. An agency can't offer objective advice about all your options for dealing with debt, including bankruptcy, if it has a financial incentive to put you on a DMP.

The Institute for Financial Literacy is a good agency that doesn't offer DMPs (phone 866-662-4932; website www.financiallit.org).

Here are some additional questions that the Federal Trade Commission suggests you ask prospective counseling agencies you may hire:

- ✔ **What are your fees? Are there setup and/or monthly fees?** Get a specific price quote in writing.

- ✔ **What if I can't afford to pay your fees or make contributions?** If an organization won't help you because you can't afford to pay, look elsewhere for help.

- ✔ **Will I have a formal written agreement or contract with you?** Don't sign anything without reading it first. Make sure all verbal promises are in writing.

- ✔ **Are you licensed to offer your services in my state?** You should work only with a licensed agency.

- ✔ **What are the qualifications of your counselors? Are they accredited or certified by an outside organization? If so, by whom? If not, how are they trained?** Try to use an organization whose counselors are trained by a nonaffiliated party.

- ✔ **What assurance do I have that information about me (including my address, phone number, and financial information) will be kept confidential and secure?** A reputable agency can provide you with a clearly written privacy policy.

- ✔ **How are your employees compensated? Are they paid more if I sign up for certain services, if I pay a fee, or if I make a contribution to your organization?** Employees who work on an incentive basis are less likely to have your best interests in mind than those who earn a straight salary that isn't influenced by your choices.

Filing Bankruptcy

For consumers in over their heads, the realization that their monthly income is increasingly exceeded by their bill payments is usually a traumatic one. In many cases, years can pass before people consider a drastic measure like filing bankruptcy. Both financial and emotional issues come into play in one of the most difficult and painful, yet potentially beneficial, decisions.

When Helen, a mother of two and a sales representative, contacted a bankruptcy attorney, her total credit-card debt equaled her annual gross income. As a result of her crushing debt load, she couldn't meet her minimum monthly credit-card payments. Rent and food gobbled up most of her earnings. What little was left over went to the squeakiest wheel.

Creditors were breathing down Helen's back. "I started getting calls from collection departments at home and work — it was embarrassing," she said. Helen's case is typical in that credit-card debt was the prime cause of her bankruptcy.

As the debt load grew (partly exacerbated by the high interest rates on the cards), more and more purchases got charged — from the kids' clothing to repairs for the car. Finally, after running out of cash, she had to take a large cash advance on her credit cards to pay for rent and food.

Despite trying to work out lower monthly payments to keep everyone happy, most of the banks to which Helen owed money were inflexible. "When I asked one bank's Visa department if it preferred that I declare bankruptcy because it was unwilling to lower my monthly payment, the representative said yes," Helen says. After running out of options, Helen filed personal bankruptcy.

Understanding bankruptcy benefits

Bankruptcy allows certain types of debts to be completely eliminated or *discharged.* Debts that typically can be discharged include credit-card, medical, auto, utilities, and rent.

Debts that may *not* be canceled generally include child support, alimony, student loans, taxes, and court-ordered damages (for example, drunk driving settlements). Helen, the subject of the preceding section, was an ideal candidate for bankruptcy because her debts (credit cards) were dischargeable. Helen also met another important criterion — her level of high-interest consumer debt relative to her annual income was high (100 percent). When this ratio (discussed in Chapter 2) exceeds 25 percent, filing bankruptcy may be your best option.

What you can keep if you file bankruptcy

In every state, you can retain certain property and assets when you file for bankruptcy. You may be surprised to discover that in some states, you can keep your home regardless of its value! Most states, though, allow you to protect a certain amount of home equity.

Additionally, you're allowed to retain some other types and amounts of personal property and assets. For example, most states allow you to retain household furnishings, clothing, pensions, and money in retirement accounts. So don't empty your retirement accounts or sell off personal possessions to pay debts unless you're absolutely sure that you won't be filing bankruptcy.

Eliminating your debt also allows you to start working toward your financial goals. Depending on the amount of debt you have outstanding relative to your income, you may need a decade or more to pay it all off. In Helen's case, at the age of 48, she had no money saved for retirement, and she was increasingly unable to spend money on her children.

Filing bankruptcy offers not only financial benefits but emotional benefits, as well. "I was horrified at filing, but it is good to be rid of the debts and collection calls — I should have filed six months earlier. I was constantly worried. When I saw homeless families come to the soup kitchen where I sometimes volunteer, I thought that someday that could be me and my kids," says Helen.

Coming to terms with bankruptcy drawbacks

Filing bankruptcy, needless to say, has a number of drawbacks. First, bankruptcy appears on your credit report for up to ten years, so you'll have difficulty obtaining credit, especially in the years immediately following your filing. However, if you already have problems on your credit report (because of late payments or a failure to pay previous debts), the damage has already been done. And without savings, you're probably not going to be making major purchases (such as a home) in the next several years anyway.

If you do file bankruptcy, getting credit in the future is still possible. You may be able to obtain a *secured credit card,* which requires you to deposit money in a bank account equal to the credit limit on your credit card. Of course, you'll be better off without the temptation of any credit cards and better served with a debit card. Also, know that if you can hold down a stable job, most creditors will be willing to give you loans within a few years of your filing bankruptcy. Almost all lenders ignore bankruptcy after five to seven years.

Another drawback of bankruptcy is that it costs money, and those expenses have jumped higher due to the requirements of bankruptcy laws (more on that in a moment). I know this expense seems terribly unfair. You're already in financial trouble — that's why you're filing bankruptcy! Court filing and legal fees can easily exceed $1,000, especially in higher cost-of-living areas.

And finally, most people find that filing bankruptcy causes emotional stress. Admitting that your personal income can't keep pace with your debt obligations is painful. Although filing bankruptcy clears the decks of debt and gives you a fresh financial start, feeling a profound sense of failure (and sometimes shame) is common. Despite the increasing incidence of bankruptcy, bankruptcy filers are reluctant to talk about it with others, including family and friends.

Another part of the emotional side of filing bankruptcy is that you must open your personal financial affairs to court scrutiny and court control during the several months it takes to administer a bankruptcy. A court-appointed bankruptcy trustee oversees your case and tries to recover as much of your property as possible to satisfy the *creditors* — those to whom you owe money.

Some people also feel that they're shirking responsibility by filing for bankruptcy. One client I worked with should have filed, but she couldn't bring herself to do it. She said, "I spent that money, and it's my responsibility to pay it back."

If you file for bankruptcy, don't feel bad about not paying back the bank. Credit cards are one of the most profitable lines of business for banks. (Now you know why your mailbox is always filled with solicitations for more cards.) The nice merchants from whom you bought the merchandise have already been paid. *Charge-offs* — the banker's term for taking the loss on debt that you discharge through bankruptcy — are the banker's cost, which is another reason why the interest rate is so high on credit cards and why borrowing on them is a bad idea.

Deciphering the bankruptcy laws

The Bankruptcy Abuse and Prevention Act of 2005 has had a significant effect on consumers who are considering filing for bankruptcy. As you may be able to tell from the bill's name, major creditors, such as credit-card companies, lobbied heavily for new laws. Although they didn't get everything they wanted, they got a lot, which — not surprisingly — doesn't benefit those folks in dire financial condition contemplating bankruptcy. Don't despair, though; help and information can overcome the worst provisions of this law. Here are the major elements of the personal bankruptcy laws:

- ✔ **Required counseling:** Before filing for bankruptcy, individuals must complete credit counseling, the purpose of which is to explore your options for dealing with debt, including (but not limited to) bankruptcy and developing a debt repayment plan.

    Historically, many supposed "counseling" agencies have provided highly biased advice. Be sure to read the "Turning to Credit Counseling Agencies" section in this chapter to find out what conflicts of interest agencies have and to get advice on how to pick a top-notch agency.

    To actually have debts discharged through bankruptcy, the new law requires a second type of counseling called "Debtor Education." All credit counseling and debtor education must be completed by an approved organization on the U.S. Trustee's website (www.justice. gov/ust). Click on the link Credit Counseling & Debtor Education.

- ✔ **Means testing:** Some high-income earners may be precluded from filing the form of bankruptcy that actually discharges debts (called Chapter 7) and instead be forced to use the form of bankruptcy that involves a repayment plan (called Chapter 13).

    Recognizing that folks living in higher cost-of-living areas tend to have higher incomes, the law allows for differences in income by making adjustments based upon your state of residence and family size. The expense side of the equation is considered as well, and allowances are determined by county and metropolitan area. I won't bore you with the details and required calculations here. Few potential filers are affected by this provision. For more information, click on the Means Testing Information section on the U.S. Trustee's website (www.justice.gov/ ust).

- ✔ **Increased requirements placed on filers and attorneys:** The means testing alone has created a good deal of additional work for bankruptcy filers, work generally done by attorneys. Filers, including lawyers, must also attest to the accuracy of submitted information, which has attorneys doing more verification work. Thus, it's no surprise that when the new bankruptcy laws were passed, legal fees increased significantly — jumps of 30 to 40 percent were common.

- ✔ **New rules for people who recently moved:** Individual states have their own provisions for how much personal property and home equity you can keep. Prior to the passage of the 2005 laws, in some cases, shortly before filing bankruptcy, people actually moved to a state that allowed them to keep more. Under the new law, you must live in the state for at least two years before filing bankruptcy in that state and using that state's personal property exemptions. To use a given state's *homestead exemption,* which dictates how much home equity you may protect, you must have lived in that state for at least 40 months.

Choosing between Chapter 7 and 13

You can file one of two forms of personal bankruptcy: Chapter 7 or Chapter 13. Here are the essentials regarding each type:

✔ **Chapter 7 allows you to discharge, or cancel, certain debts.** This form of bankruptcy makes the most sense when you have significant debts that you're legally allowed to cancel. (See "Understanding bankruptcy benefits" earlier in this chapter for details on which debts can be canceled, or discharged.)

✔ **Chapter 13 comes up with a repayment schedule that requires you to pay your debts over several years.** Chapter 13 stays on your credit record (just like Chapter 7), *but it doesn't eliminate debt,* so its value is limited — usually to dealing with debts like taxes that can't be discharged through bankruptcy. Chapter 13 can keep creditors at bay until you work out a repayment schedule in the courts.

Seeking bankruptcy advice

If you want to find out more about the pros, cons, and details of filing for bankruptcy, pick up a copy of *The New Bankruptcy: Will It Work for You?* by attorneys Leon Bayer and Stephen R. Elias (Nolo Press). If you're comfortable with your decision to file and you think you can complete the paperwork, check out *How to File for Chapter 7 Bankruptcy,* by attorneys Stephen R. Elias and Albin Renauer (Nolo Press), which comes with all the necessary filing forms.

Hiring a paralegal typing service to prepare the forms, which can be a cost-effective way to get help with the process if you don't need heavy-duty legal advice, is an intermediate approach. To find a paralegal typing service in your area, check your local yellow page listings under "Paralegals."

Stopping the Spending/ Consumer Debt Cycle

Regardless of how you deal with paying off your debt, you're in real danger of falling back into old habits. Backsliding happens not only to people who file bankruptcy but also to those who use savings or home equity to eliminate their debt. This section speaks to that risk and tells you what to do about it.

Resisting the credit temptation

Getting out of debt can be challenging, but I have confidence that you can do it with this book by your side. In addition to the ideas I discuss earlier in this chapter (such as eliminating all your credit cards and getting a debit card), the following list provides some additional tactics you can use to limit the influence credit cards hold over your life. (If you're concerned about the impact that any of these tactics may have on your credit rating, please see Chapter 2.)

- ✔ **Reduce your credit limit.** If you choose not to take my advice and get rid of all your credit cards or get a debit card, be sure to keep a lid on your credit card's *credit limit* (the maximum balance allowed on your card). You don't have to accept the increase just because your bank keeps raising your credit limit to reward you for being such a profitable customer. Call your credit-card service's toll-free phone number and lower your credit limit to a level you're comfortable with.

- ✔ **Replace your credit card with a charge card.** A *charge card* (such as the American Express Card) requires you to pay your balance in full each billing period. You have no credit line or interest charges. Of course, spending more than you can afford to pay when the bill comes due is possible. But you'll be much less likely to overspend if you know you have to pay in full monthly.

- ✔ **Never buy anything on credit that depreciates in value.** Meals out, cars, clothing, and shoes all depreciate in value. Don't buy these things on credit. Borrow money only for sound investments — education, real estate, or your own business, for example.

- ✔ **Think in terms of total cost.** Everything sounds cheaper in terms of monthly payments — that's how salespeople entice you into buying things you can't afford. Take a calculator along, if necessary, to tally up the sticker price, interest charges, and upkeep. The total cost will scare you. *It should.*

- ✔ **Stop the junk mail avalanche.** Look at your daily mail — I bet half of it is solicitations and mail-order catalogs. You can save some trees and some time sorting junk mail by removing yourself from most mailing lists. To remove your name from mailing lists, contact the Direct Marketing Association (you can register through its website at www.dmachoice.org or call 212-768-7277 between 9 a.m. and 2 p.m. Eastern Standard Time, Monday through Thursday).

To remove your name from the major credit reporting agency lists that are used by credit-card solicitation companies, call 888-567-8688. Also, tell any credit-card companies you keep cards with that you want your account marked to indicate that you don't want any of your personal information shared with telemarketing firms.

✔ **Limit what you can spend.** Go shopping with a small amount of cash and no plastic or checks. That way, you can spend only what little cash you have with you!

Identifying and treating a compulsion

No matter how hard they try to break the habit, some people become addicted to spending and accumulating debt. It becomes a chronic problem that starts to interfere with other aspects of their lives and can lead to problems at work and with family and friends.

Debtors Anonymous (DA) is a nonprofit organization that provides support (primarily through group meetings) to people trying to break their debt accumulation and spending habits. DA is modeled after the 12-step Alcoholics Anonymous (AA) program.

Like AA, Debtors Anonymous works with people from all walks of life and socioeconomic backgrounds. You can find people who are financially on the edge, $100,000-plus income earners, and everybody in between at DA meetings. Even former millionaires join the program.

DA has a simple questionnaire that helps determine whether you're a problem debtor. If you answer "yes" to at least 8 of the following 15 questions, you may be developing or already have a compulsive spending and debt accumulation habit:

✔ Are your debts making your home life unhappy?

✔ Does the pressure of your debts distract you from your daily work?

✔ Are your debts affecting your reputation?

✔ Do your debts cause you to think less of yourself?

✔ Have you ever given false information in order to obtain credit?

✔ Have you ever made unrealistic promises to your creditors?

✔ Does the pressure of your debts make you careless when it comes to the welfare of your family?

✔ Do you ever fear that your employer, family, or friends will learn the extent of your total indebtedness?

✔ When faced with a difficult financial situation, does the prospect of borrowing give you an inordinate feeling of relief?

✔ Does the pressure of your debts cause you to have difficulty sleeping?

✔ Has the pressure of your debts ever caused you to consider getting drunk?

✔ Have you ever borrowed money without giving adequate consideration to the rate of interest you're required to pay?

✔ Do you usually expect a negative response when you're subject to a credit investigation?

✔ Have you ever developed a strict regimen for paying off your debts, only to break it under pressure?

✔ Do you justify your debts by telling yourself that you are superior to the "other" people, and when you get your "break," you'll be out of debt?

To find a Debtors Anonymous (DA) support group in your area, visit the DA website at www.debtorsanonymous.org or contact the DA's national headquarters by phone at 800-421-2383 or 781-453-2743.

Chapter 6

Reducing Your Spending

*T*elling people how and where to spend their money is a risky undertaking, because most people like to spend money and hate to be told what to do. So in this chapter I detail numerous strategies that I have seen work for other people. The final decision for what to cut rests solely on you. Only you can decide what's important to you and what's dispensable (should you cut out your weekly poker games or cut back on your shoe collection?).

With these recommendations, I assume that you value your time. Therefore, I don't tell you to scrimp and save by doing things like cutting open a tube of toothpaste so that you can use every last bit of it. And I don't tell you to have your spouse do your ironing to reduce your dry-cleaning bills — no point in having extra money in the bank if your significant other walks out on you!

The fact that you're busy all the time may be part of the reason you spend money as you do. Therefore, the recommendations in this chapter focus on methods that produce significant savings but don't involve a lot of time. In other words, these strategies provide bang for the buck.

Unlocking the Keys to Successful Spending

For most people, spending money is a whole lot easier and more fun than earning it. Far be it from me to tell you to stop having fun and turn into a penny-pinching, stay-at-home miser. Of course you can spend money. But there's a world of difference between spending money carelessly and spending money *wisely*.

If you spend too much and spend unwisely, you put pressure on your income and your future need to continue working. Savings dwindle, debts may accumulate, and you can't achieve your financial (and perhaps personal) goals.

If you dive into details too quickly, you may miss the big picture. So before I jump into the specific areas where you can trim your budget, I give you my four overall keys to successful spending. These four principles run through my recommendations in this chapter:

- ✔ Living within your means
- ✔ Finding the best values
- ✔ Cutting excess spending
- ✔ Rejecting consumer credit

Living within your means

Spending too much is a *relative* problem. Two people can each spend $40,000 per year (including their taxes) yet still have drastically different financial circumstances. How? Suppose that one of them earns $50,000 annually, while the other makes $35,000. The $50,000 income earner saves $10,000 each year. The $35,000 wage earner, on the other hand, accumulates $5,000 of new debt (or spends that amount from prior savings). So, spend within your means. If you do nothing else in this chapter, please be sure to do this!

Don't let the spending habits of others dictate yours. Certain people — and you know who they are — bring out the big spender in you. Do something else with them besides shopping and spending. If you can't find any other activity to share with them, try shopping with limited cash and no credit cards. That way, you can't overspend on impulse.

How much you can safely spend while working toward your financial goals depends on what your goals are and where you are financially. Save first for your goals and then live on what's left over. Chapter 4 assists you with figuring how much you should be saving and what you can afford to spend while still accomplishing your financial goals.

Looking for the best values

You can find high quality and low cost in the same product. Conversely, paying a high price is no guarantee that you're getting high quality. Cars are a good example. Whether you're buying a subcompact, a sports car, or a luxury four-door sedan, some cars are more fuel-efficient and cheaper to maintain than rivals that carry the same sticker price.

When you evaluate the cost of a product or service, think in terms of total, long-term costs. Suppose that you're comparing the purchase of two used cars: the Solid Sedan, which costs $11,995, and the Clunker Convertible, which weighs in at $9,995. On the surface, the convertible appears to be cheaper. However, the price that you pay for a car is but a small portion of what that car ultimately costs you. If the convertible is costly to operate, maintain, and insure over the years, it could end up costing you much more than the sedan would. Sometimes, paying a reasonable amount more upfront for a higher-quality product or service ends up saving you money in the long run.

People who sell particular products and services may initially appear to have your best interests at heart when they steer you toward something that isn't costly. However, you may be in for a rude awakening when you discover the ongoing service, maintenance, and other fees you face in the years ahead. Salespeople are generally trained to pitch you a lower-cost product if you indicate that's what you're after.

Don't waste money on brand names

You don't want to compromise on quality, especially in the areas where quality is important to you. But you also don't want to be duped into believing that brand-name products are better or worth a substantially higher price. Be suspicious of companies that spend gobs on image-oriented advertising. Why? Because heavy advertising costs many dollars, and as a consumer of those companies' products and services, you pay for all that advertising.

All successful companies advertise their products. Advertising is cost-effective and good business if it brings in enough new business. But you need to consider the products and services and the claims that companies make. In grocery stores, for example, you can often find name brands and store brands for the same product sitting in close proximity to one another. Upon reading the label, you can see that the products may in fact be identical and the only difference between the two products is that the name brand product costs more (because of the branding and associated advertising and marketing).

Branding is used in many fields to sell overpriced, mediocre products and services to consumers. Does a cola beverage really taste better if it's "the real thing" or "the choice of a new generation"? Consider all the silly labels and fluffy marketing of beers. Blind taste-testing demonstrates little if any difference between the more expensive brand-name products and the cheaper, less heavily advertised ones.

Now, if you can't live without your Coca-Cola or Samuel Adams beer, and you think that these products are head and shoulders above the rest, drink them to your heart's content. But question the importance of the name and image of the products you buy. Companies spend a lot of money creating and cultivating an image, which has zero impact on how their products taste or perform.

Tread carefully online

Online shopping has grown in popularity for some good reasons. It's reasonably fast and convenient, and you can quickly research different products and services before buying. But there are clear downsides to online shopping. In your rush, you may make unwise purchases. This slip-up may happen in part because so many reviews online are biased. Also, be careful when ordering from newer, smaller sites that may not stand behind what they sell. (See the next section for more shopping advice.)

Getting your money back

Take a look around your home for items you never use. Odds are you have some (maybe even many). Returning such items to where you bought them can be cathartic; it also reduces your home's clutter and puts more money in your pocket.

Also, think about the last several times you bought a product or service and didn't get what was promised. What did you do about it? Most people do nothing and let the derelict company off the hook. Why? Here are some common explanations for this type of behavior:

- ✔ **Low standards:** Consumers have come to expect shoddy service and merchandise because of the common lousy experiences they've had.

- ✔ **Conflict avoidance:** Most people shun confrontation. It makes them tense and anxious, and it churns their stomachs.

- ✔ **Hassle aversion:** Most companies don't make it easy for complainers to get their money back or obtain satisfaction. To get restitution from some companies, you need the tenacity and determination of a pit bull.

You can increase your odds of getting what you expect for your money by doing business with companies that

- ✔ **Have fair return policies:** Don't purchase any product or service until you understand the company's return policy. Be especially wary of buying from companies that charge hefty "restocking" fees for returned merchandise or simply don't allow returns at all. Reputable companies offer full refunds and don't make you take store credit (although taking credit is fine if you're sure that you'll use it soon and that the company will still be around).

- ✔ **Can provide good references:** Suppose that you're going to install a fence on your property, and, as a result, you're going to be speaking with fencing contractors for the first time. You can sift out many inferior firms by asking each contractor that you interview for at least three references from people in your local area who have had a fence installed in the past year or two.

- ✔ **Are committed to the type of product or service they provide:** Suppose that your chosen fencing contractor does a great job, and now that you're in the market for new gutters on your home, the contractor says that he does gutters, too. Although the path of least resistance would be to simply hire the same contractor for your gutters, you should inquire about how many gutters the contractor has installed and also interview some other firms that specialize in such work. Because your fencing contractor may have done only a handful of gutter jobs, he may not know as much about that type of work.

Recognizing the Better Business Bureau's conflicts of interest

The Better Business Bureau (BBB) states that its mission is "to promote and foster the highest ethical relationship between businesses and the public." The reality of the typical consumer's experience of dealing with the BBB doesn't live up to the BBB's marketing. BBBs are nonprofits and are not agencies of any governmental body.

"It's a business trade organization, and each local BBB is basically independent, like a franchise," says John Bear, an author of consumer advocacy books. "By and large, when somebody has a problem with a company and they fill out a complaint form with the BBB, if the company is a member of the BBB, there's ample evidence that consumers often end up not being satisfied. The BBB protects their members."

Particularly problematic among the BBB's pro-business practices are the company reports the BBB keeps on file. The BBB often considers a legitimate complaint satisfactorily resolved even when you're quite unhappy and the company is clearly not working to satisfy the problems for which it's responsible.

Bear also cites examples of some truly troubling BBB episodes. In one case, he says that a diploma mill (a company that sells degrees but provides little, if any, education) in Louisiana was a member of the local BBB. "When complaints started coming in," says Bear, "the BBB's response was always that the company met their standards and that the complaints were resolved. The reality was that the complaints weren't satisfactorily resolved, and it took about two years until complaints reached into the hundreds for the BBB to finally cancel the diploma mill's membership and give out a bland statement about complaints. Two months later, the FBI raided the company. Millions of consumers' dollars were lost because the BBB didn't do its job."

In another case, the president of a South Florida BBB (the fifth largest in the country, according to Bear) was ultimately imprisoned for taking bribes from companies in exchange for maintaining favorable reports on file.

Following these guidelines can greatly diminish your chances of having unhappy outcomes with products or services you buy. And here's another important tip: Whenever possible and as long as you can pay the balance in full when due, buy with a credit card if your credit's in good standing. Doing so enables you to dispute a charge within 60 days and gives you leverage for getting your money back.

If you find that you're unable to make progress when trying to get compensation for a lousy product or service, here's what I recommend you do:

- ✔ **Document:** Taking notes whenever you talk to someone at a company can help you validate your case down the road should problems develop. Obviously, the bigger the purchase and the more you have at stake, the more carefully you should document what you've been promised. In many cases, though, you probably won't start carefully noting each conversation until a conflict develops. Keep copies of companies' marketing literature, because such documents often make promises or claims that companies fail to live up to in practice.

- ✔ **Escalate:** Some frontline employees either aren't capable of resolving disputes or lack the authority to do so. No matter what the cause, speak with a department supervisor and continue escalating from there. If you're still not making progress, lodge a complaint to whatever state regulatory agency (if any) oversees such companies. Consider posting your beefs on some of the numerous consumer complaint-compiling websites and possibly social media outlets, but be careful to stick to the facts and avoid saying something false or incendiary that could lead to your being sued. Tell your friends and colleagues not to do business with the company (and let the company know that you're doing so until your complaint is resolved to your satisfaction). Also consider contacting a consumer help group — these groups are typically sponsored by broadcast or print media in metropolitan areas. They can be helpful in resolving disputes or shining adverse publicity on disreputable companies or products.

- ✔ **Litigate:** If all else fails, consider taking the matter to small claims court if the company continues to be unresponsive. (Depending on the amount of money at stake, this tactic may be worth your time.) The maximum dollar limit that you may recover varies by state, but you're usually limited to a few thousand dollars. For larger amounts than those allowed in small claims court in your state, you can, of course, hire an attorney and pursue the traditional legal channels — although you may end up throwing away more of your time and money. Mediation and arbitration are generally a better option than following through on a lawsuit.

Eliminating the fat from your spending

If you want to reduce your overall spending by, say, 10 percent, you can just cut all of your current expenditures by 10 percent. Or, you can reach your 10 percent goal by cutting some categories a lot and others not at all. You need to set priorities and make choices about where you want and don't want to spend your money.

What you spend your money on is sometimes a matter of habit rather than a matter of what you really want or value. For example, some people shop at whatever stores are close to them. But eliminating fat doesn't necessarily mean cutting back on your purchases: You can save money by buying in bulk. Some stores specialize in selling larger packages or quantities of a product at a lower price because they save money on the packaging and handling. If you're single, shop with a friend and split the bulk purchases. You can also do some comparison shopping online, but be sure you're surveying reputable websites that stand behind what they sell and that provide high quality customer service.

Turning your back on consumer credit

As I discuss in Chapters 3 and 5, buying items that depreciate — such as cars, clothing, and vacations — on credit is hazardous to your long-term financial health. Buy only what you can afford today. If you'll be forced to carry a debt for months or years on end, you can't really afford what you're buying on credit today.

Without a doubt, *renting-to-own* is the most expensive way to buy. Here's how it works: You see a huge ad blaring "$12.95 for a DVD player!" Well, the ad has a big hitch: That's $12.95 per week, for many weeks. When all is said and done (and paid), buying a $100 DVD player through a rent-to-own store costs a typical buyer more than $375! Welcome to the world of rent-to-own stores, which offer cash-poor consumers the ability to lease consumer items and, at the end of the lease, an option to buy.

If you think that paying an 18 percent interest rate on a credit card is expensive, consider this: The effective interest rate charged on many rent-to-own purchases exceeds 100 percent; in some cases, it may be 200 percent or more! Renting-to-own makes buying on a credit card look like a great deal. I'm not sharing this information to encourage you to buy on credit cards but to point out what a rip-off renting-to-own is. Such stores prey on cashless consumers who either can't get credit cards or don't understand how expensive renting-to-own really is. Forget the instant gratification and save a set amount each week until you can afford what you want.

Consumer credit is expensive, and it reinforces a bad financial habit: spending more than you can afford.

Budgeting to Boost Your Savings

When most people hear the word *budgeting,* they think unpleasant thoughts — like those associated with *dieting* — and rightfully so. But budgeting can help you move from knowing how much you spend on various things to successfully reducing your spending.

The first step in the process of *budgeting,* or planning your future spending, is to analyze where your current spending is going (refer to Chapter 3). After you do that, calculate how much more you'd like to save each month. Then comes the hard part: deciding where to make cuts in your spending.

Suppose that you're currently not saving any of your monthly income and you want to save 10 percent for retirement. If you can save and invest through a tax-sheltered retirement account — for example, a 401(k) or 403(b), or a SEP-IRA — you don't actually need to cut your spending by 10 percent to reach a savings goal of 10 percent (of your gross income). When you contribute money to a tax-deductible retirement account, you reduce your federal and state taxes. If you're a moderate-income-earner paying, say, 30 percent in federal and state taxes on your marginal income, you actually need to reduce your spending by only 7 percent to save 10 percent. The other 3 percent of the savings comes from the lowering of your taxes. (The higher your tax bracket, the less you need to cut your spending to reach a particular savings goal.)

So to boost your savings rate to 10 percent, go through your current spending category by category until you come up with enough proposed cuts to reduce your spending by 8 percent. Make your cuts in the areas that will be the least painful and where you're getting the least value from your current level of spending. (If you don't have access to a tax-deductible retirement account, budgeting still involves the same process of assessment and making cuts in various spending categories, but your cuts need to add up to the entire amount you want to save, in this example, 10 percent rather than 8 percent.)

Another method of budgeting involves starting completely from scratch rather than examining your current expenses and making cuts from that starting point. Ask yourself how much you'd like to spend on different categories. The advantage of this approach is that it doesn't allow your current spending levels to constrain your thinking. You'll likely be amazed at the discrepancies between what you think you should be spending and what you actually are spending in certain categories.

Reducing Your Spending

As you read through the following strategies for reducing your spending, please keep in mind that some of these strategies will make sense for you and some of them won't. Start your spending reduction plan with the strategies that come easily. Work your way through them. Keep a list of the options that are more challenging for you — ones that may require more of a sacrifice but may be workable if necessary to achieve your spending and savings goals.

No matter which of the ideas in this chapter you choose, rest assured that keeping your budget lean and mean pays enormous dividends. After you implement a spending reduction strategy, you'll reap the benefits for years to come. Take a look at Figure 6-1: For every $1,000 that you shave from your annual spending (that's just $83 per month), check out how much more money you'll have down the road. (This chart assumes that you invest your newfound savings in a tax-deferred retirement account, you average 8-percent-per-year returns on your investments, and you're in a combined federal and state tax bracket of 35 percent — see Chapter 7 for information on tax brackets.)

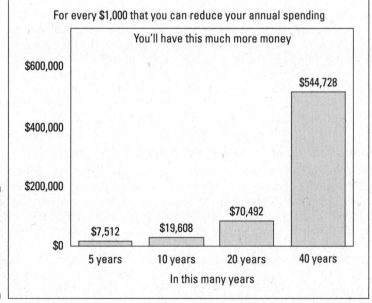

Figure 6-1:
Reducing your spending can yield large investment sums.

© John Wiley & Sons

Managing food costs

Not eating is one way to reduce food expenditures; however, this method tends to make you weak and dizzy, so it's probably not a viable long-term strategy. The following culinary cutbacks can keep you on your feet — perhaps even improve your health — and help you save money.

Eating out frugally

Eating meals out and getting takeout can be timesavers, but they rack up big bills if done too often and too lavishly. Eating out is a luxury — think of it as hiring someone to shop, cook, and clean up for you. Of course, some people either hate to cook or don't have the time, space, or energy to do much in the kitchen. If this sounds like you, choose restaurants carefully and order from the menu selectively. Here are a couple of tips for eating out:

- ✔ **Avoid beverages, especially alcohol.** Most restaurants make big profits on beverages. Drink water instead. (Water is healthy, and it reduces the likelihood that you'll want a nap after a big meal.)

- ✔ **Order vegetarian.** Vegetarian dishes generally cost less than meat-based entrees (and they're generally better for you).

I don't want to be a killjoy. I'm not saying that you should live on bread and water. You can have dessert — heck, have some wine, too, for special occasions! Just try not to eat dessert with every meal. Try eating appetizers and dessert at home, where they're a lot less expensive.

Also, if you aren't skilled in the kitchen, consider learning how to cook. Folks who eat out a lot do so in part because they don't really know how to cook. Take a cooking class and read some good books on the topic.

Eating healthy at home without spending a fortune

As evidenced by the preponderance of diet and weight-loss books on health book bestseller lists — and the growth of the natural and organic grocery stores like Whole Foods and Trader Joe's — Americans are trying to eat healthier. Concerned about all the pesticides, antibiotics, and hormones that end up in the food supply, organic food purchases are growing at a fast rate.

Problem is, financially speaking, better quality food, especially organic foods, can cost more, sometimes much more — but not always. A number of studies I've seen demonstrate that highly processed foods, which are less nutritious and worse for your health, can be as costly as or even more expensive than fresh, so-called whole foods. The key to not overspending on fresher, healthier, and organic foods is to be flexible when you're at the grocery store. Buy more of what is seasonal and therefore currently less expensive, stock up on sale items that aren't perishable, and buy more at stores like Trader Joe's (go to www.traderjoes.com or call 800-SHOPTJS [800-746-7857]) that have competitive pricing. Many larger grocery chains carry some organic foods; just be sure to comparison price. Local food co-ops, which source food locally, are another great source for competitively priced food and sometimes pay dividends annually to members.

According to various studies, spending the money to buy organic food makes the most sense when buying the following foods:

- ✔ **Produce:** Apples, bell peppers, celery, cherries, hot peppers, imported grapes, nectarines, peaches, pears, potatoes, red raspberries, spinach, and strawberries have historically been found to carry the greatest amount of pesticides, even after washing.

- ✔ **Meat, poultry, eggs, and dairy:** By going organic, you avoid supplemental hormones and antibiotics. You also greatly reduce the risk of exposure to the agent believed to cause mad cow disease, and you minimize your exposure to other potential toxins in nonorganic feed.

- ✔ **Baby food:** Baby food is typically loaded with condensed fruits and vegetables, which thus contain concentrated pesticide residues. Also, children's small and developing bodies are especially vulnerable to toxins.

One area where many folks are wasting money is in buying bottled water. Although tap water often does leave something to be desired, bottled water is typically not as pure as some folks think. You can save hundreds of dollars annually and drink cleaner water by installing a water filtration system at home and improving your tap (or well) water. (For more information, see my website, www.erictyson.com.)

Joining a wholesale superstore

Superstores such as Costco and Sam's Club enable you to buy groceries in bulk at wholesale prices. And contrary to popular perception, you don't have to buy 1,000 rolls of toilet paper at once — just 24.

I've performed price comparisons between wholesale superstores and retail grocery stores and found that wholesalers charge about 30 percent less for the exact same stuff — all without the hassle of clipping coupons or hunting for the store that has the best price on paper towels this month! (At these discount prices, you only need to buy about $150 per year to recoup Costco and Sam's Club's membership fees, which start at $55 and $45 per year, respectively.) In addition to saving you lots of money, buying in bulk requires fewer shopping trips. You'll have more supplies around your humble abode, so you'll have less need to eat out (which is costly) or make trips (which wastes time and gasoline) to the local grocer, who may be really nice but charges the most.

Perishables run the risk of living up to their name, so only buy what you can reasonably use. Repackage bulk packs into smaller quantities and store them in the freezer if possible. If you're single, shop with a friend and split the order. Also, be careful when you shop at the warehouse clubs — you may be tempted to buy things you don't really need. These stores carry all sorts of items, including the newest TVs, computers, furniture, clothing, complete sets of baseball cards, and giant canisters of biscotti — so wallet and waist-line beware! Try not to make impulse purchases, and be especially careful when you have kids in tow.

To find a Costco store near you, visit the Costco website at www.costco.com or call 800-774-2678. Sam's Club is online at www.samsclub.com.

Saving on shelter

Housing and all the costs associated with it (utilities, furniture, appliances, and, if you're a homeowner, maintenance, repairs, and home insurance) can gobble a large chunk of your monthly income. I'm not suggesting that you live in an igloo or teepee (though they're probably less costly), but people often overlook opportunities to save money in this category.

Reducing rental costs

Rent can take up a sizable chunk of your monthly take-home pay. Many people consider rent to be a fixed and inflexible part of their expenses, but it's not. Here's what you can do to cut down your rental costs:

- ✔ **Move to a lower-cost rental.** Of course, a lower-cost rental may not be as nice — it may be smaller, lack a private parking spot, or be located in a less popular area. Remember that the less you spend renting, the more you can save toward buying your own place. Just be sure to factor in all the costs of a new location, including the possible higher commuting costs.

- ✔ **Share a rental.** Living alone has some benefits, but financially speaking, it's a luxury. If you rent a larger place with roommates, your rental costs should be a good deal less, and you'll get more home for your rental dollars. You have to be in a sharing mood, though. Roommates can be a hassle at times, but they can also be a plus — you get to meet all sorts of new people, and you have someone else to blame when the kitchen's a mess.

- ✔ **Negotiate your rental increases.** Every year, like clockwork, your landlord bumps up your rent by a certain percentage. If your local rental market is soft or your living quarters are deteriorating, stand up for yourself! You have more leverage and power than you probably realize.

A smart landlord doesn't want to lose good tenants who pay rent on time. Filling vacancies takes time and money. State your case: You've been a responsible tenant, and your research shows comparable rentals going for less. Crying "poor" may help, too. At the very least, if you can't stave off the rent increase, maybe you can wrangle some improvements to the place.

✔ **Buy rather than rent.** Purchasing your own place may seem costly but in the long run, owning is cheaper than renting, and you have something to show for it in the end. (The decline in home prices in the late 2000s coupled with low interest rates made housing the most affordable it was in decades and even less costly than renting in some areas.) If you purchase real estate with a 30-year fixed-rate mortgage, your mortgage payment (which is your biggest ownership expense) remains constant. Only your property taxes, maintenance, and insurance costs are exposed to the vagaries of inflation. As a renter, your entire monthly housing cost can rise with increases in the cost of living (unless you're the beneficiary of a rent-controlled apartment). See Chapter 14 to find out the smart way to buy real estate.

Reducing homeowner expenses

As every homeowner knows, houses suck up money. You should be especially careful to watch your money in this area of your budget.

✔ **Know what you can afford.** Whether you're on the verge of buying your first home or trading up to a more costly property, crunch some realistic numbers before you commit. Calculate how much you can afford to spend monthly on a home. Do the exercises in Chapter 3, on where you're spending your money, and Chapter 4, on saving for retirement, to help you calculate the amount you can afford.

Although real estate can be a good long-term investment, you can end up pouring a large portion of your discretionary dollars into your home. In addition to decorating and remodeling, some people feel the need to trade up to a bigger home every few years. Of course, after they're in their new home, the remodeling and renovation cycle simply begins again, which costs even more money. Most home renovations or remodels will never recoup anything close to what they cost. In addition, a major remodel may result in higher property taxes, as well as higher homeowner's insurance costs. Appreciate what you have, and remember that homes are for living in, not museums for display. If you have children, why waste a lot of money on expensive furnishings that take up valuable space and require you to constantly nag your kids to tread carefully? And don't covet — the world will always have people with bigger houses and more toys than you.

✔ **Rent out a room.** Because selling your home to buy a less expensive place can be a big hassle, consider taking in a tenant (or charge those adult "children" still living at home!) to reduce your housing expenses. Check out the renter thoroughly: Get references, run a credit report, research civil and criminal databases online, and talk about ground rules and expectations before sharing your space. Don't forget to check with your insurance company to see whether your homeowner's policy needs adjustments to cover potential liability from renting.

✔ **Refinance your mortgage.** This step may seem like common sense, but surprisingly, many people don't keep up-to-date on mortgage rates. If interest rates are lower than they were when you obtained your current mortgage, you may be able to save money by refinancing (see Chapter 14 for more information).

✔ **Appeal your property-tax assessment.** If you bought your property when housing prices were higher in your area than they are now, you may be able to save money by appealing your assessment. Also, if you live in an area where your assessment is based on how the local assessor valued the property (rather than what you paid for your home), your home may be overassessed. Check with your local assessor's office for the appeals procedure you need to follow. An appraiser's recent evaluation of your property may help — you may already have one if you refinanced your mortgage recently. Also, review how the assessor valued your property compared with similar ones nearby — mistakes happen.

✔ **Reduce utility costs.** Sometimes you have to spend money to save money. Old refrigerators, for example, can waste a lot of electricity. Insulate to save on heating and air-conditioning bills. Install water flow regulators in shower heads. When planting your yard, don't select water-guzzling plants, and keep your lawn area reasonable. Even if you don't live in an area susceptible to droughts, why waste water (which isn't free) unnecessarily? Recycle — recycling means less garbage, which translates into lower trash bills (because you won't be charged for using larger garbage containers) and benefits the environment by reducing landfill. Consider installing solar and other newer energy alternatives, but run the numbers and be sure you'll get your expenditures back within a reasonable number of years.

Cutting transportation costs

America is a car-driven society. In most other countries, cars are a luxury. If more people in the United States thought of cars as a luxury, Americans might have far fewer financial problems. Not only do cars pollute the air and clog the highways, but they also cost you a bundle.

Purchasing a quality car and using it wisely can reduce the cost of car owner-ship. Using alternative modes of transportation can also help you save.

Contrary to advertising slogans, cars aren't built to last; manufacturers don't want you to stick with the same car forever. New models are constantly intro-duced with new features and styling changes. But getting a new set of wheels every few years is an expensive luxury. Don't try to keep up with the Joneses as they show off their new cars every year — for all you know, they're run-ning themselves into financial ruin trying to impress others. Let your neigh-bors admire you for your thriftiness and wisdom instead.

Research before you buy a car

When you buy a car, you don't just pay the initial sticker price: You also have to pay for gas, insurance, registration fees, maintenance, and repairs. You may also owe sales and/or personal property taxes. Don't compare simply sticker prices; think about the total, long-term costs of car ownership and see whether they fit into your budget while still allowing you to save toward your goals.

Speaking of total costs, remember that you're also trusting your life to the car. With about 33,000 Americans killed in auto accidents annually (about one-third of which are caused by drunk drivers), safety should be an impor-tant consideration as well. (If you take care of your health, probably the most dangerous thing you'll ever do is get behind the wheel.) Air bags, for exam-ple, may save your life. The National Highway Traffic Safety Administration's website (www.safercar.gov) has lots of crash test data, as well as informa-tion on other car safety issues.

IntelliChoice (website www.intellichoice.com) provides information about all categories of ownership costs, warranties, and dealer costs for new cars, which are rated based on total ownership costs. Edmunds (web-site www.edmunds.com) provides more general information about different makes and models of both new and used cars. Please be aware that these sites have advertising and may receive referral fees if you buy a car through a dealer their website refers you to. Consumer Reports's annual car guide also has good information and data.

Don't lease, don't borrow: Buy your car with cash

The main reason people end up spending more than they can afford on a car is that they finance the purchase. As I discuss in Part I, you should avoid bor-rowing money for consumption purchases, especially for items that depreci-ate in value (like cars). A car is most definitely *not* an investment.

Leasing is generally more expensive than borrowing money to buy a car. Leasing is like a long-term car rental. Everyone knows how well rental cars get treated — leased cars are treated just as well, which is one of the reasons leasing is so costly.

"But I can't buy a new car with cash," you may be thinking. Some people feel that it's unreasonable of me to expect them to use cash to buy a new car, but I'm trying to look out for your best long-term financial interests. Please consider the following:

- ✔ **If you lack sufficient cash to buy a new car, don't buy a new car!** Most of the world's population can't even afford a car, let alone a new one! Buy a car that you can afford — which for most people is a used one.

- ✔ **Don't fall for the rationale that says buying a used car means lots of maintenance, repair expenses, and problems.** Do your homework and buy a good quality used car (see the preceding section). That way, you can have the best of both worlds. A good used car costs less to buy and, thanks to lower insurance costs (and possibly property taxes), less to operate.

- ✔ **You don't need a fancy car to impress people for business purposes.** Some people I know say that they absolutely must drive a nice, brand-spanking-new car to set the right impression for business purposes. I'm not going to tell you how to manage your career, but I will ask you to consider that if clients and others see you driving an expensive new car, they may think that you spend money wastefully or that you're getting rich off of them!

If you absolutely must finance a portion or all of your new car, and you are a homeowner, consider using a home equity line of credit. Interest rates on these loans are low right now, and interest on amounts of up to $100,000 of debt is currently tax deductible.

Replace high-cost cars

Maybe you realize by now that your car is too expensive to operate because of insurance, gas, and maintenance costs. Or maybe you bought too much car — people who lease or borrow money for a car frequently buy a far more expensive car than they can realistically afford.

Sell your expensive car and get something more financially manageable. The sooner you switch, the more money you'll save. Getting rid of a car on a lease is a challenge, but it can be done. I had a client who, when he lost his job and needed to slash expenses, convinced the dealer (by writing a letter to the owner) to take the leased car back.

Keep cars to a minimum

For most households, maintaining two or more cars is an expensive extravagance. Try to find ways to make do with fewer cars. You can move beyond the confines of owning a car by either carpooling or riding buses or trains to work. Some employers give incentives for taking public transit to work, and some cities and counties offer assistance for setting up vanpools or carpools along popular routes. By leaving the driving to someone else, you can catch up on reading or just relax on the way to and from work. You also help reduce pollution.

When you're considering the cost of living in different areas, don't forget to factor in commuting costs. One advantage of living close to work, or at least close to public transit systems, is that you may be able to make do with fewer cars (or no car at all) in your household.

Buy commuter passes

In many areas, you can purchase train, bus, or subway passes to help reduce the cost of commuting. Many toll bridges also have booklets of tickets or passes that you can buy at a discount. Electronic passes like E-Z Pass help you keep moving through toll plazas and eliminate sitting in toll collection lines that waste your time and gas. Some areas even allow before-tax dollars to be withheld from your paycheck to buy commuter passes.

Use regular unleaded gas

A number of studies have shown that "premium" gasoline isn't worth the extra expense. But make sure that you buy gasoline that has the minimum octane rating recommended for your vehicle by consulting your owner's manual. Paying more for higher-octane gasoline just wastes money. Your car doesn't run better; you just pay more for gas. Fill up your tank when you're on a shopping trip to the warehouse wholesalers (discussed earlier in this chapter). These superstores are usually located in lower-cost areas, so the gas is often cheaper there, too. Also, don't use credit cards to buy your gas if you have to pay a higher price to do so.

Service your car regularly

Sure, servicing your car (for example, changing the oil every 5,000 miles) costs money, but it saves you dough in the long run by extending the operating life of your car. Servicing your car also reduces the chance that your car will conk out in the middle of nowhere, which requires a hefty towing charge to a service station. Stalling on the freeway during peak rush hour and having thousands of angry commuters stuck behind you is even worse.

Lowering your energy costs

Escalating energy prices remind all of us how much we depend upon and use oil, electricity, and natural gas in our daily lives. A number of terrific websites are packed with suggestions and tips for how to lower your energy costs. Before I present those to you, however, here are the basics:

- **Drive fuel-efficient cars and drive efficiently.** If you're safety minded, you know how dangerous driving can be and aren't willing to risk your life driving a pint-size vehicle just to get 50 miles per gallon. That said, you can drive safe cars (see the earlier section "Research before you buy a car") that are fuel-efficient. Also, take it easy on the gas pedal and brakes; do both gradually and don't speed on the highway because doing so gobbles more gas.

- **Be thrifty at home.** Get all family members on the same page, without driving them crazy, to turn off lights they don't need. Turn down the heat at night, which saves money and helps you sleep better, and turn it down when no one is home. *Hint:* If people are walking around your home during the winter with shorts on instead of wearing sweaters, turn the heat down!

- **Service and maintain what you have.** Anything that uses energy — from your cars to your furnace — should be regularly serviced. For instance, make sure you clean your filters.

- **Investigate energy efficiency before you buy.** This advice applies not only to appliances but also to an entire home. Some builders are building energy efficiency into their new homes.

My favorite energy information and tip websites are the Database of State Incentives for Renewables & Efficiency (www.dsireusa.org) and the U.S. Department of Energy's Energy Efficiency and Renewable Energy (www.energysavers.gov).

Controlling clothing costs

Given the amount of money that some people spend on clothing and related accessories, I've come to believe that people in nudist colonies must be great savers! But you probably live among the clothed mainstream of society, so here's a short list of economical ideas:

- **Avoid clothing that requires dry-cleaning.** When you buy clothing, try to stick with cottons and machine-washable synthetics rather than wools or silks that require dry-cleaning. Check labels before you buy clothing.

✔ **Don't chase the latest fashions.** Fashion designers and retailers are constantly working to tempt you to buy. Don't do it. Ignore publications that pronounce this season's look. In most cases, you simply don't need to buy racks of new clothes or an entire new wardrobe every year. True fashion, as defined by what people wear, changes quite slowly. In fact, the classics never go out of style. If you want the effect of a new wardrobe every year, store last year's purchases away next year and then bring them out the year after. Or rotate your clothing inventory every third year. Set your own fashion standards. Buy basic and buy classic — if you let fashion gurus be your guide, you'll end up with the biggest wardrobe in the poorhouse!

✔ **Minimize accessories.** Shoes, jewelry, handbags, and the like can gobble large amounts of money. Again, how many of these accessory items do you really need? The answer is probably very few, because each one should last many years.

Go to your closet or jewelry box and tally up the loot. What else could you have done with all that cash? Do you see things you regret buying or forgot you even had? Don't make the same mistake again. Have a garage sale if you have a lot of stuff that you don't want. Return recent unused purchases to stores.

Repaying your debt

In Chapter 5, I discuss strategies for reducing the cost of carrying consumer debt. The *best* way to reduce the costs of such debt is to avoid it in the first place when you're making consumption purchases.

You can avoid consumer debt by eliminating your access to credit or by limiting your purchase of consumer items to what you can pay off each month. Borrow only for long-term investments (see Chapter 2 for more information).

Don't keep a credit card that charges you an annual fee, especially if you pay your balance in full each month. Many no-fee credit cards exist — and some even offer you a benefit for using them:

✔ **Discover Card** (phone 800-347-2683; website www.discover.com) rebates up to 1 percent of purchases in cash.

✔ **Armed Forces Benefit Association (AFBA)/5Star Bank** (phone 800-776-2265; website www.afba.com) offers no-fee cards that accumulate points toward rewards such as airline tickets, merchandise, gift cards, or cash back.

✔ **USAA Federal Savings** (phone 800-922-9092; website www.usaa.com) offers no-fee cards for members of the military and their immediate relatives.

Consider the cards in the preceding list only if you pay your balance in full each month, because no-fee cards typically don't offer the lowest interest rates for balances carried month-to-month. The small rewards that you earn really won't do you much good if they're negated by high interest charges.

If you have a credit card that charges an annual fee, try calling the company and saying that you want to cancel the card because you can get a competitor's card without an annual fee. Many banks will agree to waive the fee on the spot. Some require you to call back yearly to cancel the fee — a hassle that can be avoided by getting a true no-fee card.

Some cards that charge an annual fee and offer credits toward the purchase of a specific item, such as a car or airline ticket, may be worth your while if you pay your bill in full each month and charge $10,000 or more annually. *Note:* Be careful — you may be tempted to charge more on a card that rewards you for more purchases. Spending more in order to rack up bonuses defeats the purpose of the credits.

Indulging responsibly in fun and recreation

Having fun and taking time out for R and R can be money well spent. But when it comes to fun and recreation, financial extravagance can wreck an otherwise good budget.

Looking at low-cost entertainment

If you adjust your plans and expectations, entertainment doesn't have to cost a great deal of money. Many movies, theaters, museums, and restaurants offer discount prices on certain days and/or at certain times.

Cultivate some interests and hobbies that are free or low-cost. Visiting with friends, hiking, reading, and playing sports can be good for your finances as well as your health.

Vacationing for less

For many people, vacations are a luxury. For others, regular vacations are essential parts of their routine. Regardless of how you recharge your batteries, remember that vacations aren't investments, so you shouldn't borrow through credit cards to finance your travels. After all, how relaxed will you feel when you have to pay all those bills?

Try taking shorter vacations that are closer to home. Have you been to a state or national park recently? Great places that you've always wanted to see but haven't visited for one reason or another are probably located within 200 miles of you. Or you may want to just block out some time and do what family pets do: Relax around your home and enjoy some naps.

If you do travel a long way to a popular destination, travel during the off-season for the best deals on airfares and hotels. Keep an eye out for discounts. The *Consumer Reports Travel* newsletter and numerous websites, such as www.priceline.com, www.expedia.com, and www.travelocity.com can help you find low-cost travel options as well. Senior citizens generally qualify for special fares at most airlines — ask the airline what programs it offers.

Also, be sure to shop around, even when working with a travel agent. Travel agents work on commission, so they may not work hard to find you the best deals. Tour packages, when they meet your interests and needs, can also save you money.

Using thrift with gifts

Think about how you approach buying gifts throughout the year — especially during the holidays. I know people who spend so much on their credit cards during the year-end holidays that it takes them until late spring or summer to pay their debts off! Some people forget their thrifty shopping habits when gift-buying, perhaps because they don't like to feel cheap when buying a gift. As with other purchases you make, paying careful attention to where and what you buy can save you significant dollars. Don't make the mistake of equating the value of a gift with its dollar cost.

Although I don't want to deny your loved ones gifts from the heart — or deny you the pleasure of giving them — spend wisely. Homemade gifts are less costly to the giver and may be dearer to recipients. Many children actually love durable, classic, basic toys. If the TV commercials and web ads dictate your kids' desires, it may be time to limit the TV and Internet usage or set better rules for what the kids are allowed to watch. Use TiVo or similar DVR services to record desired shows so you can zap through the ubiquitous commercials.

And here's a good suggestion for getting rid of those old, unwanted gifts: a *white elephant* gift exchange. Everyone brings a wrapped, unwanted gift from the past and exchanges it with someone else. After the gifts are opened, trading is allowed. (Just be sure not to bring a gift that was given to you by any of the exchange participants!) Can't be bothered with this? Consider donating unwanted items for a tax write-off if you itemize on Schedule A — see Chapter 7.

Lowering your phone bills

Thanks to increased competition and technology, telephoning costs continue to fall. If you haven't looked for lower rates in recent years, you're probably paying more than you need to for quality phone service. Unfortunately, shopping among the many service providers is difficult. Plans come with different restrictions, minimums, and bells and whistles.

You may have to switch companies to reduce your bill, but I find that many people can save significantly with their current phone company simply by getting onto a better calling plan. So before you spend hours shopping around, contact your current local and long distance providers and ask them which of their calling plans offer the lowest cost for you based on the patterns of your calls.

Cellphones are ubiquitous. And although being able to make calls from wherever you are can be enormously convenient, you can spend a lot of money for service given the myriad extra charges. On the other hand, if you take advantage of the included minutes many plans offer, a good cellphone service can save you money.

The primary reason that some parents elect to provide cellphones to their teenage children is for safety, the ability to call home for a ride, and so on. Thus, you don't need all the costly bells and whistles. A cellphone need only be set up to place and receive calls.

In addition to downloads, text messaging, web surfing, and other services, kids (and adults) can find all sorts of entertaining ways to run up huge cellphone bills each month. Also, I hear a lot of complaints from parents about kids racking up data charges or texting too much.

To deal with going over plan allowances, you have a few options:

- ✔ **Examine family plan options that don't limit usage in the categories most important to you.** Shop around and make sure you sign up with the best plan and carrier given your typical usage. Reputable carriers let you test out their services. They also offer full refunds if you're not satisfied after a week or two of service.

- ✔ **Set and enforce limits.** If you provide a cellphone to a child, keep in mind that kids don't need to use their phones for hours daily. This point is especially important with data usage, which you can block so that your kids can only use Wi-Fi when available. With teens, why not tie having good grades to being able to have some of the extra features?

- ✔ **Check out prepaid or no-contract plans.** Look at companies like Consumer Cellular or TracFone.

Cellphones and kids can be a dangerous mix

Everywhere you look these days, it seems as if every teen (and just as often, every adult) has a cellphone. Cellphones are a great way for parents to keep in contact with their children, especially in emergencies. Important safety issues come up when teens get caught up in using cellphones. Keep the following in mind:

✔ A number of studies have raised concerns about the impact of repeated cellphone usage on the brain and the possible linkage between brain tumors and usage of cellphones held near the side of one's head. Getting teens who talk on the phone to use earpieces connected to the cellphone is easier said than done.

✔ A second health concern with cellphone usage is the common occurrence of older teens being on their phones while driving. Horrible accidents have happened with teens fiddling with their phones not only while placing and receiving calls but also while typing out text messages. Increasing numbers of states have passed laws requiring cellphone users to have hands-free devices and laws banning texting while driving.

Technology: Spending wisely

Americans today have email, cellphones, smartphones, voicemail, tablets, satellite TV, the Internet, and too many other ways to stay in touch and entertained 24/7. Visit a store that sells electronics, and you'll find no end to new gadgets.

Although I enjoy choices and convenience as much as the next person, I also see the detrimental impact these technologies have on people's lives. As it is, most families struggle to find quality time together given their work obligations, long school days, and various other activities. At home, all these technology choices and options compete for attention and often pull families apart. The cost for all these services and gadgets adds up, leading to continued enslavement to your job. Err on the side of keeping your life simple. Doing so costs less, reduces stress, and allows more time for the things that really do matter in life.

The worst way to shop for electronics and technology-based products is to wander around stores selling lots of these goods while a salesperson pitches you things. These folks are trained in what buttons to push to get you to whip out your Visa card and be on your way with things you don't know how you ever could've lived without. Educate yourself (check out Consumer Reports and CNET's website at www.cnet.com) and determine what you really need instead of going to a store and being seduced by a salesperson.

Curtailing personal care costs

You have to take care of yourself, but as with anything else, you can find ways to do it that are expensive, and you can find ways that save you money. Try this money-saving advice:

- **Hair care:** Going bald is one way to save money in this category. I'm working on this one myself. In the meantime, if you have hair to be trimmed, a number of no-frills, low-cost, hair-cutting joints can do the job. Supercuts is one of the larger hair-care chains. You may insist that your stylist is the only one who can manage your hair the way you like it. At the prices charged by some of the trendy hair places, you have to really adore what they do to justify the price. Consider going periodically to a no-frills stylist for maintenance after getting a fabulous cut at a more expensive place. If you're daring, you can try getting your hair cut at a local training school.

  For parents of young children, buying simple-to-use home haircutting electric clippers (such as Wahl's) can be a great time- and money-saver — no more agonizing trips with little ones to have their hair cut by a "stranger." The kit pays for itself after just two haircuts!

- **Other personal-care services:** As long as I'm on the subject of outward beauty, I have to say that, in my personal opinion, the billions spent annually on cosmetics are largely a waste of money (not to mention all the wasted time spent applying and removing them). Women look fine without makeup. (In most cases, they look better.) And having regular facials, pedicures, and manicures can add up quickly.

- **Health club expenses:** Money spent on exercise is almost always money well spent. But you don't have to belong to a trendy club to receive the benefits of exercise. Local schools, colleges, and universities often have tennis courts, running tracks, swimming pools, basketball courts, and exercise rooms, and they may provide instruction as well. Community centers offer fitness programs and classes, too. Metropolitan areas that have lots of health clubs undoubtedly have the widest range of options and prices. *Note:* When figuring the cost of membership, be sure to factor in the cost of travel to and from the club, as well as any parking costs (and the realistic likelihood of going there regularly to work out).

  Don't forget that healthy exercise can be done indoors or out, free of charge. Isn't hiking in the park more fun than pedaling away on a stationary bike, anyway? You may want to buy some basic gym equipment for use at home. Be careful, though: Lots of rowing machines and weights languish in a closet after their first week at home.

Paring down professional expenses

Accountants, lawyers, and financial advisors can be worth their expense if they're good. But be wary of professionals who create or perpetuate work and have conflicts of interest with their recommendations.

Make sure that you get organized before meeting with professionals for tax, legal, or financial advice. Do some background research to evaluate their strengths and biases. Set goals and estimate fees in advance so you know what you're getting yourself into.

Computer-based and printed resources (see Chapters 19 and 20) can be useful, low-cost alternatives and supplements to hiring professionals.

Managing medical expenses

The cost of healthcare continues going up fast. Your health insurance — if you have health insurance, that is — probably covers most of your healthcare needs. (Chapter 16 explains how to shop for health insurance.) But many plans require you to pay for certain expenses out of your own pocket.

Medical care and supplies are like any other services and products — prices and quality vary. And medicine in the United States, like any other profession, is a business. A conflict of interest exists whenever the person recommending treatment benefits financially from providing that treatment. Many studies have documented some of the unnecessary surgeries and medical procedures that have resulted from this conflict of interest.

Remember to shop around when seeking health insurance. Don't take any one physician's advice as gospel. Always get a second opinion for any major surgery. Most health insurance plans, out of economic self-interest, require a second opinion, anyway.

Therapy can be useful and even lifesaving. Have a frank talk with your therapist about how much total time and money you can expect to spend and what kind of results you can expect to receive. As with any professional service, a competent therapist gives you a straight answer if he's looking out for your psychological *and* financial well-being.

Alternative medicine (holistic, for example) is gaining attention because of its focus on preventive care and the treatment of the whole body or person. Although alternative medicine can be dangerous if you're in critical condition, alternative treatment for some forms of chronic pain or disease may be worth investigating. Alternative medicine may lead to better *and* lower-cost healthcare.

If you have to take certain drugs on an ongoing basis and pay for them out-of-pocket, ordering through a mail-order company can bring down your costs and help make refilling your prescriptions more convenient. Ask your health plan provider for more information about this option. Also inquire about generic versions of drugs.

Examine your employer's benefit plans. Take advantage of being able to put away a portion of your income before taxes to pay for out-of-pocket health-care expenses. Make sure that you pay close attention to the "use it or lose it" provisions of some plans. (Uncover more about health savings accounts in Chapter 16.)

Eliminating costly addictions

Human beings are creatures of habit. Everybody has habits he wishes he didn't have, and breaking those habits can be very difficult. Costly habits are the worst. The following tidbits may nudge you in the right direction toward breaking your own financially-draining habits.

✔ **Kick the smoking habit.** Check with local hospitals for smoking-cessation programs. The American Lung Association (phone 800-LUNGUSA; website www.lung.org) also offers Freedom from Smoking clinics around the country. The National Cancer Institute (phone 800-422-6237 or 800-4CANCER; website www.cancer.gov/) and the Office on Smoking and Health at the Centers for Disease Control (phone 800-784-8669 or 800-QUIT NOW; website www.cdc.gov/tobacco/about/osh/index.htm) offer free information online and in guides that contain effective methods for stopping smoking.

✔ **Stop abusing alcohol and other drugs.** The National Clearinghouse for Alcohol and Drug Information (phone 800-729-6686) can refer you to local treatment programs such as Alcoholics Anonymous. It also provides pamphlets and other literature about the various types of substance abuse. The National Substance Abuse Information and Treatment Hotline (phone 800-662-4357 or 800-662-HELP) can refer you to local drug treatment programs. It provides literature as well.

✔ **Don't gamble.** The house *always* comes out ahead in the long run. Why do you think so many governments run lotteries? Because governments make money on people who gamble, that's why. Casinos, horse and dog racetracks, and other gambling establishments are sure long-term losers for you. So, too, is the short-term trading of stocks, which isn't investing but gambling. Getting hooked on the dream of winning is easy. And sure, occasionally you win a little bit (just enough to keep you coming back). Every now and then, a few folks win a lot. But your hard-earned capital mostly winds up in the pockets of the casino owners.

If you gamble just for entertainment, take only what you can afford to lose. Gamblers Anonymous (phone 626-960-3500; website www. gamblersanonymous.org) helps those for whom gambling has become an addiction.

Keeping an eye on insurance premiums

Insurance is a vast minefield. In Part IV, I explain the different types of coverage, suggest what to buy and avoid, and detail how to save on policies. The following list explains the most common ways people waste money on insurance:

✔ **Keeping low deductibles.** The *deductible* is the amount of a loss that must come out of your pocket. For example, if you have an auto insurance policy with a $100 collision deductible and you get into an accident, you pay for the first $100 of damage, and your insurance company picks up the rest. Low deductibles, however, translate into much higher premiums for you. In the long run, you save money with a higher deductible, even when factoring in the potential for greater out-of-pocket costs to you when you do have a claim. Insurance should protect you from economic disaster. Don't get carried away with a really high deductible, which can cause financial hardship if you have a claim and lack savings.

If you have a lot of claims, you won't come out ahead with lower deductibles, because your insurance premiums will escalate. Plus, low deductibles mean more claim forms to file for small losses (creating more hassle). Filing an insurance claim usually isn't an enjoyable or quick experience.

✔ **Covering small potential losses.** You shouldn't buy insurance for anything that won't be a financial catastrophe if you have to pay for it out of your own pocket. Although the postal service isn't perfect, insuring inexpensive gifts sent in the mail isn't worth the price. Buying dental or home warranty plans, which also cover relatively small potential expenditures, doesn't make financial sense for the same reason. And if no one's dependent on your income, you don't need life insurance either. (Who will be around to collect when you're gone?)

✔ **Failing to shop around.** Rates vary *tremendously* from insurer to insurer. In Part IV, I recommend the best companies to call for quotes and other cost-saving strategies.

Trimming your taxes

Taxes are probably one of your largest — if not *the* largest — expenditures. (So why is it last here? Read on to find out.)

Retirement savings plans are one of the best and simplest ways to reduce your tax burden. (I explain more about retirement savings plans in Chapter 11.) Unfortunately, most people can't take full advantage of these plans because they spend everything they make. So not only do they have less savings, but they also pay higher income taxes — a double whammy.

I've attended many presentations where a fast-talking investment guy in an expensive suit lectures about the importance of saving for retirement and explains how to invest your savings. Yet details and tips about finding the money to save (the hard part for most people) are left to the imagination.

In order to take advantage of the tax savings that come through retirement savings plans, you must first spend less than you earn. Only then can you afford to contribute to these plans. That's why the majority of this chapter is about strategies to reduce your spending.

Reduced sales tax is another benefit of spending less and saving more. When you buy most consumer products, you pay sales tax. Therefore, when you spend less money and save more in retirement accounts, you reduce your income and sales taxes. (See Chapter 7 for detailed tax-reduction strategies.)

Chapter 7

Trimming Your Taxes

You pay a lot of money in taxes — probably more than you realize. Few people know just how much they pay in taxes each year. Most people remember whether they received a refund or owed money on their return. But when you file your tax return, all you're doing is settling up with tax authorities over the amount of taxes you paid during the year versus the total tax you owe based on your income and deductions.

Understanding the Taxes You Pay

Some people feel lucky when they get a refund, but all a refund really indicates is that you overpaid in taxes during the year. You should have had this money in your own account all along. If you're consistently getting big refunds, you need to pay less tax throughout the year. (Fill out a W-4 to determine how much you should be paying in taxes throughout the year. You can obtain a W-4 through your employer's payroll department. If you're self-employed, you can obtain Form 1040-ES by calling the IRS at 800-TAX-FORM [800-829-3676] or visiting its website at www.irs.gov. The IRS website also has a helpful withholding calculator at www.irs.gov/Individuals/IRS-Withholding-Calculator.)

Instead of focusing on whether you're going to get a refund when you complete your annual tax return, concentrate on the *total* taxes you pay, which I discuss in the following section.

Focusing on your total taxes

To find out the *total* taxes you pay, you need to get out your federal and state tax returns. On each of those returns is a line that shows the *total tax you owed for the year:* This is Line 63 on the most recent federal 1040 returns. If you add up the totals from your federal and state income tax returns, you'll probably see one of your largest expenses.

The goal of this chapter is to help you legally and permanently reduce your total taxes. Understanding the tax system is the key to reducing your tax burden — if you don't, you'll surely pay more taxes than necessary. Your tax ignorance can lead to mistakes, which can be costly if the IRS and state government catch your underpayment errors. With the proliferation of computerized information and data tracking, discovering mistakes has never been easier.

The tax system, like other public policy, is built around incentives to encourage desirable behavior and activity. For example, saving for retirement is considered desirable because it encourages people to prepare for a time in their lives when they may be less able or interested in working so much and when they may have additional healthcare expenses. Therefore, the tax code offers all sorts of tax perks, which I discuss later in this chapter, to encourage people to save in retirement accounts.

Now, it's a free country, and you should make choices that work best for your life and situation. However, keep in mind that the *fewer* desirable activities you engage in, the more you will generally pay in taxes. If you understand the options, you can choose the ones that meet your needs as you approach different stages of your financial life.

Recognizing the importance of your marginal tax rate

When it comes to taxes, *not all income is treated equally.* This fact is far from self-evident. If you work for an employer and earn a constant salary during the course of a year, a steady and equal amount of federal and state taxes is deducted from each paycheck. Thus, it appears as though all that earned income is being taxed equally.

In reality, however, you pay less tax on your first dollars of earnings and more tax on your *last* dollars of earnings. For example, if you're single and your taxable income (see the next section) totals $45,000 during 2016, you pay federal tax at the rate of 10 percent on the first $9,275 of taxable income,

15 percent on income between $9,275 and $37,650, and 25 percent on income from $37,650 up to $45,000.

Table 7-1 gives federal tax rates for singles and married households filing jointly.

Table 7-1	2016 Federal Income Tax Brackets and Rates	
Singles Taxable Income	*Married-Filing-Jointly Taxable Income*	*Federal Tax Rate (Bracket)*
$0–$9,275	$0–$18,550	10%
$9,275–$37,650	$18,550–$75,300	15%
$37,650–$91,150	$75,300–$151,900	25%
$91,150–$190,150	$151,900–$231,450	28%
$190,150–$413,350	$231,450–$413,350	33%
$413,350–$415,050	$413,350–$466,950	35%
More than $415,050	More than $466,950	39.6%

Your *marginal tax rate* is the rate of tax you pay on your *last,* or so-called *highest,* dollars of income. A single person with taxable income of $45,000 has a federal marginal tax rate of 25 percent. In other words, she effectively pays 25-percent federal tax on her last dollars of income — those dollars in excess of $37,650.

Marginal tax rates are a powerful concept. Your marginal tax rate allows you to quickly calculate the additional taxes you'd have to pay on additional income. Conversely, you can enjoy quantifying the amount of taxes you save by reducing your taxable income, either by decreasing your income or by increasing your deductions.

As you're probably already painfully aware, you pay not only federal income taxes but also state income taxes — that is, unless you live in one of the handful of states (Alaska, Florida, Nevada, South Dakota, Texas, Washington, or Wyoming) that have no state income tax. ***Note:*** Some states, such as New Hampshire and Tennessee, don't tax employment income but do tax other income, such as investment income.

Your *total marginal rate* includes your federal *and* state tax rates (not to mention local income tax rates in the municipalities that have them).

You can look up your state tax rate in your current state income tax preparation booklet.

Defining taxable income

Taxable income is the amount of income on which you actually pay income taxes. (In the sections that follow, I explain strategies for reducing your taxable income.) The following reasons explain why you don't pay taxes on your total income:

- ✔ **Not all income is taxable.** For example, you pay federal tax on the interest you earn on a bank savings account but not on the interest you earn from municipal bonds. As I discuss later in this chapter, some income, such as from stock dividends and long-term capital gains, is taxed at lower rates.

- ✔ **You get to subtract deductions from your income.** Some deductions are available just for being a living, breathing human being. In 2016, single people get an automatic $6,300 standard deduction, and married couples filing jointly get $12,600. (People over age 65 and those who are blind get a slightly higher deduction.) Other expenses, such as mortgage interest and property taxes, are deductible in the event that these so-called itemized deductions exceed the standard deductions. When you contribute to qualified retirement plans, you also effectively get a deduction.

Being mindful of the second tax system: Alternative minimum tax

You may find this hard to believe, but a second tax system actually exists (as if the first tax system weren't already complicated enough). This second system may raise your taxes even higher than they would normally be.

Over the years, as the government grew hungry for more revenue, taxpayers who slashed their taxes by claiming lots of deductions or exclusions from taxable income came under greater scrutiny. So the government created a second tax system — the alternative minimum tax (AMT) — to ensure that those with high deductions or exclusions pay at least a certain percentage of taxes on their incomes.

If you have a lot of deductions or exclusions from state income taxes, real-estate taxes, certain types of mortgage interest, and passive investments (for example, rental real estate), you may fall prey to AMT. You may also get tripped up by AMT if you exercise certain types of stock options or if you have a high amount of capital gains relative to your other ordinary income.

AMT restricts you from claiming certain deductions and requires you to add back in income that is normally tax-free (like certain municipal-bond interest). So you have to figure your tax under the AMT system and under the other system and then pay whichever amount is higher.

Watching for tax reform

In the aftermath of the 2016 presidential and Congressional elections, there is likely to be some tax reform unless control of Congress again becomes divided. There has been some talk and discussion of tax reform, but the two political parties can't reach agreement.

Republicans generally don't want anyone's tax rates to increase, and they demand that the federal budget deficit be reduced through spending cuts and by fostering faster economic growth through tax policy that encourages investment. Democrats, meanwhile, prefer raising taxes on the highest income earners while making more minimal spending cuts. (Please visit my website, www.erictyson.com, for updates on important pending tax law changes.)

Trimming Employment Income Taxes

You're supposed to pay taxes on income you earn from work. Countless illegal methods can reduce your taxable employment income — for example, not reporting it — but if you use them, you can very well end up paying a heap of penalties and extra interest charges on top of the taxes you owe. And you may even get tossed in jail. Because I don't want you to serve jail time or lose even more money by paying unnecessary penalties and interest, this section focuses on the best *legal* ways to reduce your income taxes on your earnings from work.

Contributing to retirement plans

A retirement plan is one of the few relatively painless and authorized ways to reduce your taxable employment income. Besides reducing your taxes, retirement plans help you build up a nest egg so you don't have to work for the rest of your life.

You can exclude money from your taxable income by tucking it away in employer-based retirement plans, such as 401(k) or 403(b) accounts, or self-employed retirement plans, such as SEP-IRAs. If your combined federal and state marginal tax rate is, say, 33 percent and you contribute $1,000 to one of these plans, you reduce your federal and state taxes by $330. Do you like the sound of that? How about this: Contribute another $1,000, and your taxes drop *another* $330 (as long as you're still in the same marginal tax rate). And when your money is inside a retirement account, it can compound and grow without taxation.

Many people miss this great opportunity to reduce their taxes because they *spend* all (or too much) of their current employment income and, therefore, have nothing (or little) left to put into a retirement account. If you're in this predicament, you first need to reduce your spending before you can contribute money to a retirement plan. (Chapter 6 explains how to decrease your spending.)

If your employer doesn't offer the option of saving money through a retirement plan, lobby the benefits and human resources departments. If they resist, you may want to add this to your list of reasons for considering another employer. Many employers offer this valuable benefit, but some don't. Some company decision-makers either don't understand the value of these accounts or feel that they're too costly to set up and administer.

If your employer doesn't offer a retirement savings plan, individual retirement account (IRA) contributions may or may not be tax-deductible, depending on your circumstances. You should first maximize contributions to the previously mentioned tax-deductible accounts. Chapter 11 can help you determine whether you should contribute to an IRA, what type you should contribute to, and whether your IRA contributions are tax-deductible.

Married couples filing jointly with adjusted gross incomes (AGIs) of less than $61,500 and single taxpayers with an AGI of less than $30,750 can earn a tax credit (claimed on Form 8880) for retirement account contributions. (For info on how the AGI is calculated, see "Deducting miscellaneous expenses.") Unlike a deduction, a *tax credit* directly reduces your tax bill by the amount of the credit. This credit, which is detailed in Table 7-2, is a percentage of the first $2,000 contributed (or $4,000 on a joint return). The credit is not available to those under the age of 18, full-time students, or people who are claimed as dependents on someone else's tax return.

Table 7-2	Special Tax Credit for Retirement Plan Contributions	
Singles Adjusted Gross Income	**Married-Filing-Jointly Adjusted Gross Income**	**Tax Credit for Retirement Account Contributions**
$0–$18,500	$0–$37,000	50%
$18,500–$20,000	$37,000–$40,000	20%
$20,000–$30,750	$40,000–$61,500	10%

Shifting some income

Income shifting, which has nothing to do with money laundering, is a more esoteric tax-reduction technique that's an option only to those who can control *when* they receive their income.

For example, suppose your employer tells you in late December that you're eligible for a bonus. You're offered the option to receive your bonus in either December or January. If you're pretty certain that you'll be in a higher tax bracket next year, you should choose to receive your bonus in December.

Or, suppose you run your own business and you think that you'll be in a lower tax bracket next year. Perhaps you plan to take time off to be with a newborn or take an extended trip. You can send out some invoices later in the year so your customers won't pay you until January, which falls in the next tax year.

Increasing Your Deductions

Deductions are amounts you subtract from your adjusted gross income before calculating the tax you owe. To make things more complicated, the IRS gives you two methods for determining your total deductions. The good news is that you get to pick the method that leads to greater deductions — and hence, lower taxes. This section explains your options.

Choosing standard or itemized deductions

The first method for figuring deductions requires no thinking or calculating. If you have a relatively uncomplicated financial life, taking the so-called *standard deduction* is generally the better option.

Single folks qualify for a $6,300 standard deduction, and married couples filing jointly get a $12,600 standard deduction in 2016. If you're 65 or older, or blind, you get a slightly higher standard deduction.

Itemizing your deductions on your tax return is the other method for determining your allowable deductions. This method is definitely more of a hassle, but if you can tally up more than the standard amounts noted in the preceding section, itemizing will save you money. Use Schedule A of IRS Form 1040 to sum up your itemized deductions.

Even if you take the standard deduction, take the time to peruse all the line items on Schedule A to familiarize yourself with the many legal itemized deductions. Figure out what's possible to deduct so you can make more-informed financial decisions year-round.

Organizing your deductions

Locating Form 1098 and all the other scraps of paper you need when completing your tax return can be a hassle. Setting up a filing system can be a big timesaver:

- **Folder or shoe box:** If you have a simple financial life (that is, you haven't saved receipts throughout the year), you can confine your filing to January and February. During those months, you receive tax summary statements on wages paid by your employer (Form W-2), investment income (Form 1099), and home mortgage interest (Form 1098) in the mail. Label the shoe box or folder with something easy to remember ("2015 Taxes" is a logical choice) and dump these papers and your tax booklet into it. When you're ready to crunch numbers, you'll have everything you need to complete the form.

- **Accordion-type file:** Organizing the bills you pay into individual folders during the entire year is a more thorough approach. This method is essential if you own your own business and need to tabulate your expenditures for office supplies each year. No one is going to send you a form totaling your office expenditures for the year — you're on your own.

- **Software:** Software programs can help organize your tax information during the year and save you time and accounting fees come tax-preparation time. See Chapter 19 for more information about tax and financial software.

The following sections explain commonly *overlooked* deductions and deduction strategies. Some are listed on Schedule A, and others appear on Form 1040.

Shifting or bunching deductions

When you total your itemized deductions on Schedule A and the sum is lower than the standard deduction, you should take the standard deduction. This total is worth checking each year, because you may have more deductions in some years, and itemizing may make sense.

Because you can control when you pay particular expenses that are eligible for itemizing, you can *shift* or *bunch* more of them into the select years where you have enough deductions to take advantage of itemizing. Suppose, for example, that you're using the standard deduction this year because you don't have many itemized deductions. Late in the year, though, you become certain that you're going to buy a home next year. With mortgage interest and property taxes to write off, you also know that you can itemize next year. If you typically make more charitable contributions in December because of the barrage of solicitations you receive when you're in the giving mood, you may want to write the checks in January rather than in December.

When you're sure that you're not going to have enough deductions in the current year to itemize, try to shift as many expenses as you can into the next tax year.

Purchasing real estate

When you buy a home, you can claim two big ongoing expenses of home ownership as deductions on Schedule A: your property taxes and the interest on your mortgage. You're allowed to claim mortgage interest deductions for a primary residence (where you actually live) and on a second home for mortgage debt totaling $1 million (and a home equity loan of up to $100,000). There's no limit on property tax deductions.

In order to buy real estate, you need to first collect a down payment, which requires maintaining a lid on your spending. See Part I for help with prioritizing and achieving important financial goals. Check out Chapter 14 for more on investing in real estate.

Trading consumer debt for mortgage debt

When you own real estate, you haven't borrowed the maximum, and you've run up high-interest consumer debt, you may be able to trade one debt for another. You may be able to save on interest charges by refinancing your mortgage or taking out a home equity loan and pulling out extra cash to pay off your credit card, auto loan, or other costly credit lines. You can usually borrow at a lower interest rate for a mortgage and get a tax deduction as a bonus, which lowers the effective borrowing cost further. Consumer debt, such as that on auto loans and credit cards, isn't tax-deductible.

This strategy involves some danger. Borrowing against the equity in your home can be an addictive habit. I've seen cases where people run up significant consumer debt three or four times and then refinance their home the same number of times over the years to bail themselves out.

An appreciating home creates the illusion that excess spending isn't really costing you. But debt is debt, and all borrowed money ultimately has to be repaid (unless you file bankruptcy). In the long run, you wind up with greater mortgage debt, and paying it off takes a bigger bite out of your monthly income. Refinancing and establishing home equity lines cost you more in terms of loan application fees and other charges (points, appraisals, credit reports, and so on).

At a minimum, the continued expansion of your mortgage debt handicaps your ability to work toward other financial goals. In the worst case, easy access to borrowing encourages bad spending habits that can lead to bankruptcy or foreclosure on your debt-ridden home.

Contributing to charities

You can deduct contributions to charities if you itemize your deductions. Consider the following possibilities:

- Most people know that when they write a check for $50 to their favorite church or college, they can deduct it. *Note:* Make sure that you get a receipt for contributions of $250 or more.

- Many taxpayers overlook the fact that you can deduct expenses for work you do with charitable organizations. For example, when you go to a soup kitchen to help prepare and serve meals, you can deduct some of your transportation costs. Keep track of your driving mileage and other commuting expenses.

- You can deduct the fair market value (which can be determined by looking at the price of similar merchandise in thrift stores) of donations of clothing, household appliances, furniture, and other goods to charities. (Some charities will drive to your home to pick up the stuff.) Find out whether organizations such as the Salvation Army, Goodwill, or others are interested in your donation. Just make sure that you keep some documentation — write up an itemized list and get it signed by the charity. Take pictures of your more valuable donations.

✔ You can even donate securities and other investments to charity. In fact, donating an appreciated investment gives you a tax deduction for the full market value of the investment and eliminates your need to pay tax on the (unrealized) profit.

Remembering auto registration fees and state insurance

If you don't currently itemize, you may be surprised to discover that your state income taxes can be itemized. When you pay a fee to the state to register and license your car, you can itemize a portion of the expenditure as a deduction (on Schedule A, Line 7, "Personal Property Taxes"). The IRS allows you to deduct the part of the fee that relates to the value of your car. The state organization that collects the fee should be able to tell you what portion of the fee is deductible. (Some states detail on the invoice what portion of the fee is tax-deductible.)

Several states have state disability insurance funds. If you pay into these funds (check your W-2), you can deduct your payments as state and local income taxes on Line 5 of Schedule A. You may also claim a deduction on this line for payments you make into your state's unemployment compensation fund.

Deducting miscellaneous expenses

A number of so-called *miscellaneous expenses* are deductible on Schedule A. Most of these expenses relate to your job or career and the management of your finances:

✔ **Educational expenses:** You may be able to deduct the cost of tuition, books, and travel to and from classes if your education is related to your career. Specifically, you can deduct these expenses if your course work improves your work skills. Courses required by law or your employer to maintain your position are deductible if you pay for them. Continuing education classes for professionals may also be deductible. *Note:* Educational expenses that lead to your moving into a new field or career are not deductible.

✔ **Job searches and career counseling:** After you obtain your first job, you may deduct legitimate costs related to finding another job within your field. You can even deduct the cost of courses and trips for new job interviews — *even if you don't change jobs.* And if you hire a career counselor to help you, you can deduct that cost as well.

✔ **Expenses related to your job that aren't reimbursed:** When you pay for your own subscriptions to trade journals to keep up with your field or buy a new desk and chair to ease back pain, you can deduct these costs. If your job requires you to wear special clothes or a uniform (for example, you're an EMT), you can write off the cost of purchasing and cleaning these clothes, as long as they aren't suitable for wearing outside of work. When you buy a computer for use outside the office at your own expense, you may be able to deduct the cost if the computer is for the convenience of your employer, is a condition of your employment, and is used more than half the time for business. Union dues and membership fees for professional organizations are also deductible.

✔ **Investment and tax-related expenses:** Investment and tax-advisor fees are deductible when paid from taxable accounts (although fees associated with tax-exempt investments, such as municipal bonds, are not), as are subscription costs for investment-related publications. Accounting fees for preparing your tax return or conducting tax planning during the year are deductible; legal fees related to your taxes are also deductible. If you purchase a home computer to track your investments or prepare your taxes, you can deduct that expense, too.

When you deduct miscellaneous expenses, you get to deduct only the amount that exceeds 2 percent of your AGI (adjusted gross income). *AGI* is your total wage, interest, dividend, and all other income minus retirement account contributions, self-employed health insurance, alimony paid, and losses from investments.

Deducting self-employment expenses

When you're self-employed, you can deduct a multitude of expenses from your income before calculating the tax you owe. If you buy a computer or office furniture, you can deduct those expenses. (Sometimes they need to be gradually deducted, or *depreciated,* over time.) Salaries for your employees, office supplies, rent or mortgage interest for your office space, and phone/communications expenses are also generally deductible.

Many self-employed folks don't take all the deductions they're eligible for. In some cases, people simply aren't aware of the wonderful world of deductions. Others are worried that large deductions will increase the risk of an audit. Spend some time finding out more about tax deductions; you'll be convinced that taking full advantage of your eligible deductions makes sense and saves you money.

The following are common mistakes made by people who are their own bosses:

- ✔ **Being an island unto yourself.** When you're self-employed, going it alone is usually a mistake when it comes to taxes. You must educate yourself to make the tax laws work for rather than against you. Hiring tax help is well worth your while. (See "Hiring professional help" later in this chapter for information on hiring tax advisors.)

- ✔ **Making administrative tax screwups.** As a self-employed individual, you're responsible for the correct and timely filing of all taxes owed on your income and employment taxes on your employees. You need to make estimated tax payments on a quarterly basis. And if you have employees, you also need to withhold taxes from each paycheck they receive and make timely payments to the IRS and the appropriate state authorities. In addition to federal and state income tax, you also need to withhold and send in Social Security and any other state or locally mandated payroll taxes.

  To pay taxes on your income, use Form 1040-ES. This form, along with instructions, can be obtained from the IRS (phone 800-829-3676; website www.irs.gov). The form comes complete with an estimated tax worksheet and the four payment coupons you need to send in with your quarterly tax payments. If you want to find the rules for withholding and submitting taxes from employees' paychecks, ask the IRS for Form 941 and Form 940, which is for unemployment insurance. And unless you're lucky enough to live in a state with no income taxes, you need to call for your state's estimated income tax package. Another alternative is to hire a payroll firm, such as Paychex, to do all this drudgery for you. Scrutinize and negotiate the expenses.

- ✔ **Failing to document expenses.** When you pay with cash, following the paper trail for all the money you spent can be hard for you to do (and for the IRS, in the event you're ever audited). At the end of the year, how are you going to remember how much you spent for parking or client meals if you fail to keep a record? How will you survive an IRS audit without proper documentation?

Debit cards are accepted most places and provide a convenient paper trail. (Be careful about getting a debit card in your business's name, because some banks don't offer protection against fraudulent use of business debit cards.) Otherwise, you need a record of your daily petty cash purchases. Most pocket calendars or daily organizers include ledgers that allow you to track these small purchases. (Some apps can help with this as well.) If you aren't that organized, at least get receipts for cash transactions and write on each receipt what the purchase was for. Then stash the receipts in a file folder in your desk or keep the receipts in envelopes labeled with the month and year.

✔ **Failing to fund a retirement plan.** You should be saving money toward retirement anyway, and you can't beat the tax break. People who are self-employed are allowed to save a substantial portion of their net income on an annual basis. To find out more about SEP-IRAs and other retirement plans, see Chapter 11.

✔ **Failing to use numbers to help manage business.** If you're a small-business owner who doesn't track her income, expenses, staff performance, and customer data on a regular basis, your tax return may be the one and only time during the year when you take a financial snapshot of your business. After you go through all the time, trouble, and expense to file your tax return, make sure you reap the rewards of all your work; use those numbers to help analyze and manage your business.

Some bookkeepers and tax preparers can provide you with management information reports on your business from the tax data they compile for you. Just ask! See "Using software and websites" later in this chapter for my recommendations.

✔ **Failing to pay family help.** If your children, spouse, or other relatives help with some aspect of your business, consider paying them for the work. Besides showing them that you value their work, this practice may reduce your family's tax liability. For example, children are usually in a lower tax bracket. By shifting some of your income to family members, you not only cut your tax bill, but can also make them eligible for attractive savings options like IRAs.

Reducing Investment Income Taxes

The distributions and profits on investments that you hold outside of tax-sheltered retirement accounts are exposed to taxation when you receive them. Interest, dividends, and *capital gains* (profits from the sale of an investment at a price that's higher than the purchase price) are all taxed.

Although this section explains some of the best methods for reducing the taxes on investments exposed to taxation, Chapter 12 discusses how and where to invest money held outside of tax-sheltered retirement accounts such as IRAs and 401(k) plans.

Investing in tax-free money-market funds and bonds

When you're in a high enough tax bracket, you may find that you come out ahead with tax-free investments. Tax-free investments pay investment income, which is exempt from federal tax, state tax, or both. (See Part III for details.)

Tax-free investments normally yield less than comparable investments that produce taxable income. But because of the difference in taxes, the earnings from tax-free investments *can* end up being greater than what you're left with from taxable investments.

Tax-free money-market funds can be a better alternative to bank savings accounts (where interest is subject to taxation). Likewise, tax-free bonds are intended to be longer-term investments that pay tax-free interest, so they may be a better investment option for you than bank certificates of deposit, Treasury bills and bonds, and other investments that produce taxable income. (See Chapter 12 for specifics on which tax-free investments may be right for your situation.)

Selecting other tax-friendly investments

Too often, when selecting investments, people mistakenly focus on past rates of return. Everyone knows that the past is no guarantee of the future. But choosing an investment with a reportedly high rate of return without considering tax consequences is an even worse mistake. What you get to keep — after taxes — is what matters in the long run.

For example, when comparing two similar funds, most people prefer a fund that averages returns of 14 percent per year to one that earns 12 percent per year. But what if the 14-percent-per-year fund, because of greater taxable distributions, causes you to pay a lot more in taxes? What if, after factoring in taxes, the 14-percent-per-year fund nets just 9 percent, while the 12-percent-per-year fund nets an effective 10-percent return? In such a case, you'd be unwise to choose a fund solely on the basis of the higher (pre-tax) reported rate of return.

I call investments that appreciate in value and don't distribute much in the way of highly taxed income *tax-friendly.* (Some in the investment business use the term *tax-efficient.*) See Chapter 10 for more information on tax-friendly stocks and stock mutual funds.

Real estate is one of the few areas with privileged status in the tax code. In addition to deductions allowed for mortgage interest and property taxes, you can depreciate rental property to reduce your taxable income. *Depreciation* is a special tax deduction allowed for the gradual wear and tear on rental real estate. When you sell investment real estate, you may be eligible to conduct a tax-free exchange into a replacement rental property. See Chapter 14 for a crash course in real estate.

Making your profits long-term

As I discuss in Part III, when you buy growth investments such as stocks and real estate, you should do so for the long-term — ideally ten or more years. The tax system rewards your patience with lower tax rates on your profits.

When you're able to hold on to an investment (outside of a retirement account) such as a stock, bond, or mutual fund for more than one year, you get a tax break if you sell that investment at a profit. Specifically, your profit is taxed under the lower capital gains tax rate schedule. If you're in the 25 percent to 35 percent federal income tax brackets, you pay just 15 percent of your long-term capital gains' profit in federal taxes. (The same lower tax rate applies to stock dividends.) If you're in the 10- or 15-percent federal income tax brackets, the long-term capital gains tax rate is 0 percent.

High income taxpayers (with total taxable income above $200,000 for singles; $250,000 for marrieds filing jointly), are now subject to a 3.8-percent-higher tax on their investment income (for example, interest, dividends, and capital gains) to help pay for Obamacare. The Bush tax cuts also expired, causing the tax rate on long-term capital gains for higher income investors (those in the highest — 39.6 percent — income tax bracket) to increase back to 20 percent. This increase combined with the new 3.8-percent tax from the healthcare bill produces a top long-term capital gains rate of nearly 24 percent — a significant increase from the previous 15 percent level. Depending on the outcome of the 2016 presidential election, these rates may change again. (Democratic candidates generally want to increase them, while Republicans would generally lower them.)

Does funding retirement accounts still make sense?

Historically, taking advantage of opportunities to direct money into retirement accounts gives you two possible tax benefits. First, your contributions to the retirement account may be immediately tax-deductible (see Chapter 11 for details). Second, the returns on the investments in the retirement accounts aren't generally taxed until withdrawal.

In the preceding section, I mention a tax break for long-term capital gains and on stock dividends. This break, unfortunately, applies only to investments held *outside* of retirement accounts. If you realize a long-term capital gain or receive stock dividends *inside* a retirement account, those investment returns are taxed, upon withdrawal, at the relatively higher ordinary income tax rates. Thus, some people argue that you shouldn't fund retirement accounts. In most cases, the people making those arguments have a vested interest.

One good reason not to fund a retirement account is having a specific goal, such as saving to purchase a home or start a business, that necessitates having access to your money. Not funding a retirement account may make sense in only two atypical situations:

- ✔ **You're temporarily in a very low tax bracket.** This circumstance can come about if, for example, you lose your job for an extended period of time or are in school. In these cases, you're unlikely to have lots of spare money to contribute to a retirement account anyway! If you have some employment income, consider the Roth IRA (see Chapter 11).

- ✔ **You have too much money socked away already.** If you have a large net worth inside retirement accounts, which could get hit by estate taxes (see Chapter 17), continuing to fund your retirement may be counter-productive.

Enlisting Education Tax Breaks

The government offers several tax reduction opportunities for those with educational expenses. Knowing that you don't want to read the dreadful tax code, here's a summary of key provisions you should know about for yourself and your kids if you have them:

- ✔ **Student loan interest deduction:** You may take up to a $2,500 deduction for student loan interest that you pay on IRS Form 1040 for college costs as long as your modified adjusted gross income (AGI) is less than or equal to $65,000 for single taxpayers and $130,000 for married couples filing jointly. (*Note:* Your deduction is phased out if your AGI is between $65,000 and $80,000 for single taxpayers and between $130,000 and $160,000 for married couples filing jointly.)

- ✔ **Tax-free investment earnings in special accounts:** Money invested in section 529 plans is sheltered from taxation and is not taxed upon withdrawal as long as the money is used to pay for eligible education expenses. Subject to eligibility requirements, 529 plans allow you to sock away $200,000+. Please be aware, however, that funding such accounts may harm your potential financial aid. (See Chapter 13 for details on these accounts.)

- ✔ **Tax credits:** The American Opportunity (AO) credit and Lifetime Learning (LL) credit provide tax relief to low- and moderate-income earners facing education costs. The AO credit may be up to $2,500 per student per year of undergraduate education, while the LL credit may be up to $2,000 per taxpayer. Each student may take only one of these credits per tax year, and they are subject to income limitations. And in a year in which a credit is taken, you may not withdraw money from a 529 plan nor take a tax deduction for your college expenses.

Please be sure to read Chapter 13 for the best ways and strategies to pay for educational expenses.

Getting Help from Tax Resources

There are all sorts of ways to prepare your tax return. Which approach makes sense for you depends on the complexity of your situation and your knowledge of taxes.

Regardless of which approach you use, you should be taking financial steps during the year to reduce your taxes. By the time you actually file your return in the following year, it's often too late for you to take advantage of many tax-reduction strategies.

Obtaining IRS assistance

If you have a simple, straightforward tax return, filing it on your own using only the IRS instructions is fine. This approach is as cheap as you can get. The main costs are time, patience, photocopying expenses (you should always keep a copy for your files), and postage for mailing the completed tax return (unless you're filing electronically).

IRS publications don't have Tip or Warning icons. And the IRS has been known to give wrong information from time to time. When you call the IRS with a question, be sure to take notes about your conversation to protect yourself in the event of an audit. Date your notes and include the name and identification number of the tax employee you talked to, the questions you asked, and the employee's responses. File your notes in a folder with a copy of your completed return.

In addition to the standard instructions that come with your tax return, the IRS offers some free (actually, paid for with your tax dollars) and sometimes-useful booklets. Publication 17, *Your Federal Income Tax,* is designed for individual tax-return preparation. Publication 334, *Tax Guide for Small Businesses,* is for (you guessed it) small-business tax-return preparation. These publications are more comprehensive than the basic IRS instructions. Call 800-829-3676 to request these booklets or visit the IRS website at www.irs.gov.

Consulting preparation and advice guides

Books about tax preparation and tax planning that highlight common problem areas and are written in clear, simple English are invaluable. They supplement the official instructions not only by helping you complete your return correctly but also by showing you how to save as much money as possible.

Using software and websites

If you have access to a computer, good tax-preparation software can be helpful. TurboTax and H&R Block Tax Software are programs that I have reviewed and rated as the best. If you go the software route, I highly recommend having a good tax advice book by your side.

For you web surfers, the Internal Revenue Service website (www.irs.gov) is among the better Internet tax sites, believe it or not.

Hiring professional help

Competent tax preparers and advisors can save you money — sometimes more than enough to pay their fees — by identifying tax-reduction strategies you may overlook. They can also help reduce the likelihood of an audit, which can be triggered by blunders. Mediocre and lousy tax preparers, on the other hand, may make mistakes and be unaware of sound ways to reduce your tax bill.

Tax practitioners come with varying backgrounds, training, and credentials. The four main types of tax practitioners are preparers, enrolled agents (EAs), certified public accountants (CPAs), and tax attorneys. The more training and specialization a tax practitioner has (and the more affluent her clients), the higher her hourly fee usually is. Fees and competence vary greatly. If you hire a tax advisor and you're not sure of the quality of the work performed or the soundness of the advice, try getting a second opinion.

Preparers

Preparers generally have the least amount of training of all the tax practitioners, and a greater proportion of them work part-time. As with financial planners, no national regulations apply to preparers, and no licensing is required.

Preparers are appealing because they're relatively inexpensive — they can do most basic returns for around $100 or so. The drawback of using a preparer is that you may hire someone who doesn't know much more than you do.

Preparers make the most sense for folks who have relatively simple financial lives, who are budget-minded, and who hate doing their own taxes. If you're not good about hanging on to receipts or you don't want to keep your own files with background details about your taxes, you should definitely shop around for a tax preparer who's committed to the business. You may need all that stuff someday for an audit, and many tax preparers keep and organize their clients' documentation rather than return everything each year. Also, going with a firm that's open year-round may be a safer option (some small shops are open only during tax season) in case tax questions or problems arise.

Enrolled agents (EAs)

A person must pass IRS scrutiny in order to be called an *enrolled agent*. This license allows the agent to represent you before the IRS in the event of an audit. Continuing education is also required; an EA's training is generally longer and more sophisticated than that of a typical preparer.

Enrolled agents' fees tend to fall between those of a preparer and a CPA (see the next section). Returns that require a few of the more common schedules (such as Schedule A for deductions and Schedule D for capital gains and losses) shouldn't cost more than $200 to $300 to prepare.

EAs are best for people who have moderately complex returns and don't necessarily need complicated tax-planning advice throughout the year (although some EAs provide this service as well). You can get names and telephone numbers of EAs in your area by contacting the National Association of Enrolled Agents (NAEA). You can call the NAEA at 202-822-6232 or visit its website at www.naea.org.

Certified public accountants (CPAs)

Certified public accountants go through significant training and examination before receiving the CPA credential. In order to maintain this designation, a CPA must also complete a fair number of continuing education classes every year.

CPA fees vary tremendously. Most charge $100+ per hour, but CPAs at large companies and in high-cost-of-living areas tend to charge somewhat more.

If you're self-employed and/or you file lots of other schedules, you may want to hire a CPA. But you don't need to do so year after year. If your situation grows complex one year and then stabilizes, consider getting help for the perplexing year and then using preparation guides, software, or a lower-cost preparer or enrolled agent in the future.

Tax attorneys

Tax attorneys deal with complicated tax problems and issues that usually have some legal angle. Unless you're a super-high-income earner with a complex financial life, hiring a tax attorney to prepare your annual return is prohibitively expensive. In fact, many tax attorneys don't prepare returns, but they may offer tax preparation as an ancillary service through others in their office.

Because of their level of specialization and training, tax attorneys tend to have the highest hourly billing rates — $200 to $300+ per hour is not unusual.

Dealing with an Audit

On a list of real-life nightmares, most people would rank tax audits right up there with root canals, rectal exams, and court appearances. Many people are traumatized by audits because they feel like they're on trial and being accused of a crime. Take a deep breath and don't panic.

You may be getting audited simply because someone at the IRS or a business that reports tax information on you made an error regarding the data on your return. In the vast majority of cases, the IRS conducts its audit by corresponding with you through the mail.

Audits that require you to schlep to the local IRS office are the most feared type of audit. In these cases, about 20 percent of such audited returns are left unchanged by the audit — in other words, the taxpayer doesn't end up owing more money. In fact, if you're the lucky sort, you may be one of the 5 percent of folks who actually gets a refund because the audit finds a mistake in your favor!

Unfortunately, you'll most likely be one of the roughly 75 percent of audit survivors who end up owing more tax money. The amount of additional tax that you owe in interest and penalties hinges on how your audit goes.

Getting your act together

Preparing for an audit is sort of like preparing for a test at school. The IRS lets you know which sections of your tax return it wants to examine.

The first decision you face when you get an audit notice is whether to handle it yourself or hire a tax advisor to represent you. Hiring representation may help you save time, stress, and money.

If you normally prepare your own return and you're comfortable with your understanding of the areas being audited, handle the audit yourself. When the amount of tax money in question is small compared to the fee you'd pay the tax advisor to represent you, self-representation is probably your best option. However, if you're likely to turn into a babbling, intimidated fool and you're unsure of how to present your situation, hire a tax advisor to represent you. (See "Hiring professional help" earlier in this chapter for information about whom to hire.)

If you decide to handle the audit yourself, get your act together sooner rather than later. Don't wait until the night before to start gathering receipts and other documentation. You may need to contact others to get copies of documents you can't find.

You need to document and be ready to speak only about the areas the audit notice says are being investigated. Organize the various documents and receipts into folders. You want to make it as easy as possible for the auditor to review your materials. *Don't* show up, dump shopping bags full of receipts and paperwork on the auditor's desk, and say, "Here it is — *you* figure it out."

Whatever you do, *don't ignore your audit request letter.* The IRS is the ultimate bill-collection agency. And if you end up owing more money (the unhappy result of most audits), the sooner you pay, the less interest and penalties you'll owe.

Surviving the day of reckoning

Two people with identical situations can walk into an audit and come out with very different results. The loser can end up owing much more in taxes and have the audit expanded to include other parts of the return. The winner can end up owing no additional tax or even owing less.

Here's how to be a winner in your tax audit:

✔ **Treat the auditor as a human being.** This advice may be obvious, but it isn't practiced by taxpayers very often. You may be resentful or angry about being audited. You may be tempted to gnash your teeth and tell the auditor how unfair it is that an honest taxpayer like you had to spend hours getting ready for this ordeal. You may feel like ranting and raving about how the government wastes too much of your tax money, or how the party in power is out to get you. Bite your tongue.

Believe it or not, most auditors are decent people just trying to do their jobs. They're well aware that taxpayers don't like seeing them. Don't suck up, either — just relax and be yourself. Behave as you would around a boss you like — with respect and congeniality.

✔ **Stick to the knitting.** Your audit is for discussing *only* the sections of your tax return that are in question. The more you talk about other areas or things that you're doing, the more likely the auditor is to probe into other items. Don't bring documentation for parts of your return that aren't being audited. Besides creating more work for yourself, you may be opening up a can of worms that doesn't need to be opened. Should the auditor inquire about areas that aren't covered by the audit notice, politely say that you're not prepared to discuss those other issues and that another meeting should be scheduled.

✔ **Don't argue when you disagree.** State your case. When the auditor wants to disallow a deduction or otherwise increase the taxes you owe and you disagree, state once why you don't agree with her assessment. If the auditor won't budge, don't get into a knock-down, drag-out confrontation. She may not want to lose face and is inclined to find additional tax money — that's the auditor's job.

When necessary, you can plead your case with several people who work above your auditor. If this method fails and you still feel wronged, you can take your case to tax court.

✔ **Don't be intimidated.** Most auditors are not tax geniuses. The work is stressful — being in a job where people dislike seeing you isn't easy. Turnover is quite high. Thus, many auditors are fairly young, just-out-of-school types who majored in something like English, history, or sociology. They may know less about tax and financial matters than you do. The basic IRS tax boot camp that auditors go through doesn't come close to covering all the technical details and nuances in the tax code. So you may not be at such a disadvantage in your tax knowledge after all, especially if you work with a tax advisor (most tax advisors know more about the tax system than the average IRS auditor).

Part III
Building Wealth through Investing

Allocating 401(k) Investments			
	25-Year-Old, Aggressive Risk Investor	45-Year-Old, Moderate Risk Investor	60-Year-Old, Moderate Risk Investor
Bond fund	0%	35%	50%
Balanced fund (50% stock/50% bond)	10%	0%	0%
Blue-chip/larger company stock fund(s)	30–40%	20–25%	25%
Smaller company stock fund(s)	20–25%	15–20%	10%
International stock fund(s)	25–35%	20–25%	15%

You may not know what to do when the stock market starts fluctuating wildly. Check out the free article at www.dummies.com/extras/personalfinance for advice on keeping calm in an uncertain market.

In this part . . .

✔ Master critical investment concepts such as major types of investments, expected returns, risks, and diversification.

✔ Understand the specific types of investments to choose among.

✔ Discover how to use mutual funds and exchange-traded funds.

✔ Find out how to invest inside and outside of retirement accounts and for future educational expenses.

✔ Master the fundamentals of investing in real estate through your own home and beyond.

Chapter 8

Considering Important Investment Concepts

- -

In This Chapter

▶ Determining your investment goals

▶ Evaluating returns and risks

▶ Keeping your eggs in more than one basket: Asset allocation

▶ Distinguishing the best investment firms from the rest

- -

Making wise investments need not be complicated. However, many investors get bogged down in the morass of the thousands of investment choices out there and the often-conflicting perspectives on how to invest. This chapter helps you grasp the important "bigger picture" issues that can help you ensure that your investment plan meshes with your needs and the realities of the investment marketplace.

Establishing Your Goals

Before you select a specific investment, first determine your investment needs and goals. Why are you saving money — what are you going to use it for? You don't need to earmark every dollar, but you should set some major objectives. Establishing objectives is important because the expected use of the money helps you determine how long to invest it. And that, in turn, helps you determine which investments to choose.

The risk level of your investments should factor in your time frame and your comfort level. Investing in high-risk vehicles doesn't make sense if you'll need to spend the funds within the next few years or if you'll have to spend all your profits on stress-induced medical bills. For example, suppose you've been accumulating money for a down payment on a home you want to buy in a few years. You can't afford much risk with that money because you're going to need it sooner rather than later. Putting that money in the stock market, then, is foolish. As I discuss later in this chapter, the stock market can drop a lot in a year or over several years. So stocks are probably too risky a place to invest money you plan to use soon.

Perhaps you're saving toward a longer-term goal, such as retirement, that's 20 or 30 years away. In this case, you're in a position to make riskier investments, because your holdings have more time to bounce back from temporary losses or setbacks. You may want to consider investing in growth investments, such as stocks, within a retirement account that you leave alone for 20 years or longer. (If stocks aren't to your liking, I discuss other growth investments throughout Part III.) You can tolerate year-to-year volatility in the market — you have time on your side. If you haven't yet done so, take a tour through Chapter 4, which helps you contemplate and set your financial goals.

Understanding the Primary Investments

For a moment, forget all the buzzwords, jargon, and product names you've heard tossed around in the investment world — in many cases, they obscure, sometimes intentionally, what an investment really is and hide the hefty fees and commissions.

Imagine a world with only two investment flavors — think of chocolate and vanilla ice cream (or low-fat frozen yogurt for you health-minded folks). The investment world is really just as simple. You have only two major investment choices: You can be a lender or an owner.

Looking at lending investments

You're a lender when you invest your money in a bank certificate of deposit (CD), a treasury bill, or a bond issued by a company like Exxon Mobil, for example. In each case, you lend your money to an organization — a bank, the federal government, or Exxon Mobil. You're paid an agreed-upon rate of interest for lending your money. The organization also promises to have your original investment (the *principal*) returned to you on a specific date.

Getting paid all the interest in addition to your original investment (as promised) is the best that can happen with a lending investment. Given that the investment landscape is littered with carcasses of failed investments, this is not a result to take for granted.

The worst that can happen with a lending investment is that you don't get everything you're promised. Promises can be broken under extenuating circumstances. When a company goes bankrupt, for example, you can lose all or part of your original investment.

Another risk associated with lending investments is that even if you get what you were promised, the ravages of inflation may reduce the purchasing power of your money. Also, the value of a bond may drop below what you paid for it if interest rates rise or the quality/risk of the issuing company declines.

Table 8-1 shows the reduction in the purchasing power of your money at varying rates of inflation after just ten years.

Table 8-1	Reduction in Purchasing Power Due to Inflation
Inflation Rate	*Reduction in Purchasing Power after Ten Years*
2 percent	−18 percent
4 percent	−32 percent
6 percent	−44 percent
8 percent	−54 percent
10 percent	−61 percent

Some investors make the common mistake of thinking that they're diversifying their long-term investment money by buying several bonds, some CDs, and an annuity. The problem, however, is that all these investments pay a relatively low fixed rate of return that's exposed to the vagaries of inflation.

A final drawback to lending investments is that you don't share in the success of the organization to which you lend your money. If the company doubles or triples in size and profits, your principal and interest rate don't double or triple in size along with it; they stay the same. Of course, such success does ensure that you'll get your promised interest and principal.

Exploring ownership investments

You're an *owner* when you invest your money in an asset, such as a company or real estate, that has the ability to generate earnings or profits. Suppose that you own 100 shares of Verizon Communications stock. With billions of shares of stock outstanding, Verizon is a mighty big company — your

100 shares represent a tiny piece of it. What do you get for your small slice of Verizon? As a stockholder, although you don't get free calling, you do share in the profits of the company in the form of annual dividends and an increase (you hope) in the stock price if the company grows and becomes more profitable. Of course, you receive these benefits if things are going well. If Verizon's business declines, your stock may be worth less (or even worthless!).

Real estate is another one of my favorite financially rewarding and time-honored ownership investments. Real estate can produce profits when it's rented out for more than the expense of owning the property or sold at a price higher than what you paid for it. I know numerous successful real-estate investors (myself included) who have earned excellent long-term profits.

The value of real estate depends not only on the particulars of the individual property but also on the health and performance of the local economy. When companies in the community are growing and more jobs are being produced at higher wages, real estate often does well. When local employers are laying people off and excess housing is sitting vacant because of previous over-building, rent and property values fall, as they did in the late 2000s.

Finally, many Americans have also built substantial wealth through small business. According to *Forbes* magazine, more of the United States' (and the world's) wealthiest individuals have built their wealth through their stake in small businesses than through any other vehicle. Small business is the engine that drives much of the country's economic growth. You can participate in small business in a variety of ways. You can start your own business, buy and operate an existing business, or simply invest in promising small businesses. In the chapters ahead, I explain each of these major investment types in detail.

Shunning Gambling Instruments and Behaviors

Although investing is often risky, it's not gambling. *Gambling* is putting your money into schemes that are sure to lose you money over time. That's not to say that everyone loses or that you lose every time you gamble. However, the deck is stacked against you. The house wins most of the time.

Horse-racing tracks, gambling casinos, and lotteries are set up to pay out 50 to 60 cents on the dollar. The rest goes to profits and covering the costs of those businesses — don't forget that they are businesses. Sure, your chosen horse may win a race or two, but in the long run, you're almost guaranteed to lose about 40 to 50 percent of what you bet. Would you put your money in an "investment" where your expected return over the long-term was negative 40 percent?

Forsaking futures, options, and other derivatives

Futures, options, and commodity futures are *derivatives,* or financial investments whose value is derived from the performance of another security, such as a stock or bond.

Suppose you hear a radio ad from the firm Fleecem, Cheatem, and Leavem advocating that you buy heating oil futures because of conflicts in the Middle East and the upcoming rise in heating oil usage due to the cold-weather months. You call the firm and are impressed by the smooth-talking vice president. His logic makes sense, and he spends a lot of time with little ol' you, so you send him a check for $10,000.

Buying futures isn't much different from blowing $10,000 at the craps tables in Las Vegas. Futures prices depend on short-term, highly volatile price movements. As with gambling, you occasionally win when the market moves the right way at the right time. But in the long run, you're gonna lose. In fact, you can lose it all.

Options are as risky as futures. With options, you're betting on the short-term movements of a specific security. If you have inside information (such as knowing in advance when a major corporate development is going to occur), you can get rich. But insider trading is illegal and will land you in jail.

Honest brokers who help their clients invest in stocks, bonds, and mutual funds tell them the truth about commodities, futures, and options. A former broker I know who worked for various major brokerage firms for 12 years told me, "I had just one client who made money in options, futures, or commodities, but the only reason he came out ahead was because he was forced to pull money out to close on a home purchase just when he happened to be ahead. The commissions were great for me, but there's no way a customer will make money in them." Remember these words if you're tempted to gamble with futures, options, and the like.

Futures and options are not always used for speculation and gambling. Some sophisticated professional investors use them to hedge, or actually reduce the risk of, their broad investment holdings. When futures and options are used in this fashion, things don't often work out the way that the pros hoped. You, the individual investor, should steer clear of futures and options.

Ditching day trading

Day trading — which is the rapid buying and selling of securities online — is an equally foolish vehicle for individual investors to pursue. This is speculation and gambling, not investing. Placing trades via the Internet is far cheaper than the older methods of trading (such as telephoning a broker), but the more you trade, the more trading costs eat into your investment capital.

Frequent trading also increases your tax bill as profits realized over short periods of time are taxed at your highest possible tax rate (see Chapter 7). You can certainly make some profits when day trading. However, over an extended period of time, you'll inevitably underperform the broad market averages. In those rare instances where you may do a little better than the market averages, the profits are rarely worth the time and personal sacrifices that you, your family, and your friendships endure.

Understanding Investment Returns

The previous sections describe the difference between ownership and lending investments, and they help you distinguish gambling and speculation from investing. "That's all well and good," you say, "but how do I choose which type of investments to put my money into? How much can I make, and what are the risks?"

Good questions. I'll start with the returns you *might* make. I say "might" because this requires looking at history, and history is a record of the past. Using history to predict the future — especially the near future — is dangerous. History may repeat itself, but not always in exactly the same fashion and not necessarily when you expect it to.

During this past century, ownership investments such as stocks and investment real estate returned around 9 percent per year, handily beating lending investments such as bonds (around 5 percent) and savings accounts (roughly 4 percent) in the investment performance race. Inflation has averaged 3 percent per year.

If you already know that the stock market can be risky, you may be wondering why investing in stocks is worth the anxiety and potential losses. Why bother for a few extra percent per year? Well, over many years, a few extra percent per year can really magnify the growth of your money (see Table 8-2). The more years you have to invest, the greater the difference a few percent makes in your returns.

Table 8-2	The Difference a Few Percent Makes	
At This Rate of Return on $10,000 Invested	*You'll Have This Much in 25 Years*	*You'll Have This Much in 40 Years*
4% (savings account)	$26,658	$48,010
5% (bond)	$33,863	$70,400
9% (stocks and investment real estate)	$86,231	$314,094

Investing is not a spectator sport. You can't earn good returns on stocks and real estate if you keep your money in cash on the sidelines. If you invest in growth investments such as stocks and real estate, don't chase one new investment after another trying to beat the market average returns. *The biggest value comes from being in the market, not from beating it.*

Sizing Investment Risks

Many investors have a simplistic understanding of what risk means and how to apply it to their investment decisions. For example, when compared to the yo-yo motions of the stock market, a bank savings account may seem like a less risky place to put your money. Over the long term, however, the stock market usually beats the rate of inflation, while the interest rate on a savings account does not, especially when factoring in taxes. Thus, if you're saving your money for a long-term goal like retirement, a savings account can be a "riskier" place to put your money.

Before you invest, ask yourself these questions:

- ✔ **What am I saving and investing this money for?** In other words, what's my goal?

- ✔ **What is my timeline for this investment?** When will I use this money?

- ✔ **What is the historical volatility of the investment I'm considering?** Does that suit my comfort level and timeline for this investment?

After you answer these questions, you'll have a better understanding of risk and you'll be able to match your savings goals to their most appropriate investment vehicles. In Chapter 4, I help you consider your savings goals and timeline. I address investment risk and returns in the sections that follow.

Comparing the risks of stocks and bonds

Given the relatively higher historic returns I mention for ownership investments in the previous section, some people think they should put all their money in stocks and real estate. So what's the catch?

The risk with ownership investments is the short-term fluctuations in their value. During the last century, stocks declined, on average, by more than 10 percent once every five years. Drops in stock prices of more than 20 percent occurred, on average, once every ten years. Real-estate prices suffer similar periodic setbacks.

Therefore, in order to earn those generous long-term returns from ownership investments like stocks and real estate, you must be willing to tolerate volatility. You absolutely should not put all your money in the stock or real-estate market. Investing your emergency money or money you expect to use within the next five years in such volatile investments is not a good idea.

The shorter the time period that you have for holding your money in an investment, the less likely growth-oriented investments like stocks are to beat out lending-type investments like bonds. Table 8-3 illustrates the historical relationship between stock and bond returns based on number of years held.

Table 8-3	Stocks versus Bonds
Number of Years Investment Held	*Likelihood of Stocks Beating Bonds*
1	60%
5	70%
10	80%
20	91%
30	99%

Some types of bonds have higher yields than others, but the risk-reward relationship remains intact (see Chapter 9 for more on bonds). A bond generally pays you a higher rate of interest when it has a

- ✔ **Lower credit rating:** To compensate for the higher risk of default and the higher likelihood of losing your investment

- ✔ **Longer-term maturity:** To compensate for the risk that you'll be unhappy with the bond's set interest rate if the market level of interest rates moves up

Focusing on the risks you can control

I always asked students in my personal finance class that I used to teach at the University of California to write down what they'd like to learn. Here's what one student had to say: "I want to learn what to invest my money in now, as the stock market is overvalued and interest rates are about to go up, so bonds are dicey and banks give lousy interest — HELP!"

This student recognized the risk of price fluctuations in her investments, but she also seemed to believe, like too many people, that you can predict what's going to happen. How did she know that the stock market was overvalued, and why hadn't the rest of the world figured it out? How did she know that interest rates were about to go up, and why hadn't the rest of the world figured that out, either?

When you invest in stocks and other growth-oriented investments, you must accept the volatility of these investments. That said, you can take several actions, which I discuss in this chapter and the remainder of Part III, to greatly reduce your risk when investing in these higher potential return investments. Invest the money that you have earmarked for the longer term in these vehicles. Minimize the risk of these investments through diversification. Don't buy just one or two stocks; buy a number of stocks. Later in this chapter, I discuss what you need to know about diversification.

Discovering low-risk, high-return investments

Despite what professors teach in the nation's leading business and finance graduate-school programs, low-risk investments that almost certainly lead to high returns are available. I can think of at least four such investments:

- ✔ **Paying off consumer debt.** If you're paying 10-, 14-, or 18-percent interest or more on an outstanding credit card or other consumer loan, pay it off before investing. To get a comparable return through other investment vehicles (after the government takes its share of your profits), you'd have to start a new career as a loan shark. If, between federal and state taxes, you're in a 33-percent tax bracket and you're paying 14-percent interest on consumer debt, you need to annually earn a whopping pretax return of 21 percent on your investments to justify not paying off the debt. Good luck!

When your only source of funds for paying off debt is a small emergency reserve equal to a few months' living expenses, paying off your debt may involve some risk. Tap into your emergency reserves only if you have a backup source — for example, the ability to borrow from a willing family member or against a retirement account balance.

✔ **Investing in your health.** Eat healthy, exercise, and relax.

✔ **Investing in friends and family.** Invest time and effort in improving your relationships with loved ones.

✔ **Investing in personal and career development.** Pick up a new hobby or reinvigorate your interest in an old one, improve your communication skills, or read widely. Take an adult education course or go back to school for a degree. Your investment will most likely lead to greater happiness and perhaps even higher paychecks.

Diversifying Your Investments

Diversification is one of the most powerful investment concepts. It refers to saving your eggs (or investments) in different baskets. Diversification requires you to place your money in different investments with returns that are not completely correlated, which is a fancy way of saying that when some of your investments are down in value, odds are that others are up in value.

To decrease the chances of all your investments getting clobbered at the same time, you must put your money in different types of investments, such as bonds, stocks, real estate, and small business. (I cover all these investments and more in Chapter 9.) You can further diversify your investments by investing in domestic as well as international markets.

Within a given class of investments, such as stocks, investing in different types of that class (such as different types of stocks) that perform well under various economic conditions is important. For this reason, *mutual funds,* which are diversified portfolios of securities such as stocks or bonds, are a highly useful investment vehicle. When you buy into a mutual fund, your money is pooled with the money of many others and invested in a vast array of stocks or bonds.

You can look at the benefits of diversification in two ways:

✔ Diversification reduces the volatility in the value of your whole portfolio. In other words, your portfolio can achieve the same rate of return that a single investment can provide with less fluctuation in value.

✔ Diversification allows you to obtain a higher rate of return for a given level of risk.

Keep in mind that no one, no matter whom he works for or what credentials he has, can guarantee returns on an investment. You can do good research and get lucky, but no one is free from the risk of losing money. Diversification allows you to hedge the risk of your investments. See Figures 8-1, 8-2, and 8-3 to get an idea of how diversifying can reduce your risk. (The figures in these charts are adjusted for inflation.) Notice that different investments did better during different economic environments and time periods.

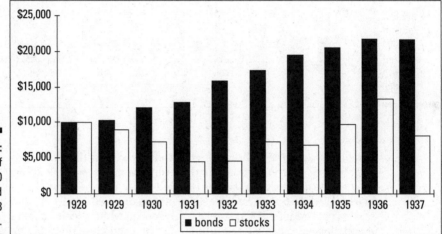

Figure 8-1: Value of $10,000 invested from 1928 to 1937.

© John Wiley & Sons, Inc.

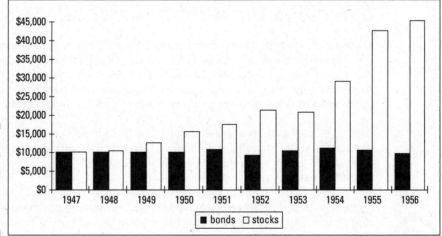

Figure 8-2: Value of $10,000 invested from 1947 to 1956.

© John Wiley & Sons, Inc.

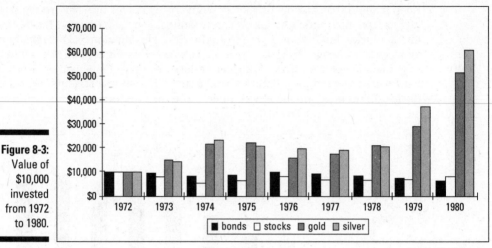

Figure 8-3:
Value of
$10,000
invested
from 1972
to 1980.

Recent decades have shown fluctuations as well. In the 1990s, stocks appreciated greatly, and bonds did pretty well, too, while gold and silver did poorly. In the 2000s, stocks treaded water (except those in emerging markets) while bonds and precious metals did well. Since the end of the severe recession in 2009, stocks have soared while precious metals have greatly lagged. Because the future can't be predicted, diversifying your money into different investments is safer.

Spreading the wealth: Asset allocation

Asset allocation refers to how you spread your investing dollars among different investment options (stocks, bonds, money-market accounts, and so on). Before you can intelligently decide how to allocate your assets, you need to ponder a number of issues, including your present financial situation, your goals and priorities, and the pros and cons of various investment options.

Although stocks and real estate offer attractive long-term returns, they can sometimes suffer significant declines. Thus, these investments are not suitable for money that you think you may want or need to use within, say, the next five years.

Money-market and shorter-term bond investments are good places to keep money that you expect to use soon. Everyone should have a reserve of money — about three to six months' worth of living expenses in a money-market fund — that's accessible in an emergency. Shorter-term bonds or bond mutual funds can serve as a higher-yielding, secondary emergency cushion. (Refer to Chapter 4 for more on emergency reserves.)

Bonds can also be useful for some longer-term investing for diversification purposes. For example, when investing for retirement, placing a portion of your money in bonds helps buffer stock market declines. The remaining chapters in Part III detail your various investment options and explain how to select those that best meet your needs.

Allocating money for the long term

Investing money for retirement is a classic long-term goal that most people have. Your current age and the number of years until you retire are the biggest factors to consider when allocating money for long-term purposes. The younger you are and the more years you have before retirement, the more comfortable you can afford to be with growth-oriented (and more volatile) investments, such as stocks and investment real estate.

One useful guideline for dividing or allocating your money between longer-term-oriented growth investments, such as stocks, and more-conservative lending investments, such as bonds, is to subtract your age from 110 (or 120 if you want to be aggressive; 100 to be more conservative) and invest the resulting percentage in stocks. You then invest the remaining amount in bonds.

For example, if you're 30 years old, you invest from 70 (100 – 30) to 90 (120 – 30) percent in stocks. You invest the remaining 10 to 30 percent in bonds.

Table 8-4 lists some guidelines for allocating long-term money based on your age and the level of risk you desire.

Table 8-4	Allocating Long-Term Money	
Your Investment Attitude	*Bond Allocation (%)*	*Stock Allocation (%)*
Play it safer	= Age	= 100 – age
Middle-of-the-road	= Age – 10	= 110 – age
Aggressive	= Age – 20	= 120 – age

For example, if you're the conservative sort who doesn't like a lot of risk but recognizes the value of striving for some growth and making your money work harder, you're a *middle-of-the-road* type. Using Table 8-4, if you're 40 years old, you may consider putting 30 percent (40 – 10) in bonds and 70 percent (110 – 40) in stocks.

In most employer retirement plans, mutual funds are the typical investment vehicle. If your employer's retirement plan includes more than one stock mutual fund as an option, you may want to try discerning which options are best by using the criteria I discuss in Chapter 10. In the event that all your retirement plan's stock fund options are good, you can simply divide your stock allocation among the choices.

When one or more of the choices is an international stock fund, consider allocating a percentage of your stock fund money to overseas investments: at least 20 percent for play-it-safe investors, 25 to 35 percent for middle-of-the-road investors, and as much as 35 to 50 percent for aggressive investors.

If the 40-year-old middle-of-the-roader from the previous example is investing 70 percent in stocks, about 25 to 35 percent of the stock fund investments (which works out to be about 18 to 24 percent of the total) can be invested in international stock funds.

In the past, most employees haven't had to make their own investing decisions with retirement money. That's because pension plans, in which the company directs the investments, were more common in previous years. It's interesting to note that in a typical pension plan, companies choose to allocate the majority of money to stocks (about 60 percent), with a bit less placed in bonds (about 35 percent) and other investments. For more information on investing in retirement accounts, see Chapter 11.

Sticking with your allocations: Don't trade

Your goals and desire to take risk should drive the allocation of your investment dollars. As you get older, gradually scaling back on the riskiness (and therefore growth potential and volatility) of your portfolio generally makes sense.

Don't tinker with your portfolio daily, weekly, monthly, or even annually. (Every two to three years or so, you may want to rebalance your holdings to get your mix to a desired asset allocation, as discussed in the preceding section.) Don't engage in trading with the hopes of buying into a hot investment and selling your losers. Jumping onto a "winner" and dumping a "loser" may provide some short-term psychological comfort, but in the long-term, such an investment strategy often produces below-average returns.

When an investment gets front-page coverage and everyone is talking about its stunning rise, it's definitely time to take a reality check. The higher an investment's price rises, the greater the danger that it's overpriced. Its next move may be downward. Don't follow the herd.

During the late 1990s, many technology (especially Internet) stocks had spectacular rises, thus attracting a lot of attention. However, the fact that the U.S. economy is increasingly becoming technology-based doesn't mean that any price you pay for a technology stock is fine. Some investors who neglected to do basic research and bought into the attention-grabbing, high-flying technology stocks lost 80 percent or more of their investments in the early 2000s — ouch!

Conversely, when things look bleak (as when stocks in general suffered significant losses in the early 2000s and then again in the late 2000s), giving up hope is easy — who wants to be associated with a loser? However, investors who forget about their overall asset allocation plan and panic and sell *after* a major decline miss out on a tremendous buying opportunity.

Many people like buying everything from clothing to cars to ketchup on sale — yet whenever the stock market has a clearance sale, most investors stampede for the exits instead of snatching up great buys. Demonstrate your courage; don't follow the herd.

Investing lump sums via dollar-cost averaging

When you have a large chunk of cash to invest — whether you received it from an accumulation of funds over the years, an inheritance, or a recent windfall from work you've done — you may have a problem deciding what to do with it. Many people, of course, would like to have your problem. (You're not complaining, right?) You want to invest your money, but you're a bit skittish — if not outright terrified — at the prospect of investing the lump of money all at once.

If the money is residing in a savings or money-market account, you may feel like it's wasting away. You want to put it to work! My first words of advice are "Don't rush." Nothing is wrong with earning a small return in a money-market account. (See Chapter 12 for my recommendations of the best money funds.) Remember that a money-market fund beats the heck out of rushing into an investment in which you may lose 20 percent or more. I sometimes get calls from people in a state of near panic. Typically, these folks have CDs coming due, and they feel that they must decide exactly where they want to invest the money in the 48 hours before the CD matures.

Take a deep breath. You have absolutely no reason to rush into an important decision. Tell your friendly banker that when the CD matures, you want to put the proceeds into the bank's highest-yielding savings or money-market account. That way, your money continues to earn interest while you buy yourself some breathing room.

One approach to investing is called *dollar-cost averaging* (DCA). With DCA, you invest your money in equal chunks on a regular basis — such as once a month — into a diversified group of investments. For example, if you have $60,000 to invest, you can invest $2,500 per month until it's all invested, which takes a couple of years. The money awaiting future investment isn't lying fallow; you keep it in a money-market account so it can earn a bit of interest while waiting its turn.

The attraction of DCA is that it allows you to ease into riskier investments instead of jumping in all at once. If the price of the investment drops after some of your initial purchases, you can buy some later at a lower price. If you dump your entire chunk of money into an investment all at once and then it drops like a stone, you'll be kicking yourself for not waiting.

The flip side of DCA is that when your investment of choice appreciates in value, you may wish that you had invested your money faster. Another drawback of DCA is that you may get cold feet as you continue to pour money into an investment that's dropping in value. Many people who are attracted to DCA because they fear that they may buy before a price drop end up bailing out of what feels like a sinking ship.

DCA can also cause headaches with your taxes when the time comes to sell investments held outside retirement accounts. When you buy an investment at many different times and prices, the accounting becomes muddied as you sell blocks of the investment.

DCA is most valuable when the money you want to invest represents a large portion of your total assets and you can stick to a schedule. Make DCA automatic so you're less likely to chicken out if the investment falls after your initial purchases. Most of the investment firms I recommend in the next few chapters provide automatic exchange services.

Acknowledging Differences among Investment Firms

Thousands of firms sell investments and manage money. Banks, mutual-fund companies, securities brokerage firms, and even insurance companies all vie for your dollars.

Just to make matters more complicated, each industry plays in the others' backyards. You can find mutual-fund companies that offer securities brokerage, insurance firms that are in the mutual-fund business, and mutual-fund companies that offer banklike accounts and services. You may benefit from this competition and one-stop shopping convenience. On the other hand, some firms are novices at particular businesses and count on folks shopping by brand-name recognition.

Focusing on the best firms

Make sure you do business with a firm that

✔ **Offers the best value investments in comparison to its competitors:** Value is the combination of performance (including service) and cost. Given the level of risk that you're comfortable with, you want investments that offer higher rates of return, but you don't want to have to pay a small fortune for them. Commissions, management fees, maintenance fees, and other charges can turn a high-performance investment into a mediocre or poor one.

✔ **Employs representatives who don't have an inherent self-interest in steering you into a particular type of investment:** This criterion has nothing to do with whether an investment firm hires polite, well-educated, or well-dressed people. The most important factor is the way the company compensates its employees. If the investment firm's personnel are paid on commission, be wary. Give preference to investing firms that don't tempt their employees to push one investment over another in order to generate more fees.

No-load (commission-free) mutual-fund companies

Mutual funds are an ideal investment vehicle for most investors. *No-load mutual-fund companies* are firms through which you can invest in mutual funds without paying sales commissions. In other words, every dollar you invest goes to work in the mutual funds you choose — nothing is siphoned off to pay sales commissions. Many of these firms also offer exchange-traded funds (ETFs), which are similar to mutual funds in many ways, are (in the best cases) lower cost, and trade on a major stock exchange and thus can be bought and sold during the trading day. See Chapter 10 for details on investing in mutual funds and ETFs.

Discount brokers

In one of the most beneficial changes for investors in the past century, the Securities and Exchange Commission (SEC) deregulated the retail brokerage industry on May 1, 1975. Prior to this date, investors were charged fixed commissions when they bought or sold stocks, bonds, and other securities. In other words, no matter which brokerage firm an investor did business with, the cost of the firm's services was set (and the level of commissions was high). After the 1975 deregulation, brokerage firms could charge people whatever their little hearts desired.

Competition inevitably resulted in more and better choices. Many new brokerage firms (that didn't do business the old way) opened. They were dubbed *discount brokers* because the fees they charged customers were substantially lower than what brokers charged under the old fixed-fee system.

Even more important than saving customers money, discount brokers established a vastly improved compensation system that greatly reduced conflicts of interest. Discount brokers generally pay the salaries of their brokers. The term *discount broker* is actually not an enlightening one. Certainly, this new breed of brokerage firm saves you lots of money when you invest; you can easily save 50 to 80 percent through the major discount brokers. But these firms' investments are not "on sale" or "second-rate." Discount brokers are simply brokers without major conflicts of interest. Of course, like any other for-profit enterprise, they're in business to make money, but they're much less likely to steer you in the wrong direction for their own benefit.

Be wary of discount brokers selling load mutual funds. (I discuss the reasons you should shun these brokers in Chapter 10.)

Places to consider avoiding

The worst places to invest are those that charge you a lot, have mediocre- or poor-performing investments, and have major conflicts of interest. The prime conflict of interest arises when investment firms pay their brokers commissions on the basis of what and how much they sell. The result: The investment firms sell lots of stuff that pays fat commissions, and they *churn,* or cause a rapid turnover of, your account. (Because each transaction has a fee, the more you buy and sell, the more money they make.)

Some folks who call themselves *financial planners* or *financial consultants* work on commission. In addition to working at the bigger brokerage firms, many of them belong to so-called *broker-dealer networks,* which provide back-office support and investment products to sell. When a person claiming to be a financial planner or advisor is part of a broker-dealer network, odds are quite high that you're dealing with an investment salesperson. See Chapter 18 for more background on the financial-planning industry and questions to ask an advisor you're thinking about hiring.

Commissions and their impact on human behavior

Investment products bring in widely varying commissions. The products that bring in the highest commissions tend to be the ones that money-hungry brokers push the hardest.

Table 8-5 lists the commissions that you pay — and that come out of your investment dollars — when you work with brokers, financial consultants, and financial planners who work on commission.

Table 8-5	Investment Sales Commissions	
Investment Type	*Average Commission on a $20,000 Investment*	*Average Commission on a $100,000 Investment*
Annuities	$1,400	$7,000
Initial public offerings (new stock issue)	$1,000	$5,000
Limited partnerships	$1,800	$9,000
Load mutual funds	$1,200	$5,000
Options and futures	$2,000+	$10,000+

Besides the fact that you can never be sure that you're getting an unbiased recommendation from a salesperson working on commission, you're wasting money unnecessarily. The best investments can be bought on a *no-load* (commission-free) basis.

When you're unsure about an investment product that's being pitched to you (and even when you *are* sure), ask for a copy of the prospectus. In the first few pages, check out whether the investment includes a commission (also known as a *load*). Although salespeople can hide behind obscure titles such as vice president or financial consultant, a prospectus must detail whether the investment carries a commission.

Investment salespeople's conflicts of interest

Financial consultants (also known as stockbrokers), financial planners, and others who sell investment products can have enormous conflicts of interest when recommending strategies and specific investment products. Commissions and other financial incentives can't help but skew the advice of even the most earnest and otherwise well-intentioned salespeople.

Numerous conflicts of interest can damage your investment portfolio. The following are the most common conflicts to watch out for:

- **Pushing higher-commission products:** As I discuss earlier in this chapter, commissions on investment products vary tremendously. Products like limited partnerships, commodities, options, and futures are at the worst end of the spectrum for you (and the best end of the spectrum for a salesperson). Investments such as no-load mutual funds, exchange-traded funds, and Treasury bills that are 100-percent commission-free are at the best end of the spectrum for you (and, therefore, the worst end of the spectrum for a salesperson).

   Surprisingly, commission-based brokers and financial planners don't have to give you the prospectus (where commissions are detailed) before you buy a financial product that carries commissions (as with a load mutual fund). In contrast, commission-free investment companies, such as no-load mutual-fund companies, must send a prospectus before taking a mutual-fund order. (Commission-based investment salespeople should also be required to provide a prospectus and disclose any commissions upfront and in writing before making a sale.)

- **Recommending active trading:** Investment salespeople often advise you to trade frequently into and out of different securities. They usually base their advice on current news events or an analyst's comments on the security. Sometimes these moves are valid, but more often they're not. In extreme cases, brokers trade on a monthly basis. By the end of the year, they've churned through your entire portfolio. Needless to say, all these transactions cost you big money in trading fees.

Diversified mutual funds and exchange-traded funds (see Chapter 10) make more sense for most people. You can invest in funds free of sales commissions. Besides saving money on commissions, you earn better long-term returns by having an expert money manager work for you.

✔ **Failing to recommend investing through retirement plans:** If you're not taking advantage of retirement savings plans (see Chapter 11), you may be missing out on valuable tax benefits. The initial contributions to most retirement plans are tax-deductible, and your money compounds without taxation over the years. An investment salesperson is not likely to recommend that you contribute to your employer's retirement plan — a 401(k) for example. Such contributions cut into the money you have available to invest with your friendly salesperson.

If you're self-employed, salespeople are somewhat more likely to recommend that you fund a retirement plan because they can set up such plans for you. You're better off setting up a retirement plan through a no-load mutual-fund company (see Chapters 10 and 11).

✔ **Pushing high-fee products:** Many of the brokerage firms that used to sell investment products only on commission moved into fee-based investment management. This change is an improvement for investors because it reduces some of the conflicts of interest caused by commissions.

On the other hand, these brokers charge extraordinarily high fees, which are usually quoted as a percentage of assets under management on their managed-investment (or wrap) accounts (see the sidebar "Wrap (or managed) accounts" for more info).

Valuing brokerage research

Brokerage firms and the brokers who work for them frequently argue that their research is better. With their insights and recommendations, they say, you'll do better and "beat the market averages."

Wall Street analysts are often overly optimistic when it comes to predicting corporate profits. If analysts were simply inaccurate or bad estimators, you'd expect that they'd sometimes underestimate and, at other times, overestimate companies' earnings. The discrepancy identifies yet another conflict of interest among many of the brokerage firms.

Brokerage firm analysts are reluctant to write a negative report about a company because the firms these analysts work for also solicit companies to issue new stock to the public. What better way to show businesses your potential for selling shares to the public at a high price than by showing how much you believe in certain companies and writing glowing reports about their future prospects?

What to do when you're fleeced by a broker

You can't sue a broker just because you lose money on that person's investment recommendations. However, if you have been the victim of one of the following cardinal financial sins, you may have some legal recourse:

- **Misrepresentation and omission:** If you were told, for example, that a particular investment guaranteed returns of 15 percent per year and then the investment ended up plunging in value by 50 percent, you were misled. Misrepresentation can also be charged if you're sold an investment with hefty commissions after you were originally told that it was commission-free.

- **Unsuitable investments:** Retirees who need access to their capital are often advised to invest in limited partnerships (or LPs, discussed in Chapter 9) for safe, high yields. The yields on most LPs end up being anything but safe. LP investors have also discovered how *illiquid* (or not readily converted into cash) their investments are — some can't be liquidated for up to ten years or more.

- **Churning:** If your broker or financial planner is constantly trading your investments, odds are that his weekly commission check is benefiting at your expense.

- **Rogue elephant salespeople:** When your planner or broker buys or sells without your approval or ignores your request to make a change, you may be able to collect for losses caused by these actions.

Two major types of practitioners — securities lawyers and arbitration consultants — stand ready to help you recover your lost money.

You can find securities lawyers by searching for "Attorneys — Securities" online or calling your local bar association for referrals. Arbitration consultants can be found in phone directories under "Arbitrators." If you come up dry, try contacting business writers at a major newspaper in your area or at your favorite personal finance magazine. These sources may be able to give you names and numbers of folks they know.

Most lawyers and consultants work on a *contingency-fee* basis — they get a percentage (about 20 to 40 percent) of the amount collected. They also often ask for an up-front fee, ranging from several hundred to several thousand dollars, to help them cover their expenses and time. If they take your case and lose, they generally keep the up-front money. Securities lawyers are usually a more expensive option.

You may want to go to *arbitration* — in fact, you may have agreed to do just that (probably without realizing it) when you set up an account to work with the broker or planner. Arbitration is usually much quicker, cheaper, and easier than going to court. You can even choose to represent yourself. Both sides present their cases, typically to a panel of three arbitrators. The arbitrators then make a decision that neither side can squabble over or appeal. If you decide to prepare for arbitration by yourself, the nonprofit American Arbitration Association can send you a package of background materials to help with your case. Contact the association's headquarters (phone 800-778-7879; website www.adr.org). Their website also provides contact information organized by state for local branches.

Seeing through Experts Who Predict the Future

Hoping that you can increase your investment returns by following the prognostications of certain gurus is a common mistake that some investors make, especially during more trying and uncertain times. Many people may want to believe that some experts can predict the future of the investment world and keep them out of harm's way. Trusting in gurus makes it easier to accept the risk you know you're taking when trying to make your money grow. The sage predictions that you read in an investment newsletter or hear from an "expert" who is repeatedly quoted in financial publications make you feel protected — sort of like Linus and his security blanket.

Investment newsletter subscribers and guru followers would be better off buying a warm blanket instead — it has a lot more value and costs a whole lot less! No one can predict the future. If they could, they'd be so busy investing their own money and getting rich that they wouldn't have the time and desire to share their secrets with you.

Investment newsletters

Many investment newsletters purport to time the markets, telling you exactly the right time to get into and out of certain stocks or mutual funds (or the financial markets in general). Such an approach is doomed to failure in the long run. By failure, I mean that this approach won't beat the tried-and-true strategy of buying and holding.

I see people paying hundreds of dollars annually to subscribe to all sorts of market-timing and stock-picking newsletters. One client of mine, an attorney, subscribed to several newsletters. When I asked him why, he said that their marketing materials claimed that if you followed their advice, you would make a 20-percent-per-year return on your money. But in the four years that he'd followed their advice, he'd actually *lost* money, despite appreciating financial markets overall.

Before I ever consider subscribing to any investment newsletter, I examine its historic track record through avenues such as *Hulbert Financial Digest*. The investment newsletter's marketing materials typically hype the supposed returns that the publication's recommendations have produced. Sadly, newsletters seem to be able to make lots of bogus claims without suffering the timely wrath of securities regulators.

Don't get predictive advice from newsletters. If newsletter writers were so smart about the future of financial markets, they'd be making lots more money as money managers. The only types of investment newsletters and periodicals that you should consider subscribing to are those that offer research and information rather than predictions. I discuss the investment newsletters that fill the bill in the subsequent investment chapters. My website, www.erictyson.com, provides excerpts and updates from the best newsletters to which I subscribe and read. Also check out the "Guru Watch" section of my site in which I evaluate commonly quoted gurus.

Investment gurus

Investment gurus come and go. Some of them get their 15 minutes of fame on the basis of one or two successful predictions that someone in the press remembers (and makes famous).

During the financial crisis of 2008 and 2009, all sorts of pundits were coming out of the woodwork claiming that they had predicted what was unfolding. Chief among them was an economist named Nouriel Roubini, whom few people had previously heard of. Many news services credited Roubini for supposedly predicting the recession. My research uncovered that Roubini had indeed predicted a recession. The only problem, however, is that Roubini predicted a recession in 2004, 2005, 2006, and 2007. So he was wrong for four long years in a row. In 2008, his prediction of a recession finally came true.

When the stock market dropped sharply and the recession worsened in late 2008, Roubini maintained a breakneck schedule with the news media. So he made even more predictions. For example, in late October 2008, Roubini predicted that ". . . hundreds of hedge funds are poised to fail as frantic investors rush to redeem their assets and force managers into a fire sale of assets. . . . We've reached a situation of sheer panic. Don't be surprised if policymakers need to close down markets for a week or two in coming days." This prediction sounded absurd to me at the time, which prompted me to write an article warning folks not to blindly follow Roubini's advice. This prediction was indeed absurd and, of course, never happened. Roubini was wrong.

In January 2009, Roubini predicted oil prices would stay below $40 per barrel for all of 2009. It didn't take long for that prediction to be proven wrong: Oil jumped above $50 per barrel by April and $70 by June.

When the Dow Jones Industrial Average fell to 6,500 in early 2009, Roubini said the market was likely to fall much farther, and he described any rally from that level as a "sucker's rally." Those people who panicked and sold in early 2009 because of Roubini's dire prediction were soon disappointed again as the stock market rebounded sharply.

The sad part about hyped articles with hyped predictions is that they cause some individual investors to panic and do the wrong thing — selling good assets like stocks at depressed prices. The media shouldn't irresponsibly publicize hyped predictions, especially without clearly and accurately disclosing the predictor's track record. Don't fall victim to such hype.

Commentators and experts who publish predictive commentaries and newsletters and who are interviewed in the media can't predict the future. Ignore the predictions and speculations of self-proclaimed gurus and investment soothsayers. The few people who have a slight leg up on everyone else aren't going to share their investment secrets — they're too busy investing their own money! If you have to believe in something to offset your fears, believe in good information and proven investment managers. And don't forget the value of optimism, faith, and hope — regardless of *what* or *whom* you believe in!

Leaving You with Some Final Advice

I cover a lot of ground in this chapter. In the remaining chapters in Part III, I detail different investment choices and accounts and how to build a champion portfolio! Before you move on, here are several other issues to keep in mind as you make important investing choices:

- **Don't invest based on sales solicitations.** Companies that advertise and solicit prospective customers aggressively with tactics such as telemarketing offer some of the worst financial products with the highest fees. All companies have to do some promotion, but the companies with the best investment offerings don't have to use the hard-sell approach; they get plenty of new business through the word-of-mouth recommendations of satisfied customers.

- **Don't invest in what you don't understand.** When you don't understand an investment, odds are good that it won't be right for you. Slick-tongued brokers (who may call themselves financial consultants, advisors, or planners) who earn commissions based on what they sell can talk you into inappropriate investments. Before you invest in anything, you need to know its track record, its true costs, and how liquid (easily convertible to cash) it is.

Wrap (or managed) accounts

Wrap accounts (also called managed accounts) are all the rage among commission-based brokerage firms. These accounts go by a variety of names, but they're all similar in that they charge a fixed percentage of the assets under management to invest your money through money managers.

Wrap accounts can be poor investments because their management expenses may be extraordinarily high — up to 3 percent per year (some even higher) of assets under management. Remember that in the long haul, stocks can return about 10 percent per year before taxes. So if you're paying 3 percent per year to have your money managed in stocks, 30 percent of your return (before taxes) is siphoned off. But don't forget — because the government sure won't — that you pay a good chunk of money in taxes on your 10 percent return as well. So the 3 percent wrap actually ends up depleting 40 to 50 percent of your after-tax profits!

The best no-load (commission-free) mutual funds and exchange-traded funds (ETFs) offer investors access to the nation's best investment managers for a fraction of the cost of wrap accounts. You can invest in dozens of top-performing funds for an annual expense of 1 percent per year or less. Some of the best fund companies offer excellent funds for a cost as low as 0.1 to 0.5 percent (see Chapter 10).

You may be told, in the marketing of wrap accounts, that you're getting access to investment managers who don't normally take money from small-fry investors like you. Not a single study shows that the performance of money managers has anything to do with the minimum account they handle. Besides, no-load funds hire many of the same managers who work at other money management firms. You also may be told that you'll earn a higher rate of return, so the extra cost is worth it. "You could have earned 18 to 25 percent per year," they say, "had you invested with the 'Star of Yesterday' investment management company." The key word here is *had.* History is history. Many of yesterday's winners become tomorrow's losers or mediocre performers.

You also need to remember that, unlike mutual funds and ETFs, wrap account performance records may include unaudited marketing hype. Showing only the performance of selected accounts — those that performed the best — is the most common ploy.

✔ **Minimize fees.** Avoid investments that carry high sales commissions and management expenses (usually disclosed in a prospectus). Virtually all investments today can be purchased without a salesperson. Besides paying unnecessary commissions, the bigger danger in investing through a salesperson is that you may be directed to a path that's not in your best interests. Management fees create a real drag on investment returns. Not surprisingly, higher-fee investments, on average, perform worse than alternatives with lower fees. High ongoing management fees often go toward lavish offices, glossy brochures, and skyscraper salaries, or toward propping up small, inefficient operations. Do you want your hard-earned dollars to support these types of businesses?

✔ **Pay attention to tax consequences.** Even if you never become an investment expert, you're smart enough to know that the more money you pay in taxes, the less you have for investing and playing with. See Chapter 11 for info on how retirement accounts can help boost your investment returns. For investments outside retirement accounts, you need to match the types of investments to your tax situation (see Chapter 12).

Chapter 9

Understanding Your Investment Choices

*W*hich vehicle you choose for your investment journey depends on where you're hoping to go, how fast you want to get there, and what risks you're willing to take. If you haven't yet read Chapter 8, you may want to do so now. In it, I cover a number of investment concepts, such as the difference between lending and ownership investments, which will enhance your ability to choose among the common investment vehicles I discuss in this chapter.

Slow and Steady Investments

Everyone should have some money in stable, safe investment vehicles, including money that you've earmarked for your short-term bills, both expected and unexpected. Likewise, if you're saving money for a home purchase within the next few years, you certainly don't want to risk that money on the roller coaster of the stock market.

The investment options that follow are appropriate for money you don't want to put at great risk.

Transaction/checking accounts

Transaction/checking accounts are best used for depositing your monthly income and paying for your expenditures. If you want to have unlimited check-writing privileges and access to your money with an ATM card, checking accounts at local banks are often your best bet.

Here's how not to be taken by banks:

- **Consider small banks, credit unions, and online banks.** You may get a better checking account deal at a credit union, a smaller bank, or one that operates online only. Because you can easily obtain cash through ATM outlets in supermarkets and other retail stores, you may not need to do business with Big City Bank, which has ATMs and branch offices at every intersection. Whatever institution you use, make sure your deposits are fully insured by the FDIC or NCUA.

- **Shop around.** Some banks don't require you to maintain a minimum balance to avoid a monthly service charge when you direct-deposit your paychecks. Make sure that you shop around for accounts that don't ding you $1.50 here for the use of an ATM and $12 there for a low balance.

- **Limit the amount you keep in checking.** Keep only enough money in the account for your monthly bill payment needs. If you consistently keep more than a few thousand dollars in a checking account, get the excess out. You can generally earn more in a savings or money-market account, which I describe in the following section. And, if you're a high roller, be sure to limit the total amount you invest at any one institution to avoid exceeding insurance limits.

- **Don't do your checking through the bank.** Some folks (me included) don't have a bank checking account. Discount brokerage accounts offer unlimited check-writing within a money-market fund. (See Chapter 10 for recommended firms; also see my discussion in Chapter 19 about paying your bills via your computer and through other automatic means.)

Savings accounts and money-market funds

Savings accounts are available through banks; money-market funds are available through mutual-fund companies. Savings accounts and money-market funds are nearly identical, except that money-market funds generally pay a better rate of interest. The interest rate paid to you, also known as the *yield,* fluctuates over time, depending on the level of interest rates in the overall economy. (Note that some banks offer money-market accounts, which are basically like savings accounts and shouldn't be confused with money-market mutual *funds.*)

The federal government backs bank savings accounts with Federal Deposit Insurance Corporation (FDIC) insurance. Money-market funds are not insured. But don't give preference to a bank account just because your investment (principal) is insured. In fact, your preference should lean toward money-market funds, because the better ones are higher-yielding than the better bank savings accounts. And money-market funds offer check-writing and other easy ways to access your money (for more on money funds, please see Chapter 10).

Money-market funds generally have several advantages over bank savings accounts:

✔ The best money-market funds have higher yields.

✔ If you're in a higher tax bracket, you may net more after factoring in taxes using tax-free money-market funds. No savings account pays tax-free interest.

✔ Most money-market funds come with free check-writing privileges. (The only stipulation is that each check must be written for a minimum amount — $250 is common.)

As with money you put into bank savings accounts, money-market funds are suitable for money that you can't afford to see dwindle in value.

Bonds

When you invest in a bond, you effectively lend your money to an organization. When a bond is issued, it includes a specified maturity date at which time the principal will be repaid. Bonds are also issued at a particular interest rate, or what's known as a *coupon*. This rate is fixed on most bonds. So, for example, if you buy a five-year, 6 percent bond issued by Home Depot, you're lending your money to Home Depot for five years at an interest rate of 6 percent per year. (Bond interest is usually paid in two equal, semi-annual installments.)

The value of a bond generally moves opposite of the directional change in interest rates. For example, if you're holding a bond issued at 6 percent and rates increase to 8 percent for comparable, newly issued bonds, your 6 percent bond will decrease in value. (Why would anyone want to buy your bond at the price you paid if it yields just 6 percent and 8 percent can be obtained elsewhere?)

The overused certificate of deposit

A *certificate of deposit* (CD) is another type of bond that's issued by a bank. With a CD, as with a real bond, you agree to lend your money to an organization (in this case, a bank) for a predetermined number of months or years. Generally, the longer you agree to lock up your money, the higher the interest rate you receive.

With CDs, you pay a penalty for early withdrawal. If you want your money back before the end of the CD's term, you get whacked with the loss of a number of months' worth of interest. CDs also don't tend to pay very competitive interest rates. You can usually beat the interest rate on shorter-term CDs (those that mature within a year or so) with the best money-market mutual funds, which offer complete liquidity without any penalty.

Some bonds are tied to variable interest rates. For example, you can buy bonds that are adjustable-rate mortgages, on which the interest rate can fluctuate. As an investor, you're actually lending your money to a mortgage borrower — indirectly, you're the banker making a loan to someone buying a home.

Bonds differ from one another in the following major ways:

- **The type of institution to which you're lending your money:** With municipal bonds, you lend your money to the state or local government or agency; with Treasuries, you lend your money to the federal government; with GNMAs (Ginnie Maes), you lend your money to a mortgage holder (and the federal government backs the bond); with corporate bonds, you lend your money to a corporation.

- **The credit quality of the borrower to whom you lend your money:** Credit quality refers to the probability that the borrower will pay you the interest and return your principal as agreed.

- **The length of maturity of the bond:** Short-term bonds mature within a few years, intermediate bonds within 3 to 10 years, and long-term bonds within 30 years. Longer-term bonds generally pay higher yields but fluctuate more with changes in interest rates.

Bonds are rated by major credit-rating agencies for their safety, usually on a scale where AAA is the highest possible rating. For example, high-grade corporate bonds (AAA or AA) are considered the safest (that is, most likely to pay you back). Next in safety are general bonds (A or BBB), which are still safe but just a little less so. Junk bonds rated BB or B are actually not all that junky; they're just lower in quality and have a slight (1 or 2 percent) probability of default over long periods of time. Junk bonds with even lower ratings — such as C or lower — carry higher default rates.

Some bonds are *callable,* which means that the bond's issuer can decide to pay you back earlier than the previously agreed-upon date. This event usually occurs when interest rates fall and the lender wants to issue new, lower-interest-rate bonds to replace the higher-rate, outstanding bonds. To compensate you for early repayment, the lender typically gives you a small premium over what the bond is currently valued at.

Building Wealth with Ownership Vehicles

The three best legal ways to build wealth are to invest in stocks, real estate, and small business. I've found this to be true from observing many clients and other investors and from my own personal experiences. Check out the following sections for more details about these three options.

Socking your money away in stocks

Stocks, which represent shares of ownership in a company, are the most common ownership investment vehicle. When companies *go public,* they issue shares of stock that people like you and me can purchase on the major stock exchanges, such as the New York Stock Exchange and NASDAQ (National Association of Securities Dealers Automated Quotation system), or on the over-the-counter market.

As the economy grows and companies grow with it, earning greater profits, stock prices (and dividend payouts on those stocks) generally follow suit. Stock prices and dividends don't move in lockstep with earnings, but over the years, the relationship is pretty close. In fact, the *price/earnings ratio* — which measures the level of stock prices relative to (or divided by) company earnings — of U.S. stocks has averaged approximately 15 (although it has tended to be higher during periods of low inflation and interest rates). A price-earnings ratio of 15 simply means that stock prices per share, on average, are selling at about 15 times those companies' earnings per share.

Companies that issue stock (called *publicly held* companies) include automobile manufacturers, computer software producers, fast-food restaurants, hotels, publishers, supermarkets, wineries, and everything in between! (You can also invest overseas — see the "International stocks" sidebar.) By contrast, some companies are *privately held,* which means that they've elected to have senior management and a small number of affluent investors own their stock. Privately held companies' stocks do not trade on a stock exchange, so folks like you and me can't buy stock in such firms.

International stocks

Not only can you invest in company stocks that trade on the U.S. stock exchanges, but you can also invest in stocks overseas. Why would you want to invest in international stocks?

I can give you several reasons. First, many investing opportunities exist overseas. If you look at the total value of all stocks outstanding worldwide, the value of foreign stocks now exceeds the value of U.S. stocks. Another reason for investing in international stocks is that when you confine your investing to U.S. securities, you miss a world of opportunities, not only because of business growth available in other countries but also because you get the opportunity to diversify your portfolio even further. International securities markets don't move in tandem with U.S. markets. During various U.S. stock market drops, some international stock markets drop less, while others actually rise in value.

Some people hesitate to invest in overseas securities out of concern that overseas investing hurts the U.S. economy and contributes to a loss of American jobs. I have some counterarguments. First, if you don't profit from the growth of economies overseas, someone else will. If there's money to be made, Americans may as well be there to participate. Profits from a foreign company are distributed to all stockholders, no matter where they live. Dividends and stock price appreciation know no national boundaries.

Also, recognize that you already live in a global economy. Making a distinction between U.S. and non-U.S. companies is no longer appropriate. Many companies that are headquartered in the United States also have overseas operations. Some U.S. firms derive a large portion of their revenue from their international divisions. Conversely, many firms based overseas also have U.S. operations. An increasing number of companies are worldwide operations.

Companies differ in what industry or line of business they're in and also in size. In the financial press, you often hear companies referred to by their *market capitalization,* which is the value of their outstanding stock (the number of total shares multiplied by the market price per share). When describing the sizes of companies, Wall Street has done away with such practical adjectives as *big* and *small* and replaced them with expressions like *large cap* and *small cap* (where *cap* is shorthand for *market capitalization*). Such is the language of financial geekiness.

Investing in the stock market involves occasional setbacks and difficult moments (just like raising children or going mountain climbing), but the overall journey is almost certainly worth the effort. Over the past two centuries, the U.S. stock market has produced an annual average rate of return of about 9 to 10 percent. However, the market, as measured by the Dow Jones Industrial Average, fell more than 20 percent during 16 different periods in the 20th century. On average, these periods of decline lasted less than two years. So if you can withstand a temporary setback over a few years, the stock market is a proven place to invest for long-term growth.

You can invest in stocks by making your own selection of individual stocks or by letting mutual (or exchange-traded) funds (discussed in Chapter 10) do it for you.

Discovering the relative advantages of mutual funds

Efficiently managed mutual funds offer investors low-cost access to high-quality money managers. Mutual funds span the spectrum of risk and potential returns, from nonfluctuating money-market funds (which are similar to savings accounts) to bond funds (which generally pay higher yields than money-market funds but fluctuate with changes in interest rates) to stock funds (which offer the greatest potential for appreciation but also the greatest short-term volatility).

Investing in individual securities should be done only by those who really enjoy doing it and are aware of and willing to accept the risks in doing so. Mutual funds and exchange-traded funds (see the next section), if properly selected, are a low-cost, quality way to hire professional money managers. Over the long haul, you're highly unlikely to beat full-time professional managers who are investing in securities of the same type and at the same risk level. Chapter 10 is devoted to mutual funds.

Understanding exchange-traded funds, hedge funds, and managed accounts

Mutual funds aren't the only game in town when it comes to hiring a professional money manager. Three additional options you may hear about include

- ✔ **Exchange-traded funds (ETFs):** These funds are the most similar to mutual funds except that they trade on a major stock exchange and thus can be bought and sold during the trading day. The best ETFs have low fees and, like an index fund (see Chapter 10), invest to track the performance of a stock market index.

- ✔ **Hedge funds:** These privately managed funds are for wealthier investors and are generally riskier (some even go bankrupt) than a typical mutual fund. The fees can be steep — typically 20 percent of the hedge fund's annual returns as well as an annual management fee of 1 percent or so. They're also generally illiquid — there are usually lock-up periods, and it can still be difficult to get your money back out later when needed. I generally don't recommend them.

- ✔ **Managed accounts:** The major brokerage firms, which employ brokers on commission, offer access to private money managers. In reality, this option isn't really different from getting access to fund managers via mutual funds, but you'll generally pay a much higher fee, which reduces this option's attractiveness.

Investing in individual stocks

My experience is that plenty of people choose to invest in individual securities because they think that they're smarter or luckier than the rest. I don't know you personally, but it's safe to say that in the long run, your investment choices are highly unlikely to outperform those of the best full-time investment professionals and index funds.

When I was a financial counselor, I noticed a distinct difference between the sexes on this issue. Perhaps because of the differences in how people are raised, testosterone levels, or whatever, men tend to have more of a problem swallowing their egos and admitting that they're better off not selecting their own individual securities. Maybe the desire to be a stock picker is genetically linked to not wanting to ask for directions!

Investing in individual stocks entails numerous drawbacks and pitfalls:

- ✔ **You need to spend a significant amount of time doing research.** When you're considering the purchase of an individual security, you need to know a lot about the company in which you're thinking about investing. Relevant questions to ask about the company include the following:

    - What products or services does it sell?

    - What are its prospects for future growth and profitability?

    - How much debt does the company have?

    You need to do your homework not only before you make your initial investment but also on an ongoing basis for as long as you hold the investment. Research takes your valuable free time and sometimes costs money.

- ✔ **Your emotions will probably get in your way.** Analyzing financial statements, corporate strategy, and competitive position requires great intellect and insight. However, those skills aren't nearly enough. Will you have the stomach to hold on after what you thought was a sure-win stock plunges 20, 30, 40, or 50 percent? Will you have the courage to dump such a stock if your new research suggests that the plummet is the beginning of the end rather than just a big bump in the road? When your money is on the line, emotions often kick in and undermine your ability to make sound long-term decisions. Few people have the psychological constitution to invest in individual stocks and handle and outfox the financial markets.

- ✔ **You're less likely to diversify.** Unless you have tens of thousands of dollars to invest in different stocks, you probably can't cost-effectively afford to develop a diversified portfolio. For example, when you're investing in stocks, you should hold companies in different industries, different companies within an industry, and so on. By not diversifying, you unnecessarily add to your risk.

✔ **You'll face accounting and bookkeeping hassles.** When you invest in individual securities outside retirement accounts, every time you sell a specific security, you must report that transaction on your tax return. Even if you pay someone else to complete your tax return, you still have the hassle of keeping track of statements and receipts.

Of course, you may find some people (with a vested interest) who try to convince you that picking your own stocks and managing your own portfolio of stocks is easy and more profitable than investing in, say, a mutual fund. In my experience, such stock-picking cheerleaders fall into at least one of the following categories:

✔ **Newsletter writers:** Whether in print, on television, or on a website, some pundits pitch the notion that professional money managers are just overpaid buffoons and that you can handily trounce the pros with little of your time by simply putting your money into the pundits' stock picks. Of course, what these self-anointed gurus are really selling is either an ongoing newsletter (which can run upward of several hundred dollars per year) or your required daily visitation of their advertising-stuffed websites. How else will you be able to keep up with their announced buy-and-sell recommendations? These supposed experts want you to be dependent on continually following their advice. (I discuss investment newsletters in Chapter 8 and websites in Chapter 19.)

✔ **Book authors:** Go into any bookstore with a decent-sized investing section, and you'll find plenty of books claiming that they can teach you a stock-picking strategy for beating the system. Never mind the fact that the author has no independently audited track record demonstrating her success! The book publisher of at least one investment group (Beardstown Ladies) was successfully sued over hyping and misrepresenting the group's actual investment success.

✔ **Stockbrokers:** Some brokers steer you toward individual stocks for several reasons that benefit the broker and not you. First, as I discuss in Chapter 8, the high-commission brokerage firms can make handsome profits for themselves by getting you to buy stocks. Second, brokers can use changes in the company's situation to encourage you to then sell and buy different stocks, generating even more commissions. Third, as with newsletter writers, this whole process forces you to be dependent on the broker, leaving you broker!

Researching individual stocks can be more than a full-time job, and if you choose to take this path, remember that you'll be competing against the professionals who do so on a full-time basis. If you derive pleasure from picking and following your own stocks, or you want an independent opinion of some stocks you currently own, useful research reports are available from Value Line (call 800-833-0046 or visit www.valueline.com). I also recommend that you limit your individual stock picking to no more than 20 percent of your overall investments.

Individual stock dividend reinvestment plans

Many corporations allow existing shareholders to reinvest their dividends (their share in company profits) in more shares of stock without paying brokerage commissions. In some cases, companies allow you to make additional cash purchases of more shares of stock, also commission-free.

In order to qualify, you must first generally buy some shares of stock through a broker (although some companies allow the initial purchases to be made directly from them). Ideally, you should purchase these initial shares through a discount broker to keep your commission burden as low as possible.

Some investment associations also have plans that allow you to buy one or just a few shares to get started. You typically need to complete some forms to invest in a number of different companies' stock. Life is too short to bother with these plans for this reason alone.

Finally, even with those companies that do sell stock directly without charging an explicit commission like a brokerage firm, you pay plenty of other fees. Many plans charge an up-front enrollment fee, fees for reinvesting dividends, and a fee when you want to sell.

Generating wealth with real estate

Over the generations, real-estate owners and investors have enjoyed rates of return comparable to those produced by the stock market, thus making real estate another time-tested method for building wealth. However, like stocks, real estate goes through good and bad performance periods. Most people who make money investing in real estate do so because they invest over many years and do their homework when they buy to ensure that they purchase good property at an attractive price.

 Buying your own home is the best place to start investing in real estate. The *equity* (the difference between the market value of the home and the loan owed on it) in your home that builds over the years can become a significant part of your net worth. Among other things, you can tap this equity to help finance other important personal goals, such as retirement, college, and starting or buying a business. Moreover, throughout your adult life, owning a home should be less expensive than renting a comparable home. See Chapter 14 for the best ways to buy and finance real estate.

Real estate: Not your ordinary investment

Real estate differs from most other investments in several respects. Here's what makes real estate unique as an investment:

✔ **You can live in it.** You can't live in a stock, bond, or mutual fund (although I suppose you could glue together a substantial fortress with all the paper some of these companies fill your mailbox with each year). Real estate is the only investment you can use (by living in it or renting it out) to produce income.

✔ **Land is in limited supply.** The percentage of the Earth occupied by land is relatively constant. And because humans like to reproduce, the demand for land and housing continues to grow. Consider the areas that have the most expensive real-estate prices in the world — Hong Kong, Tokyo, Hawaii, San Francisco, and Manhattan. In these densely populated areas, virtually no new land is available for building new housing.

✔ **Zoning shapes potential value.** Local government regulates the zoning of property, and zoning determines what a property can be used for. In most communities these days, local zoning boards are against big growth. This position bodes well for future real-estate values. Also know that in some cases, a particular property may not have been developed to its full potential. If you can figure out how to develop the property, you can reap large profits.

✔ **You don't need a lot of cash up-front.** Real estate is also different from other investments because you can borrow a lot of money to buy it — up to 80 to 90 percent or more of the value of the property. This borrowing is known as exercising *leverage:* With only a small investment of 10 to 20 percent down, you're able to purchase and own a much larger investment. When the value of your real estate goes up, you make money on your investment and on all the money you borrowed. (In case you're curious, you can leverage nonretirement-account stock and bond investments through margin borrowing. However, you have to make a much larger "down payment" — about double to triple the percentage you need to buy real estate.)

For example, suppose you plunk down $20,000 to purchase a property for $100,000. If the property appreciates to $120,000, you make a profit of $20,000 (on paper) on your investment of just $20,000. In other words, you make a 100 percent return on your investment. But leverage cuts both ways. If your $100,000 property decreases in value to $80,000, you actually lose (on paper) 100 percent of your original $20,000 investment, even though the property value drops only 20 percent.

✔ **You can discover hidden value.** In an *efficient market,* the price of an investment accurately reflects its true worth. Some investment markets are more efficient than others because of the large number of transactions and easily accessible information. Real-estate markets can be inefficient at times. Information is not always easy to come by, and you may find an ultramotivated or uninformed seller. If you're willing to do some homework, you may be able to purchase a property below its fair market value (perhaps by as much as 10 to 20 percent).

Just as with any other investment, real estate has its drawbacks. For starters, buying or selling a property generally takes time and significant cost. When you're renting property, you discover firsthand the occasional headaches of being a landlord. And especially in the early years of rental property ownership, the property's expenses may exceed the rental income, producing a net cash drain.

The best real-estate investment options

Although real estate is unique in some ways, it's also like other types of investments in that prices are driven by supply and demand. You can invest in homes or small apartment buildings and then rent them out. In the long run, investment-property buyers hope that their rental income and the value of their properties will increase faster than their expenses.

When selecting real estate for investment purposes, remember that local economic growth is the fuel for housing demand. In addition to a vibrant and diverse job base, you want to look for limited supplies of both existing housing and land on which to build. When you identify potential properties in which you may want to invest, run the numbers to understand the cash demands of owning the property and the likely profitability. See Chapter 14 for help determining the costs of real-estate ownership.

Although few will admit it, some real-estate investors get an ego rush from a tangible display of their wealth. Sufferers of this "edifice complex" can't obtain similar pleasure from a stock portfolio detailed on a piece of paper (although others have been known to boast of their stock-picking prowess). When you want to invest directly in real estate, residential housing — such as single-family homes or small multi-unit buildings — may be an attractive investment. Buying properties close to home offers the advantage of allowing you to more easily monitor and manage what's going on. The downside is that your investments will be less diversified — more of them will be dependent on the local economy.

If you don't want to be a landlord — one of the biggest drawbacks of investment real estate — consider investing in real estate through real-estate investment trusts (REITs). *REITs* are diversified real-estate investment companies that purchase and manage rental real estate for investors. A typical REIT invests in one or two types of property, such as shopping centers, apartments, and other rental buildings. You can invest in REITs either by purchasing them directly on the major stock exchanges or by investing in a real-estate mutual fund (see Chapter 10) that invests in numerous REITs.

Comparing real estate and stocks

Real estate and stocks have historically produced comparable returns. Deciding between the two depends less on the performance of the markets than on you and your situation. Consider the following major issues when deciding which investment may be better for you:

✔ The first and most important question to ask yourself is whether you're cut out to handle the responsibilities that come with being a landlord. Real estate is a time-intensive investment (property managers can help, but their cost takes a sizable chunk of your rental income). Investing in stocks can be time-intensive as well, but it doesn't have to be if you use professionally managed mutual funds and exchange-traded funds (see Chapter 10).

✔ An often-overlooked drawback to investing in real estate is that you earn no tax benefits while you're accumulating your down payment. Retirement accounts such as 401(k)s, SEP-IRAs, 403(b)s, and so on (see Chapter 11) give you an immediate tax deduction as you contribute money to them. If you haven't exhausted your tax-deductible contributions to these accounts, consider doing so before chasing after investment real estate.

✔ Ask yourself which investments you have a better understanding of. Some folks feel uncomfortable with stocks and mutual funds because they don't understand them. If you have a better handle on what makes real estate tick, you have a good reason to consider investing in it.

✔ Figure out what will make you happy. Some people enjoy the challenge that comes with managing and improving rental property; it can be a bit like running a small business. If you're good at it and you have some good fortune, you can make money and derive endless hours of enjoyment.

The worst real-estate investments

Not all real-estate investments are good; some aren't even real investments. The bad ones are characterized by burdensome costs and problematic economic fundamentals:

✔ **Limited partnerships:** Avoid limited partnerships (LPs) sold through brokers and financial consultants. LPs are inferior investment vehicles. They're so burdened with high sales commissions and ongoing management fees that deplete your investment that you can do better elsewhere. The investment salesperson who sells you such an investment stands to earn a commission of up to 10 percent or more — so only 90 cents of each dollar gets invested. Each year, LPs typically siphon off another several percent for management and other expenses. Most partnerships have little or no incentive to control costs. In fact, they have a conflict of interest that forces them to charge more to enrich the managing partners.

Unlike a mutual fund, you can't vote with your dollars. If the partnership is poorly run and expensive, you're stuck. LPs are *illiquid* (not readily convertible into cash without a substantial loss). You can't access your money until the partnership is liquidated, typically seven to ten years after you buy in.

Many of the yields on LPs have turned out to be bogus. In some cases, partnerships prop up their yields by paying back investors' principals (without telling them, of course). As for returns — well — historically too many LPs have been turkeys. The only thing limited about a limited partnership is its ability to make you money.

✔ **Time shares:** Time shares are another nearly certain money loser. With a time share, you buy a week or two of ownership, or usage, of a particular unit (usually a condominium in a resort location) per year. If, for example, you pay $8,000 for a week (in addition to ongoing maintenance fees), you're paying the equivalent of more than $400,000 for the whole unit, when a comparable unit nearby may sell for only $150,000. The extra markup pays the salespeople's commissions, administrative expenses, and profits for the time-share development company.

People usually get enticed into buying a time share when they're enjoying a vacation someplace. They're easy prey for salespeople who want to sell them a souvenir of the trip. The "cheese in the mousetrap" is an offer of something free (for example, a free night's stay in a unit) for attending the sales presentation.

If you can't live without a time share, consider buying a used one. Many previous buyers, who more than likely have lost a good chunk of money, are trying to dump their shares (which should tell you something). In this case, you may be able to buy a time share at a fair price. But why commit yourself to taking a vacation in the same location and building at the same time each year? Many time shares let you trade your weeks for other times and other places; however, doing so is a hassle — you're charged an extra fee, and your choices are usually limited to time slots that other people don't want (that's why they're trading them!).

✔ **Second homes:** The weekend getaway is a sometimes romantic notion and an extended part of the so-called American dream. When your vacation home is not in use, you may be able to rent it out and earn some income to help defray the expense of keeping it up. However, most second-home owners seldom rent out their property — they typically do so 10 percent or less of the time. As a result, second homes are usually money drains, not investments.

The supposed tax benefits are part of the attraction of a second home. Even when you qualify for some or all of them, tax benefits only partially reduce the cost of owning a property. In some cases, the second home is such a cash drain that it prevents its owners from contributing to and taking advantage of tax-deductible retirement savings plans.

If you aren't going to rent out a second home most of the time, ask your-self whether you can afford such a luxury. Can you accomplish your other financial goals — saving for retirement, paying for the home in which you live, and so on — with this added expense? Keeping a second home is more of a consumption than an investment decision. Few people can afford more than one home.

Investing in small business (and your career)

Small business is the leading investment through which folks have built the greatest wealth. You can invest in small business by starting one yourself (and thus finding yourself the best boss you've probably ever had), buying an existing business, or investing in someone else's small business. Even if small business doesn't interest you, hopefully your own job does, so I pres-ent some tips on making the most of your career.

Launching your own enterprise

When you have self-discipline and a product or service you can sell, starting your own business can be both profitable and fulfilling. Consider first what skills and expertise you possess that you can use in your business. You don't need a "eureka"-type idea or invention to start a small business. Millions of people operate successful businesses that are hardly unique, such as dry cleaners, restaurants, tax preparation firms, and so on.

Begin exploring your idea by first developing a written business plan. Such a plan should detail your product or service, how you're going to market it, your potential customers and competitors, and the economics of the busi-ness, including the start-up costs.

Of all the small-business investment options, starting your own business involves the most work. Although you can do this work on a part-time basis in the beginning, most people end up running their business full-time — it's your new job, career, or whatever you want to call it.

I've been running my own business for most of my working years, and I wouldn't trade that experience for the corporate life. That's not to say that running my own business doesn't have its drawbacks and down moments. But in my experience counseling small-business owners, I've seen many people of varied backgrounds, interests, and skills succeed and be happy with running their own businesses.

In most people's eyes, starting a new business is the riskiest of all small-business investment options. But if you're going into a business that uses your skills and expertise, the risk isn't nearly as great as you may think. Many businesses can be started with little cash by leveraging your existing skills and expertise. You can build a valuable company and job if you have the time to devote. As long as you check out the competition and offer a valued service at a reasonable cost, the principal risk with your business comes from not doing a good job marketing what you have to offer. If you can market your skills and have a plan to get through the inevitable economic down cycles that affect every business, you're home free.

As long as you're thinking about the risks of starting a business, consider the risks of staying in a job you don't enjoy or that doesn't challenge or fulfill you. If you never take the plunge, you may regret that you didn't pursue your dreams.

Buying an existing business

If you don't have a specific product or service you want to sell but you're skilled at managing and improving the operations of a company, buying a small business may be for you. Finding and buying a good small business takes much time and patience, so be willing to devote at least several months to the search. You may also need to enlist financial and legal advisors to help inspect the company, look over its financial statements, and hammer out a contract.

Although you don't have to go through the riskier start-up period if you buy a small business, you'll likely need more capital to buy an established enterprise. You'll also need to be able to deal with stickier personnel and management issues. The history of the organization and the way things work will predate your ownership of the business. If you don't like making hard decisions, firing people who don't fit with your plans, and coercing people into changing the way they do things, buying an existing business likely isn't for you.

Some people perceive buying an existing business as being safer than starting a new one. Buying someone else's business may actually be riskier. You're likely to shell out far more money upfront, in the form of a down payment, to buy an existing business. If you don't have the ability to run the business and it does poorly, you have more to lose financially. In addition, the business may be for sale for a reason — it may not be very profitable, it may be in decline, or it may generally be a pain in the neck to operate.

Good businesses don't come cheap. If the business is a success, the current owner has already removed the start-up risk from the business, so the price of the business should be at a premium to reflect this lack of risk. When you have the capital to buy an established business and you have the skills to run it, consider going this route.

Investing in someone else's small business

Are you someone who likes the idea of profiting from successful small businesses but doesn't want the day-to-day headaches of being responsible for managing the enterprise? Then investing in someone else's small business may be for you. Although this route may seem easier, few people are actually cut out to be investors in other people's businesses. The reason: Finding and analyzing opportunities isn't easy.

Are you astute at evaluating corporate financial statements and business strategies? Investing in a small, privately held company has much in common with investing in a publicly traded firm (as is the case when you buy stock), but it also has a few differences. One difference is that private firms aren't required to produce comprehensive, audited financial statements that adhere to certain accounting principles. Thus, you have a greater risk of not having sufficient or accurate information when evaluating a small, private firm.

Another difference is that unearthing private, small-business investing opportunities is harder. The best private companies who are seeking investors generally don't advertise. Instead, they find prospective investors through networking with people such as business advisors. You can increase your chances of finding private companies to invest in by speaking with tax, legal, and financial advisors who work with small businesses. You can also find interesting opportunities through your own contacts or experience within a given industry.

Don't consider investing in someone else's business unless you can afford to lose all of what you're investing. Also, you should have sufficient assets so that what you're investing in small, privately held companies represents only a small portion (20 percent or less) of your total financial assets.

Investing in your career

In my work with financial counseling clients over the years and from observing friends and colleagues, I've witnessed plenty of people succeed working for employers. So I don't want to leave you with the impression that financial success equates with starting, buying, or investing in someone else's small business.

You can and should invest in your career. Some time-tested, proven ways to do that include

✔ **Networking:** Some people wait to network until they've been laid off or are really hungry to change jobs. Take an interest in what others do for a living and you'll learn and grow from the experience, even if you choose to stay with your current employer or in your chosen field.

✔ **Making sure you keep learning:** Whether it's reading quality books or other publications or taking some night courses, find ways to build on your knowledge base.

✔ **Considering the risk in the status quo:** Many folks are resistant to change and get anxious thinking about what could go wrong when taking a new risk. I know when I was ready to walk away from a six-figure consulting job with a prestigious firm and open my own financial counseling firm, a number of my relatives and friends thought I had lost my marbles. That's not to say that they didn't have some valid concerns; they just weren't really considering the risks inherent in my staying put and didn't see the upside of my small-business venture.

Off the Beaten Path: Investment Odds and Ends

The investments that I discuss in this section sometimes belong on their own planet (because they're not an ownership or lending vehicle). Here are the basics on these other common, but odd, investments.

Precious metals

Gold and silver have been used by many civilizations as currency or a medium of exchange. One advantage of precious metals as a currency is that they can't be debased by the government. With paper currency, such as U.S. dollars, the government can simply print more. This process can lead to the devaluation of a currency and inflation.

Holdings of gold and silver can provide a so-called *hedge* against inflation. In the late 1970s and early 1980s, inflation rose dramatically in the United States. This largely unexpected rise in inflation depressed stocks and bonds. Gold and silver, however, rose tremendously in value — in fact, more than 500 percent (even after adjusting for inflation) from 1972 to 1980 (see Chapter 8). Such periods are unusual. Precious metals produced decent returns in the 2000s, but, after peaking in 2011, precious metals prices fell steeply.

Over many decades, precious metals tend to be lousy investments. Their rate of return tends to keep up with the rate of inflation but not surpass it.

When you want to invest in precious metals as an inflation hedge, your best option is to do so through mutual funds or exchange-traded funds (see Chapter 10). Don't purchase precious metals futures. They're not investments; they're short-term gambles on which way gold or silver prices may head over a short period of time. I also recommend staying away from firms and shops that sell coins and *bullion* (not the soup, but bars of gold or silver). Even if you can find a legitimate firm (not an easy task), the cost of storing and insuring gold and silver is quite costly. You won't get good value for your money — markups can be substantial.

Annuities

Annuities are a peculiar type of insurance and investment product. They're a sort of savings-type account with slightly higher yields, and they're backed by insurance companies. *Fixed annuities* pay a preset interest rate determined by the insurance company. This rate is typically set one year ahead at a time. *Variable annuities'* return varies over time depending on the returns provided by which investment is chosen within the annuity offerings.

As with other types of retirement accounts, money placed in an annuity compounds without taxation until it's withdrawn. However, unlike most other types of retirement accounts, such as 401(k)s, SEP-IRAs, and 403(b)s, you don't receive upfront tax breaks on contributions you make to an annuity. Ongoing investment expenses also tend to be much higher than in retirement plan accounts. Therefore, consider an annuity generally only after you fully fund tax-deductible retirement accounts. There's one other possible personal use for annuities: Those nearing or in retirement with limited resources can insure against the risk of outliving their assets by buying an annuity and annuitizing it — again, at a cost, so proceed carefully. (For more help on deciding whether to invest in an annuity, see Chapter 12.)

Collectibles

The collectibles category is a catchall for antiques, art, autographs, baseball cards, clocks, coins, comic books, diamonds, dolls, gems, photographs, rare books, rugs, stamps, vintage wine, and writing utensils — in other words, any material object that, through some kind of human manipulation, has become more valuable to certain humans.

Notwithstanding the few people who discover on *Antiques Roadshow* that they own an antique of significant value, collectibles are generally lousy investment vehicles. Dealer markups are enormous, maintenance and protection costs are draining, research is time-consuming, and people's tastes are quite fickle. All this for returns that, after you factor in the huge markups, rarely keep up with inflation. Furthermore, investment gains you do earn on collectibles are currently taxed at a higher maximum federal tax rate (28 percent) than capital gains on stocks, real estate, and small business (20 percent) held for a year or more.

Buy collectibles for your love of the object, not for financial gain. Treat collecting as a hobby rather than as an investment. When buying a collectible, try to avoid the big markups by cutting out the middlemen. Buy directly from the artist or producer if you can.

Chapter 10

Investing in Funds

In This Chapter

▶ Grasping the advantages of mutual funds and exchange-traded funds (ETFs)

▶ Checking out the different types of funds

▶ Choosing the best funds

▶ Evaluating your fund's performance

▶ Monitoring and selling your funds

When you invest in a mutual fund or its close sibling, an exchange-traded fund (ETF) that trades on a stock exchange, an investment company pools your money with the money of many other like-minded individuals and invests it in stocks, bonds, and other securities. Think of it as a big investment club without the meetings! When you invest through a typical fund, several hundred million to billions of dollars are typically invested along with your money.

If you're thinking of joining the club, read on to discover the benefits of investing in mutual funds and ETFs and the types of funds available (see Chapter 9 for a discussion of mutual-fund alternatives). In this chapter, I advise you on analyzing and choosing your funds, explain how to track your investments, and help you decide when to sell.

Understanding the Benefits of Mutual Funds and Exchange-Traded Funds

Mutual funds and exchange-traded funds (ETFs) rank right up there with microwave ovens, sticky notes, and plastic wrap as one of the best modern inventions. To understand their success is to grasp how and why these funds can work for you. Here are the benefits you receive when you invest in mutual funds and ETFs:

- ✔ **Professional management:** Mutual funds and ETFs are managed by a portfolio manager and research team whose full-time jobs are to screen the universe of investments for those that best meet the fund's stated objectives. These professionals call and visit companies, analyze companies' financial statements, and speak with companies' suppliers and customers. In short, the team does more research and analysis than you could ever hope to do in your free time.

  Fund managers are typically graduates of the top business and finance schools in the country, where they learn the principles of portfolio management and securities valuation and selection. The best fund managers typically have a decade of experience or more in analyzing and selecting investments, and many measure their experience in decades rather than years.

- ✔ **Low fees:** The most efficiently managed stock mutual funds and ETFs cost much less than 1 percent per year in fees (bond and money-market funds cost even less). Because funds typically buy or sell tens of thousands of shares of a security at a time, the percentage of commissions these funds pay is far less than what you pay to buy or sell a few hundred shares on your own. In addition, when you buy a *no-load fund,* you avoid paying sales commissions (known as *loads*) on your transactions. I discuss these types of funds throughout this chapter. You can buy an ETF for a low transaction fee through the best online brokers (see Chapter 19).

- ✔ **Diversification:** Fund investing enables you to achieve a level of diversification that's difficult to reach without tens of thousands of dollars and a lot of time to invest. If you go it alone, you should invest money in at least 8 to 12 different securities in different industries to ensure that your portfolio can withstand a downturn in one or more of the investments. Proper diversification allows a fund to receive the highest possible return at the lowest possible risk given its objectives. The most unfortunate investors during major stock market downswings have been individuals who had all their money riding on only a few stocks that plunged in price by 90 percent or more.

- ✔ **Low cost of entry:** Most mutual funds have low minimum-investment requirements, especially for retirement account investors. (ETFs essentially have no minimum, although you don't want to do transactions involving small amounts because the brokerage fee takes up a larger percentage of your investment amount.) Even if you have a lot of money to invest, consider funds for the low-cost, high-quality money-management services they provide.

> ✔ **Audited performance records and expenses:** In their prospectuses,
> all funds are required to disclose historical data on returns, operating
> expenses, and other fees. The U.S. Securities and Exchange Commission
> (SEC) and accounting firms check these disclosures for accuracy. Also,
> several firms (such as Morningstar, Inc.) report hundreds of fund statis-
> tics, allowing comparisons of performance, risk, and many other factors.
>
> ✔ **Flexibility in risk level:** Among the different funds, you can choose a
> level of risk that you're comfortable with and that meets your personal
> and financial goals. If you want your money to grow over a long period
> of time, you may want to select funds that invest more heavily in stocks.
> If you need current income and don't want investments that fluctuate
> in value as widely as stocks, you may choose more-conservative bond
> funds. If you want to be sure that your invested principal doesn't drop
> in value (perhaps because you may need your money in the short term),
> you can select a money-market fund.

Exploring Various Fund Types

When fund companies package and market funds, the names they give their
funds aren't always completely accurate or comprehensive. For example, a
stock fund may not be *totally* invested in stocks. Twenty percent of it may be
invested in bonds. Don't assume that a fund invests exclusively in U.S. companies, either — it may invest in international firms, as well.

Note: If you haven't yet read Chapters 8 and 9, which provide an overview of
investment concepts and vehicles, doing so can enhance your understanding
of the rest of this chapter.

Money-market funds

Money-market funds are the safest type of mutual funds (although not
insured or guaranteed) for people concerned about losing their invested dollars. As with bank savings accounts, the value of your original investment
does not fluctuate. (For more background on the advantages of money funds,
see Chapter 9.)

These funds are closely regulated by the SEC. Trillions of dollars of individuals' and institutions' money are invested in money-market funds. General-
purpose money-market funds invest in safe, short-term bank certificates of
deposit, U.S. Treasuries, and *corporate commercial paper* (short-term debt),
which is issued by the largest and most creditworthy companies.

Since their origination in the early 1970s, money-market funds have been extremely safe. The risk difference versus a bank account is nil. Only twice have funds broken the buck (one by 6 percent, the other by 3 percent), and both funds were used by institutional investors. Hundreds of trillions of dollars have flowed into and out of money funds over the decades without any retail investors losing principal.

Money-market-fund investments can exist only in the most creditworthy securities and must have an average maturity of less than 120 days. In the unlikely event that an investment in a money-market-fund's portfolio goes sour, the mutual-fund company that stands behind the money-market fund will almost certainly cover the loss.

If the lack of insurance on money-market funds still spooks you, select a money-market fund that invests exclusively in U.S. government securities, which are virtually risk-free because they're backed by the full strength and credit of the federal government (as is the FDIC insurance system). These types of accounts typically pay less interest, although the interest is free of state income tax.

Bond funds

Bonds are IOUs. When you buy a newly issued bond, you typically lend your money to a corporation or government agency. A bond fund is nothing more than a large group of bonds.

Bond funds typically invest in bonds of similar *maturity* (the number of years that elapse before the borrower must pay back the money you lend). The names of most bond funds include a word or two that provides clues about the average length of maturity of their bonds. For example, a *short-term bond fund* typically concentrates its investments in bonds maturing in the next two to three years. An *intermediate-term fund* generally holds bonds that come due within three to ten years. The bonds in a *long-term fund* usually mature in more than ten years.

In contrast to an individual bond that you buy and hold until it matures, a bond fund is always replacing bonds in its portfolio to maintain its average maturity objective. Therefore, if you know that you absolutely, positively must have a certain principal amount back on a particular date, individual bonds may be more appropriate than a bond fund.

Like money-market funds, bond funds can invest in tax-free bonds, which are appropriate for investing money you hold outside retirement accounts if you're in a reasonably high tax bracket.

Bond funds are useful when you want to live off interest income or you don't want to put all your money in riskier investments such as stocks and real estate (perhaps because you plan to use the money soon). Also, making small incremental investments in a bond fund is easier, as opposed to the cost of buying a single individual bond, which can be many thousands of dollars. Bonds (especially municipal bonds) are among the most inefficient parts of the U.S. securities markets. Most individuals can't easily determine the bonds' true value and pay steep markups or markdowns, all of which a larger institutional trader (like a mutual fund) can more easily avoid.

Stock funds

Stock funds, as their name implies, invest in stocks. These funds are often referred to as *equity funds*. *Equity* — not to be confused with equity in real estate — is another word for stocks. Stock funds are often categorized by the type of stocks they primarily invest in.

Stock types are first defined by size of company (small, medium, or large). The total market value *(capitalization)* of a company's outstanding stock determines its size. Small-company stocks, for example, are usually defined as companies with total market capitalization of less than $1 billion. Stocks are further categorized as growth or value stocks:

- **Growth stocks** represent companies that are experiencing rapidly expanding revenues and profits and typically have high stock prices relative to their current earnings or asset (book) values. These companies tend to reinvest most of their earnings in their infrastructure to fuel future expansion. Thus, growth stocks typically pay low dividends. (See the later "Dividends" section for more information.)

- **Value stocks** are at the other end of the spectrum. Value stock investors look for good buys. They want to invest in stocks that are cheaply priced in relation to the profits per share and book value (assets less liabilities) of the company. Value stocks are usually less volatile than growth stocks.

These categories are combined in various ways to describe how a mutual fund invests its money. One fund may focus on large-company growth stocks, while another fund may limit itself to small-company value stocks. Funds are further classified by the geographical focus of their investments: U.S., international, worldwide, and so on (see the section "U.S., international, and global funds").

Balancing bonds and stocks: Hybrid funds

Hybrid funds invest in a mixture of different types of securities. Most commonly, they invest in bonds and stocks. These funds are usually less risky and volatile than funds that invest exclusively in stocks. In an economic downturn, bonds usually hold up in value better than stocks do. However, during good economic times when the stock market is booming, the bond portions of these funds tend to drag down their performance a bit.

Hybrid mutual funds are typically known as *balanced funds,* which generally try to maintain a fairly constant percentage of investments in stocks and bonds, or *asset allocation funds,* which tend to adjust the mix of different investments according to the portfolio manager's expectations of the market. Of course, exceptions do exist — some balanced funds make major shifts in their allocations, whereas some asset allocation funds maintain a relatively fixed mix.

Most funds that shift money around instead of staying put in good investments rarely beat the market averages over a number of years.

There are also now increasing numbers of *target-maturity funds* (also known as target-date or retirement-date funds), which tend to decrease their risk (and stock allocation) over time. Such funds appeal to investors who are approaching a particular future goal, such as retirement or a child's college education, and want their fund to automatically adjust as that date approaches.

Hybrid funds are a way to make fund investing simple. They give you extensive diversification across a variety of investing options. They also make it easier for stock-skittish investors to invest in stocks while avoiding the high volatility of pure stock funds.

U.S., international, and global funds

Unless they have words like *international, global, worldwide,* or *world* in their names, most American-issued funds focus their investments in the United States. But even funds without one of these terms attached may invest money internationally.

The only way to know for sure where a fund is currently invested (or where the fund may invest in the future) is to investigate. You can start by calling the toll-free number of the fund company you're interested in. A fund's annual report (which often can be found on the fund company's website) also details where the fund is investing (the prospectus will also detail where the fund can be invested).

Funds of funds

An increasing number of fund providers are responding to overwhelmed investors by offering a simplified way to construct a portfolio: a fund that diversifies across numerous other funds — or a *fund of funds.* When a fund of funds is done right, it helps focus fund investors on the important big-picture issue of asset allocation — how much of your investment money you put into bonds versus stocks. Although the best funds of funds appear to deliver a high-quality, diversified portfolio of funds in one fell swoop, funds of funds are not all created equal, and not all are worthy of your investment dollars.

The fund of funds idea isn't new. In fact, the concept has been around for many years. High fees gave the earlier funds of funds, run in the 1950s by the late Bernie Cornfeld, a bad name. Cornfeld established a fund of funds outside the United States and tacked on many layers of fees. Although the funds were profitable for his enterprise, duped investors suffered a continual drain of high fees. The Cornfeld episode is an important reason why the SEC has been careful in approving new funds of funds.

The newer funds of funds developed by the larger fund companies are investor friendly and ones that I recommend. Vanguard's LifeStrategy, Fidelity's Freedom, and T. Rowe Price's Spectrum funds of funds add no extra fees for packaging together the individual funds. Long-term performance of many of these is solid. Annual operating fees on the underlying funds at Vanguard are less than 0.2 percent.

When a fund has the term *international* or *foreign* in its name, it typically means that the fund invests anywhere in the world *except* the United States. The term *worldwide* or *global* generally implies that a fund invests everywhere in the world, *including* the United States.

Index funds

Index funds are funds that can be (and are, for the most part) managed by a computer. An index fund's assets are invested to replicate an existing market index such as Standard & Poor's 500, an index of 500 large U.S. company stocks. (Some exchange-traded funds are index funds with the added twist that they trade on a major stock exchange.)

Over long periods (ten years or more), index funds outperform about three-quarters of their peers! How is that possible? How can a computer making mindless, predictable decisions beat an intelligent, creative, MBA-endowed portfolio manager with a crack team of research analysts scouring the market for the best securities? The answer is largely cost. The computer doesn't demand a high salary or need a big corner office. And index funds don't need a team of research analysts.

Most active fund managers can't overcome the handicap of high operating expenses that pull down their funds' rates of return. As I discuss later in this chapter, operating expenses include all the fees and profit that a mutual fund extracts from a fund's returns before the returns are paid to you. For example, the average U.S. stock fund has an operating expense ratio of 1.2 percent per year. So a U.S. stock index fund (or its peer exchange-traded fund, which is an index fund that trades on a stock exchange) with an expense ratio of just 0.1 to 0.2 percent per year has an advantage of 1.0 to 1.1 percent per year.

Another not-so-inconsequential advantage of index funds is that they can't underperform the market. Some funds do just that because of the burden of high fees and/or poor management. For money invested outside retirement accounts, index funds have an added advantage: Lower taxable capital gains distributions are made to shareholders because less trading of securities is conducted and a more stable portfolio is maintained.

Yes, index funds may seem downright boring. When you invest in them, you give up the opportunity to brag to others about your shrewd investments that beat the market averages. On the other hand, with a low-cost index fund, you have no chance of doing much worse than the market (which more than a few mutual-fund managers do).

Index funds and exchange-traded funds make sense for a portion of your investments, because beating the market is difficult for portfolio managers. The Vanguard Group (phone 800-662-7447; website www.vanguard.com), headquartered in Valley Forge, Pennsylvania, is the largest and lowest-cost mutual-fund provider of these funds.

Specialty (sector) funds

Specialty funds don't fit neatly into the previous categories. These funds are often known as *sector funds,* because they tend to invest in securities in specific industries.

In most cases, you should avoid investing in specialty funds. Investing in stocks of a single industry defeats one of the major purposes of investing in funds — diversification. Another good reason to avoid specialty funds is that they tend to carry much higher expenses than other funds.

Specialty funds that invest in real estate or precious metals may make sense for a small portion (10 percent or less) of your investment portfolio. These types of funds can help diversify your portfolio, because they can do better during times of higher inflation.

Identifying socially responsible funds

Select funds label themselves *socially responsible.* This term means different things to different people. In most cases, though, it implies that the fund avoids investing in companies whose products or services harm people or the world at large — tobacco manufacturers, for example. Because cigarettes and other tobacco products kill hundreds of thousands of people and add billions of dollars to healthcare costs, most socially responsible funds shun tobacco companies.

Socially responsible investing presents challenges. For example, your definition of social responsibility may not match the definition offered by the investment manager who's running a fund. Another problem is that even if you can agree on what's socially irresponsible (such as selling tobacco products), funds aren't always as clean as you would think or hope. Even though a fund avoids tobacco manufacturers, it may well invest in retailers that sell tobacco products. Another drawback is that these funds tend to have higher-than-average costs, even when they take an indexing approach.

If you want to consider a socially responsible fund, review the fund's recent annual report, which lists the specific investments the fund owns. Also consider giving directly to charities (and getting a tax deduction) instead.

Selecting the Best Funds

When you go camping in the wilderness, you can do a number of things to maximize your chances for happiness and success. You can take maps and a GPS to keep you on course, food for nourishment, proper clothing to stay dry and warm, and some first-aid gear to treat minor injuries. But regardless of how much advance preparation you do, you may have a problematic experience. You may take the wrong trail, trip on a rock and break your ankle, or lose your food to a tenacious bear that comes romping through camp one night.

And so it is with funds. Although most fund investors are rewarded for their efforts, you get no guarantees. You can, however, follow some simple, common-sense guidelines to help keep you on the trail and increase your odds of investment success and happiness. The issues in the following sections are the main ones to consider.

Reading prospectuses and annual reports

Fund companies produce information that can help you make decisions about fund investments. Every fund is required to issue a *prospectus.* This legal document is reviewed and audited by the SEC. The most valuable information — the fund's investment objectives, costs, performance history, and primary risks — is summarized in the first few pages of the prospectus. Make sure that you read this part. Skip the rest, which is comprised mostly of tedious legal details. Funds also produce what's called a *summary prospectus,* which is an abbreviated version of the full length (*statutory*) prospectus and which hits the important highlights.

Funds also produce *annual reports* that discuss how the fund has been doing and provide details on the specific investments a fund holds. If, for example, you want to know which countries an international fund invests in, you can find this information in the fund's annual report.

Keeping costs low

The charges you pay to buy or sell a fund, as well as the fund's ongoing operating expenses, can have a big impact on the rate of return you earn on your investments. Many novice investors pay too much attention to a fund's prior performance (in the case of stock funds) or to the fund's current yield (in the case of bond funds) and too little attention to fees. Doing so is dangerous because a fund can inflate its return or yield in many (risky) ways. And what worked yesterday may flop tomorrow.

Fund costs are an important factor in the return you earn from a fund. Fees are deducted from your investment. All other things being equal, high fees and other charges depress your returns. What are a fund's fees, you ask? Good question — read on to find the answers.

Eliminating loads

Loads are upfront or ongoing annual commissions paid to brokers who sell mutual funds. Loads typically range from 3 percent to as high as 8.5 percent of your investment. Sales loads have two problems:

✔ **Sales loads are an extra cost that drags down your investment returns.** Because commissions are paid to the salesperson and not to the fund manager, the manager of a load fund doesn't work any harder and isn't any more qualified than a manager of a no-load fund. Common sense suggests, and studies confirm, that load funds perform *worse,* on average, than no-loads when factoring in the load because the load charge is subtracted from your payment before your payment is invested.

✔ **The power of self-interest can bias your broker's advice.** Although this issue is rarely discussed, it's even more problematic than the issue of sales loads. Brokers who work for a commission are interested in selling you commission-based investment products; therefore, their best interests often conflict with your best interests.

Although you may be mired in high-interest debt or underfunding your retirement plan, salespeople almost never advise you to pay off your credit cards or put more money into your 401(k). To get you to buy, they tend to exaggerate the potential benefits and obscure the risks and drawbacks of what they sell. They don't take the time to educate investors. I've seen too many people purchase investment products through brokers without understanding what they're buying, how much risk they're taking, and how these investments will affect their overall financial lives.

Invest in no-load (commission-free) funds. The only way to be sure that a fund is truly no-load is to look at the prospectus for the fund. Only there, in black and white and without marketing hype, must the truth be told about sales charges and other fund fees. When you want investing advice, hire a financial advisor on a fee-for-service basis (see Chapter 18), which should cost less and minimize potential conflicts of interest.

Minimizing operating expenses

All funds charge ongoing fees. The fees pay for the operational costs of running the fund — employees' salaries, marketing, servicing the toll-free phone lines, printing and mailing published materials, computers for tracking investments and account balances, accounting fees, and so on. Despite being labeled "expenses," the profit a fund company earns for running the fund is added to the tab as well.

The fund's operating expenses are quoted as an annual percentage of your investment and are essentially invisible to you, because they're deducted before you're paid any return. The expenses are charged on a daily basis, so you don't need to worry about trying to get out of a fund before these fees are deducted. You can find a fund's operating expenses in the fund's prospectus. Look in the expenses section and find a line that says something like "Total Fund Operating Expenses." You can also call the fund's toll-free number and ask a representative.

Within a given sector of funds (for example, money-market, short-term bond, or international stock), funds with low annual operating fees can more easily produce higher total returns for you. Although expenses matter on all funds, some types of funds are more sensitive to high expenses than others. Expenses are critical on money-market funds and very important on bond funds. Fund managers already have a hard time beating the averages in these markets; with higher expenses added on, beating the averages is nearly impossible.

With stock funds, expenses are a less important (but still significant) factor in a fund's performance. Don't forget that, over time, stocks average returns of about 10 percent per year. So if one stock fund charges 1 percent more in operating expenses than another fund, you're already giving up an extra 10 percent of your expected returns.

Some people argue that investing in stock funds that charge high expenses may be justified if those funds generate higher rates of return. However, evidence doesn't show that these stock funds actually generate higher returns. In fact, funds with higher operating expenses tend to produce *lower* rates of return. This trend makes sense, because operating expenses are deducted from the returns a fund generates. (One additional cost not included in a fund's expense ratio is trading costs. The SEC now requires funds to report these costs in their annual reports.)

Stick with funds that maintain low total operating expenses and don't charge loads (commissions). Both types of fees come out of your pocket and reduce your rate of return. You have no reason to pay a lot for the best funds. (In Chapters 11 and 12, I provide some specific fund recommendations as well as sample portfolios for investors in different situations.)

Evaluating historic performance

A fund's *performance,* or historic rate of return, is another factor to weigh when selecting a fund. As all funds are supposed to tell you, past performance is no guarantee of future results. An analysis of historic fund performance proves that some of yesterday's stars turn into tomorrow's skid-row bums.

Many former high-return funds achieved their results by taking on high risk. Funds that assume higher risk should produce higher rates of return. But high-risk funds usually decline in price faster during major market declines. Thus, in order for a fund to be considered a *best* fund, it must consistently deliver a favorable rate of return given the degree of risk it takes.

When assessing an individual fund, compare its performance and volatility over an extended period of time (five or ten years will do) to a relevant market index. For example, compare funds that focus on investing in large U.S. companies to the Standard & Poor's 500 Index. Compare funds that invest in U.S. stocks of all sizes to the Dow Jones U.S. Total Stock Market Index. Indexes also exist for bonds, foreign stock markets, and almost any other type of security you can imagine.

Assessing fund manager and fund family reputations

Much is made of who manages a specific mutual fund. As Peter Lynch, the retired and famous former manager of the Fidelity Magellan fund, said, "The financial press made us Wall Street types into celebrities, a notoriety that was largely undeserved. Stock stars were treated as rock stars. . . ."

Although the individual fund manager is important, no fund manager is an island. The resources and capabilities of the parent company are equally important. Different companies have different capabilities and levels of expertise in relation to the different types of funds. When you're considering a particular fund — for example, the Barnum & Barney High-Flying Foreign Stock fund — examine the performance history and fees not only of that fund but also of similar foreign stock funds at the Barnum & Barney company. If Barnum's other foreign stock funds have done poorly, or Barnum & Barney offers no other such funds because it's focused on its circus business, those are strikes against its High-Flying fund. Also be aware that "star" fund managers tend to be associated with higher-expense funds to help pay their rock-star salaries. (And star managers tend to leave or get hired away after three to five years of stellar performance, so you may not be getting the manager who created that good past performance in the first place. Index and asset class funds that use a team approach avoid this issue.)

Rating tax friendliness

Investors often overlook tax implications when selecting funds for nonretirement accounts. Numerous funds effectively reduce their shareholders' returns because of their tendency to produce more taxable distributions — that is, capital gains (especially short-term gains, which are taxed at the highest federal income tax rate) and dividends. (See the "Dividends" and "Capital gains" sections later in this chapter.)

Fund capital-gains distributions have an impact on an investor's after-tax rate of return. All fund managers buy and sell stocks over the course of a year. Whenever a fund manager sells securities, any gain or loss from those securities must be distributed to fund shareholders. Securities sold at a loss can offset securities sold at a profit. When a fund manager has a tendency to cash in more winners than losers, investors in the fund receive taxable gains. So, even though some funds can lay claim to producing higher total returns, *after* you factor in taxes, they actually may not produce higher total returns.

Choosing funds that minimize capital-gains distributions helps you defer taxes on your profits. By allowing your capital to continue compounding as it would in a retirement account, you receive a higher total return. When you're a long-term investor, you benefit most from choosing funds that minimize capital-gains distributions. The more years that appreciation can compound without being taxed, the greater the value to you as the investor.

If you're purchasing shares in funds outside tax-sheltered retirement accounts, consider the time of year when making your purchases. December is the most common month in which funds make capital-gains distributions. When making purchases late in the year, ask if and when the fund may make a significant capital-gains distribution. Consider delaying purchases in such funds until after the distribution date.

Determining your needs and goals

Selecting the best funds for you requires an understanding of your investment goals and risk tolerance. What may be a good fund for your next-door neighbor may not necessarily be a good fund for you. You have a unique financial profile.

If you've already determined your needs and goals — terrific! If you haven't, refer to Chapter 4. Understanding yourself is a good part of the battle. But don't shortchange yourself by not being educated about the investment you're considering. If you don't understand what you're investing in and how much risk you're taking, stay out of the game.

Deciphering Your Fund's Performance

As a fund investor, you can't simply calculate your return by comparing the share price of the fund today to the share price you originally paid. Why not? Because funds make distributions of dividends and capital gains, which, when reinvested, give you more shares of the fund.

Even if you don't reinvest distributions, they create an accounting problem, because they reduce the share price of a fund. (Otherwise, you could make a profit from the distribution by buying into a fund just before a distribution is made.) Therefore, over time, following just the share price of your fund doesn't tell you how much money you've made or lost.

The only way to figure out exactly how much you've made or lost on your investment is to compare the total value of your holdings in the fund today with the total dollar amount you originally invested. If you invested chunks of money at various points in time and you want to factor in the timing of your various investments, this exercise becomes complicated. (Check out my investment software recommendations in Chapter 19 if you want your computer to help you crunch the numbers.)

The *total return* of a fund is the percentage change of your investment over a specified period. For example, a fund may tell you that in 2015, its total return was 15 percent. Therefore, if you invested $10,000 in the fund on the last day of 2014, your investment would be worth $11,500 at the end of 2015. To find out a fund's total return, you can call the fund company's toll-free number, visit the company's website, or read the fund's annual report.

The following three components make up your total return on a fund:

- ✔ Dividends (includes interest paid by money-market or bond funds)
- ✔ Capital gains distributions
- ✔ Share price changes

In short, you calculate a fund's total return as follows:

> Dividends + Capital Gains Distributions + Share Price Changes = Total Return

The following sections discuss each of these components in more detail.

Dividends

Dividends are income paid by investments. Both bond funds and stocks can pay dividends. Bond fund dividends (the interest paid by the individual bonds in a fund) tend to be higher (as a percentage of the amount you have invested in a fund). When a dividend distribution is made, you can receive it as cash (which is good if you need money to live on) or reinvest it into more shares in the fund. In either case, the share price of the fund drops to offset the payout. So if you're hoping to strike it rich by buying into a bunch of funds just before their dividends are paid, don't bother. You'll just end up paying more in income taxes.

If you hold your mutual fund outside a retirement account, the dividend distributions are taxable income (unless they come from a tax-free municipal bond fund). Dividends are taxable whether or not you reinvest them as additional shares in the fund. Stock dividends are taxed at a low rate — 0 percent for those in the federal 10- and 15-percent tax brackets, 15 percent for most people in the higher federal tax brackets, and 20 percent for those in the highest federal income tax bracket of 39.6 percent. (Tax reform may be coming in 2017, especially if a Republican is elected to the White House, so stay tuned to www.erictyson.com for up-to-date information on tax law changes affecting your investments.)

Capital gains

When a fund manager sells a security in the fund, net gains realized from that sale (the difference from the purchase price) must be distributed to you as a *capital gain.* Typically, funds make one annual capital gains distribution in December, but distributions can be paid multiple times per year.

As with a dividend distribution, you can receive your capital-gains distribution as cash or as more shares in the fund. In either case, the share price of the fund drops to offset the distribution.

For funds held outside retirement accounts, your capital-gains distribution is taxable. As with dividends, capital gains are taxable whether or not you reinvest them in additional shares in the fund. Capital-gains distributions can be partly comprised of short-term and long-term gains. As I discuss in Chapter 7, profits realized on securities sold after more than a one-year holding period are taxed at the lower long-term capital gains rate. Short-term gains are taxed at the ordinary income tax rate.

If you want to avoid making an investment in a fund that is about to make a capital-gains distribution, check with the fund to determine when capital gains are distributed. Capital-gains distributions increase your current-year tax liability for investments made outside of retirement accounts. (I discuss this concept in more detail in Chapter 12.)

Share price changes

You also make money with a fund when the share price increases. This occurrence is just like investing in a stock or piece of real estate. If the fund is worth more today than it was when you bought it, you've made a profit (on paper, at least). In order to realize or lock in this profit, you need to sell your shares in the fund.

Evaluating and Selling Your Funds

How closely you follow your funds is up to you, depending on what makes you happy and comfortable. I don't recommend tracking the share prices of your funds (or other investments, for that matter) on a daily basis; it's time-consuming and nerve-racking, and it can make you lose sight of the (long-term) big picture. When you track your investments too closely, you're more likely to panic when times get tough. And with investments held outside of retirement accounts, every time you sell an investment at a profit, you get hit with taxes.

A monthly or quarterly check-in is more than frequent enough for following your funds. Many publications carry total return numbers over varying periods so you can determine the exact rate of return you're earning.

Trying to time and trade the markets so you buy at lows and sell at highs rarely works. Yet an entire industry of investment newsletters, hotlines, online services, and the like purport to be able to tell you when to buy and sell. Don't waste your time and money on such predictive nonsense. (See Chapter 8 for more info about gurus and newsletters.)

Consider selling a fund only when it no longer meets the criteria mentioned in "Selecting the Best Funds" earlier in this chapter. If a fund underperforms its peers for at least a two-year period, or if a fund jacks up its management fees, it may be a good time to sell. But if you do your homework and buy good funds from good fund companies, you shouldn't have to do much trading.

Finding and investing in good funds isn't rocket science. Chapters 11 and 12 recommend some specific funds using the criteria discussed earlier in this chapter. If you're still not satiated, pick up a copy of the latest edition of my book *Mutual Funds For Dummies* (Wiley) and visit my website at www. erictyson.com for more details on the best exchange-traded funds and mutual funds.

Chapter 11

Investing in Retirement Accounts

. . . .

. . . .

T his chapter helps you make sense of the various retirement account options and decide how to invest money you currently hold inside — or plan to contribute to — retirement accounts. (To see how much money you should be saving toward retirement, see Chapter 4.)

Looking at Types of Retirement Accounts

Retirement accounts offer numerous benefits. In most cases, your contributions to retirement accounts are tax-deductible. And when you place your money inside the retirement account, it compounds without taxation until you withdraw it. (Some accounts, such as the Roth IRA, even allow for tax-free withdrawal of investment earnings.) If you're not a high-income earner, you may be eligible for a tax credit for making retirement account contributions — please refer to Table 7-2 in Chapter 7. The following sections detail the types of retirement accounts and explain how to determine whether you're eligible and how to make the best use of them.

Employer-sponsored plans

Your employer sets up this type of retirement plan and usually provides a limited number of investment options. All you have to do is contribute and choose how to divide your money among the menu of investment choices.

INVESTIGATE

Can your employer steal your retirement plan money?

The short answer, unfortunately, is yes. However, the vast majority of employees, particularly those who work for larger and more established companies, need not worry.

Some companies that administer 401(k) plans have been cited by the U.S. Labor Department for being too slow in putting money that employees had deferred from their paychecks into employee 401(k) investment accounts. In the worst cases, companies diverted employees' 401(k) money to pay corporate bills. Many business owners who engaged in such practices used 401(k) money as a short-term emergency fund.

In cases where companies failed and funds were diverted from employee 401(k) accounts, the funds were lost. In situations where the employer delayed placing the money into the employees' 401(k) accounts, employees simply lost out on earning returns on their investments during the period. When your contributions are in your 401(k) account, they're financially and legally separate from your employer. Thus, your funds are still protected even if your employer goes bankrupt.

The Labor Department requires employers to contribute employee retirement contributions to their proper accounts as soon as they can reasonably be segregated from the employer's general assets, but absolutely not later than the 15th business day of the month immediately after the month in which the contributions were either withheld or received by the employer. (Employers can get into trouble, for example, if they make a deposit later than they typically do — taking, say, ten days when they normally deposit the money within a few days.) In addition to keeping tabs on your employer to ensure that money withheld from your paycheck is contributed into your account within this time frame, you should also periodically check your 401(k) statement to make sure that your contributions are being invested as you instructed.

401(k) plans

For-profit companies offer *401(k) plans*. The silly name comes from the section of the tax code that establishes and regulates these plans. A 401(k) generally allows you to save up to $18,000 per year (for 2016), usually through payroll deductions. If you're age 50 or older, you can stash away even more — $24,000 (for 2016). Your employer's plan may have lower limits, though. Your contributions to a 401(k) are excluded from your reported income and thus are generally free from federal and state income taxes (although they are subject to Social Security and Medicare taxes). Future year limits will increase in $500 increments to keep pace with inflation. (Some employers are offering a Roth 401(k) option, which doesn't offer an up-front tax deduction but does enable you to put away more money to compound without taxation. Also, withdrawals after age 59½ are tax-free as long as you've had the account for at least five years.)

Some employers don't allow you to contribute to a 401(k) plan until you work for them for a full year. Others allow you to start contributing right away. Some employers also match a portion of your contributions. They may, for example, match half of your first 6 percent of contributions; so in addition to saving a lot of taxes, you get a bonus from the company.

If you're a high-income earner and you contribute such a significant percentage of each paycheck that you hit the plan maximum before the end of the year, you may lose out on some matching money. You may be better off spreading your contributions over the full calendar year. Check with your company's benefits department for your plan's specifics.

Smaller companies (those with fewer than 100 employees) can offer 401(k) plans, too. If your company is interested in this option, contact some of the leading mutual fund organizations and discount brokerage firms that I discuss in Chapter 12 and in the section "Allocating money in plans you design" later in this chapter.

403(b) plans

Nonprofit organizations offer *403(b) plans* to their employees. As with 401(k)s, your contributions to these plans are excluded from federal and state income taxes. (Some employers are offering a Roth 403(b) option: There are no up-front tax breaks on contributions, but investment earnings compound without taxation and withdrawals past age 59½ aren't taxed as long as you've had the account for five years.) The 403(b) plans are often called *tax-sheltered annuities,* the name for insurance company investments that satisfy the requirements for 403(b) plans. For the benefit of 403(b) retirement plan participants, *no-load* (commission-free) mutual funds can be used in 403(b) plans. (See Chapter 10 for more on mutual funds.)

Nonprofit employees are allowed to annually contribute up to $18,000 of their salary ($24,000 if age 50 or older) for tax year 2016. (Future year limits will increase with the cost of living in $500 increments.) Employees who have 15 or more years of service may be allowed to contribute beyond the standard limits. Ask your employee benefits department or the investment provider for the 403(b) plan about eligibility requirements and the details of your personal contribution limit.

If you work for a nonprofit or public-sector organization that doesn't offer this benefit, lobby for it. Nonprofit organizations have no excuse not to offer a 403(b) plan to their employees. Unlike a 401(k), this type of plan requires virtually no out-of-pocket expenses from the employer. The only requirement is that the organization must deduct the appropriate contribution from employees' paychecks and send the money to the investment company handling the 403(b) plan.

When compared to insurance company annuities, no-load (no sales charge) mutual funds are superior investment vehicles on several fronts:

- ✔ Mutual fund companies have a longer and more successful investment track record than do insurance companies, many of which have only recently entered the mutual fund arena.

- ✔ Insurance annuities charge higher annual operating expenses, often two to three times those of efficiently managed no-load mutual funds. These high expenses reduce your returns.

- ✔ Insurance company *insolvency* (bankruptcy) can risk the safety of your investment in an annuity, whereas the value of a mutual fund depends only on the value of the securities in the fund. (If a mutual fund company fails, your securities investments aren't lost because they're held separately from the assets of the fund company itself.)

- ✔ Insurance annuities come with significant charges for early surrender; 403(b) plans with mutual funds don't include these charges.

With some 403(b) plans, you may borrow against your fund balance without penalty. If this capability is important to you, check with your employer to see whether the company plan allows loans. Although many insurance annuities advertise borrowing as an advantage, it can also be a drawback, because it may encourage you to raid your retirement money.

As long as your employer allows it, you may want to open a 403(b) account at the investment companies I suggest in the section "Allocating money in plans you design" later in this chapter.

457 plans

Some nonprofit organizations and state and local governments offer 457 plans. Like 403(b) or 401(k) plans, 457 plans offer participants the ability to contribute money from their paychecks on a pretax basis and thus save on federal and state taxes.

Money that you contribute to a tax-exempt organization's 457 plan is not separate from the organization's finances. Thus, if the nonprofit goes belly up — a rare but not impossible occurrence in the nonprofit world — your retirement funds could be in jeopardy.

Don't consider contributing to a 457 plan until you exhaust contributions to your 403(b). The 2016 tax year contribution limits for a 457 plan are $18,000 per year ($24,000 if age 50 or older). Future year limits will increase with inflation in $500 increments.

Self-employed plans

When you work for yourself, you don't have an employer to do the legwork necessary for setting up a retirement plan. You need to take the initiative. Although setting up a retirement account on your own requires more work, you can select and design a plan that meets your needs. Self-employment retirement savings plans often allow you to put *more* money away on a tax-deductible basis than do employers' plans.

When you have employees, you're required to provide coverage for them under these plans with contributions comparable to the company owners' (as a percentage of salary).

Some part-time (fewer than 1,000 hours per year) and newer (those with less than a few years of service) employees may be excluded. Many small-business owners either don't know about this requirement or choose to ignore it; they set up plans for themselves but fail to cover their employees.

 The danger is that the IRS and state tax authorities may discover small-business owners' negligence, sock them with big penalties, and disqualify their prior contributions. Remember: Self-employed people and small businesses get their tax returns audited at a relatively high rate.

 To get the most from contributions as an employer, consider the following advice:

- ✔ **Educate your employees** about the value of retirement savings plans. You want them to understand, but more importantly, you want them to appreciate your investment.

- ✔ **Select a profit-sharing plan** that requires employees to stay a certain number of years before they vest fully in their contributions. Reward long-term contributors to your company's success.

- ✔ **Consider offering a 401(k) or SIMPLE** IRA (Savings Incentive Match Plan for Employees of Small Employers) if you have 100 or fewer employees. (For more information on the SIMPLE IRA, see the Department of Labor's website at www.dol.gov/ebsa/publications/simple.html.)

Making retirement contributions doesn't have to increase your personnel costs. In the long run, you build the contributions you make for your employees into their total compensation package — which includes salary and benefits such as health insurance.

Don't be duped into a "private pension plan"

Employers who don't want to make retirement plan contributions on behalf of their employees are bait for insurance salespeople selling so-called "private pension plans." Basically, these plans are cash value life insurance policies that combine life insurance protection with a savings-type account. (See Chapter 16 for more details.)

The selling hook of these plans is that you can save money for yourself, but you don't need to contribute money on your employees' behalf (as you must with self-employed retirement plans). And your contributions compound without taxation over the years.

Sound too good to be true? Well, life insurance salespeople who earn hefty commissions from selling cash value life policies won't tell you about the big negatives of these plans. Unlike contributions to true retirement savings plans such as SEP-IRAs and 401(k)s, you derive *no* up-front tax deduction. Your long-term investment returns will be quite mediocre, especially due to these plans' high and hidden fees.

Also, if you don't need life insurance protection, the cost of such coverage is wasted when you save through these plans.

SEP-IRA (Simplified Employee Pension Individual Retirement Account) plans require little paperwork to set up. SEP-IRAs allow you to sock away 20 percent of your net self-employment income (business revenue minus deductions), up to a maximum of $53,000 (for tax year 2016). Future contribution limits will rise with inflation.

Each year, you decide the amount you want to contribute — with no minimums. Your contributions to a SEP-IRA are deducted from your taxable income, saving you big-time on federal and state taxes. As with other retirement plans, your money compounds without taxation until you withdraw it.

Individual Retirement Accounts (IRAs)

Anyone with employment income can contribute to an Individual Retirement Account (IRA). You may contribute up to $5,500 each year — $6,500 if you're age 50 or older. If you earn less than these contribution limits, you can contribute up to the amount you earn. This rule has an exception if you're a nonworking spouse: As long as the working spouse earns at least $11,000 in income, the nonworking spouse can put up to $5,500 per year into a so-called *spousal IRA;* likewise, the working spouse can put up to $5,500 into his or her own IRA. Another exception to earning employment income makes you eligible to contribute to an IRA: receiving alimony.

Your contributions to an IRA may or may not be tax-deductible. For tax year 2016, if you're single and your adjusted gross income is $61,000 or less for the year, you can deduct your full IRA contribution. If you're married and file your taxes jointly, you're entitled to a full IRA deduction if your AGI (adjusted gross income) is $98,000 per year or less. If you make more than these amounts, you can take a full IRA deduction if and only if you're *not* an active participant in any other retirement plan. The only way to know for certain whether you're an active participant is to look at your W-2 Form — that smallish (4-x-8½-inch) document your employer sends you early in the year to file with your tax returns. An "X" mark in a little box in Section 13 on that form indicates that you're an active participant in an employer retirement plan.

If your adjusted gross income is higher than the previously mentioned amounts by less than $10,000 for singles ($20,000 for married couples filing jointly), you're eligible for a partial IRA deduction, even if you're an active participant in another plan. The IRS 1040 instruction booklet comes with a worksheet that allows you to do the calculations for your situation.

If you can't deduct your contribution to a standard IRA, consider making a contribution to a type of IRA called the Roth IRA. With the *Roth IRA,* the contribution is not deductible (you're contributing after-tax dollars), but earnings inside the account are shielded from tax; and unlike a standard IRA, qualified withdrawals from the account, including investment earnings, are free from income tax. Single taxpayers with an AGI less than $117,000, and joint filers with an AGI less than $184,000 can contribute up to $5,500 per year to a Roth IRA ($6,500 for those age 50 and older), provided that they have at least that amount in earned income. (Reduced contributions are allowed for taxpayers with AGIs above these amounts up to $132,000 for single taxpayers and $194,000 for married taxpayers filing jointly.)

To make a qualified (tax-free) withdrawal, you must be at least 59½ and have held the account for at least five years. An exception to the age rule is made for first-time home buyers, who can withdraw up to $10,000 toward the down payment on a principal residence.

Annuities: An odd investment

Annuities are peculiar investment products. They're contracts that are backed by an insurance company. If you, the annuity holder (investor), die during the so-called *accumulation phase* (that is, prior to receiving payments from the annuity), your designated beneficiary is guaranteed to receive the amount of your contribution. In this sense, annuities look a bit like life insurance.

Inappropriate retirement account investments

Some investments for retirement accounts simply don't make sense. Investments that produce income that is tax-free at either the federal or state level don't generally make much sense inside retirement accounts. Because tax-free securities generally yield less than their taxable counterparts, you're essentially giving away free yield when you invest in such securities inside retirement accounts.

Investing in municipal bonds inside a retirement account is a big no-no, and the better investment firms won't let you make this mistake. Municipals are free from federal taxation (and state tax, too, if you buy such a bond issued in your state). As such, they yield significantly less than an equivalent bond that pays fully taxable dividends.

Lots of people make the mistake (albeit a smaller one) of investing in Treasuries — that is, U.S. Treasury bills, notes, or bonds — inside retirement accounts. When you buy Treasuries, you get the safety net of a government guarantee, but you also get a bond that produces interest free of state tax. Fully taxable bonds yield more than state-tax-free Treasuries. And the safety of Treasuries can be replicated in other bonds.

Although annuities are retirement vehicles, as noted earlier in this chapter, they have no place inside retirement accounts. Annuities allow your investment dollars to compound without taxation. In comparison to other investments that don't allow such tax deferral, annuities carry much higher annual operating expenses, which depress your returns.

Purchasing an annuity inside an IRA, 401(k), or other type of retirement account is like wearing a belt and suspenders together. Either you have a peculiar sense of style, or you're spending too much time worrying about your pants falling down. In my experience, many people who mistakenly invest in annuities inside retirement accounts have been misled by investment salespeople.

Limited partnerships (LPs) are treacherous, high-commission, high-cost (and hence low-return) investments sold through investment salespeople. Part of their supposed allure, however, is the tax benefits they generate. But when you buy and hold a limited partnership in a retirement account, you lose the ability to take advantage of many of the tax deductions. The illiquidity of LPs may also mean that you can't make required retirement account withdrawals when needed. These are just some of the many reasons to avoid investing in limited partnerships. (For more reasons, see Chapter 9.)

Annuities, like IRAs, allow your capital to grow and compound without taxation. You defer taxes until withdrawal. Annuities carry the same penalties for withdrawal prior to age 59½ as do other retirement accounts.

Unlike an IRA, which has an annual contribution limit, you can deposit as much as you want into an annuity in any year — even a million dollars or more if you have it! As with a so-called nondeductible IRA, you get no up-front tax deduction for your contributions.

Contributing to an annuity may make sense if

✔ **You have exhausted contributions to employer-sponsored and self-employed plans.** Your contributions to these retirement accounts are tax-deductible, while annuity contributions are not.

✔ **You have made the maximum contribution possible to an IRA, even if it's not tax-deductible.** Annuities carry higher fees (which reduce your investment returns) because of the insurance that comes with them; IRA investments offer you slightly better returns. Roth IRAs also allow for tax-free withdrawal of investment earnings.

✔ **You expect to leave the money compounding in the annuity for at least 15 years.** It typically takes this long for the benefits of tax-deferred compounding to outweigh the higher annuity fees and treatment of all withdrawn annuity earnings at the higher ordinary income tax rates. If you're close to or are actually in retirement, tax-friendly investments made outside of retirement accounts are preferable.

For details about other investment options and the best places to purchase annuities, see Chapter 12, where I discuss investing money outside of retirement accounts.

Allocating Your Money in Retirement Plans

With good reason, people are concerned about placing their retirement account money in investments that can decline in value. You may feel that you're gambling with dollars intended for the security of your golden years.

Most working folks need to make their money work hard in order for it to grow fast enough to provide this security. This need involves taking some risk; you have no way around it. Luckily, if you have 15 to 20 years or more before you need to draw on the bulk of your retirement account assets, time is on your side. As long as the value of your investments has time to recover, what's the big deal if some of your investments drop a bit over a year or two? The more years you have before you're going to retire, the greater your ability to take risk.

Think of your retirement accounts as part of your overall plan to generate retirement income. Then allocate different types of investments between your tax-deferred retirement accounts and other taxable investment accounts to get the maximum benefit of tax deferral. This section helps you determine how to distribute your money in retirement plans. Chapter 8 can help you decide how to divide your money among different nonretirement investment options based on your time frame and risk tolerance.

Prioritizing retirement contributions

When you have access to various retirement accounts, prioritize which account you're going to use first by determining how much each gives you in return. Your first contributions should be to employer-based plans that match your contributions. After that, contribute to any other employer or self-employed plans that allow tax-deductible contributions. After you contribute as much as possible to these tax-deductible plans (or if you don't have access to such plans), contribute to an IRA. If you max out on contributions to an IRA or you don't have this choice because you lack employment income, consider an annuity (see "Annuities: An odd investment" earlier in this chapter).

Setting up a retirement account

Investments and account types are different issues. People sometimes get confused when discussing the investments they make in retirement accounts — especially people who have a retirement account, such as an IRA, at a bank. They don't realize that you can have your IRA at a variety of financial institutions (for example, a mutual fund company or brokerage firm). At each financial institution, you can choose among the firm's investment options for putting your IRA money to work.

No-load, or commission-free, mutual fund and discount brokerage firms are your best bets for establishing a retirement account. For more specifics, see my recommendations throughout the remainder of this chapter.

Allocating money when your employer selects the investment options

In some company-sponsored plans, such as 401(k)s, you're typically limited to the predetermined investment options your employer offers. In the following sections, I discuss common investment options for 401(k) plans in order of increasing risk and, hence, likely return. Then I follow with examples for how to allocate your money across the different types of common employer retirement plan options.

Money market/savings accounts

For regular contributions that come out of your paycheck, the money-market or savings account option makes little sense. Some people who are skittish about the stock and bond markets are attracted to money-market and savings accounts because they can't drop in value. However, the returns are low — so low that you have a great risk that your investment will not stay ahead of, or even keep up with, inflation and taxes (which are due upon withdrawal of your money from the retirement account).

Don't be tempted to use a money-market fund as a parking place until you think stocks and bonds are cheap. In the long run, you won't be doing yourself any favors. As I discuss in Chapter 8, timing your investments to attempt to catch the lows and avoid the peaks isn't possible.

You may need to keep money in the money-market investment option if you use the borrowing feature that some retirement plans allow. Check with your employee benefits department for more details. After you retire, you may also want to use a money-market account to hold money you expect to withdraw and spend within a year or so.

Bond mutual funds

Bond mutual funds (which I describe in Chapter 10) invest in a mixture of typically high-quality bonds. Bonds pay a higher rate of interest or dividends than money funds. Depending on whether your plan's option is a short-term, intermediate-term, or long-term fund (maybe you have more than one type), the bond fund's current yield is probably a percent or two higher than the money-market fund's yield. (*Note:* During certain time periods, the yield difference may be more, whereas during other time periods, it may be less.)

Bond funds carry higher yields than money-market funds, but they also carry greater risk, because their value can fall if interest rates increase. However, bonds tend to be more stable in value over the shorter term (such as a few years) than stocks.

Aggressive, younger investors should keep a minimum amount of money in bond funds. Older folks who want to invest conservatively can place more money in bonds (see the asset allocation discussion in Chapter 8).

Guaranteed-investment contracts (GICs)

Guaranteed-investment contracts (GICs) are backed by an insurance company, and they typically quote you a rate of return projected one or a few years forward. Thus, you don't have the uncertainty that you normally face with bond or stock investments (unless, of course, the insurance company fails).

The attraction of these investments is that your account value doesn't fluctuate (at least, not that you can see). Insurers normally invest your money mostly in bonds and maybe a bit in stocks. The difference between what these investments generate for the insurer and what they pay in interest to GIC investors is profit to the insurer. A GIC's yield is usually comparable to that of a bond fund.

For people who hit the eject button the moment a bond fund slides a bit in value, GICs are soothing to the nerves. And they're certainly higher yielding than a money-market or savings account.

Like bonds, however, GICs don't give you the opportunity for much long-term growth above the rate of inflation. Over the long haul, you can expect to earn a better return in a mixture of bond and stock investments. In GICs, you pay for the peace of mind of a guaranteed return with lower long-term returns.

GICs also have another minor drawback: Insurance companies, unlike mutual funds, can and do fail, putting GIC investment dollars at risk. Some employers' retirement plans have been burned by insurance company failures.

Balanced/target-date mutual funds

Balanced mutual funds invest primarily in a mixture of stocks and bonds. This one-stop-shopping concept makes investing easier and smoothes out fluctuations in the value of your investments — funds investing exclusively in stocks or in bonds make for a rougher ride. These funds are solid options and, in fact, can be used for a significant portion of your retirement plan contributions. See Chapter 10 to find out more about balanced funds.

Some fund companies offer funds of funds known as a *target date fund*. These funds include a mixture of stocks and bonds; the mix gets gradually more conservative (less risky) over the years as a person nears retirement.

Stock mutual funds

Stock mutual funds invest in stocks, which often provide greater long-term growth potential but also wider fluctuations in value from year to year. Some companies offer a number of different stock funds, including funds that invest overseas. Unless you plan to borrow against your funds to purchase a home (if your plan allows), you should have a healthy helping of stock funds. See Chapter 10 for an explanation of the different types of stock funds as well as for details on how to evaluate a stock fund.

Stock in the company you work for

Some companies offer employees the option of investing in the company's stock. I generally advocate avoiding this option for the simple reason that your future income and other employee benefits are already riding on the success of the company. If the company hits the skids, you may lose your job and your benefits. You certainly don't want the value of your retirement account to depend on the same factors.

In the early 2000s, you may have heard all the hubbub about companies such as Enron going under and employees losing piles of money in their retirement savings plans. Enron's bankruptcy in and of itself shouldn't have caused direct problems in Enron's 401(k) plan. The problem was that Enron required employees to hold substantial amounts of Enron company stock. Thus, when the company tanked, employees lost their jobs *and* their retirement savings balances invested in their company's stock.

Thanks to the Employee Retirement Income Security Act (ERISA), companies are no longer allowed to force employees to hold retirement plan money in company stock. Specifically, ERISA rules require companies to offer prudent and adequately diversified investments within their retirement savings plans. An option to invest in the employer's stock can be offered, but investing in the stock is now strictly optional, and it must be one of numerous investment options offered to employees.

If you think that your company has its act together and the stock is a good buy, investing a portion of your retirement account is fine — but no more than 20 to 25 percent. Now, if your company is on the verge of hitting it big and the stock is soon to soar, you'll of course be kicking yourself for not putting more of your money into the company's stock. But when you place a big bet on your company's stock, be prepared to suffer the consequences if the stock tanks. Don't forget that lots of smart investors track companies' prospects, so odds are that the current value of your company's stock is reasonably fair.

Some employers offer employees an additional option to buy company stock outside a tax-deferred retirement plan at a discount, sometimes as much as 15 percent, when compared to its current market value. If your company offers a discount on its stock, take advantage of it. When you sell the stock, you'll usually be able to lock in a decent profit over your purchase price.

Some asset allocation examples

Using the methodology that I outline in Chapter 8 for allocating money, Table 11-1 shows a couple examples of how people in different employer plans may choose to allocate their 401(k) investments among the plan's investment options.

Please note that making allocation decisions is not a science. Use the formulas in Chapter 8 as a guideline.

Table 11-1	Allocating 401(k) Investments		
	25-Year-Old, Aggressive Risk Investor	**45-Year-Old, Moderate Risk Investor**	**60-Year-Old, Moderate Risk Investor**
Bond fund	0%	35%	50%
Balanced fund (50% stock/50% bond)	10%	0%	0%
Blue-chip/larger company stock fund(s)	30–40%	20–25%	25%
Smaller company stock fund(s)	20–25%	15–20%	10%
International stock fund(s)	25–35%	20–25%	15%

Allocating money in plans you design

With self-employed plans (SEP-IRAs and self-employed 401(k)s), certain 403(b) plans for nonprofit employees, and IRAs, you may select the investment options as well as the allocation of money among them. In the sections that follow, I give some specific recipes that you may find useful for investing at some of the premier investment companies.

To establish your retirement account at one of these firms, dial the company's toll-free number and ask the representative to mail you an account application for the type of account (for example, SEP-IRA, 403(b), and so on) you want to set up. You can also have the company mail you background information on specific mutual funds. Furthermore, many investment firms provide downloadable account applications on their websites, and some allow you to complete the application online.

Note: In the examples, I make recommendations for a conservative portfolio and an aggressive portfolio for each firm. I use the terms *conservative* and *aggressive* in a relative sense. Because some of the funds I recommend don't maintain fixed percentages of their different types of investments, the actual percentage of stocks and bonds that you end up with may vary slightly from the targeted percentages. Don't sweat it.

Where you have more than one fund choice, you can pick one or split the suggested percentage among them. If you don't have enough money today to divvy up your portfolio as I suggest, you can achieve the desired split over time as you add more money to your retirement accounts.

Vanguard

Vanguard (phone 877-662-7447; website www.vanguard.com) is a mutual fund and exchange-traded fund powerhouse, and it also operates a discount brokerage division. It's the largest no-load fund company, and it consistently has the lowest operating expenses in the business. Historically, Vanguard's funds have shown excellent performance when compared to those of the company's peers, especially among conservatively managed bond and stock funds.

A conservative portfolio with 50 percent stocks, 50 percent bonds

If you don't want to risk too much, try this:

- ✔ Vanguard Total Bond Market Index — 25 percent
- ✔ Vanguard Star (balanced fund of funds) — 60 percent
- ✔ Vanguard International Value *and/or* Vanguard Total International Stock Index — 15 percent

An aggressive portfolio with 80 percent stocks, 20 percent bonds

If you want to be aggressive, try this:

- ✔ Vanguard Star (fund of funds) — 50 percent
- ✔ Vanguard Total Stock Market Index — 30 percent
- ✔ Vanguard International Value *and/or* Vanguard Total International Stock Index — 20 percent

Or you can place 100 percent in Vanguard LifeStrategy Growth (fund of funds). Note that this portfolio places less money overseas than the preceding example.

Should I use more than one investment firm?

The firms I recommend in this chapter offer a large-enough variety of investment options, managed by different fund managers, that you can feel comfortable concentrating your money at one firm. Your investments themselves aren't at risk based on the financial health of the fund company itself. Discovering the nuances and choices of just one firm rather than several and having fewer administrative hassles are the advantages of a focused approach.

If you like the idea of spreading your money around, you may want to invest through a number of different firms using a discount brokerage account (see Chapter 8). You can diversify across different mutual fund companies through one brokerage firm. However, you'll pay small transaction fees on some of your purchases and sales of funds.

Fidelity

Fidelity Investments (phone 800-343-3548; website www.fidelity.com) is a large provider of funds, and it operates a discount brokerage division. However, some Fidelity funds assess sales charges (no such funds are recommended in the sections that follow).

A conservative portfolio with 50 percent stocks, 50 percent bonds

If you want to maintain a conservative portfolio, try this:

- ✔ Fidelity Puritan (balanced fund) — 50 percent
- ✔ Dodge & Cox Balanced — 50 percent

An aggressive portfolio with 80 percent stocks, 20 percent bonds

If you want to maintain an aggressive portfolio, try this:

- ✔ Fidelity Puritan (balanced fund) — 35 percent
- ✔ Sequoia — 25 percent
- ✔ Fidelity Low-Priced Stock — 20 percent
- ✔ Vanguard Total International Stock Index *and/or* Litman Gregory Masters' International — 20 percent

Discount brokers

As I discuss in Chapter 8, a discount brokerage account can allow you centralized, one-stop shopping and the ability to hold funds from a variety of leading fund companies. Some funds are available without transaction fees, although most of the better funds require you to pay a small transaction fee when you buy funds through a discount broker. The reason: The discounter is a middleman between you and the fund companies. You have to weigh the convenience of being able to buy and hold funds from multiple fund companies in a single account versus the lower cost of buying funds directly from their providers. A $25 to $30 transaction fee can gobble a sizeable chunk of what you have to invest, especially if you're investing smaller amounts.

Among brokerage firms or brokerage divisions of mutual fund companies, for breadth of fund offerings and competitive pricing, I like TD Ameritrade (phone 800-454-9272; website www.tdameritrade.com), T. Rowe Price (phone 800-225-5132; website www.troweprice.com), and Vanguard (phone 877-662-7447; website www.vanguard.com).

A conservative portfolio with 50 percent stocks, 50 percent bonds

If you want to set up a conservative portfolio, try this:

- ✔ Vanguard Short-Term Investment-Grade — 20 percent
- ✔ Harbor Bond *and/or* Dodge & Cox Income — 20 percent
- ✔ Dodge & Cox Balanced — 20 percent
- ✔ T. Rowe Price Spectrum Growth (global stock fund of funds) — 30 percent
- ✔ Litman Gregory Masters' International *and/or* Vanguard Total International Stock Index — 10 percent

An aggressive portfolio with 80 percent stocks, 20 percent bonds

If you want to set up an aggressive portfolio, try this:

- ✔ Harbor Bond *and/or* Vanguard Total Bond Market Index — 20 percent
- ✔ Vanguard Total Stock Market Index *and/or* Dodge & Cox Stock *and/or* Sequoia — 50 percent
- ✔ Litman Gregory Masters' International *and/or* Vanguard International Growth *and/or* Vanguard Total International Stock — 30 percent

Transferring Retirement Accounts

With the exception of plans maintained by your current employer that limit your investment options, such as most 401(k)s, you can move your money held in an SEP-IRA, a self-employed 401(k), a traditional IRA, and many 403(b) plans (also known as *tax-sheltered annuities*) or 401(k) plans you hold at former employers, to almost any major investment firm. Moving the money is pretty simple: If you can fill out some forms and send them back in a postage-paid envelope (or complete them online), you can transfer an account. The investment firm to which you're transferring your account does the rest.

Transferring accounts you control

Here's a step-by-step list of what you need to do to transfer a retirement account to another investment firm. Even if you're working with a financial advisor, you should be aware of this process (called a *direct trustee-to-trustee transfer*) to ensure that no hanky-panky takes place on the advisor's part and to ensure that the transfer is not taxable.

1. **Decide where you want to move the account.**

   I recommend several investment companies in this chapter, along with some sample portfolios within those firms. You may also want to consult the latest editions of some of my other books, including *Mutual Funds For Dummies* and *Investing For Dummies* (Wiley) and visit my website at www.erictyson.com.

2. **Obtain an account application and asset transfer form.**

   Call the toll-free number of the firm you're transferring the money to and ask for an *account application and asset transfer form* for the type of account you're transferring — for example, SEP-IRA, self-employed 401(k), IRA, 403(b), or 401(k). You can also visit the firm's website, but for this type of request, I think most people find it easier to speak directly to someone.

   Ask for the form for the same type of account you currently have at the company from which you're transferring the money. You can determine the account type by looking at a recent account statement — the account type should appear near the top of the statement or in the section with your name and address. If you can't figure out the account type on a cryptic statement, call the firm where the account is currently held and ask a representative to tell you what kind of account you have.

Never, ever sign over assets such as checks and security certificates to a financial advisor, no matter how trustworthy and honest she may seem. Transfers should not be completed this way. The advisor could bolt with them quicker than you can say "Bonnie and Clyde." Besides, you'll find it easier to handle the transfer by following the information in this section.

3. **Figure out which securities you want to transfer and which need to be liquidated.**

Transferring existing investments in your account to a new investment firm can sometimes be a little sticky. Transferring such assets as cash (money-market funds) or securities that trade on any of the major stock exchanges is not a problem.

If you own publicly traded securities, transferring them as is (also known as transferring them *in kind*) to your new investment firm is better, especially if the firm offers discount brokerage services. You can then sell your securities through that firm more cheaply.

If you own mutual funds unique to the institution you're leaving, check with your new firm to see whether it can accept them. If not, you need to contact the firm that currently holds them to sell them.

Certificates of deposit are tricky to transfer. Ideally, you should send in the transfer forms several weeks or so before the CDs mature — few people do this. If the CD matures soon, call the bank and tell it that when the CD matures, you would like the funds to be invested in a savings or money-market account that you can access without penalty when your transfer request lands in the bank's mailbox.

4. **Complete and mail the account application and asset transfer form.**

Completing these for your new investment firm opens your new account and authorizes the transfer.

Don't take possession of the money in your retirement account when moving it over to the new firm. The tax authorities impose huge penalties if you perform a transfer incorrectly. Let the company to which you're transferring the money do the transfer for you. If you have questions or problems, the firm(s) to which you're transferring your account has armies of capable employees waiting to help you. Remember, these firms know that you're transferring your money to them, so they should roll out the red carpet.

5. **Let the firm from which you're transferring the money know that you're doing so. (This step is optional.)**

If the place you're transferring the money from doesn't assign a specific person to your account, you can definitely skip this step. When you're moving your investments from a brokerage firm where you dealt with a particular broker, deciding whether to follow this step can be more difficult.

Most people feel obligated to let their representative know that they're moving their money. In my experience, calling the person with the "bad news" is usually a mistake. Brokers or others who have a direct financial stake in your decision to move your money will try to sell you on staying. Some may try to make you feel guilty for leaving, and some may even try to bully you.

Writing a letter may seem like the coward's way out, but writing usually makes leaving your broker easier for both of you. You can polish what you have to say, and you don't put the broker on the defensive. Although I don't want to encourage lying, not telling the *whole* truth may be an even better idea. Excuses, such as that you have a family member in the investment business who will manage your money for free, may help you avoid an uncomfortable confrontation.

Then again, telling an investment firm that its charges are too high or that it misrepresented and sold you a bunch of lousy investments may help the firm improve in the future. Don't fret too much — do what's best for you and what you're comfortable with. Brokers are not your friends. Even though the broker may know your kids' names, your favorite hobbies, and your birthday, you have a *business* relationship with him.

Transferring your existing assets typically takes two to four weeks to complete. If the transfer is not completed within one month, get in touch with your new investment firm to determine the problem. If your old company isn't cooperating, call a manager there to help get the ball rolling.

The unfortunate reality is that an investment firm will cheerfully set up a new account to *accept* your money on a moment's notice, but it will drag its feet, sometimes for months, when the time comes to relinquish your money. To light a fire under the behinds of the folks at the investment firm, tell a manager at the old firm that you're going to send letters to the Financial Industry Regulatory Authority (FINRA) and the Securities and Exchange Commission (SEC) if it doesn't complete your transfer within the next week.

Moving money from an employer's plan

When you leave a job, particularly if you're retiring or being laid off after many years of service, money-hungry brokers and financial planners probably will be on you like a pack of bears on a tree leaking sweet syrup. If you seek financial help, tread carefully — Chapter 18 helps you avoid the pitfalls of hiring such assistance.

When you leave a job, you're confronted with a slightly different transfer challenge: moving money from an employer plan into one of your own retirement accounts. (As long as your employer allows it, you may be able to leave your money in your old employer's plan. Evaluate the quality of the investment choices using the information I provide in this part of the book.) Typically, employer retirement plan money can be rolled over into your own IRA. Check with your employer's benefits department or a tax advisor for details.

Federal tax law requires employers to withhold, as a tax, 20 percent of any retirement account disbursements to plan participants. So if you personally take possession of your retirement account money in order to transfer it to an IRA, you must wait until you file your annual tax return to be reimbursed by the government for this 20-percent withholding. This withholding creates a problem, because if you don't replace the 20-percent withholding into the rollover IRA and deposit the entire rollover within 60 days in the new account, the IRS treats the shortfall as an early distribution subject to income tax and penalties.

Never take personal possession of money from your employer's retirement plan. To avoid the 20-percent tax withholding and a lot of other hassles, simply inform your employer of where you want your money to be sent. Prior to doing so, establish an appropriate account (an IRA, for example) at the investment firm you intend to use. Then tell your employer's benefits department where you'd like your retirement money transferred. You can send your employer a copy of your account statement, which contains the investment firm's mailing address and your account number.

Chapter 12

Investing in Taxable Accounts

. . . .

In This Chapter

▶ Taking advantage of overlooked, attractive investment options

▶ Factoring taxes into your investment decisions

▶ Bolstering your emergency reserves

▶ Looking at longer-term investments

. . . .

*I*n this chapter, I discuss investment options for money held outside retirement accounts, and I include some sample portfolio recommendations. (Chapter 11 reviews investments for money *inside* retirement accounts.) This distinction may seem somewhat odd — it's not one that's made in most financial books and articles. However, thinking of these two types of investment accounts differently can be useful because

✔ **Investments held outside retirement accounts are subject to taxation.** You have a whole range of different investment options to consider when taxes come into play.

✔ **Money held outside retirement accounts is more likely to be used sooner than funds held inside retirement accounts.** Why? Because you'll generally have to pay far more in income taxes to access money inside rather than outside retirement accounts. (And you may be subject to penalties if you need to make early withdrawals from retirement accounts.)

✔ **Funds inside retirement accounts have their own nuances.** For example, when you invest through your employer's retirement plan, your investment options are usually limited to a handful of choices. And special rules govern transfer of your retirement account balances.

Getting Started

Suppose that you have some money sitting in a bank savings account or money-market mutual fund, earning a pitiful amount of interest, and you want to invest it more profitably. You need to remember two things about investing this type of money:

> ✔ **Earning a little is better than losing 20 to 50 percent or more.** Just talk to anyone who didn't do his homework and ended up buying a lousy investment. Be patient. Educate yourself *before* you invest.

> ✔ **To earn a higher rate of return, you must be willing to take more risk.** In order to earn a better rate of return, you need to consider investments that fluctuate in value — of course, the value can drop as well as rise.

You approach the vast sea of investment options and start stringing up your rod to go fishing. You hear stories of people catching big ones — cashing in big on stocks or real estate that they bought years ago. Even if you don't have delusions of grandeur, you'd at least like your money to grow faster than the cost of living.

But before you cast your investment line, consider the following often over-looked ways to put your money to work and earn higher returns without much risk. These options may not be as exciting as hunting the big fish out there, but they can easily improve your financial health.

Paying off high-interest debt

Many folks have credit card or other consumer debt that costs more than 10 percent per year in interest. Paying off this debt with savings is like putting your money in an investment with a guaranteed return that's equal to the interest rate you're paying on the debt.

For example, if you have credit card debt outstanding at 14-percent interest, paying off that loan is the same as putting your money to work in an investment with a sure 14-percent annual return. Remember that the interest on consumer debt is not tax-deductible, so you actually need to earn *more* than 14 percent investing your money elsewhere in order to net 14 percent after paying taxes. (See Chapter 5 for more details if you're still not convinced.)

Paying off some of or your entire mortgage may make sense, too. This financial move isn't as clear as erasing consumer debt, because the mortgage interest rate is lower than it is on consumer debt and is usually tax-deductible. (See Chapter 14 for more details on this strategy.)

Taking advantage of tax breaks

Make sure that you take advantage of the tax benefits offered on retirement accounts. If you work for a company that offers a retirement savings plan such as a 401(k), fund it at the highest level you can manage. If you earn self-employment income, consider a SEP-IRA. (I discuss retirement-plan options in Chapter 11.)

If you need to save money outside retirement accounts for shorter-term goals (for example, to buy a car or a home, or to start or buy a small business), then by all means, do so. This chapter can assist you with thinking through investing money in taxable accounts (nonretirement accounts exposed to taxation).

Understanding Taxes on Your Investments

When you invest money outside of a retirement account, *investment distributions* — such as interest, dividends, and capital gains — are subject to current taxation. Too many folks (and too many of their financial advisors) ignore the tax impact of their investment strategies. You need to pay attention to the tax implications of your investment decisions *before* you invest your money.

Consider a person in a combined 40-percent tax bracket (federal plus state taxes) who keeps extra cash in a taxable bond paying 4-percent interest. If he pays 40 percent of his interest earnings in taxes, he ends up keeping just 2.4 percent. With a similar but tax-free bond, he could earn more than this amount, completely free of federal and/or state taxes. (Make sure you do an apples-to-apples comparison: Both the taxable and tax-free bonds must be of similar risk, which means that they should have the same credit rating/risk of default and mature in about the same number of years.)

Another mistake some people make is investing in securities that produce tax-free income when they're not in a high enough tax bracket to benefit. Now consider a person in a combined 20-percent tax bracket who's investing in securities that produce tax-free income. Suppose he invests in a tax-free investment that yields 4.5 percent. A comparable taxable investment is yielding 7 percent. If he had instead invested in the taxable investment at a 7-percent yield, the after-tax yield would have been 5.6 percent. Thus, he's losing out on yield by being in the tax-free investment, even though he may feel happy in it because the yield isn't taxed.

To decide between comparable taxable and tax-free investments, you need to know your *marginal tax bracket* (the tax rate you pay on an extra dollar of taxable income) and the rates of interest or yield on each investment. (Check out Table 7-1 in Chapter 7 to see what federal income tax bracket you're in.)

Fortifying Your Emergency Reserves

In Chapter 4, I explain the importance of keeping sufficient money in an emergency reserve account. From such an account, you need two things:

- ✔ **Accessibility:** When you need to access your money for an emergency, you want to be able to do so quickly and without penalty.

- ✔ **Highest possible return:** You want to get the highest rate of return possible without risking your principal. This factor doesn't mean that you should simply pick the money-market or savings option with the highest yield, because other issues, such as taxes, are a consideration. What good is earning a slightly higher yield if you pay a lot more in taxes?

The following sections give you information on investments that are suitable for emergency reserves.

Bank and credit union accounts

When you have a few thousand dollars or less, your best and easiest path may be to keep this excess savings in a local bank or credit union. Look first to the institution where you keep your checking account.

Keeping this stash of money in your checking account, rather than in a separate savings account, makes financial sense if the extra money helps you avoid monthly service charges when your balance occasionally dips below the minimum. Compare the service charges on your checking account with the interest earnings from a savings account.

For example, suppose you're keeping $4,000 in a savings account to earn 1 percent interest versus earning no interest on your checking account money. Over the course of a year, you earn $40 in interest on that savings account. If you incur a $9 per month service charge on your checking account, you pay $108 per year. So keeping your extra $4,000 in a checking account may be better financially if it keeps you above a minimum balance and erases that monthly service charge. (However, if you're more likely to spend the extra money in your checking account, keeping it in a separate savings account where you won't be tempted to spend it may be better.)

Money-market mutual funds

Money-market funds, a type of mutual fund (see Chapter 10), are just like bank savings accounts — but better, in most cases. The best money-market funds pay higher yields than bank savings accounts and allow check-writing. And if you're in a high tax bracket, you can select a tax-free money-market fund, which pays interest that's free from federal and/or state tax — a feature you can't get with a bank savings account.

The yield on a money-market fund is an important consideration. The operating expenses deducted before payment of dividends is the single biggest determinant of yield. All other things being equal (which they usually are with different money-market funds), lower operating expenses translate into higher yields for you. With interest rates as low as they have been in recent years, seeking out money funds with the lowest operating expenses is more vital than ever.

Doing most or all of your fund shopping (money-market and otherwise) at one good fund company can reduce the clutter in your investing life. Chasing after a slightly higher yield offered by another company sometimes isn't worth the extra paperwork and administrative hassle. On the other hand, there's no reason why you can't invest in funds at multiple firms (as long as you don't mind the extra paperwork), using each for its relative strengths.

Most mutual fund companies don't have many local branch offices, so you may have to open and maintain your money-market mutual fund through the fund's toll-free phone line, website, or the mail. Distance has its advantages. Because you can conduct business by mail, the Internet, and the phone, you don't need to go schlepping into a local branch office to make deposits and withdrawals. I'm *happy* to report that I haven't visited a bank office in many years.

Despite the distance between you and your mutual fund company, your money is still accessible via check-writing, and you can also have money electronically transferred to your local bank on any business day. Don't fret about a deposit being lost in the mail; it rarely happens, and no one can legally cash a check made payable to you, anyway. Just be sure to endorse the check with the notation "for deposit only" under your signature.

Watch out for "sales"

Beware of money-market mutual funds that have a "sale" by temporarily waiving (sometimes called *absorbing*) operating expenses, which lets a fund boost its yield. These sales rarely last long; the operating expenses come back and deflate that too-good-to-be-true yield like a nail in a bike tire. Some fund companies run sales because they know that a major portion of the fund buyers who are lured in won't bother leaving when they jack up operating expenses.

You're better off sticking with funds that maintain "everyday low operating expenses" to get the highest long-term yield. I recommend such funds in the next section. However, if you want to move your money to companies having specials and then move it back out when the special is over, be my guest. If you have lots of money and don't mind paperwork, it may be worth the bother.

Recommended money-market mutual funds

In this section, I recommend good money-market mutual funds. As you peruse this list, remember that the money-market fund that works best for you depends on your tax situation. Throughout the list, I try to guide you to funds that generally make sense for people in particular tax brackets.

- **Money-market funds that pay taxable dividends** are appropriate when you're not in a high tax bracket. Some of my favorites include

    - Fidelity Cash Reserves (phone 800-343-3548; website www.fidelity.com)

    - USAA Money Market (phone 800-531-8722; website www.usaa.com)

    - Vanguard Prime Money Market (phone 877-662-7447; website www.vanguard.com)

- **U.S. Treasury money-market funds** are appropriate if you prefer a money fund that invests in U.S. Treasuries, which have the safety of government backing, or if you're in a high state tax bracket (5 percent or higher) but not in a high federal tax bracket. Vanguard (phone 877-662-7447; website www.vanguard.com) offers the Vanguard Admiral Treasury Money Market fund.

- **State-focused tax-free money-market funds** are appropriate when you're in high federal and state tax brackets. Fidelity (phone 800-343-3548; website www.fidelity.com), USAA (phone 800-531-8722; website www.usaa.com), and Vanguard (phone 877-662-7447; website www.vanguard.com) offer the best selection.

    Residents of many states won't find attractive state-specific money-market funds or won't find any at all. In some cases, no options exist. In other cases, the funds available for that particular state have such high annual operating expenses, and therefore such low yields, that you're better off in one of the more competitively run federal-tax-free-only funds that I note in the next bullet.

✔ **Federal-tax-free-only money-market funds** (the dividends on these are state taxable) are appropriate when you're in a high federal but not state bracket, or if you live in a state that doesn't have competitive state- and federal-tax-free funds available. Here are a few to choose from:

- Vanguard Tax-Exempt Money Market (phone 877-662-7447; website www.vanguard.com)

- Fidelity Tax-Free Money Market (phone 800-343-3548; website www.fidelity.com)

- T. Rowe Price Summit Municipal Money Market and Tax-Exempt Money Market (phone 800-225-5132; website www.troweprice.com)

- USAA Tax-Exempt Money Market (phone 800-531-8722; website www.usaa.com)

Investing for the Longer Term (Several Years or Decades)

Note: This section (together with its recommended investments) assumes that you have a sufficient emergency reserve stashed away and are taking advantage of tax-deductible retirement account contributions. (Please see Chapter 4 for more on these goals.)

Asset allocation refers to the process of figuring out what portion of your wealth to invest in different types of investments. You often (and most appropriately) practice asset allocation with retirement accounts, because this money is earmarked for the long term. Ideally, more of your saving and investing should be conducted through tax-sheltered retirement accounts. These accounts generally offer the best way to lower your long-term tax burden (see Chapter 11 for details).

If you plan to invest outside retirement accounts, asset allocation for these accounts depends on how comfortable you are with risk. But your choice of investments should also be suited to how much *time* you have until you plan to use the money. That's not because you won't be able to sell these investments on short notice if necessary (in most cases, you can). Investing money in a more volatile investment is simply riskier if you need to liquidate it in the short term.

For example, suppose that you're saving money for a down payment on a house and are about one to two years away from having enough to make your foray into the real-estate market. If you had put this "home" money into the U.S. stock market near the beginning of one of the stock market's 20- to 50-percent declines (such as what happened in the early 2000s and then again in the late 2000s), you'd have been mighty unhappy. You would have seen a substantial portion of your money *vanish* in short order and would've seen your home ownership dreams put on hold.

Defining your time horizons

The different investment options in the remainder of this chapter are organized by time frame. All the recommended investment funds that follow assume that you have *at least* a several-year time frame, and they're all *no-load* (commission-free) mutual funds and exchange-traded funds (ETFs). Funds can be sold on any business day, usually with a simple phone call or the click of a mouse. Funds come with all different levels of risk, so you can choose funds that match your time frame and desire to take risk. (Chapter 10 discusses all the basics of mutual funds.)

The recommended investments are also organized by your tax situation. (If you don't know your current tax bracket, be sure to review Chapter 7.) Following are summaries of the different time frames associated with each type of fund:

✔ **Short-term investments:** These investments are suitable for a period of a few years — perhaps you're saving money for a home or some other major purchase in the near future. When investing for the short-term, look for liquidity and stability — features that rule out real estate and stocks. Recommended investments include shorter-term bond funds, which are higher-yielding alternatives to money-market funds. If interest rates increase, these funds drop slightly in value — a couple of percent or so (unless rates rise tremendously). I also discuss Treasury bonds and certificates of deposit (CDs) later in this chapter.

✔ **Intermediate-term investments:** These investments are appropriate for more than a few years but less than ten years. Investments that fill the bill are intermediate-term bonds and well-diversified hybrid funds (which include some stocks as well as bonds).

✔ **Long-term investments:** If you have a decade or more for investing your money, you can consider potentially higher-return (and therefore riskier) investments. Stocks, real estate, and other growth-oriented investments can earn the most money if you're comfortable with the risk involved. See Chapter 8 for information on investing the portion that you intend to hold for the long term.

Bonds and bond funds

Bond funds that pay taxable dividends are generally appropriate when you're not in a high tax bracket. Here are some of my favorites:

- ✔ **Short-term:** Vanguard Short-Term Investment-Grade (phone 877-662-7447; website www.vanguard.com)

- ✔ **Intermediate-term:** Dodge & Cox Income (phone 800-621-3979; website www.dodgeandcox.com); Harbor Bond (phone 800-422-1050; website www.harborfunds.com); Vanguard Total Bond Market Index (phone 877-662-7447; website www.vanguard.com)

- ✔ **Long-term:** Vanguard Long-Term Investment-Grade (phone 877-662-7447; website www.vanguard.com)

Please note that Vanguard also offers ETF versions of many of its leading bond funds. The following sections discuss other bond funds, as well as the individual bonds you can buy through Treasury Direct.

U.S. Treasury bond funds

U.S. Treasury bond funds are appropriate if you prefer a bond fund that invests in U.S. Treasuries (which have the safety of government backing), or when you're in a high state tax bracket (5 percent or higher) but not a high federal tax bracket. For good Treasury bond funds, look no further than the Vanguard Group, which offers short-, intermediate-, and long-term U.S. Treasury funds with a low 0.20-percent operating expense ratio. With a $50,000 minimum, Vanguard's Admiral series of U.S. Treasury funds offers even higher yields thanks to an even lower expense ratio of 0.10 percent.

Buying Treasuries from the Federal Reserve Bank

If you want an even cheaper method of investing in Treasury bonds than you can get through the thrifty Vanguard Treasury funds, try this: Purchase Treasuries directly from the Federal Reserve Bank. To open an account through the Treasury Direct program, call 844-284-2676, or visit its website at www.treasurydirect.gov.

You do sacrifice a bit of liquidity, however, when purchasing Treasury bonds directly from the government. You can sell your bonds prior to maturity; however, you'll have to go through the hassle of having your Treasury bond(s) transferred to a brokerage account and you'll pay brokerage fees to sell them. If you want daily access to your money, buy a recommended Vanguard fund and pay the company's low management fee.

Inflation-indexed Treasury bonds

Like a handful of other nations, the U.S. Treasury now offers *inflation-indexed* government bonds. Because a portion of these Treasury bonds' return is pegged to the rate of inflation, the bonds offer investors a safer type of Treasury bond investment option.

To understand the relative advantages of an inflation-indexed bond, take a brief look at the relationship between inflation and a normal bond. When an investor purchases a normal bond, he's committing himself to a fixed payment over a set period of time — for example, a bond that matures in ten years and pays 5 percent interest. However, changes in the cost of living (inflation) aren't fixed, so they're difficult to predict.

Suppose that an investor put $10,000 into a regular bond in the 1970s. During the life of his bond, he would've unhappily watched inflation escalate. During the time he held the bond, and by the time his bond matured, he would've witnessed the erosion of the purchasing power of his $500 of annual interest and $10,000 of returned principal.

Enter the inflation-indexed Treasury bond. Suppose that you have $10,000 to invest and you buy a ten-year, inflation-indexed bond that pays you a real rate of return (the return above and beyond the rate of inflation) of, say, 2 percent (or $200). This portion of your return is paid out in interest. The other portion of your return is from the inflation adjustment to the principal you invested. The inflation portion of the return gets put back into the principal. So if inflation were running at about 2 percent, as it has in recent years, your $10,000 of principal would be indexed upward after one year to $10,200. In the second year of holding this bond, the 2 percent real return of interest ($204), would be paid on the increased ($10,200) principal base.

If inflation skyrocketed and was running at, say, 8 percent rather than 2 percent per year, your principal balance would grow 8 percent per year, and you'd still get your 2 percent real rate of return on top of that. Thus, an inflation-indexed Treasury bond investor doesn't see the purchasing power of his invested principal or annual interest earnings eroded by unexpected inflation.

The inflation-indexed Treasuries can be a good investment for conservative bond investors who are worried about inflation, as well as taxpayers who want to hold the government accountable for increases in inflation. The downside: Inflation-indexed bonds may yield slightly lower returns, because they're less risky compared to regular Treasury bonds.

State- and federal-tax-free bond funds

State- and federal-tax-free bond funds are appropriate when you're in high federal and state (5 percent or higher) tax brackets. Vanguard (phone 877-662-7447; website www.vanguard.com) has the best selection of state-specific tax-free bond funds. USAA (phone 800-531-8722; website www.usaa.com) and, to a lesser extent, Fidelity (phone 800-343-3548; website www.fidelity.com) offer some of the better state-specific bond funds. Fidelity does have higher balance ($10,000) requirements.

Federal-tax-free-only bond funds

Federal-tax-free-only bond funds (the dividends on them are state-taxable) are appropriate when you're in a high federal bracket but a low state bracket (less than 5 percent) or when you live in a state that doesn't have state- and federal-tax-free funds available. Vanguard (phone 877-662-7447; website www. vanguard.com) offers the best selection of federal-tax-free bond funds.

Certificates of deposit (CDs)

For generations, bank CDs have been a popular investment for folks with some extra cash that isn't needed in the near future. With a CD, you generally get a higher rate of return than you get on a bank savings account. And unlike with bond funds, your principal doesn't fluctuate in value.

Compared to bonds, however, CDs have a couple drawbacks:

- ✔ **Inaccessibility:** In a CD, your money isn't accessible unless you cough up a fairly big penalty — typically six months' interest. With a no-load (commission-free) bond fund, you can access your money without penalty — whether you need some or all of your money next week, next month, or next year.

- ✔ **Taxability:** CDs come in only one tax flavor — taxable. Bonds, on the other hand, come in tax-free (federal and/or state) and taxable flavors. So if you're a higher-tax-bracket investor, bonds offer you a tax-friendly option that CDs can't.

In the long run, you can expect to earn more — perhaps 1 to 2 percent more per year — and have better access to your money in bond funds than in CDs. Bond funds make particular sense when you're in a higher tax bracket and you'd benefit from tax-free income on your investments. If you're not in a high tax bracket and you have a bad day whenever your bond fund takes a dip in value, consider CDs. Just make sure that you shop around to get the best interest rate.

One final piece of advice: Don't buy CDs simply for the FDIC (Federal Deposit Insurance Corporation) insurance. Much is made, particularly by bankers, of the FDIC government insurance that comes with bank CDs. The lack of this insurance on high-quality bonds shouldn't be a big concern for you. High-quality bonds rarely default; even if a fund were to hold a bond that defaulted, that bond would probably represent only a tiny fraction (less than 1 percent) of the value of the fund, having little overall impact.

Besides, the FDIC itself is no Rock of Gibraltar. Banks have failed and will continue to fail. Yes, you are insured if you have less than $250,000 in a bank. However, if the bank crashes, you may have to wait a long time and settle for less interest than you thought you were getting. You're not immune from harm, FDIC or no FDIC.

If the government backing you receive through FDIC insurance allows you to sleep better, you can invest in Treasuries (see "Bonds and bond funds" earlier in this chapter), which are government-backed bonds.

Stocks and stock funds

Stocks have stood the test of time for building wealth. (In Chapter 9, I discuss picking individual stocks versus investing through stock funds.) Remember that when you invest in stocks in taxable (nonretirement) accounts, all the distributions on those stocks, such as dividends and capital gains, are taxable. Stock dividends and long-term capital gains do benefit from lower tax rates (the maximum 20 percent).

Some stock-picking advocates argue that you should shun stock funds due to tax considerations. I disagree. You can avoid stock funds that generate a lot of short-term capital gains, which are taxed at the relatively high ordinary income tax rates. Additionally, increasing numbers of fund companies offer *tax-friendly* stock funds, which are appropriate if you don't want current income or you're in a high federal tax bracket and seek to minimize receiving taxable distributions on your funds. Vanguard (phone 877-662-7447; website www.vanguard.com) offers the best menu of tax-managed stock funds. Alternatively, you can invest in a wider variety of diversified stock funds inside an annuity (see the following section). Also consider some of the stock funds I recommend in Chapter 11.

Annuities

As I discuss in Chapter 11, *annuities* are accounts that are partly insurance but mostly investment. Consider contributing to an annuity only after you exhaust contributions to all your available retirement accounts. Because annuities carry higher annual operating expenses than comparable mutual funds, you should consider them only if you plan to leave your money invested, preferably for 15 years or more. Even if you leave your money invested for that long, the tax-friendly funds discussed in the previous sections of this chapter can allow your money to grow without excessive annual taxation.

The best annuities can be purchased from no-load (commission-free) mutual fund companies such as Vanguard (phone 877-662-7447; website www.vanguard.com) or Fidelity (phone 800-343-3548; website www.fidelity.com).

Real estate

Real estate can be a financially and psychologically rewarding investment. It can also be a money pit and a real headache if you buy the wrong property or get a "tenant from hell." (I discuss the investment particulars of real estate in Chapter 9 and the nuts and bolts of buying real estate in Chapter 14.)

Small-business investments

Investing in your own business or someone else's established small business can be a high-risk but potentially high-return investment. The best options are those you understand well. See Chapter 9 for more information about small-business investments.

Chapter 13

Investing for Educational Expenses

*I*f you're like most parents (or potential future parents), just turning to this chapter makes you anxious. Such trepidation is understandable. According to much of what you read about educational expenses (particularly college expenses), if costs keep rising at the current rate, you'll soon have to spend upward of $250,000 dollars to give your youngster a quality college education. (And, if you add in graduate school, you could be pushing $400,000 to $500,000.)

Whether you're about to begin a regular college investment plan or you've already started saving, your emotions may lead you astray. The hype about educational costs may scare you into taking a financially detrimental path. However, quality education for your child doesn't have to — and probably won't — cost you as much as those gargantuan projections suggest. In this chapter, I explain the inner workings of the financial aid system, help you gauge how much money you'll need, and discuss educational investment options so you can keep a cool head (and some money in your pocket) when all is said and done.

Figuring Out How the Financial Aid System Works

Your child shouldn't choose to apply to a college on the basis of whether you think you can afford it. Except for the affluent who have plenty of cash available to pay for the full cost of college, everyone else should apply for financial aid. More than a few parents who don't think that they qualify for financial aid are pleasantly surprised to find that their children have access to loans as well as grants, which don't have to be repaid. (And your ability to pay often isn't a consideration when scholarship committees hand out money — see "Tips for getting loans, grants, and scholarships" later in this chapter for info on scholarships.)

Completing the Free Application for Federal Student Aid (FAFSA), which is available from any high school or college, is the first step in the financial aid process. (Internet users can fill out the form online at www.fafsa.ed.gov.) As its name implies, you pay nothing for submitting this application other than the time to complete the paperwork. Some schools also supplement the FAFSA with the College Board's CSS/Financial Aid PROFILE form; these forms are mainly used by costly private schools to differentiate need among financial aid applicants.

States have their own financial aid programs, so apply to these programs as well if your child plans to attend an in-state college. You and your child can check with your local high school or college financial aid office to get the necessary forms. Some colleges also require submission of supplementary forms directly to them.

The data you supply through student aid forms is run through a *financial needs analysis,* a standard methodology approved by the U.S. Congress. The needs analysis considers a number of factors, such as your income and assets, age and need for retirement income, number of dependents, number of family members in college, and unusual financial circumstances, which you explain on the application.

The financial needs analysis calculates how much money you, as the parent(s), and your child, as the student, are expected to contribute toward educational expenses. Even if the needs analysis determines that you don't qualify for need-based financial aid, you may still have access to loans that are *not* based on need if you go through the financial aid application process. So make sure you apply for financial aid!

Treatment of retirement accounts

Under the current financial needs analysis, the value of your retirement plans is *not* considered an asset. By contrast, money that you save *outside* retirement accounts, especially money in the child's name, is counted as an asset and reduces financial aid eligibility.

Therefore, forgoing contributions to your retirement savings plans in order to save money in a taxable account for Junior's college fund doesn't make sense. When you do, you pay higher taxes both on your current income and on the interest and growth of the college fund money. In addition to paying higher taxes, you're expected to contribute more to your child's educational expenses.

Let me stress the need to get an early start on saving for retirement. Most retirement accounts limit how much you can contribute each year. See Chapter 11 for more on saving for your golden years.

Treatment of money in the kids' names

If you plan to apply for financial aid, save money in your name rather than in your children's names (such as via custodial accounts). Colleges expect a much greater percentage of the money in your children's names (20 percent) to be used annually for college costs than the money in your name (about 6 percent).

However, if you're affluent enough to foot your child's college bill without outside help, investing in your kid's name can save you some money in taxes. Read on.

Traditional custodial accounts

Parents control a *custodial account* until the child reaches either the age of 18 or 21, depending upon the state in which you reside. For 2015, prior to your child's reaching age 18 the first $1,050 of interest and dividend income is tax-free; the next $1,050 is taxed at 10 percent. Any unearned income above $2,100 is taxed at 10 percent. Any income above $2,100 is taxed at the parents' marginal tax rate. Upon reaching age 18 (or age 24 if your offspring are still full-time students), all income generated by investments in your child's name is taxed at your child's rate, which is presumably a lower tax rate.

Education Savings Accounts

The Education Savings Account (ESA) is another option that, like a traditional custodial account, may make sense for affluent parents who don't expect to apply for or need any type of financial aid. As with regular custodial accounts, parents who have their kids apply for financial aid will be penalized by college financial aid offices for having ESA balances.

Subject to eligibility requirements, you can put up to $2,000 per child per year into an ESA. Single taxpayers with adjusted gross incomes (AGIs) of $110,000 or more and couples with AGIs of $220,000 or more may not contribute to an ESA (although another individual, such as a grandparent, may make the contribution to the child's account). Although the contribution is not tax-deductible, the future investment earnings compound without taxation. Upon withdrawal, the investment earnings are not taxed (unlike a traditional retirement account) as long as the money is used for qualified education expenses. These expenses can include pre-college expenses as well, such as private K–12 school expenses.

State-sponsored college savings plans: 529

The 529 plans (named after Internal Revenue Code Section 529 and also known as *qualified state tuition plans*) are educational savings plans. A parent or grandparent can generally put more than $300,000 per beneficiary into one of these plans. Up to $70,000 per donor or $140,000 per married couple may be placed in a child's college savings account immediately, and this amount counts for the next five years' worth of $14,000 annual tax-free gifts per donor allowed under current gifting laws. (Money contributed to the account is not considered part of the donor's taxable estate. However, if the donor gives $70,000 and then dies before five years are up, a proportionate amount of that gift will be charged back to the donor's estate.)

Of course, you can contribute much smaller amounts to a 529 plan if you so desire. Though plans vary by state, some offer investment minimums as low as $25 to get you started. But before you jump into one of these plans, you should understand and weigh the overall tax and financial aid consequences of doing so.

The attraction of the 529 plans is that money inside the plans compounds without tax, and if it's used to pay for college tuition, room and board, and other related qualifying higher-education (post-secondary) expenses, the investment earnings and appreciation can be withdrawn tax-free. You can generally invest in any state plan to pay college expenses in any state, regardless of where you live.

In addition to paying college costs, the money in 529 plans may be used for graduate school expenses. Some states provide additional tax benefits on contributions to their state-sanctioned plan.

Unlike the money in a custodial account, with which a child may do as she pleases when she reaches either the age of 18 or 21 (the age varies by state), these state tuition plans must be used for higher-education expenses. However, most state plans do allow you to change the beneficiary. You can also take the money out of the plan if you change your mind. (You will, however, owe tax on the withdrawn earnings plus a penalty — typically 10 percent.)

A potential drawback of the 529 plans — especially for families hoping for some financial aid — is that college financial aid offices treat assets in these plans as parental nonretirement assets. If your family isn't wealthy and you aren't fully funding your retirement accounts, you gain better tax benefits and help your financial aid profile if you instead put your extra dollars into your retirement account(s). Also, be aware that the assets can be considered as belonging to an older child (independent young adult) who no longer reports parental financial information for financial aid purposes.

With some plans, you can't control how the money is invested, although this may be a positive. The farther your child is from college age, the more aggressive the investment mix. As your child approaches college age, the investment mix is tilted to more conservative investments. The best plans offer both individually selected investments and age-based options.

Some state plans have high investment management fees, and some plans don't allow transfers to other plans. Avoid such plans. Look for proven low-cost, performing investment options from companies such as TIAA-CREF, T. Rowe Price, and Vanguard.

Please also be aware that a future Congress could change the tax laws affecting these plans, diminishing the tax breaks or increasing the penalties for nonqualified withdrawals.

Clearly, these plans have both pros and cons. They generally make the most sense for affluent parents (or grandparents) who don't expect their children to qualify for financial aid. Do a lot of research and homework before investing in any plan. Check out the investment track record, allocations, and fees of each plan, as well as restrictions on transferring to other plans or changing beneficiaries. (See my website at www.erictyson.com for more information on these plans.) Parents who do establish a 529 plan should be careful on financial aid forms to list those assets as their own and not the child's to avoid harming your aid chances even more, as explained earlier in this chapter.

Treatment of home equity and other assets

Your family's assets may include equity in real estate and businesses that you own. Although the federal financial aid analysis no longer counts equity in your primary residence as an asset, many private (independent) schools continue to ask parents for this information when making their own financial aid determinations. Therefore, paying down your home mortgage more quickly instead of funding retirement accounts can harm you financially: You may end up with less financial aid and a higher tax bill.

Strategizing to Pay for Educational Expenses

Now I get more specific about what college may cost your kids and how you're going to pay for it. I don't have just one solution, because how you help pay for your child's college costs depends on your own unique situation and personal philosophy. However, in most cases, you may have to borrow *some* money, even if you have some available cash that can be directed to pay the college bills as you receive them.

Ask yourself what the best way is to "help" pay for college and what you want/expect in the way of contribution(s) by your children. Even parents who can afford to pay the entire costs often require their children to contribute something meaningful in terms of costs — whether from savings over summer work, loans, and so on. This strategy increases the chances of the kids having more focus via some "skin in the game" and helps ensure that they don't walk away after four or five years with a degree but no direction or purpose.

Estimating college costs

College can cost a lot. The total costs — including tuition, fees, books, supplies, room, board, and transportation — vary substantially from school to school. The total average annual cost is running around $47,000 per year at private colleges and around $24,000 at public colleges and universities (at the in-state rate). The more expensive schools can cost up to one-third more. Ouch!

Is all this expense worth it? Although many critics of higher education claim that the cost of a college education shouldn't be rising faster than inflation and that costs can, and should, be contained, denying the value of going to college is hard. Whether you're considering a local community college, your state's university, or a selective Ivy League institution, investing in education is usually worth the effort and the cost.

An *investment* is an outlay of money for an expected profit. Unlike a car, which depreciates in value, an investment in education generally yields monetary, social, and intellectual profits. A car is more tangible in the short term, but an investment in education (even if it means borrowing money) gives you more bang for your buck in the long run.

Colleges are now finding themselves subject to the same types of competition that companies confront. As a result, some colleges are finally beginning to clamp down on rising costs. As with any other product or service purchase, it pays to shop around. You can find good values — colleges that offer competitive pricing *and* provide a quality education. Although you don't want your son or daughter to choose a college simply because it costs less, you also shouldn't allow a college choice without any consideration of cost.

Setting realistic savings goals

If you have money left over *after* taking advantage of retirement accounts, by all means, try to save for your children's college costs. You should save in your name unless you know you aren't going to apply for financial aid, including those loans that are available regardless of your economic situation.

Be realistic about what you can afford for college expenses given your other financial goals, especially saving for retirement (see Chapter 4). Being able to personally pay 100 percent of the cost of a college education, especially at a four-year private college, is a luxury of the affluent. If you're not a high-income earner, consider trying to save enough to pay a third or, at most, half of the cost. You can make up the balance through loans, your child's employment before and during college, and the like.

Use Table 13-1 to help get a handle on how much you should be saving for college.

Table 13-1	How Much to Save for College*
Figure Out This	*Write It Here*
1. *Four-year total cost of the school you think your child will attend	$_____
2. Percent of costs you'd like to pay (for example, 20% or 40%)	×_____%
3. Line 1 times line 2 (the amount you'll pay in today's dollars)	= $_____
4. Number of months until your child reaches college age	÷_____ months
5. **Line 3 divided by line 4 (amount to save per month in today's dollars)	= $_____ / month

*The average cost of a four-year private college education today is about $188,000; the average cost of a four-year public college education is about $96,000. If your child has an expensive taste in schools, you may want to tack 20 to 30 percent onto the average figures.
**The amount you need to save (calculated in line 5) "in today's dollars" does need to be increased once per year to reflect the increase in college inflation — 5 percent should do.

Tips for getting loans, grants, and scholarships

A host of financial aid programs, including a number of loan programs, allow you to borrow at reasonable interest rates. Federal government educational loans have *variable interest rates* — which means that the interest rate you're charged *floats,* or varies, with the overall level of interest rates. Most programs add a few percent to the current interest rates on three-month to one-year Treasury bills. Thus, current rates on educational loans for students are in the vicinity of rates charged on fixed-rate mortgages (parents' loan rates are a little higher). The rates are also capped so the interest rate on your student loan can never exceed several percent more than the initial rate on the loan.

A number of loan programs, such as unsubsidized Stafford Loans and Parent Loans for Undergraduate Students (PLUS), are available even when your family is not deemed financially needy. Only subsidized Stafford Loans, on which the federal government pays the interest that accumulates while the student is still in school, are limited to students deemed financially needy.

Most loan programs limit the amount that you can borrow per year, as well as the total you can borrow for a student's educational career. If you need more money than your limits allow, PLUS loans can fill the gap: Parents can borrow the full amount needed after other financial aid is factored in. The only obstacle is that you must go through a credit qualification process. Unlike privately funded college loans, you can't qualify for a federal loan if you have negative credit (recent bankruptcy, more than three debts over three months past due, and so on). For more information from the federal government about these student loan programs, call the Federal Student Aid Information Center at 800-433-3243 or visit its website at `studentaid.ed.gov`.

If you're a homeowner, you may be able to borrow against the *equity* (market value less the outstanding mortgage loan) in your property. This option is useful because you can borrow against your home at a reasonable interest rate, and the interest is generally tax-deductible on up to $100,000 borrowed. Some company retirement plans — for example, 401(k)s — allow borrowing as well.

Parents are allowed to make penalty-free withdrawals from individual retirement accounts if the funds are used for college expenses. Although you won't be charged an early-withdrawal penalty, the IRS (and most states) will treat the amount withdrawn as taxable income. On top of that, the financial aid office will look at your beefed-up income and assume that you don't need as much financial aid. Because of these negative ramifications, funding college costs in this fashion should only be done as an absolute last resort.

In addition to loans, a number of grant programs are available through schools, the government, and independent sources. You can apply for federal government grants via the FAFSA (see "Figuring Out How the Financial Aid System Works," earlier in this chapter). Grants available through state government programs may require a separate application. Specific colleges and other private organizations (including employers, banks, credit unions, and community groups) also offer grants and scholarships.

One of the most important aspects of getting financial aid is choosing to apply, even if you're not sure whether you qualify. You may be able to lower your expected contribution by reducing your qualifying assets. (For more information on how those in charge of handing out financial aid evaluate how much of the bill you can foot, see "Figuring Out How the Financial Aid System Works.")

Many scholarships and grants don't require any extra work on your part — simply apply for financial aid through colleges. Other aid programs need seeking out — check directories and databases at your local library, your child's school counseling department, and college financial aid offices. You can also contact local organizations, churches, employers, and so on. You have a better chance of getting scholarship money through these avenues.

Your child can work and save money during high school and college. In fact, if your child qualifies for financial aid, she is expected to contribute a certain amount to education costs from savings and employment during the school year or summer breaks. Besides giving your child a stake in her own future, this training encourages sound personal financial management.

Investing Educational Funds

Financial companies pour big bucks into advertising for investment and insurance products that they claim are best for making your money grow for your children. Don't get sucked in by these ads.

What makes for good and bad investments in general applies to investments for educational expenses, too. Stick with basic, proven, lower-cost investments. (Chapter 9 explains what you generally need to look for and beware of.) The following sections focus on considerations specific to college funding.

Good investments: No-load mutual funds and exchange-traded funds

As I discuss in Chapter 10, the professional management and efficiency of the best no-load mutual funds and exchange-traded funds makes them a tough investment to beat. Chapters 11 and 12 provide recommendations for investing money in funds both inside and outside tax-sheltered retirement accounts.

Gearing the investments to the time frame involved until your children will need to use the money is the most important issue with funds. The closer your child gets to attending college and using the money saved, the more conservatively the money should be invested.

Bad investments

Life insurance policies that have cash values are among the most oversold investments for funding college costs. Here's the usual pitch: "Because you need life insurance to protect your family, why not buy a policy that you can borrow against to pay for college?"

One reason you shouldn't invest in this type of policy to fund college costs is that you're better off contributing to retirement accounts that give you an immediate tax deduction that saving through life insurance doesn't offer. Because life insurance that comes with a cash value is more expensive (largely due to the higher commissions these policies pay out to agents who sell them), parents are more likely to make a second mistake — not buying enough coverage. If you need and want life insurance, you're better off buying lower-cost term life insurance (see Chapter 16).

Another poor investment for college expenses is one that fails to keep you ahead of inflation, such as savings or money-market accounts. You need your money to grow so you can afford educational costs down the road.

Prepaid tuition plans should generally be avoided. A few states have developed plans that allow you to pay college costs at a specific school (calculated for the age of your child). The allure of these plans is that by paying today, you eliminate the worry of not being able to afford rising costs in the future.

This logic doesn't work for several reasons. First, odds are quite high that you don't have the money today to pay in advance. Second, putting money into such plans reduces your eligibility for financial aid dollar for dollar. If you have that kind of extra dough around, you're better off using it for other purposes. You can invest your own money — that's what the school's going to do with it, anyway.

Besides, how do you know which college your child will want to attend and how long it may take her to finish? Coercing your child into the school you've already paid for is a sure ticket to long-term problems in your relationship.

Overlooked investments

Too often, I see parents knocking themselves out to make more money so they can afford to buy a bigger home, purchase more expensive cars, take costly vacations, and send their kids to more expensive (and therefore supposedly better) private schools and colleges. Sometimes families want to send younger children to costly elementary schools, too. Families stretch themselves with outrageous mortgages or complicated living arrangements so they can get into neighborhoods with top-rated public schools or send their kids to expensive private elementary schools.

The best school in the world for your child is you and your home. The reason many people I know (including my siblings and I) were able to attend some of the top educational institutions is that concerned parents worked hard, not just at their jobs, but at spending time with the kids when they were growing up. Rather than working to make more money (with the best intentions of buying educational games or trips, or sending the kids to better schools), try focusing more attention on your kids. In my humble opinion, you can do more for your kids by spending more time with them.

I see parents scratching their heads about their child's lack of academic interest and achievement — they blame the school, TV, video games, or society at large. These factors may contribute to the problem, but education begins in the home. Schools can't do it alone.

Living within your means not only allows you to save more of your income but also frees up more of your time for raising and educating your children. Don't underestimate the value of spending more time with your kids and giving them your attention.

Chapter 14

Investing in Real Estate: Your Home and Beyond

*B*uying a home or investing in real estate can be financially and psychologically rewarding. On the other hand, owning real estate can be a real pain in the posterior, because purchasing and maintaining property can be quite costly, time-consuming, and emotionally draining. Perhaps you're looking to escape your rented apartment and buy your first home. Or maybe you're interested in becoming a local real-estate investing tycoon. In either case, you can learn many lessons from real-estate buyers who've traveled before you.

Note: Although this chapter focuses primarily on real estate in which you're going to live — otherwise known by those in the trade as *owner-occupied property* — much of what this chapter covers is relevant to real-estate investors. (For additional information on buying *investment real estate* — property that you rent out to others — see Chapter 9.)

Deciding Whether to Buy or Rent

You may be tired of moving from rental to rental. Perhaps your landlord doesn't adequately keep up the place, or you have to ask permission to hang a picture on the wall. You may desire the financial security and rewards that seem to come with home ownership. Or maybe you just want a place to call your own.

Any one of these reasons is good enough to *want* to buy a home. But before you commit to buy, you should take stock of your life and your financial health so you can decide whether you still want to buy a home and how much you can really afford to spend. You need to ask yourself some bigger questions.

Assessing your timeline

From a financial standpoint, you really shouldn't buy a place unless you can anticipate being there for at least three years (preferably five or more). Buying and selling a property entails a lot of expenses, including the cost of getting a mortgage (points, application, and appraisal fees), inspection expenses, moving costs, real-estate agents' commissions, and title insurance. *To cover these transaction costs plus the additional costs of ownership, a property needs to appreciate about 15 percent.*

If you need or want to move in a couple of years, counting on 15 percent appreciation is risky. If you're fortunate and you happen to buy before a sharp upturn in housing prices, you may get it. If you're unlucky, you'll probably lose money on the deal.

Some people are willing to invest in real estate even when they don't expect to live in it for long and are open to turning their home into a rental. Doing so can work well financially in the long haul, but don't underestimate the responsibilities that come with being a landlord. Also, most people need to sell their current home in order to tap all the cash that they have in it so they can buy the next one.

Determining what you can afford

Although buying and owning your own home can be a wise financial move in the long run, it's a major purchase that can send shock waves through the rest of your personal finances. You'll probably have to take out a 15- to 30-year mortgage to finance your purchase. The home you buy will need maintenance over the years. Owning a home is a bit like running a marathon: Just as you should be in good physical shape to successfully run a marathon, you should be in solid financial health when you buy a home.

I've seen too many people fall in love with a home and make a rushed decision without taking a hard look at the financial ramifications. Take stock of your overall financial health (especially where you stand in terms of retirement planning) *before* you buy property and agree to a particular mortgage. Don't let the financial burdens of a home control your financial future.

Don't trust a lender when he tells you what you can "afford" according to some formulas the bank uses to figure out what kind of a credit risk you are. To determine how much a potential home buyer can borrow, lenders look primarily at annual income; they pay no attention to some major aspects of a borrower's overall financial situation. Even if you don't have money tucked away into retirement savings, or you have several children to clothe, feed, and help put through college, you still qualify for the same size loan as other people with the same income (assuming equal outstanding debts). Only you can figure out how much you can afford, because only you know what your other financial goals are and how important they are to you.

Here are some important financial questions that no lender will ask or care about but that you should ask yourself before buying a home:

- ✔ Are you saving enough money monthly to reach your retirement goals?

- ✔ How much do you spend (and want to continue spending) on fun things such as travel and entertainment?

- ✔ How willing are you to budget your expenses in order to meet your monthly mortgage payments and other housing expenses?

- ✔ How much of your children's expected college educational expenses do you want to be able to pay for?

The other chapters in this book can help you answer these important questions. Chapter 4, in particular, helps you think through saving for important financial goals.

Many homeowners run into financial trouble because they don't know their spending needs and priorities or how to budget for them. For this reason, a surprisingly large percentage — some studies say about half — of people who borrow additional money against their home equity use the funds to pay consumer debts.

Calculating how much you can borrow

Mortgage lenders want to know your ability to repay the money you borrow. So you have to pass a few tests that calculate the maximum amount the lender is willing to lend you. For a home in which you'll reside, lenders total up your monthly housing expenses. They define your housing costs as

mortgage payment + property taxes + insurance

Lenders typically limit the amount they'll loan so your total housing costs are no more than 35 to 40 percent of your monthly gross (before taxes) income for the housing expense. (If you're self-employed, take your net income from the bottom line of your federal tax form Schedule C and divide by 12 to get your monthly gross income.)

Lenders also consider your other debts when deciding how much to lend you. These other debts diminish the funds available to pay your housing expenses. Lenders add the amount you need to pay down your other consumer debts (for example, auto loans and credit cards) to your monthly housing expense. The monthly total costs of these debt payments plus your housing costs typically cannot exceed 40 to 45 percent.

One general rule says that you can borrow up to three times (or two and one-half times) your annual income when buying a home. But this rule is a really rough estimate. The maximum that a mortgage lender will loan you depends on interest rates. If rates fall, the monthly payment on a mortgage of a given size also drops. Thus, lower interest rates make real estate more affordable.

Table 14-1 gives you an estimate of the maximum amount you may be eligible to borrow. Multiply your gross annual income by the number in the second column to determine the approximate maximum you may be able to borrow. For example, if you're getting a mortgage with a fixed rate around 7 percent and your annual income is $50,000, multiply 3.5 by $50,000 to get $175,000 — the approximate maximum mortgage allowed.

Table 14-1	The Approximate Maximum You Can Borrow
When Mortgage Rates Are	*Multiply Your Gross Annual Income* by This Figure*
3%	5.0
4%	4.6
5%	4.2
6%	3.8
7%	3.5
8%	3.2
9%	2.9
10%	2.7
11%	2.5

*If you're self-employed, this is your net business income (before taxes).

Comparing owning versus renting costs

The cost of owning a home is an important financial consideration for many renters. Some people assume that owning costs more. In fact, owning a home doesn't have to cost a truckload of money; at times, it may even cost less than renting (for example, with the decline in home prices in the late 2000s in many parts of the country).

On the surface, buying a place seems a lot more expensive than renting. You're probably comparing your monthly rent (measured in hundreds of dollars to more than $1,000, depending on where you live) to the purchase price of a property, which is usually a much larger number — perhaps $150,000 to $500,000 or more. When you consider a home purchase, you may be thinking about your housing expenses in one huge chunk rather than in small monthly installments (like a rent check).

Tallying up the costs of owning a place can be a useful and not-too-complicated exercise. To make a fair comparison between ownership and rental costs, you need to figure what it will cost on a *monthly basis* to buy a place you desire versus what it will cost to rent a *comparable* place. The worksheet in Table 14-2 enables you to do such a comparison. *Note:* In the interest of reducing the number of variables, all this "figuring" assumes a fixed-rate mortgage, *not* an adjustable-rate mortgage. (For more info on mortgages, see "Financing Your Home" later in this chapter.)

Table 14-2	Monthly Expenses: Renting versus Owning
Figure Out This ($ per Month)	*Write It Here*
1. Monthly mortgage payment (see "Mortgage")	$
2. Plus monthly property taxes (see "Property taxes")	+ $
3. Equals total monthly mortgage plus property taxes	= $
4. Your income tax rate (refer to Table 7-1 in Chapter 7)	%
5. Minus tax benefits (line 3 multiplied by line 4)	− $
6. Equals after-tax cost of mortgage and property taxes (subtract line 5 from line 3)	= $
7. Plus insurance ($30 to $150/mo., depending on property value)	+ $
8. Plus maintenance (1% of property cost divided by 12 months)	+ $
9. Equals total cost of owning (add lines 6, 7, and 8)	= $

Also, I ignore what economists call the *opportunity cost of owning*. In other words, when you buy, the money you put into your home can't be invested elsewhere, and the foregone investment return on that money, say some economists, should be considered a cost of owning a home. I choose to ignore this concept because I don't agree with this line of thinking. When you buy a home, you're investing your money in real estate, which historically has offered solid returns over the decades (see Chapter 8). And second, I have you ignore opportunity cost because it greatly complicates the analysis.

Now compare line 9 in Table 14-2 with the monthly rent on a comparable place to see which costs more — owning or renting.

Mortgage

To determine the monthly payment on your mortgage, simply multiply the relevant number (or multiplier) from Table 14-3 by the size of your mortgage expressed in thousands of dollars (divided by 1,000). For example, if you're taking out a $100,000, 30-year mortgage at 6.5 percent, you multiply 100 by 6.32 for a $632 monthly payment.

Table 14-3	Your Monthly Mortgage Payment Multiplier	
Interest Rate	*15-Year Mortgage Multiplier*	*30-Year Mortgage Multiplier*
3.0%	6.91	4.22
3.5%	7.15	4.49
4.0%	7.40	4.77
4.5%	7.65	5.07
5.0%	7.91	5.37
5.5%	8.17	5.68
6.0%	8.44	6.00
6.5%	8.71	6.32
7.0%	8.99	6.65
7.5%	9.27	6.99
8.0%	9.56	7.34
8.5%	9.85	7.69
9.0%	10.14	8.05
9.5%	10.44	8.41
10.0%	10.75	8.78

Property taxes

You can ask a real-estate person, mortgage lender, or your local assessor's office what your annual property tax bill would be for a house of similar value to the one you're considering buying (the average is about 1.5 percent of your property's value). Divide this amount by 12 to arrive at your monthly property tax bill.

Tax savings in home ownership

Generally speaking, mortgage interest and property tax payments for your home are tax-deductible on Schedule A of IRS Form 1040 (see Chapter 7). Here's a shortcut that works quite well in determining your tax savings in home ownership: Multiply your federal tax rate (see Table 7-1 in Chapter 7) by the total amount of your property taxes and mortgage payment. (Technically speaking, not all of your mortgage payment is tax-deductible — only the portion of the mortgage payment that goes toward interest. In the early years of your mortgage, nearly all of your payment goes toward interest. On the other hand, you may earn state tax benefits from your deductible mortgage interest and property taxes.)

If you want to more accurately determine how home ownership may affect your tax situation, get out your tax return and try plugging in some reasonable numbers to estimate how your taxes will change. You can also speak with a tax advisor.

Considering the long-term costs of renting

When you crunch the numbers to find out what owning rather than renting a comparable place may cost you on a monthly basis, you may discover that owning isn't as expensive as you thought. Or you may find that owning costs more than renting. This discovery may tempt you to think that, financially speaking, renting is cheaper than owning.

Be careful not to jump to conclusions. Remember that you're looking at the cost of owning versus renting *today*. What about 5, 10, 20, or 30 years from now? As an owner, your biggest monthly expense — the mortgage payment — doesn't increase (assuming that you buy your home with a fixed-rate mortgage). Your property taxes, homeowner's insurance, and maintenance expenses — which are generally far less than your mortgage payment — will increase over time with the cost of living.

When you rent, however, your entire monthly rent is subject to the vagaries of inflation. Living in a rent-controlled unit, where the annual increase allowed in your rent is capped, is the exception to this rule. Rent control does not eliminate price hikes; it just limits them.

Suppose you're comparing the costs of owning a home that costs $240,000 to renting that same home for $1,200 a month. Table 14-4 compares the cost per month of owning the home (after factoring in tax benefits) to your rental costs over 30 years. This comparison assumes that you take out a mortgage loan equal to 80 percent of the cost of the property at a fixed rate of 7 percent and that the rate of inflation of your homeowner's insurance, property taxes, maintenance, and rent is 4 percent per year. I further assume that you're in a moderate, combined 35 percent federal and state tax bracket.

Table 14-4	Cost of Owning versus Renting over 30 Years	
Year	*Ownership Cost per Month*	*Rental Cost per Month*
1	$1,380	$1,200
5	$1,470	$1,410
10	$1,620	$1,710
20	$2,040	$2,535
30	$2,700	$3,750

As you can see in Table 14-4, in the first few years, owning a home costs a little more than renting it. In the long run, however, owning is less expensive, because more of your rental expenses increase with inflation. And don't forget that as a homeowner you're building equity in your property; that equity will be quite substantial by the time you have your mortgage paid off.

Recognizing advantages to renting

Although owning a home and investing in real estate generally pay off handsomely over the long-term, to be fair and balanced, I must say that renting has its advantages. Some of the financially successful renters I've seen include people who pay low rent, either because they've made housing sacrifices or they live in a rent-controlled building. If you're consistently able to save 10 percent or more of your earnings, you're probably well on your way to achieving your future financial goals.

As a renter, you can avoid worrying about or being responsible for fixing up the property — that's your landlord's responsibility. You also have more financial and psychological flexibility as a renter. If you want to move, you can generally do so a lot more easily as a renter than you can as a homeowner.

Having a lot of your money tied up in your home is another challenge that you don't face when renting over the long haul. Some people enter their retirement years with a substantial portion of their wealth in their homes. As a renter, you can have all your money in financial assets that you can tap in to more easily. Homeowners who have a major chunk of equity in their home at retirement can downsize to a less costly property to free up cash and/or take out a reverse mortgage (which I discuss later in this chapter) on their home equity.

Financing Your Home

After you look at your financial health, figure out your timeline, and compare renting costs to owning costs, you need to confront the tough task of taking on debt to buy a home (unless you're independently wealthy). A mortgage loan from a bank or other source makes up the difference between the cash you intend to put into the purchase and the agreed-upon selling price of the real estate. This section reviews the different options you have for financing your home.

Understanding the two major types of mortgages

Like many other financial products, you have more mortgages to choose from than you could ever possibly investigate. The differences can be important or trivial, expensive or not. Two major types of mortgages exist — those with a fixed interest rate and those with a variable or adjustable rate.

✔ **Fixed-rate mortgages,** which are usually issued for a 15- or 30-year period, have interest rates that never, ever change. The interest rate you pay the first month is the same rate you pay the last month (and every month in between). Because the interest rate stays the same, your monthly mortgage payment amount doesn't change. With a fixed-rate mortgage, your monthly mortgage expense is certain.

Fixed-rate loans are not risk-free, however. If interest rates fall significantly after you obtain your mortgage, you face the danger of being stuck with your higher-cost mortgage if you're unable to refinance (see "Refinancing your mortgage" later in this chapter). You can be turned down for a refinance because of deterioration in your financial situation or a decline in the value of your property. Even if you're eligible to refinance, you may have to spend significant time and money to complete the process.

✔ **Adjustable-rate mortgages** (ARMs) carry an interest rate that varies over time. With an adjustable-rate mortgage, you can start with one interest rate and then have different rates for every year (or possibly every month) during a 30-year mortgage. Thus, the size of your monthly payment fluctuates. Because a mortgage payment makes an unusually large dent in most homeowners' checkbooks anyway, signing up for an ARM without understanding its risks is dangerous.

The attraction of ARMs is the potential interest savings. For the first few years of an adjustable loan, the interest rate is typically lower than it is on a comparable fixed-rate loan. After that, the relative cost depends on the overall trends in interest rates. When interest rates drop, stay level, or rise just a little, you probably continue to pay less for your adjustable mortgage. On the other hand, when rates rise more than a percent or two and then stay elevated, the adjustable loan can cost you more than a fixed-rate loan.

Choosing between fixed- and adjustable-rate mortgages

You need to weigh the pros and cons of each mortgage type and decide what's best for your situation *before* you go out to purchase a piece of real estate or refinance a loan. In the real world, most people ignore this advice. The excitement of purchasing a home tends to cloud one's judgment. My experience has been that few people look at their entire financial picture before making major real-estate decisions. If you're one of them, you may end up with a mortgage that could someday seriously overshadow the delight you take in your charming backyard.

Consider the issues I discuss in this section before you decide which kind of mortgage — fixed or adjustable — is right for you.

How willing and able are you to take on financial risk?

Take stock of how much risk you can handle with the size of your monthly mortgage payment. You can't afford much risk, for example, if your job and income are unstable and you need to borrow a lot. I define *a lot* as "close to the maximum a bank is willing to lend you." *A lot* can also mean that you have no slack in your monthly budget — in other words you're not regularly saving money. If you're in this situation, stick with a fixed-rate loan.

Don't take an adjustable loan simply because the initially lower interest rates allow you to afford the property you want to buy (unless you're absolutely certain that your income will rise to meet future payment increases). Try setting your sights on a property that you can afford with a fixed-rate mortgage.

If interest rates rise, a mushrooming adjustable mortgage payment may test the lower limits of your checking account balance. When you don't have emergency savings you can tap to make the higher payments, how can you afford the monthly payments — much less all the other expenses of home ownership?

And don't forget to factor in reasonably predictable future expenses that may affect your ability to make payments. For example, are you planning to start a family soon? If so, your income may fall while your expenses rise (as they surely will).

If you can't afford the highest allowed payment on an adjustable-rate mortgage, *don't take out an ARM.* You shouldn't accept the chance that the interest rate may not rise that high — it might, and then you could lose your home! Ask your lender to calculate the highest possible *maximum monthly payment* on your loan. That's the payment you'd face if the interest rate on your loan were to go to the highest level allowed (the *lifetime cap*).

You need to also consider your stress level. If you have to start following interest rate movements, it's probably not worth gambling on rates. On the other hand, maybe you're in a position to take the financial risks that come with an adjustable-rate mortgage. An adjustable loan places much of the risk of fluctuating rates on you (most adjustables, however, limit, or *cap,* the rise in the interest rate allowed on your loan). In return for your accepting some interest-rate risk, lenders cut you a deal — an adjustable mortgage's interest rate starts lower and stays lower if the overall level of interest rates doesn't rise substantially. Even if rates go up, they'll probably come back down over the life of your loan. So if you can stick with your adjustable for better and for worse, you may still come out ahead over the long term. Typical caps are 2 percent per year and 6 percent over the life of the loan.

You may feel financially secure in choosing an adjustable loan if you have a hefty financial cushion accessible in the event that rates go up, you take out a smaller loan than you're qualified for, or you're saving more than 10 percent of your income.

How long do you plan to keep the mortgage?

A mortgage lender takes extra risk when committing to a fixed interest rate for 15 to 30 years. Lenders don't know what may happen in the intervening years, so they charge you a premium for their risk.

The savings on most adjustables is usually guaranteed in the first two or three years, because an adjustable-rate mortgage starts at a lower interest rate than a fixed one. If rates rise, you can end up giving back or losing the savings you achieve in the early years of the mortgage. In most cases, if you aren't going to keep your mortgage more than five to seven years, you're probably paying unnecessary interest costs to carry a fixed-rate mortgage.

Home equity loans

Home equity loans, or home equity lines of credit (HELOCs) can be a useful source of financing to help buy or improve a home. HELOCs are second mortgages and best used by someone who already owns a home and wants to simply tap some of that equity without affecting the existing first mortgage (perhaps because of its attractive interest rate).

HELOCs of up to $100,000 are generally tax deductible. Once established, most HELOCs allow you to tap in to your credit line as you need or want to so you can use the money for many purposes, including a home remodel, college expenses for your kids, or as an emergency source of funds.

HELOCs have their downsides. The biggest negative in my experience is that they encourage homeowners to view their homes as piggy banks from which they can keep borrowing. The interest rate on a HELOC can increase instantaneously. Also beware that lenders can generally cancel your HELOC at their discretion, for example, if the value of your home falls too much or your credit score deteriorates.

For more complete and detailed information on HELOCs and all other home loans, please consult *Mortgages For Dummies* (Wiley), which I coauthored with Ray Brown.

Another mortgage option is a *hybrid loan*, which combines features of both the fixed- and adjustable-rate mortgages. For example, the initial rate may hold constant for a number of years — three to five years is common — and then adjust once a year or every six months thereafter. These hybrid loans may make sense for you if you foresee a high probability of keeping your loan seven to ten years or less but want some stability in your monthly payments. The longer the initial rate stays locked in, the higher the rate.

Shopping for fixed-rate mortgages

Of the two major types of mortgages I discuss earlier in this chapter, fixed-rate loans are generally easier to shop for and compare. The following sections cover what you need to know when shopping for fixed-rate mortgages.

Trading off interest rates and points

The *interest rate* is the annual amount a lender charges you for borrowing its money. The interest rate on a fixed-rate loan should always be quoted with the points on the loan.

Points are up-front fees paid to your lender when you close on your loan. Points are actually percentages: One point is equal to 1 percent of the loan amount. So when a lender tells you that 1.5 points are on a quoted loan, you pay 1.5 percent of the amount you borrow as points. On a $100,000 loan, for example, 1.5 points cost you $1,500. Points are actually prepaid interest, so they're tax deductible like the interest portion of regular monthly mortgage payments.

If one lender offers 30-year mortgages at 5.75 percent and another lender offers them at 6 percent, the 6-percent loan isn't necessarily worse. You also need to consider how many points each lender charges.

The interest rate and points on a fixed-rate loan go together and move in opposite directions. If you're willing to pay more points on a given loan, the lender will often reduce the interest rate. Paying more in up-front points may save you a lot of money in interest, because the interest rate on your loan determines your payments over a long, long time — 15 to 30 years. If you pay fewer points, your interest rate increases. Paying less in points may appeal to you if you don't have much cash for closing on your loan.

Suppose Lender X quotes you 5.75 percent on a 30-year fixed-rate loan and charges one point (1 percent). Lender Y, who quotes 6 percent, doesn't charge any points. Which is better? The answer depends mostly on how long you plan to keep the loan.

The 5.75-percent loan is 0.25 percent less than the 6-percent loan. Year in and year out, the 5.75-percent loan saves you 0.25 percent. But because you have to pay 1 percent (one point) up-front on the 5.75-percent loan, it takes about four years to earn back the savings to cover the cost of that point. So if you expect to keep the loan less than four years, go with the 6-percent option.

To perform an apples-to-apples comparison of mortgages from different lenders, get interest rate quotes at the same point level for each mortgage. For example, ask each lender for the interest rate on a loan for which you pay one point.

Be wary of lenders who advertise no-point loans as though they're offering something for nothing. Remember, if a loan has no points, it's *guaranteed* to have a higher interest rate. That's not to say that the loan is better or worse than comparable loans from other lenders. But don't get sucked in by a no-points sales pitch. Most lenders who spend big bucks advertising these types of loans rarely have the best deals.

Understanding other lender fees

In addition to charging you points and the ongoing interest rate, lenders tack on all sorts of other up-front fees when processing your loan. You need to know the total of all lender fees so you can compare different mortgages and determine how much completing your home purchase is going to cost you.

Lenders can nickel and dime you with a number of fees other than points. Actually, you pay more than nickels and dimes — $300 here and $50 there add up in a hurry! Here are the main culprits:

- ✔ **Application and processing fees:** Most lenders charge several hundred dollars to complete your paperwork and process it through their *underwriting* (loan evaluation) department. The justification for this fee is that if your loan is rejected or you decide not to take it, the lender needs to cover the costs. Some lenders return this fee to you upon closing if you go with their loan (after you're approved).

- ✔ **Credit report:** Many lenders charge a modest fee (about $50 to $75) for obtaining a copy of your credit report. This report tells the lender whether you've paid other loans you've taken in a timely manner. If you have problems on your credit report, clean them up before you apply (see "Increasing your approval chances" later in this chapter; also check out Chapter 2 for info on checking your credit report).

- ✔ **Appraisal:** The property for which you're borrowing money needs to be valued. If you default on your mortgage, your lender doesn't want to get stuck with a property worth less than you owe. For most residential properties, the appraisal cost is typically several hundred dollars.

- ✔ **Title and escrow charges:** These not-so-inconsequential costs are discussed in the section "Remembering title insurance and escrow fees" later in this chapter.

Get a written itemization of charges from all lenders you are seriously considering so you can more readily compare different lenders' mortgages and so you have no surprises when you close on your loan. And to minimize your chances of throwing money away on a loan for which you may not qualify, ask the lender whether you may not be approved for some reason. Be sure to disclose any problems you're aware of that are on your credit report or with the property.

Some lenders offer loans without points or other lender charges. If lenders don't charge points or other fees, they have to make up the difference by charging a higher interest rate on your loan. Consider such loans only if you lack cash for closing or if you're planning to use the loan for just a few years.

Shunning balloon loans

Be wary of balloon loans. They look like fixed-rate loans, but they really aren't. With a *balloon loan,* the large remaining loan balance becomes fully due at a predetermined time — typically within three to ten years. Balloon loans are dangerous because you may not be able to refinance into a new loan to pay off the balloon loan when it comes due. What if you lose your job or your income drops? What if the value of your property drops and the appraisal comes in too low to qualify you for a new loan? What if interest rates rise and you can't qualify for a new loan at the higher rate? Taking a balloon loan is a high-risk maneuver that can backfire.

Beware of prepayment penalties

Avoid loans with prepayment penalties. You pay this charge, usually 2 to 3 percent of the loan amount, when you pay off your loan before you're supposed to.

Prepayment penalties don't typically apply when you pay off a loan because you sell the property. But if you refinance such a loan in order to take advantage of lower interest rates, you almost always get hit by the prepayment penalties if the loan calls for such penalties.

The only way to know whether a loan has a prepayment penalty is to ask. If the answer is yes, find yourself another mortgage.

Don't take a balloon loan unless all the following conditions apply:

- ✔ You really, really want a certain property.
- ✔ The balloon loan is your only financing option.
- ✔ You're certain that you're going to be able to refinance or pay off the loan entirely when the balloon loan comes due.

If you take a balloon loan, get one that allows for as much time as possible before coming due.

Inspecting adjustable-rate mortgages (ARMs)

Although sorting through myriad fixed-rate mortgage options is enough to give most people a headache, comparing the bells and whistles of ARMs can give you a mortgage migraine. Caps, indexes, margins, and adjustment periods — you can spend weeks figuring it all out. If you're clueless about personal finances — or just think that you are — shopping for adjustable mortgages scores a 9.9 degree of difficulty on the financial frustration scale.

Unfortunately, you have to wade through a number of details to understand and compare one adjustable to another. Bear with me. And remember throughout this discussion that calculating exactly which ARM is going to cost you the least is impossible, because the cost depends on so many variables. Selecting an ARM has a lot in common with selecting a home: You have to make trade-offs and compromises based on what's important to you.

Understanding the start rate

Just as the name implies, the *start rate* is the interest rate your ARM starts with. Don't judge a loan by this rate. You won't be paying this attractively low rate for long. The interest rate will rise as soon as the terms of the mortgage allow.

Start rates are probably one of the least important items to focus on when comparing adjustable loans. (You'd never know this from the way some lenders advertise them — you see ads with the start rate in 3-inch bold type and everything else in microscopic footnotes!)

The formula (which includes index and margin) and rate caps are far more important for determining what a mortgage will cost you in the long run. Some people have labeled the start rate a *teaser rate,* because the initial rate on your loan is set artificially low to entice you. In other words, even if the market level of interest rates doesn't change, your adjustable is destined to increase — 1 to 2 percent is common.

Determining the future interest rate

You'd never (I hope) agree to a loan if your lender's whim and fancy determined your future interest rate. You need to know exactly how a lender figures out how much your interest rate is going to increase. All adjustables are based on the following formula, which specifies how the future interest rate on your loan is set:

> index + margin = interest rate

Indexes are often (but not always) widely quoted in the financial press, and the specific one used on a given adjustable loan is chosen by the lender. The six-month Treasury bill rate is an example of an index that's used on some mortgages.

The *margin* is the amount added to the index to determine the interest rate you pay on your mortgage. Most loans have margins of around 2.5 percent.

So, for example, the interest rate of a mortgage could be driven by the following formula:

> six-month Treasury bill rate + 2.5 percent = mortgage interest rate

In this situation, if six-month Treasuries are yielding 3 percent, the interest rate on your loan should be 5.5 percent. This figure is known as the *fully indexed rate.* If this loan starts at a 4.0-percent rate and the rate on six-month Treasuries stays the same, your loan should eventually increase to 5.5 percent.

The margin on a loan is hugely important. When you're comparing two loans that are tied to the same index and are otherwise equivalent, the loan with the lower margin is better. The margin determines the interest rate for every year you hold the mortgage.

Indexes differ mainly in how rapidly they respond to changes in interest rates. Following are the more common indexes:

- ✔ **Treasury bills (T-bills):** These indexes are based on government IOUs (Treasury bills), and a whole lot of them are out there. Most adjustables are tied to the interest rate on 6-month or 12-month T-bills.

- ✔ **Certificates of deposit (CDs):** Certificates of deposit are interest-bearing bank investments that lock you in for a specific period of time. ARMs are usually tied to the average interest rate banks are paying on six-month CDs. Like T-bills, CDs tend to respond quickly to changes in the market level of interest rates. Unlike T-bills, CD rates tend to move up a bit more slowly when rates rise and come down faster when rates decline.

- ✔ **11th District Cost of Funds:** This index tends to be among the slower-moving indexes. ARMs tied to 11th District Cost of Funds tend to start out at a higher interest rate. (The 11th District Cost of Funds Index is the weighted average of the cost of borrowings to member banking institutions of the Federal Home Loan Bank of San Francisco, the 11th District.) A slower-moving index has the advantage of moving up less quickly when rates are on the rise. On the other hand, you need to be patient to realize the benefit of falling interest rates.

Adjustment period or frequency

Every so often, the mortgage-rate formula is applied to recalculate the interest rate on an adjustable-rate loan. Some loans adjust monthly. Others adjust every 6 or 12 months.

In advance of each rate change, the lender should send you a notice telling you what your new rate is. All things being equal, the less frequently your loan adjusts, the less financial uncertainty you have in your life. Less-frequent adjustments usually coincide with a loan starting at a higher interest rate.

Understanding rate caps

When the initial interest rate expires, the interest rate fluctuates based on the formula of the loan. Almost all adjustables come with rate caps. The *adjustment cap* limits the maximum rate change (up or down) allowed at each adjustment. On most loans that adjust every six months, the adjustment cap is 1 percent.

Avoid negative amortization and interest-only loans if you're stretching

As you make mortgage payments over time, the loan balance you still owe is gradually reduced — this process is known as *amortizing* the loan. The reverse of this process — increasing your loan balance — is called *negative amortization.*

Negative amortization is allowed by some ARMs. Your outstanding loan balance can grow even though you're continuing to make mortgage payments when your mortgage payment is less than it really should be.

Some loans cap the increase of your monthly payment, but not the interest rate. The size of your mortgage payment may not reflect all the interest you owe on your loan. So rather than paying off the interest and some of your loan balance (or principal) every month, you're paying off some, but not all, of the interest you owe. Thus, the extra unpaid interest you still owe is added to your outstanding debt.

Using negative amortization is like paying only the minimum payment required on a credit card bill. You keep racking up greater interest charges on the balance as long as you make only the artificially low payment. Doing so defeats the whole purpose of borrowing an amount that fits your overall financial goals. And you may never get your mortgage paid off! Even worse, the increased interest you start to accrue on the unpaid interest added to your mortgage balance may not be tax deductible, because it doesn't qualify as interest incurred as part of the original purchase (what the IRS calls the *acquisition debt*).

Avoid negative-amortization mortgages. The only way to know for certain whether a loan includes negative amortization is to ask; some lenders aren't forthcoming about telling you. You'll find it more frequently on loans that lenders consider risky. If you're having trouble finding lenders who are willing to deal with your financial situation, be especially careful.

Another type of loan to avoid at all costs is the interest-only mortgage. In the early years of an interest-only loan, the monthly payment is kept lower because only interest is being paid; no payment is going to reduce the loan balance. What many folks don't realize is that at a set number of years into the mortgage (for instance, three, five, or seven), principal payments kick in as well, which dramatically increases the monthly payment.

Tread carefully with interest-only mortgages; consider one only if you understand how they work and can afford the inevitable jump in payments. Do not consider interest-only loans if you're stretching to be able to afford a home.

Loans that adjust more than once per year often limit the maximum rate change allowed over the entire year as well. On most such loans, the *annual rate cap* is 2 percent.

Almost all adjustables come with *lifetime caps*, which limit the highest rate allowed over the entire life of the loan. ARMs often have lifetime caps that are 5 to 6 percent higher than the start rate (though higher lifetime caps are increasingly common during the current low-interest-rate period). Before taking an adjustable, figure out the maximum possible payment at the life-time cap to be sure you can handle it.

Other ARM fees

Just as with fixed-rate mortgages, ARMs can carry all sorts of additional lender-levied charges. See the section "Understanding other lender fees" earlier in this chapter for details.

Avoiding the down-payment blues

You can generally qualify for the most favorable mortgage terms by making a down payment of at least 20 percent of the purchase price of the property.

In addition to saving money on interest, you can avoid the added cost of private mortgage insurance (PMI) by putting down this much. (To protect against losing money in the event you default on your loan, lenders usually require PMI, which costs several hundred dollars per year on a typical mortgage.)

Many people don't have the equivalent of 20 percent or more of the purchase price of a home to avoid paying private mortgage insurance. Here are a number of solutions for coming up with that 20 percent more quickly or buying with less money down:

- ✔ **Go on a spending diet.** Take a tour through Chapter 6 to find strategies for cutting back on your spending.

- ✔ **Consider lower-priced properties.** Smaller properties and ones that need some work can help reduce the purchase price and, therefore, the required down payment.

- ✔ **Find partners.** You can often get more home for your money when you buy a building in partnership with one, two, or a few people. Prepare a legal contract to specify what's going to happen if a partner wants out, divorces, or passes away.

- ✔ **Seek reduced down-payment financing.** Some lenders will offer you a mortgage even though you may be able to put down only 10 percent (and perhaps even less) of the purchase price (typically at the cost of a much higher interest rate). You must have solid credit to qualify for such loans, and you generally have to obtain and pay for the extra expense of private mortgage insurance (PMI), which protects the lender if you default on the loan. When the property value rises enough or you pay down the mortgage enough to have 20-percent equity in the property, you can drop the PMI. You generally have to apply to your lender to have the PMI dropped; it doesn't happen automatically.

Some property owners or developers may also be willing to finance your purchase with 10 percent or less down. You can't be as picky about properties, because not as many are available under these terms — many need work or haven't been sold yet for other reasons.

✔ **Get assistance from family.** If your relatives have money dozing away in a savings or CD account, they may be willing to lend (or even give) you the down payment. You can pay them an interest rate higher than the rate they're currently earning but lower than what you'd pay to borrow from a bank — a win/win situation for both of you. Lenders generally ask whether any portion of the down payment is borrowed and will reduce the maximum amount they're willing to loan you accordingly.

For more home-buying strategies, get a copy of the latest edition of *Home Buying For Dummies* (Wiley), which I coauthored with real-estate guru Ray Brown.

Comparing 15-year and 30-year mortgages

Many people don't have a choice between 15- and 30-year mortgages. To afford the monthly payments on their desired home, they need to spread the loan payments over a longer period of time, and a 30-year mortgage is the answer. A 15-year mortgage has higher monthly payments because you pay it off faster, meaning you pay off a larger amount of the loan balance each month and thus build equity in your home quicker. With fixed-rate mortgages at 6 percent, a 15-year mortgage comes with payments that are about 35 percent higher than those for a 30-year mortgage.

Taking the 15-year option, even if you can afford these higher payments, isn't necessarily better. The money for making extra payments doesn't come out of thin air. You may have better uses (which I discuss later in this section) for your excess funds.

And if you opt for a 30-year mortgage, you maintain the flexibility to pay it off faster (except in those rare cases where you have to pay a prepayment penalty). By making additional payments on a 30-year mortgage, you can create your own 15-year mortgage. But if the need arises, you can fall back to making only the payments required on your 30-year schedule.

Locking yourself into higher monthly payments with a 15-year mortgage comes with a risk. If money gets too tight in the future, you can fall behind in your mortgage payments. You may be able to refinance your way out of the predicament, but you can't count on it. If your finances worsen or your property declines in value, you may have trouble qualifying for a refinance.

Suppose you qualify for a 15-year mortgage and you're financially comfortable with the higher payments; the appeal of paying off your mortgage 15 years sooner is enticing. Besides, the interest rate is lower — generally up to ½ percent lower — on a 15-year mortgage. So if you can afford the higher payments on the 15-year mortgage, you'd be silly not to take it, right? Not so fast. You're really asking whether you should pay off your mortgage slowly or more quickly. And the answer isn't simple — it depends. Don't spend hours crunching numbers; you can make this decision by considering some qualitative issues.

First, think about *alternative uses* for the extra money you'd be throwing into paying down the mortgage. What's best for you depends on your overall financial situation and what else you can do with the money. If you would end up blowing the extra money at the racetrack or on an expensive car, pay down the mortgage. That's a no-brainer.

But suppose you take the extra $100 or $200 per month that you were planning to add to your mortgage payment and contribute it to a retirement account instead. This step may make financial sense. Why? Because contributions to 401(k)s, SEP-IRAs, Keoghs, and other types of retirement accounts (discussed in Chapter 11) are tax-deductible.

When you add an extra $200 to your mortgage payment to pay off your mortgage faster, you receive *no* tax benefits. When you dump that $200 into a retirement account, you get to subtract that $200 from the income on which you pay taxes. If you're paying 35 percent in federal and state income taxes, you shave $70 (that's $200 multiplied by 35 percent) off your tax bill.

In most cases, you get to deduct your mortgage interest on your tax return. So if you're paying 6 percent interest, your mortgage may really cost you only around 4 percent after you factor in the tax benefits. If you think you can do better (remember to consider the taxes on investment returns) by investing elsewhere (stocks, investment real estate, and so on), go for it. Investments such as stocks and real estate have generated better returns over the long haul. These investments carry risk, though, and they're not guaranteed to produce any return.

If you're uncomfortable investing and you'd otherwise leave the extra money sitting in a money market fund or savings account, you're better off paying down the mortgage. When you pay down the mortgage, you invest your money in a sure thing with a modest return. In fact, it's equivalent to buying a risk-free bond that pays you a pretax interest rate equal to whatever your mortgage interest rate is.

With pre-college-age kids at home, you have an even better reason to fund retirement accounts before you consider paying down your mortgage quickly. Retirement account balances are generally not counted as an asset when determining financial aid for college expenses. By contrast, many schools still count equity in your home (the difference between its market value and your loan balance) as an asset that can be tapped to pay for college. Your reward for paying down your mortgage balance may be less financial aid! (See Chapter 13 for more details about financing educational expenses.)

Paying down your mortgage faster, especially when you have children, is rarely a good financial decision if you haven't exhausted contributions to your retirement accounts. Save in your retirement accounts first and get the tax benefits.

Finding the best lender

As with other financial purchases, you can save a lot of money by shopping around. It doesn't matter whether you shop around on your own or hire someone to help you. Just do it!

On a 30-year, $180,000 mortgage, for example, getting a mortgage that costs 0.5 percent less per year saves you about $20,000 in interest over the life of the loan (given current interest rate levels). That's enough to buy a decent car! On second thought, save it!

Shopping for a lender on your own

In most areas, you can find many mortgage lenders. Although having a large number of lenders to choose from is good for competition, it also makes shopping a chore.

Large banks whose names you recognize from their advertising usually don't offer the best rates. Make sure you check out some of the smaller lending institutions in your area. Also, check out mortgage bankers, who, unlike banks, only do mortgages. The better mortgage bankers offer some of the most competitive rates.

Real-estate agents can also refer you to lenders with whom they've previously done business. These lenders may not necessarily offer the most competitive rates — the agent simply may have done business with them in the past.

Web-surfers can head on over to E-Loan (www.eloan.com), Bankrate (www.bankrate.com), Realtor.com (www.realtor.com), and HSH Associates (www.hsh.com).

You can also look in the real-estate section of one of the larger Sunday news-papers (and associated websites) in your area for charts of selected lender interest rates. These tables are by no means comprehensive or reflective of the best rates available. In fact, many of them are sent to newspapers for free by firms that distribute mortgage information to mortgage brokers. Use the tables as a starting point by calling the lenders who list the best rates.

One tactic that works well, especially in refinance situations, is to gather the best quotes from various sources and then check with your current banking relationship last. Ask them to match or beat your best offer (waive or dis-count some fees, discount the interest rate, and so on). If you're a good client and they want to keep your business (or expand what they already have with you), they may give you the best deal.

Hiring a mortgage broker

Insurance agents peddle insurance, real-estate agents sell real estate, and mortgage brokers deal in mortgages. They buy mortgages at wholesale from lenders and then mark them up to retail before selling them to you. The mort-gage brokers get their income from the difference, or *spread,* in the form of a commission. The terms of the loan obtained through a broker are generally the same as the terms you obtain from the lender directly.

Mortgage brokers get paid a percentage of the loan amount — typically 0.5 to 1 percent. This commission is negotiable, especially on larger loans that are more lucrative. Ask a mortgage broker what his cut is. Many people don't ask for this information, so some brokers may act taken aback when you inquire. Remember, it's your money!

The chief advantage of using a mortgage broker is that the broker can shop among lenders to get you a good deal. If you're too busy or disinterested to shop around for a good deal on a mortgage, a competent mortgage broker can probably save you money. A broker can also help you through the tedious process of filling out all those horrible documents lenders demand before giving you a loan. And if you have credit problems or an unusual prop-erty you're financing, a broker may be able to match you up with a hard-to-find lender who's willing to offer you a mortgage.

When evaluating a mortgage broker, be on guard for those who are lazy and don't continually shop the market looking for the best mortgage lend-ers. Some brokers place their business with the same lenders all the time, and those lenders don't necessarily offer the best rates. Also watch out for salespeople who earn big commissions pushing certain loan programs that aren't in your best interests. These brokers aren't interested in taking the time to understand your needs and discuss your options. Thoroughly check a broker's references before doing business.

Even if you plan to shop on your own, talking to a mortgage broker may still be worthwhile. At the very least, you can compare what you find with what brokers say they can get for you. Just be careful. Some brokers tell you what you want to hear and then aren't able to deliver when the time comes.

When a loan broker quotes you a really good deal, ask who the lender is. (Most brokers refuse to reveal this information until you pay the few hundred dollars to cover the appraisal and credit report.) You can check with the actual lender to verify the interest rate and points the broker quotes you and make sure you're eligible for the loan.

Increasing your approval chances

A lender can take several weeks to complete your property appraisal and an evaluation of your loan package. When many people are trying to refinance their loans, typically after a large drop in interest rates, the process may even take upward of six weeks. When you're under contract to buy a property, having your loan denied after waiting several weeks can mean you lose the property as well as the money you spent applying for the loan and having the property inspected. Some property sellers may be willing to give you an extension, but others won't.

Here's how to increase your chances of having your mortgage approved:

- ✔ **Get your finances in shape before you shop.** You won't have a good handle on what you can afford to spend on a home until you whip your personal finances into shape. Do so before you begin to make offers on properties. This book can help you. If you have consumer debt, eliminate it — the more credit card, auto loan, and other consumer debt you rack up, the less mortgage you qualify for. In addition to the high interest rate and the fact that it encourages you to live beyond your means, you now have a third reason to get rid of consumer debt. Hang onto the dream of owning a home, and plug away at paying off consumer debts.

- ✔ **Clear up credit report problems.** Get a copy of your credit report before you apply for a mortgage. Chapter 2 explains how to obtain a free copy, as well as correct any mistakes or clear up blemishes.

✔ **Get preapproved or prequalified.** When you get *prequalified,* a lender speaks with you about your financial situation and then calculates the maximum amount he's willing to lend you based on what you tell him. *Preapproval* is much more in-depth and includes a lender's review of your financial statements. Don't waste your time and money getting pre-approved if you're not really ready to buy.

✔ **Be up-front about problems.** Late payments, missed payments, or debts that you never bothered to pay can come back to haunt you. The best defense against loan rejection is to avoid it in the first place. You can sometimes head off potential rejection by disclosing to your lender anything that may cause a problem before you apply for the loan. That way, you have more time to correct problems and find alternate solutions. Mortgage brokers (see the preceding section) can also help you shop for lenders who are willing to offer you a loan despite credit problems.

✔ **Work around low/unstable income.** When you've been changing jobs or you're self-employed, your recent economic history may be as unstable as a country undergoing a regime change. Making a larger down payment is one way around this problem. You may try getting a cosigner, such as a relative or good friend. As long as he isn't borrowed up to his eyeballs, he can help you qualify for a larger loan than you can get on your own. Be sure that all parties understand the terms of the agreement, including who's responsible for monthly payments!

✔ **Consider a backup loan.** You certainly should shop among different lenders, and you may want to apply to more than one for a mortgage. Although applying for a second loan means additional fees and work, it can increase your chances of getting a mortgage if you're attempting to buy a difficult-to-finance property or if your financial situation makes some lenders leery. Be sure to disclose to each lender what you're doing — the second lender to pull your credit report will see that another lender has already done so.

Finding the Right Property

Shopping for a home can be fun. You get to peek inside other people's closets. But for most people, finding the right house at the right price can take a lot of time. When you're buying with partners or a spouse (or children, if you choose to share the decision-making with them), finding the right place can also entail a lot of compromise. A good agent (or several who specialize in different areas) can help with the legwork. The following sections cover the main things you need to consider when shopping for a home to call your own.

Condo, town house, co-op, or detached home?

Some people's image of a home is a single-family dwelling — a stand-alone house with a lawn and white picket fence. In some areas, however — particularly in higher-cost neighborhoods — you find *condominiums* (you own the unit and a share of everything else), *town homes* (attached or row houses), and *cooperatives,* also known as *co-ops* (you own a share of the entire building). The allure of such higher-density housing is that it's generally less expensive. In some cases, you don't have to worry about some of the general maintenance, because the owner's association (which you pay for, directly or indirectly) takes care of it.

 If you don't have the time, energy, or desire to keep up a property, shared housing may make sense for you. You generally get more living space for your dollars, and it may also provide you with more security than a stand-alone home.

As investments, however, single-family homes generally do better in the long run. Shared housing is easier to build and thus overbuild; on the other hand, single-family houses are harder to put up because more land is required. And most people, when they can afford it, still prefer a stand-alone home.

With that being said, you should remember that a rising tide raises all boats. In a good real-estate market, all types of housing generally appreciate, although single-family homes tend to do better. Shared housing values tend to fare better in densely populated urban areas with little available land for new building.

 From an investment return perspective, if you can afford a smaller single-family home instead of a larger shared-housing unit, buy the single-family home. Be especially wary of buying shared housing in suburban areas with lots of developable land.

Casting a broad net

You may have an idea about the type of property and location you're interested in or think you can afford before you start your search. You may think, for example, that you can only afford a condominium in the neighborhood you're interested in. But if you take the time to check out other communities, you may be surprised to find one that meets most of your needs and also has single-family homes you can afford. You'd never know about this community if you were to narrow your search too quickly.

Even if you've lived in an area for a while and you believe you know it well, look at different types of properties in a number of communities before you narrow your search. Be open-minded and figure out which of your many criteria for a home you *really* care about.

Finding out actual sale prices

Don't look at just a few of the homes listed at a particular price and then get depressed because they're all dogs or you can't afford what you really want. Before you decide to renew your apartment lease, remember that properties often sell for less than the price at which they're listed.

Find out what the places you look at eventually sell for. Doing so gives you a better sense of what places are really worth and what properties you may be able to afford. Ask the agent or owner who sold the property what the sale price was, or contact the town's assessors' office for information on how to obtain property sale price information.

Researching the area

Even (and especially) if you fall in love with a house at first sight, go back to the neighborhood at various times of the day and on different days of the week. Travel to and from your prospective new home during commute hours to see how long your commute will really take. Knock on some doors and meet your potential neighbors. You may discover, for example, that a flock of chickens lives in the backyard next door or that the street and basements frequently flood.

Go visit the schools. Don't rely on statistics about test scores. Talk to parents and teachers. What's really going on at the school? Even if you don't have kids, the quality of the local school has direct bearing on the value of your property. Is crime a problem? Call the local police department. Will future development be allowed? If so, what type? Talk to the planning department. What are your property taxes going to be? Is the property located in an area susceptible to major risks, such as floods, mudslides, fires, or earthquakes? Consider these issues even if they're not important to you, because they can affect the resale value of your property. Make sure you know what you're getting yourself into *before* you buy.

Working with Real-Estate Agents

When you buy (or sell) a home, you'll probably work with a real-estate agent. Real-estate agents earn their living on commission. As such, their incentives can be at odds with what's best for you. Real-estate agents usually don't hide the fact that they get a cut of the deal. Property buyers and sellers generally understand the real-estate commission system. I credit the real-estate profession for calling its practitioners "agents" instead of coming up with some silly obfuscating title such as "housing consultants."

A top-notch real-estate agent can be a significant help when you purchase or sell a property. On the other hand, a mediocre, incompetent, or greedy agent can be a real liability. The following sections help you sort the best from the rest.

Recognizing conflicts of interest

Real-estate agents, because they work on commission, face numerous conflicts of interest. Some agents may not even recognize the conflicts in what they're doing. The following list presents the most common conflicts of interest that you need to watch out for:

✔ Because agents work on commission, it costs them when they spend time with you and you don't buy or sell. They want you to complete a deal, and they want that deal as soon as possible — otherwise, they don't get paid. Don't expect an agent to give you objective advice about what you should do given your overall financial situation. Examine your overall financial situation *before* you decide to begin working with an agent.

✔ Because real-estate agents get a percentage of the sales price of a property, they have a built-in incentive to encourage you to spend more. Adjustable-rate mortgages (see "Financing Your Home" earlier in this chapter) allow you to spend more, because the interest rate starts at a lower level than that of a fixed-rate mortgage. Thus, real-estate agents are far more likely to encourage you to take an adjustable. But adjustables are a lot riskier — you need to understand these drawbacks before signing up for one.

✔ Agents often receive a higher commission when they sell listings that belong to other agents in their office. Beware. Sometimes the same agent represents both the property seller and the property buyer in the transaction — a real problem. Agents who hold open houses for sale may try to sell to an unrepresented buyer they meet at the open house. There's no way one person can represent the best interests of both sides.

✔ Because agents work on commission and get paid a percentage of the sales price of the property, many aren't interested in working with you if you can't or simply don't want to spend a lot. Some agents may reluctantly take you on as a customer and then give you little attention and time. Before you hire an agent, check references to make sure that he works well with buyers like you.

✔ Real-estate agents typically work a specific territory. As a result, they usually can't objectively tell you the pros and cons of the surrounding regions. Most won't admit that you may be better able to meet your needs by looking in another area where they don't normally work. Before you settle on an agent (or an area), spend time figuring out the pros and cons of different territories on your own. If you want to seriously look in more than one area, find agents who specialize in each area.

✔ Some agents may refer you to a more expensive lender who has the virtue of high approval rates. If you don't get approved for a mortgage loan, your entire real-estate deal may unravel. Be sure to shop around — you can probably get a loan more cheaply. Be especially wary of agents who refer you to mortgage lenders and mortgage brokers who pay agents referral fees. Such payments clearly bias a real-estate agent's "advice."

✔ Agents may encourage you to use a particular inspector with a reputation of being "easy" — meaning he may not "find" all the house's defects. Home inspectors are supposed to be objective third parties who are hired by prospective buyers to evaluate the condition of a property. Remember, it's in the agent's best interest to seal the deal, and the discovery of problems may sidetrack those efforts.

✔ Under pressure to get a house listed for sale, some agents agree to be accomplices and avoid disclosing known defects or problems with the property. In most cover-up cases, it seems, the seller doesn't explicitly ask an agent to help cover up a problem; the agent just looks the other way or avoids telling the whole truth. Never buy a home without having a home inspector look it over from top to bottom.

Looking for the right qualities in real-estate agents

When you hire a real-estate agent, you want to find someone who's competent and with whom you can get along. Working with an agent costs a lot of money (which is built into the price of houses sold and generally deducted from the seller's proceeds) — so make sure you get your money's worth.

Buyer's agents/brokers

Some agents market themselves as buyer's agents/brokers. Supposedly, these folks represent your interests as a property buyer exclusively. Legally speaking, buyer's agents may sign a contract saying that they represent your — and only your — interests. Before this enlightened era, all agents contractually worked for the property seller. The title "buyer's agent" is one of those things that sounds better than it really is. Agents who represent you as buyer's brokers still get paid only when you buy. And they still get a commission as a percentage of the purchase price. So they still have an incentive to sell you a piece of real estate, and the more expensive it is, the more commission they make.

Interview several agents. Check references. Ask agents for the names and phone numbers of at least three clients they've worked with in the past six months (in the geographical area in which you're looking). Look for the following traits in any agent you work with:

- ✔ **Full-time employment:** Some agents work in real estate as a second or even third job. Information in this field changes constantly. The best agents work at it full time so they can stay on top of the market.

- ✔ **Experience:** Hiring someone with experience doesn't necessarily mean looking for an agent who's been kicking around for decades. Many of the best agents come into the field from other occupations, such as business or teaching. Some sales, marketing, negotiation, and communication skills can certainly be picked up in other fields, but experience in buying and selling real estate does count.

- ✔ **Honesty and integrity:** If your agent doesn't level with you about what a neighborhood or particular property is really like, you suffer the consequences.

- ✔ **Interpersonal skills:** An agent has to be able to get along not only with you but also with a whole host of other people who are typically involved in a real-estate deal: other agents, property sellers, inspectors, mortgage lenders, and so on.

- ✔ **Negotiation skills:** Is your agent going to exhaust all avenues to negotiate the best deal possible for you? Be sure to ask the agent's references how well the agent negotiated for them.

- ✔ **High-quality standards:** Sloppy work can lead to big legal or logistical problems down the road. If an agent neglects to recommend thorough and complete inspections, for example, you may be stuck with undiscovered problems after the deal is done.

Agents sometimes market themselves as *top producers,* which means that they sell a relatively large volume of real estate. This title doesn't count for much for you, the buyer. It may be a red flag for an agent who focuses on completing as many deals as possible. When you're buying a home, you need an agent who has the following additional traits:

- ✔ **Patience:** You need an agent who's patient and willing to allow you the necessary time it takes to get educated and make the best decision for yourself.

- ✔ **Local market and community knowledge:** When you're looking to buy a home in an area in which you're not currently living, an informed agent can have a big impact on your decision.

- ✔ **Financing knowledge:** As a buyer (especially a first-time buyer or someone with credit problems), you should look for an agent who knows which lenders can best handle your type of situation.

Buying real estate requires somewhat different skills than selling real estate. Few agents can do both equally well. No law or rule says that you must use the same agent when you sell a property as you do when you buy a property.

Putting Your Deal Together

After you do your homework on your personal finances, discover how to choose a mortgage, and research neighborhoods and home prices, you'll hopefully be ready to close in on your goal. Eventually you'll find a home you want to buy. Before you make that first offer, though, you need to understand the importance of negotiations, inspections, and the other elements of a real-estate deal.

Negotiating 101

When you work with an agent, the agent usually handles the negotiation process. But you need to have a plan and strategy in mind; otherwise, you may end up overpaying for your home. Here are some recommendations for getting a good deal:

- ✔ **Never fall in love with a property.** If you have money to burn and can't imagine life without the home you just discovered, pay what you will. Otherwise, remind yourself that other good properties are out there. Having a backup property in mind can help.

✔ **Find out about the property and owner before you make your offer.** How long has the property been on the market? What are its flaws? Why is the owner selling? The more you understand about the property and the seller's motivations, the better able you'll be to draft an offer that meets both parties' needs.

✔ **Get comparable sales data to support your price.** Too often, home buyers and their agents pick a number out of the air when making an offer. But if the offer has no substance behind it, the seller will hardly be persuaded to lower his asking price. Pointing to recent and comparable home sales to justify your offer price strengthens your case.

✔ **Remember that price is only one of several negotiable items.** Sometimes sellers get fixated on selling their homes for a certain amount. Perhaps they want to get at least what they paid for it years ago. You may be able to get a seller to pay for certain repairs or improvements, to pay some of your closing costs, or to offer you an attractive loan without the extra loan fees that a bank would charge. Likewise, the real-estate agent's commission is negotiable.

Inspecting before you buy

When you buy a home, you may be making one of the biggest (if not *the* biggest) purchases of your life. Unless you build homes and do contracting work, you probably have no idea what you're getting yourself into when it comes to furnaces and termites.

Spend the time and money to locate and hire good inspectors and other experts to evaluate the major systems and potential problem areas of the home. Areas that you want to check include

✔ Overall condition of the property

✔ Electrical, heating, and plumbing systems

✔ Foundation

✔ Roof

✔ Pest control and dry rot

✔ Seismic/slide/flood risk

Inspection fees often pay for themselves. When problems that you weren't aware of are uncovered, the inspection reports give you the information you need to go back and ask the property seller to fix the problems or reduce the purchase price of the property to compensate you for correcting the deficiencies yourself.

As with other professionals whose services you retain, interview several inspection companies. Ask which systems they inspect and how detailed a report they're going to prepare for you (ask for a sample copy). Request names and phone numbers of three people who have used their service within the past six months.

Never accept a seller's inspection report as your only source of information. When a seller hires an inspector, he may hire someone who won't be as diligent and critical of the property. What if the inspector is a buddy of the seller or his agent? By all means, review the seller's inspection reports if available, but get your own as well.

And here's one more inspection for you to do: The day before you close on the purchase, do a brief walk-through of the property. Make sure that everything is still in good order and that all the fixtures, appliances, curtains, and other items that were to be left per the contract are still there. Sometimes sellers (and their movers) "forget" what they're supposed to leave or try to test your powers of observation.

Remembering title insurance and escrow fees

Mortgage lenders require *title insurance* to protect against someone else claiming legal title to your property. This claim can happen, for example, when a husband and wife split up and the one who remains in the home decides to sell and take off with the money. If both spouses are listed as owners on the title, the spouse who sells the property (possibly by forging the other's signature) has no legal right to do so. Both you and the lender can get stuck holding the bag if you buy the home that the one spouse of this divided couple is selling. But title insurance acts as the salvation for you and your lender. Title insurance protects you against the risk that the spouse whose name was forged will come back and reclaim rights to the home after it's sold.

If you're in the enviable position of paying cash for a property, you should still buy title insurance, even though a mortgage lender won't prod you to do so. You need to protect your investment.

Escrow charges pay for neutral third-party services to ensure that the instructions of the purchase contract or refinance are fulfilled and that everyone gets paid.

Many people don't seem to understand that title insurance and escrow fees vary from company to company. As a result, they don't bother to comparison shop; they simply use the company that their real-estate agent or mortgage lender suggests.

Call around for title insurance and escrow fee quotes, and make sure you understand all the fees. Many companies tack on all sorts of charges for things such as courier fees and express mail. If you find a company with lower prices and want to use it, ask for an itemization in writing so you don't have any surprises. Real-estate agents and mortgage lenders can be a good starting point for referrals because they usually have a broader perspective on the cost and service quality of different companies. Call other companies as well. Agents and lenders may be biased toward a company simply because they're in the habit of using it or they've referred clients to it before.

After You Buy

After you buy a home, you'll make a number of important decisions over the months and years ahead. This section discusses the key issues you need to deal with as a homeowner and tells what you need to know to make the best decision for each of them.

Refinancing your mortgage

Three reasons motivate people to *refinance,* or obtain a new mortgage to replace an old one. One is obvious: to save money because interest rates have dropped. Refinancing can also be a way to raise capital for some other purpose. You can use refinancing to get out of one type of loan and into another. The following sections can help you decide on the best option in each case.

Spending money to save money

If your current loan has a higher rate of interest than comparable new loans, you may be able to save money by refinancing. Because refinancing costs money, whether you can save enough to justify the cost is open to question. If you can recover the expenses of the refinance within a few years, go for it. If recovering the costs will take longer, refinancing may still make sense if you anticipate keeping the property and mortgage that long.

Be wary of mortgage lenders or brokers who tout how soon your refinance will pay for itself; they usually oversimplify their calculations. For example, if the refinance costs you $2,000 to complete (for appraisals, loan fees and points, title insurance, and so on) and reduces your monthly payment by $100, lenders or brokers typically say that it's going to take 20 months for you to recoup the refinance costs. This estimate isn't accurate, however, because you lose some tax write-offs if your mortgage interest rate and payment are reduced. You can't simply look at the reduced amount of your monthly payment. (Mortgage lenders like to look at it, however, because it makes refinancing more attractive.) And your new mortgage will be reset to a different term than the number of years remaining on your old one.

If you want a better estimate of your likely cost savings but don't want to spend hours crunching numbers, take your tax rate — for example, 27 percent — and reduce your monthly payment savings on the refinance by this amount (see Chapter 7). Continuing with the example in the preceding paragraph, if your monthly payment drops by $100, you're really saving about $73 a month after factoring in the lost tax benefits. So it takes about 28 months ($2,000 divided by $73) — not 20 — to recoup the refinance costs.

Note that not all refinances cost big money. So-called no-cost refinances or no-point loans minimize your out-of-pocket expenses, but as I discuss earlier in this chapter, they may not be your best long-term options. Such loans usually come with higher interest rates.

Using money for another purpose

Refinancing to pull out cash from your home for some other purpose can make good financial sense because under most circumstances, mortgage interest is tax-deductible. Paying off other higher-interest consumer debt — such as on credit cards or on an auto loan — is a common reason for borrowing against a home. The interest on consumer debt is not tax-deductible and is generally at a much higher interest rate than what mortgages charge you.

If you're starting a business, consider borrowing against your home to finance the launch of your business. You can usually do so at a lower cost than with a business loan.

You need to find out whether a lender is willing to lend you more money against the equity in your home (which is the difference between the market value of your house and the loan balance). You can use Table 14-1 earlier in this chapter to estimate the maximum loan for which you may qualify.

Changing loans

You may want to refinance even though you aren't forced to raise cash or you're able to save money. Perhaps you're not comfortable with your current loan — holders of adjustable-rate mortgages often face this problem. You may find out that a fluctuating mortgage payment makes you anxious and wreaks havoc on your budget.

Paying money to go from an adjustable to a fixed rate is a lot like buying insurance. The cost of the refinance is "insuring" you a level mortgage payment. Consider this option only if you want peace of mind and you plan to stay with the property for a number of years.

Sometimes jumping from one adjustable to another makes sense. Suppose that you can lower the maximum lifetime interest rate cap and the refinance won't cost much. Your new loan should have a lower initial interest rate than the one you're paying on your current loan. Even if you don't save megabucks, the peace of mind of a lower ceiling can make refinancing worth your while.

Mortgage life insurance

Shortly after you buy a home or close on a mortgage, you start getting mail from all kinds of organizations that keep track of publicly available information about mortgages. Most of these organizations want to sell you something, and they don't tend to beat around the bush. "What will your dependents do if you meet with an untimely demise and they're left with a gargantuan mortgage?" these organizations ask. In fact, this is a good financial-planning question. If your family is dependent on your income, can it survive financially if you pass away?

Don't waste your money on mortgage life insurance. You may need life insurance to provide for your family and help meet large obligations such as mortgage payments or educational expenses for your children, but mortgage life insurance is typically grossly overpriced. (Check out the life insurance section in Chapter 16 for advice about term life insurance.) Consider mortgage life insurance only if you have a health problem and the mortgage life insurer doesn't require a physical examination. Be sure to compare it with term life options.

Is a reverse mortgage a good idea?

An increasing number of homeowners are finding, particularly in their later years of retirement, that they lack cash. The home in which they live is usually their largest asset. Unlike other investments, such as bank accounts, bonds, or stocks, a home does not provide any income to the owner unless he decides to rent out a room or two.

A *reverse mortgage* allows a homeowner who is 62 years of age or older and low on cash to tap home equity. For an elderly homeowner, using home equity can be a difficult thing to do psychologically. Most people work hard to pay a mortgage month after month, year after year, until it's finally all paid off. What a feat and what a relief after all those years!

Taking out a reverse mortgage reverses this process. Each month, the reverse mortgage lender sends you a check that you can spend on food, clothing, travel, or whatever you want. The money you receive each month is really a loan from the bank against the value of your home, which makes the monthly check free from taxation. A reverse mortgage also allows you to stay in your home and use its equity to supplement your monthly income.

The main drawback of a reverse mortgage is that it can diminish the estate that you may want to pass on to your heirs or use for some other purpose. Also, some loans require repayment within a certain number of years. The fees and the effective interest rate you're charged to borrow the money can be quite high.

Because some loans require the lender to make monthly payments to you as long as you live in the home, lenders assume that you'll live many years in your home so they won't lose money when making these loans. If you end up keeping the loan for only a few years because you move, for example, the cost of the loan is extremely high.

You may be able to create a reverse mortgage with your relatives. This technique can work if you have family members who are financially able to provide you with monthly income in exchange for ownership of the home when you pass away.

You have other alternatives to tapping the equity in your home. Simply selling your home and buying a less expensive property (or renting) is one option. Under current tax laws, qualifying house sellers can exclude a sizable portion of their profits from capital gains tax: up to $250,000 for single taxpayers and $500,000 for married couples.

Selling your house

The day may come when you want to sell your house. If you're going to sell, make sure you can afford to buy the next home you desire. Be especially careful if you're a trade-up buyer — that is, if you're going to buy an even more expensive home. All the affordability issues discussed at the beginning of this chapter apply. You also need to consider the following issues.

Selling through an agent

When you're selling a property, you want an agent who can get the job done efficiently and sell your house for as much as possible. As a seller, you need to seek an agent who has marketing and sales expertise and is willing to put in the time and money necessary to sell your house. Don't necessarily be impressed by an agent who works for a large company. What matters more is what the agent will do to market your property.

When you list your house for sale, the contract you sign with the listing agent includes specification of the commission to be paid if the agent is successful in selling your house. In most areas of the country, agents usually ask for a 6-percent commission. In an area that has lower-cost housing, they may ask for 7 percent.

Remember that commissions are *always* negotiable. Because the commission is a percentage, you have a much greater possibility of getting a lower commission on a higher-priced house. If an agent makes 6 percent selling both a $200,000 house and a $100,000 house, the agent makes twice as much on the $200,000 house. Yet selling the higher-priced house does not take twice as much work. (Selling a $400,000 house certainly doesn't take four times the effort of selling a $100,000 house.)

 If you're selling a higher-priced home (above $250,000), you have no reason to pay more than a 5-percent commission. For expensive properties ($500,000 and up), a 4-percent commission may be reasonable. You may find, however, that your ability to negotiate a lower commission is greatest when an offer is on the table. Because you don't want to give other agents (working with buyers) a reason not to sell your house, have your listing agent cut his take rather than reduce the commission that you advertise you're willing to pay to an agent who brings you a buyer.

In terms of the length of the listing sales agreement you make with an agent, three months is reasonable. When you give an agent a listing that's too long (6 to 12 months) in duration, the agent may simply toss your listing into the multiple listing book and expend little effort to sell your property. Practically speaking, if your home hasn't sold, you can fire your agent whenever you want, regardless of the length of the listing agreement. However, a shorter listing may be more motivating for your agent.

Selling without a real-estate agent

You may be tempted to sell without an agent so you can save the commission that's deducted from your house's sale price. If you have the time, energy, and marketing experience and you can take the time to properly value your home, you can sell your house without an agent and possibly save some money.

The major problem with attempting to sell your house on your own is that agents who are working with buyers don't generally look for or show their clients properties that are for sale by owner. Besides saving you time, a good agent can help ensure that you're not sued for failing to disclose the known defects of your property. If you decide to sell your house on your own, make sure you have access to a legal advisor who can review the contracts. Whether you sell through an agent or not, be sure to read the latest edition of *House Selling For Dummies* (Wiley), which I co-wrote with real-estate expert Ray Brown.

Should you keep your home until prices go up?

Many homeowners are tempted to hold on to their properties (when they need to move) if the property is worth less than when they bought it or if the real-estate market is soft. Renting out your property probably isn't worth the hassle, and holding on to it probably isn't worth the financial gamble. If you need to move, you're better off, in most cases, selling your house.

You may reason that, in a few years (during which you'd rent the property), the real-estate storm clouds will clear, and you'll be able to sell your property at a much higher price. Here are three risks associated with this line of thinking:

✔ You can't know whether property prices in the next few years are going to rebound, stay the same, or drop even further. A property generally needs to appreciate at least a few percent per year just to make up for all the costs of holding and maintaining it.

✔ You may be unprepared for legal issues and dealings with your tenants. If you've never been a landlord, don't underestimate the hassle and headaches associated with this job.

✔ If you convert your home into a rental property in the meantime and it appreciates in value, you're going to pay capital gains tax on your profit when you sell it (and the taxable profit will be higher if you have taken tax deductions for depreciation during the rental period). This capital gains tax wipes out much of the advantage of having held on to the property until prices recovered. (If you want to be a long-term rental property owner, you can do a *tax-free exchange* into another rental property when you sell.)

However, if you would realize little cash from selling *and* you lack other money for the down payment to purchase your next property, you have good reason for holding on to a home that has dropped in value.

Should you keep your home as investment property after you move?

Converting your home into rental property is worth considering if you need or want to move. Don't consider doing so unless it really is a long-term proposition (ten years or more). As discussed in the preceding section, selling rental property has tax consequences.

If you want to convert your home into an investment property, you have an advantage over someone who's looking to buy an investment property, because you already own your home. Locating and buying investment property takes time and money. You also know what you have with your current home. If you go out and purchase a property to rent, you're starting from scratch.

If your property is in good condition, consider what damage renters may do to it; few renters will take care of your home the way that you would. Also consider whether you're cut out to be a landlord. For more information, see the section on real estate as an investment in Chapter 9.

Part IV
Insurance: Protecting What You Have

3 Rules for Buying Insurance

- ✔ Insure for the big stuff; don't sweat the small stuff.
- ✔ Buy broad coverage.
- ✔ Shop around and buy direct.

When choosing an insurance company, you need to consider the insurer's financial health. The free article at www.dummies.com/extras/personalfinance offers advice on how to evaluate an insurer.

In this part . . .

✔ Understand the fundamentals of insurance and determine when you need it and when you don't.

✔ Find out how to secure insurance on yourself to protect your income earning ability for yourself and loved ones and shield against major medical expenses.

✔ Know what's available to protect your assets such as your home, cars, and wealth.

Chapter 15

Insurance: Getting What You Need at the Best Price

. . . .

In This Chapter

▶ Buying the right insurance at the best price

▶ Overcoming roadblocks to getting the coverage you need

▶ Securing your claim money when you've suffered a loss

. . . .

*U*nless you work in the industry, you may find insurance to be a dreadfully boring topic. Most people associate insurance with disease, death, and disaster and would rather do just about anything other than review their policies or spend money on insurance. But because you won't want to deal with money hassles when you're coping with catastrophes — illness, disability, death, fires, floods, earthquakes, and so on — you should secure insurance well before you need it.

Insurance is probably the most misunderstood and least monitored area of personal finance. Studies show that more than 90 percent of Americans purchase and carry the wrong types and amounts of insurance coverage. My own experience as a financial counselor confirms this statistic. Most people are overwhelmed by all the jargon in sales and policy statements. Thus, they pay more than necessary for their policies and get coverage they don't really need while failing to obtain coverage that they really should have.

In this chapter, I tell you how to determine what kinds of insurance you need, explain what you can do if you're denied coverage, and give you advice on getting your claims paid. Later chapters discuss types of insurance in detail, including insurance on people (Chapter 16) and possessions (Chapter 17).

Discovering My Three Laws of Buying Insurance

I know your patience and interest in finding out about insurance is surely limited, so in this section I boil the subject down to three fairly simple but powerful concepts that can easily save you big bucks. And while you're saving money, you can still get the quality coverage you need in order to avoid a financial catastrophe.

Law 1: Insure for the big stuff; don't sweat the small stuff

What if you could buy insurance that would pay for the cost of a restaurant meal if you got food poisoning? Even if you were splurging at a fancy restaurant, you wouldn't have a lot of money at stake, so you'd probably decline that coverage.

The point of insurance is to protect against losses that would be financially catastrophic to you, not to smooth out the bumps of everyday life. The preceding example about restaurant insurance is silly, but some people buy equally foolish policies without knowing it. In the following sections, I tell you how to get the most appropriate insurance coverage for your money. I start off with the "biggies" that are worth your money, and then I work down to some insurance options that are less worthy of your dollars.

Buy insurance to cover financial catastrophes

You want to insure against what could be a huge financial loss for you or your dependents. The price of insurance isn't cheap, but it's relatively small in comparison to the potential total loss from a financial catastrophe.

The beauty of insurance is that it spreads risks over millions of other people. If your home were to burn to the ground, paying the rebuilding cost out of your own pocket probably would be a financial catastrophe. If you have insurance, the premiums paid by you and all the other homeowners collectively can easily pay the bills.

Think for a moment about what your most valuable assets are. Also consider potential large expenses. Perhaps they include the following:

✔ **Future income:** During your working years, your most valuable asset is probably your future earnings. If you were disabled and unable to work, what would you live on? Long-term disability insurance exists to help you handle this type of situation. If you have a family that's financially dependent on your earnings, how would your family manage if you died? Life insurance can fill the monetary void left by your death.

✔ **Business:** If you're a business owner, what would happen if you were sued for hundreds of thousands of dollars or a million dollars or more for negligence in some work that you messed up? Liability insurance can protect you.

✔ **Health:** In this age of soaring medical costs, you can easily rack up a $100,000 hospital bill in short order. Major medical health insurance helps pay such expenses. And yet, a surprising number of people don't carry any health insurance — particularly those who work in small businesses. (See Chapter 16 for more on health insurance.)

Psychologically, buying insurance coverage for the little things that are more likely to occur is tempting. You don't want to feel like you're wasting your insurance dollars. You want to get some of your money back, darn it! You're more *likely* to get into a fender bender with your car or have a package lost in the mail than you are to lose your home to fire or suffer a long-term disability. But if the fender bender costs $500 (which you end up paying out of your pocket because you took my advice to take a high deductible; see the next section) or the postal service loses your package worth $50 or $100, you won't be facing a financial disaster.

On the other hand, if you lose your ability to earn an income because of a disability, or if you're sued for $1 million and you're not insured against such catastrophes, not only will you be extremely unhappy, but you may also face financial ruin. "Yes, but what are the odds," I hear people rationalize, "that I'll suffer a long-term disability or that I'll be sued for $1 million?" I agree that the odds are quite low, but the risk is there. The problem is that you just don't know what, or when, bad luck may befall you.

And don't make the mistake of thinking that you can figure the odds better than the insurance companies can. The insurance companies predict the probability of your making a claim, large or small, with a great deal of accuracy. They employ armies of number-crunching actuaries to calculate the odds that bad things will happen and the frequency of current policyholders' making particular types of claims. The companies then price their policies accordingly.

So buying (or not buying) insurance based on your perception of the likelihood of needing the coverage is foolish. Insurance companies aren't stupid; in fact, they're ruthlessly smart! When insurance companies price policies, they look at a number of factors to determine the likelihood of your filing a claim. Take the example of auto insurance. Who do you think will pay more for auto insurance — a single male who's age 20, lives the fast life in a high-crime city, drives a turbo sports car, and has received two speeding tickets in the past year? Or a couple in their 40s, living in a low-crime area, driving a four-door sedan, and having a clean driving record?

Take the highest deductible you can afford

Most insurance policies have *deductibles* — the maximum amount you must pay in the event of a loss before your insurance coverage kicks in and begins paying out. On many policies, such as auto and homeowner's/renter's coverage, most folks opt for a $100 to $250 deductible.

Here are some benefits of taking a higher deductible:

- ✔ **You save premium dollars.** Year in and year out, you can enjoy the lower cost of an insurance policy with a high deductible. You may be able to shave 15 to 20 percent off the cost of your policy. Suppose, for example, that you can reduce the cost of your policy by $150 per year by raising your deductible from $250 to $1,000. That $750 worth of coverage is costing you $150 per year. Thus, you'd need to have a claim of $1,000 or more every five years — highly unlikely — to come out ahead. If you're that accident-prone, guess what? The insurance company will raise your premiums.

- ✔ **You don't have the hassles of filing small claims.** If you have a $300 loss on a policy with a $100 deductible, you need to file a claim to get your $200 (the amount you're covered for after your deductible). Filing an insurance claim can be an aggravating experience that takes hours of time. In some cases, you may even have your claim denied after jumping through all the necessary hoops. Getting your due may require prolonged haggling.

When you have low deductibles, you may file more claims (although this doesn't necessarily mean that you'll get more money). After filing more claims, you may be "rewarded" with higher premiums — in addition to the headache you get from preparing all those blasted forms! Filing more claims may even cause cancellation of your coverage!

Avoid small-potato policies

A good insurance policy can seem expensive. A policy that doesn't cost much, on the other hand, can fool you into thinking that you're getting something for next to nothing. Policies that cost little also cover little — they're priced low because they don't cover large potential losses.

Following are examples of common "small-potato" insurance policies that are generally a waste of your hard-earned dollars. As you read through this list, you may find examples of policies that you bought and that you feel paid for themselves. I can hear you saying, "But I collected on that policy you're telling me not to buy!" Sure, getting "reimbursed" for the hassle of having something go wrong is comforting. But consider all such policies that you bought or may buy over the course of your life. You're not going to come out ahead in the aggregate — if you did, insurance companies would lose money! These policies aren't worth the cost relative to the small potential benefit. On average, insurance companies pay out just 60 cents in benefits on every dollar collected. Many of the following policies pay back even less — around 20 cents in benefits (claims) for every insurance premium dollar spent:

- ✔ **Extended warranty and repair plans:** Isn't it ironic that right after a salesperson or company persuades you to buy a particular television, computer, or car — in part by saying how reliable the product is — it tries to convince you to spend more money to insure against the failure of the item? If the product is so good, why do you need such insurance?

  Extended warranty and repair plans are expensive and unnecessary short-term insurance policies. Product manufacturers' warranties typically cover any problems that occur in the first year or even several years. After that, paying for a repair out of your own pocket isn't a financial catastrophe. (Some credit-card issuers automatically double the manufacturer's warranty without additional charge on items purchased with their card. However, the cards that do this typically are higher-cost premium cards, so this is no free lunch — you're paying for this protection in terms of higher fees.)

- ✔ **Home warranty plans:** If your real-estate agent or the seller of a home wants to pay the cost of a home warranty plan for you, turning down the offer would be ungracious. (As Grandma would say, you shouldn't look a gift horse in the mouth.) But don't buy this type of plan for yourself. In addition to requiring some sort of fee (around $50 to $100), home warranty plans limit how much they'll pay for problems.

  Your money is best spent hiring a competent inspector to uncover problems and fix them *before* you purchase the home. If you buy a house, you should expect to spend money on repairs and maintenance; don't waste money purchasing insurance for such expenses.

- ✔ **Dental insurance:** If your employer pays for dental insurance, you could take advantage of it. But don't pay for this coverage on your own. Dental insurance generally covers a couple of teeth cleanings each year and limits payments for more expensive work.

- ✔ **Credit life and credit disability policies:** *Credit life policies* pay a small benefit if you die with an outstanding loan. *Credit disability policies* pay a small monthly income in the event of a disability. Banks and their credit-card divisions usually sell these policies. Some companies sell insurance to pay off your credit-card bill in the event of your death or disability, or to cover minimum monthly payments for a temporary period during specified life transition events (such as loss of a job, divorce, and so on).

The cost of such insurance seems low, but that's because the potential benefits are relatively small. In fact, given what little insurance you're buying, these policies are expensive. If you need life or disability insurance, purchase it. But get enough coverage, and buy it in a separate, cost-effective policy (see Chapter 16 for more details).

If you're in poor health and you can buy these insurance policies without a medical evaluation, you may represent an exception to the "don't buy it" rule. In this case, these policies may be the only ones to which you have access — another reason these policies are expensive. The people in good health are paying for the people with poor health who can enroll without a medical examination and who undoubtedly file more claims.

✔ **Daily hospitalization insurance:** Hospitalization insurance policies that pay a certain amount per day, such as $100, prey on people's fears of running up big hospital bills. Healthcare is expensive — there's no doubt about that.

But what you really need is a comprehensive (major medical) health insurance policy. One day in the hospital can lead to thousands, even tens of thousands, of dollars in charges, so that $100-per-day policy may pay for less than an hour of your 24-hour day! Daily hospitalization policies don't cover the big-ticket expenses. If you lack a comprehensive health insurance policy, make sure you get one (see Chapter 16)!

✔ **Insuring packages in the mail:** You buy a $40 gift for a friend, and when you go to the post office to ship it, the friendly postal clerk asks whether you want to insure it. For a few bucks, you think, "Why not?" The U.S. Postal Service may have a bad reputation for many reasons, but it rarely loses or damages things. Go spend your money on something else — or better yet, invest it.

✔ **Contact lens insurance:** The things that people in this country come up with to waste money on just astound me. Contact lens insurance really does exist! The money goes to replace your contacts if you lose or tear them. Lenses are cheap. Don't waste your money on this kind of insurance.

✔ **Little stuff riders:** Many policies that are worth buying, such as auto and disability insurance, can have all sorts of riders added on. These *riders* are extra bells and whistles that insurance agents and companies like to sell because of the high profit margin they provide (for *them*). On auto insurance policies, for example, you can buy a rider for a few bucks per year that pays you $25 each time your car needs to be towed. Having your vehicle towed isn't going to bankrupt you, so it isn't worth insuring against.

Likewise, small insurance policies that are sold as add-ons to bigger insurance policies are usually unnecessary and overpriced. For example, you can buy some disability insurance policies with a small amount of life insurance added on. If you need life insurance, purchasing a sufficient amount in a separate policy is less costly.

Law II: Buy broad coverage

Purchasing coverage that's too narrow is another major mistake people make when buying insurance. Such policies often seem like cheap ways to put your fears to rest. For example, instead of buying life insurance, some folks buy flight insurance at an airport self-service kiosk. They seem to worry more about their mortality when getting on an airplane than they do when getting into a car. If they die on the flight, their beneficiaries collect. But should they die the next day in an auto accident or get some dreaded disease — which is statistically far more likely than going down in a jumbo jet — the beneficiaries get nothing from flight insurance. Buy life insurance (broad coverage to protect your loved ones financially in the event of your death no matter how you die), not flight insurance (narrow coverage).

The medical equivalent of flight insurance is cancer insurance. Older people, who are fearful of having their life savings depleted by a long battle with this dreaded disease, are easy prey for this narrow insurance. If you get cancer, cancer insurance pays the bills. But what if you get heart disease, diabetes, or some other disease? Cancer insurance won't pay these costs. Purchase major medical coverage, not cancer insurance.

Recognizing fears

Fears, such as getting cancer, are natural and inescapable. Although you may not have control over the emotions that your fears invoke, you must often ignore those emotions in order to make rational insurance decisions. In other words, getting shaky in the knees and sweaty in the palms when boarding an airplane is okay, but letting your fear of flying cause you to make poor insurance decisions is not okay, especially when those decisions affect the financial security of your loved ones.

Preparing for natural disasters — insurance and otherwise

In the chapters following this one, in which I discuss specific types of insurance such as disability insurance and homeowner's insurance, I highlight the fact that you'll find it nearly impossible to get coverage that includes every possibility of catastrophe. For example, when purchasing homeowner's coverage, you find that losses from floods and earthquakes are excluded. You can secure such coverage in separate policies, which you should do if you live in an area subject to such risks (see more on this in Chapter 17). Many people don't understand these risks, and insurers don't always educate customers about such gaping holes in their policies.

Examining misperceptions of risks

How high do you think your risks are for expiring prematurely if you're exposed to toxic wastes or pesticides, or if you live in a dangerous area that has a high murder rate? Well, actually, these risks are quite small when compared to the risks you subject yourself to when you get behind the wheel of a car or light up yet another cigarette.

Reporter John Stossel (formerly with ABC News, now with FOX News) was kind enough to share with me the results of a study done for him by physicist Bernard Cohen. In the study, Cohen compared different risks. Cohen's study showed that people's riskiest behaviors are smoking and driving. Smoking whacks an average of seven years off a person's life, whereas driving a car results in a bit more than half a year of life lost, on average. Toxic waste shaves an average of one week off an American's life span.

Unfortunately, you can't buy a formal insurance policy to protect yourself against all of life's great dangers and risks. But that doesn't mean that you must face these dangers as a helpless victim; simple changes in behavior can help you improve your security.

Personal health habits are a good example of the types of behavior you can change. If you're overweight and you eat unhealthy, highly processed foods, drink alcohol excessively, and don't exercise, you're asking for trouble, especially during post-middle age. Engage in these habits, and you dramatically increase your risk of heart disease and cancer.

You can buy all the types of traditional insurance that I recommend in this book and still not be well protected for the simple reason that you're overlooking uninsurable risks. However, not being able to buy formal insurance to protect against some dangers doesn't mean that you can't drastically reduce your exposure to such risks by modifying your behavior. For example, you can't buy an auto insurance policy that protects your personal safety against drunk drivers, who are responsible for about 10,000 American deaths annually. However, you can choose to drive a safe car, practice safe driving habits, and minimize driving on the roads during the late evening hours and on major holidays when drinking is prevalent (such as New Year's Eve, July 4th, and so on).

In addition to filling those voids, also think about and plan for the nonfinancial issues that inevitably arise in a catastrophe. For example, make sure you have

- A meeting place for you and your loved ones if you're separated during a disaster (and an out-of-area person to serve as a common point of contact)

- An escape plan in the event that your area is hit with flooding or some other natural disaster (tornado, hurricane, earthquake, fire, or mudslide)

✔ The security of having taken steps to make your home safer in the event of an earthquake or fire (for instance, securing shelving and heavy objects from falling and tipping, and installing smoke detectors and fire extinguishers)

✔ A plan for what you'll do for food, clothing, and shelter should your home become uninhabitable

You get the idea. Although you can't possibly predict what's going to happen and when, you can find out about the risks of your area. In addition to buying the broadest possible coverage, you should also make contingency plans for disasters.

Law III: Shop around and buy direct

Whether you're looking at auto, home, life, disability, or other types of coverage, some companies may charge double or triple the rates that other companies charge for the same coverage. Insurers that charge the higher rates may not be better about paying claims, however. You may even end up with the worst of both possible worlds — high prices *and* lousy service.

Most insurance is sold through agents and brokers who earn commissions based on what they sell. The commissions, of course, can bias what they recommend.

Not surprisingly, policies that pay agents the biggest commissions also tend to be more costly. In fact, insurance companies compete for the attention of agents by offering bigger commissions. When I browse publications targeted to insurance agents, I often see ads in which the largest text is the commission percentage offered to agents who sell the advertiser's products.

Besides the attraction of policies that pay higher commissions, agents also get hooked, financially speaking, on companies whose policies they sell frequently. After an agent sells a certain amount of a company's insurance policies, she is rewarded with bigger commission percentages (and other perks) on any future sales. Just as airlines bribe frequent fliers with mileage bonuses, insurers bribe agents with heftier commissions and awards such as trips and costly goods.

Shopping around is a challenge not only because most insurance is sold by agents working on commission, but also because insurers set their rates in mysterious ways. Every company has a different way of analyzing how much of a risk you are; one company may offer low rates to me but not to you, and vice versa.

Despite the obstacles, several strategies exist for obtaining low-cost, high-quality policies. The following sections offer smart ways to shop for insurance. (Chapters 16 and 17 recommend how and where to get the best deals on specific types of policies.)

Looking at employer and other group plans

When you buy insurance as part of a larger group, you generally get a lower price because of the purchasing power of the group. Most of the health and disability policies that you can access through your employer are less costly than equivalent coverage you can buy on your own.

Likewise, many occupations have professional associations through which you may be able to obtain lower-cost policies. Not all associations offer better deals on insurance — compare their policy features and costs with other options.

Life insurance is an exception to the rule that states that group policies offer better value than individual policies. Group life insurance plans usually aren't cheaper than the best life insurance policies that you can buy individually. However, group policies may have the attraction of convenience (ease of enrollment and avoidance of lengthy sales pitches from life insurance salespeople). Group life insurance policies that allow you to enroll without a medical evaluation are usually more expensive, because such plans attract more people with health problems who can't get coverage on their own. If you're in good health, you should definitely shop around for life insurance (see Chapter 16 to find out how).

Insurance agents who want to sell you an individual policy can come up with 101 reasons why buying from them is preferable to buying through your employer or some other group. In most cases, agents' arguments for buying an individual policy from them include self-serving hype.

One valid issue that agents raise is that if you leave your job, you'll lose your group coverage. Sometimes that may be true. For example, if you know that you're going to be leaving your job to become self-employed, securing an individual disability policy before you leave your job makes sense. However, your employer's health insurer may allow you to buy an individual policy when you leave.

In Chapter 16, I explain what you need in the policies you're looking for so you can determine whether a group plan meets your needs. In most cases, group plans, especially through an employer, offer good benefits. So as long as the group policy is cheaper than a comparable individual policy, you'll save money overall buying through the group plan.

The straight scoop on commissions

The commission paid to an insurance agent is never disclosed through any of the documents or materials that you receive when buying insurance. The only way you can know what the commission is and how it compares with other policies is to ask the agent. Nothing is wrong or impolite about asking. After all, your money pays the commission. You need to know whether a particular policy is being pitched harder because of its higher commission.

Commissions are typically paid as a percentage of the first year's premium on the insurance policy. (Many policies pay smaller commissions on subsequent years' premiums.) With life and disability insurance policies, for example, a 50-percent commission on the first year's premium is not unusual. With life insurance policies that have a cash value, commissions of 80 to 100 percent of your first year's premium are possible. Commissions on health insurance are lower but generally not as low as commissions on auto and homeowner's insurance.

Buying insurance without paying sales commissions

Buying policies from the increasing number of companies that are selling their policies directly to the public without the insurance agent and the agent's commission is your best bet for getting a good insurance value. Just as you can purchase no-load mutual funds directly from an investment company without paying any sales commission (see Chapter 10), you also can buy no-load insurance. Be sure to read Chapters 16 and 17 for more specifics on how to buy insurance directly from insurance companies.

Annuities, investment/insurance products traditionally sold through insurance agents, are also now available directly to the customer, without commission. Simply contact some of the leading no-load mutual fund companies (see Chapter 11).

Dealing with Insurance Problems

When you seek out insurance or have insurance policies, sooner or later you're bound to hit a roadblock. Although insurance problems can be among the more frustrating in life, in the following sections, I explain how to successfully deal with the more common obstacles.

Knowing what to do if you're denied coverage

Just as you can be turned down when you apply for a loan, you can also be turned down when applying for insurance. With life or disability insurance, a company may reject you if you have an existing medical problem (a preexisting condition) and are therefore more likely to file a claim. When it comes to insuring assets such as a home, you may have difficulty getting coverage if the property is deemed to be in a high-risk area.

Here are some strategies to employ if you're denied coverage:

- **Ask the insurer why you were denied.** Perhaps the company made a mistake or misinterpreted some information that you provided in your application. If you're denied coverage because of a medical condition, find out what information the company has on you and determine whether it's accurate.

- **Request a copy of your medical information file.** Just as you have a credit report file that details your use (and misuse) of credit, you also have a medical information report. Once per year, you can request a free copy of your medical information file (which typically highlights only the more significant problems over the past seven years, not your entire medical file or history) by calling 866-692-6901 or visiting the website at www.mib.com (click on the link on the homepage for "Consumers"). If you find a mistake on your report, you have the right to request that it be fixed. However, the burden is on you to prove that the information in your file is incorrect. Proving that your file contains errors can be a major hassle — you may even need to contact physicians you saw in the past, because their medical records may be the source of the incorrect information.

- **Shop other companies.** Just because one company denies you coverage (for example, with disability or life insurance) doesn't mean all insurance companies will do the same. Some insurers better understand certain medical conditions and are more comfortable accepting applicants with those conditions. While most insurers charge higher rates to people with blemished medical histories than they do to people with perfect health records, some companies penalize them less than others. An agent who sells policies from multiple insurers, called an *independent agent,* can be helpful, because she can shop among a number of different companies.

- **Find out about state high-risk pools.** Before the passage of the Affordable Care Act (also known as Obamacare), most states acted as the insurer of last resort and provided basic insurance, through high-risk pools, for those who couldn't get it from insurance companies.

Because health insurers can no longer deny coverage due to preexisting health problems, numerous states have ended their high-risk pools. The Health Insurance Resource Center website at `www.healthinsurance.org/obamacare/risk-pools/` provides links to all state health coverage high-risk pool websites still offering such coverage. Alternatively, you can check with your state department of insurance (see the "Government" section of your local white pages) for high-risk pools for other types of insurance, such as property coverage.

✔ **Check for coverage availability before you buy.** If you're considering buying a home, for example, and you can't get coverage, the insurance companies are trying to tell you something. What they're effectively saying is "We think that property is so high-risk, we're not willing to insure it even if you pay a high premium."

Getting your due on claims

In the event that you suffer a loss and file an insurance claim, you naturally hope that your insurance company will cheerfully and expeditiously pay your claims. Given all the money that you shelled out for coverage and all the hoops you jumped through to get approved for coverage in the first place, that's a reasonable expectation.

Insurance companies may refuse to pay you what you think they owe you for many reasons, however. In some cases, your claim may not be covered under the terms of the policy. At a minimum, the insurer wants documentation and proof of your loss. Other people who have come before you have been known to cheat, so insurers won't simply take your word, no matter how honest and ethical you are.

Some insurers view paying claims as an adversarial situation and take a "negotiate tough" stance. Thinking that all insurance companies are going to pay you a fair and reasonable amount even if you don't make your voice heard is a mistake.

The tips I discuss in this section can help you ensure that you get paid what your policy entitles you to.

Documenting your assets and case

When you're insuring assets, such as your home and its contents, having a record of what you own can be helpful if you need to file a claim. The best defense is a good offense. If you keep records of valuables and can document their cost, you should be in good shape. A video is the most efficient record for documenting your assets, but a handwritten list detailing your possessions works, too. Just remember to keep this record someplace away from your home — if your home burns to the ground, you'll lose your documentation, too!

If you're robbed or are the victim of an accident, get the names, addresses, and phone numbers of witnesses. Take pictures of property damage and solicit estimates for the cost of repairing or replacing whatever has been lost or damaged. File police reports when appropriate, if for no other reason than to bolster your documentation for the insurance claim.

Preparing your case

Filing a claim should be viewed the same way as preparing for a court trial or an IRS audit. Any information you provide verbally or in writing can and will be used against you to deny your claim. First, you should understand whether your policy covers your claim (this is why getting the broadest possible coverage helps). Unfortunately, the only way to find out whether the policy covers your claim is to read it. Policies are hard to read because they use legal language in non-user-friendly ways.

A possible alternative to reading your policy is to call the claims department and, *without* providing your name (and using caller ID blocking on your phone if you're calling from home), ask a representative whether a particular loss (such as the one that you just suffered) is covered under its policy. You have no need to lie to the company, but you don't have to tell the representative who you are and that you're about to file a claim, either. Your call is so you can understand what your policy covers. However, some companies aren't willing to provide detailed information unless a specific case is cited.

After you initiate the claims process, keep records of all conversations and copies of all the documents you give to the insurer's claims department. If you have problems down the road, this "evidence" may bail you out.

For property damage, get at least a couple of reputable contractors' estimates. Demonstrate to the insurance company that you're trying to shop for a low price, but don't agree to use a low-cost contractor without knowing that she can do quality work.

Approaching your claim as a negotiation

To get what you're owed on an insurance claim, you must approach most claims' filings for what they are — a negotiation with a party that's often uncooperative. And the bigger the claim, the more your insurer will play the part of adversary.

A number of years ago, when I filed a homeowner's insurance claim after a major rain and wind storm significantly damaged my backyard fence, I was greeted on a weekday by a perky, smiley adjuster. When the adjuster entered my yard and started to peruse the damage, her demeanor changed dramatically. She had a combative, hard-bargainer type attitude that I last witnessed when I worked on some labor-management negotiations during my days as a consultant.

The adjuster stood on my back porch, a good distance away from the fences that had been blown over by wind and crushed by two large trees, and said that my insurer preferred to repair damaged fences rather than replace them. "With your deductible of $1,000, I doubt this will be worth filing a claim for," she said.

The fence that had blown over, she reasoned, could have new posts set in concrete. Because we had already begun to clean up some of the damage for safety reasons, I presented to her some pictures of what the yard looked like right after the storm; she refused to take them. She took some measurements and said that she'd have her settlement check to us in a couple of days. The settlement she faxed was for $1,119 — nowhere near what it would cost me to fix the damage that was done.

Practicing persistency

When you take an insurance company's first offer and don't fight for what you're due, you may be leaving a lot of money on the table. To make my long fence-repair story somewhat shorter, after *five* rounds of haggling with the adjusters, supervisors, and finally managers, I was awarded payment to replace the fences and clean up most of the damage. Even though all the contractors I contacted recommended that the work be done this way, the insurance adjuster discredited their recommendations by saying, "Contractors try to jack up the price and recommended work once they know an insurer is involved."

My final total settlement came to $4,888, more than $3,700 higher than the insurer's first offer. Interestingly, my insurer backed off its preference for repairing the fence when the contractor's estimates for doing that work exceeded the cost of a new fence.

I was disappointed with the behavior of that insurance company. I know from conversations with others that my homeowner's insurance company (at that time) was not unusual in its adversarial strategy, especially with larger claims. And to think that this insurer at the time had one of the better track records for paying claims!

Enlisting support

If you're doing your homework and you're not making progress with the insurer's adjuster, ask to speak with supervisors and managers. This is the strategy I used to get the additional $3,700 needed to get things back to where they were before the storm.

When insurers (and government) move slowly

When Hurricane Katrina caused unprecedented damage and loss along the Gulf Coast, I received many complaints from folks in that region. Typical is the following note I received from a New Orleans family more than three months after Hurricane Katrina:

"We had substantial damage to our home in New Orleans due to Hurricane Katrina. We had roof damage on August 29th and three feet of water August 31st. Our flood insurance is through an insurance company acting as an agent for FEMA's program. Our adjuster has still not turned in the necessary paperwork for our claim. Our home insurer made no allowance for proper removal and disposal of asbestos shingles and we have gotten just $2,000 for living expenses out of the $21,000 we're now owed. We have just gotten a first partial payment ($40,000 out of $160,000) on the flood insurance, but it was made out to the wrong mortgage company so we had to send the check back.

"It is shocking that it has gone on this long. It has been all over the papers about the delay of some flood insurance payments being due to FEMA not having adequate money in the till. There's no doubt the insurers are overwhelmed, but why is this taking so long? I called the Louisiana Department of Insurance and was told that insurers normally have 30 days for claims according to the insurance department (who has said they can have 45 days in this case). It's been over 60 days since the adjuster came out to our home."

Stories like this make me disappointed and mad. There's simply no excuse for large insurance companies who are in the business of insuring for such events not to bring the proper resources to bear to make timely payments. The fact that they did not do so for Gulf Coast victims is even more reprehensible given the widespread problems in that area. In addition to home losses, many people also had job losses to deal with and could ill afford to be without money. Large insurers that wrote flood policies for which FEMA temporarily lacked money should have paid their policyholders. Although the federal government and FEMA officials should have been taken to task for allowing FEMA's accounts to run dry, customer-service-oriented insurers should have stepped up and advanced money that they knew would eventually come from FEMA.

In situations like this, if you do your homework and you're not making progress with the insurer's adjuster, ask to speak with supervisors and managers. If you're having problems getting a fair and timely settlement from the insurer, try contacting your state's department of insurance. This person who wrote me was from Louisiana, where the state department of insurance had more than 1,600 hurricane-related complaints in the first three months after Hurricane Katrina. To my surprise, the department's Director of Public Information told me that no insurance companies had been fined and penalized for delaying payments. It's no wonder these companies weren't getting on the stick!

The agent who sold you the policy may be helpful in preparing and filing the claim. A good agent can help increase your chances of getting paid — and getting paid sooner. If you're having difficulty with a claim for a policy obtained through your employer or other group, speak with the benefits department or a person responsible for interacting with the insurer. These folks have a lot of clout, because the agent and/or insurer doesn't want to lose the entire account.

If you're having problems getting a fair settlement from the insurer of a policy you bought on your own, try contacting the state department of insurance. You can find the phone number in the "Government" section of the white pages of your phone book or possibly in your insurance policy, or you can peruse the list at the National Association of Insurance Commissioners website at www.naic.org (click on the link for "States and Jurisdictions" on its home page to find links to department of insurance websites for each state).

Hiring a public adjuster who, for a percentage of the payment (typically 5 to 10 percent), can negotiate with insurers on your behalf is another option.

When all else fails and you have a major claim at stake, try contacting an attorney who specializes in insurance matters. You can find these specialists in the yellow pages under "Attorneys — Insurance Law" or enter those terms and your city into a search engine. Expect to pay $100+ per hour. Look for a lawyer who's willing to negotiate on your behalf, help draft letters, and perform other necessary tasks on an hourly basis without filing a lawsuit. Your state department of insurance, the local bar association, or other legal, accounting, or financial practitioners also may be able to refer you to someone.

Chapter 16

Insurance on You: Life, Disability, and Health

In This Chapter

▶ Looking into life insurance

▶ Debating disability insurance

▶ Selecting the best health insurance

During your working years, multiplying your typical annual income by the number of years you plan to continue working produces a pretty big number. That dollar amount equals what is probably your most valuable asset — your ability to earn an income. You need to protect this asset by purchasing some insurance on *you*.

This chapter explains the ins and outs of buying insurance to protect your income: life insurance in case of death, and disability insurance in case of an accident or severe medical condition that prevents you from working. I tell you what coverage you should have, where to look for it, and what to avoid.

In addition to protecting your income, you also need to insure against financially catastrophic expenses. I'm not talking about January's credit-card bill — you're on your own with that one. I'm talking about the type of bills that are racked up from a major surgery and a multi-week stay in the hospital. To protect yourself from potentially astronomical medical bills, you need to have comprehensive health insurance.

Providing for Your Loved Ones: Life Insurance

You generally need life insurance only when other people depend on your income. The following folks don't need life insurance to protect their incomes:

- Single people with no children
- Working couples who could maintain a lifestyle acceptable to them on one of their incomes
- Independently wealthy people who don't need to work
- Retired people who are living off their retirement nest egg
- Minor children (are you financially dependent upon your children?)

If others are either fully or partly dependent on your paycheck (usually a spouse and/or child), you need life insurance, especially if you have major financial commitments such as a mortgage or years of child-rearing ahead. You may also want to consider life insurance if an extended family member is currently or likely to be dependent on your future income.

Determining how much life insurance to buy

Determining how much life insurance to buy is as much a subjective decision as it is a quantitative decision. I've seen some worksheets that are incredibly long and tedious (some rivaling your tax returns). There's no need to get fancy. If you're like me, your eyes start to glaze over if you have to complete 20-plus lines of calculations. Figuring out how much life insurance you need doesn't have to be that complicated.

The main purpose of life insurance is to provide a lump sum payment to replace the deceased person's income. Ask yourself how many years of income you want to replace. Table 16-1 provides a simple way to figure how much life insurance to consider purchasing. To replace a certain number of years' worth of income, simply multiply the appropriate number in the table by your annual after-tax income.

Table 16-1	Life Insurance Calculation
Years of Income to Replace	*Multiply Annual After-Tax Income* By*
5	4.5
10	8.5
20	15
30	20

* Roughly determine your annual after-tax income in one of two ways: Get out last year's tax return (and Form W-2) and subtract the federal, state, and Social Security taxes you paid from your gross employment income; or multiply your gross income by 80 percent if you're a low-income earner, 70 percent if you're a moderate-income earner, or 60 percent if you're a high-income earner.

Another way to determine the amount of life insurance to buy is to think about how much would be needed to pay for major debts or expenditures, such as your mortgage, other loans, and college for your children. For example, suppose you want your spouse to have enough of a life insurance death benefit to pay off your mortgage and half of your children's college education. Simply add your mortgage amount to half of your children's estimated college costs (see Chapter 13 for approximate numbers) and then buy that amount of life insurance.

Social Security, if you're covered, can provide survivors benefits to your spouse and children. However, if your surviving spouse is working and earning even a modest amount of money, he or she is going to get few, if any, survivors benefits. Prior to reaching Social Security's "full retirement age" (see Chapter 4), your survivors benefits get reduced by $1 for every $2 you earn above $14,640 (in 2012).

This income threshold is higher if you reach full retirement age during the year. For example, the Social Security benefits for those reaching full retirement age during 2012 are reduced by $1 for each $3 they earn above $38,880 until the month in which they reach full retirement age. Beginning the month you reach your full retirement age, there's no limit on your earnings if you're collecting survivors benefits.

If either you or your spouse anticipates earning a low enough income to qualify for survivors benefits, you may want to factor your Social Security survivors benefits into how much life insurance to buy. Contact the Social Security Administration by phone at 800-772-1213 or visit its website at www.ssa.gov to estimate your benefits.

Examining "other" life insurance

Contemplating the possibility of your untimely demise is surely depressing. You'll likely feel some peace of mind when purchasing a life insurance policy to provide for your dependents. However, I suggest you take things a step further. Suppose you (or your spouse) pass away. Do you think that simply buying a life insurance policy will be sufficient "help" for the loved ones you leave behind? Surely your contribution to your household involves far more than being a breadwinner.

Do you have a will? See Chapter 17 for more details on wills and other estate-planning documents. Make sure all your important financial documents — investment account statements, insurance policies, employee benefits materials, small-business accounting records, and so on — are kept in one place (such as a file drawer) that your loved ones know about. You may also want to consider providing a list of key contacts — such as

who you recommend calling (or what you recommend reading) in the event of legal, financial, or tax quandaries.

So, in addition to trying to provide financially for your dependents, you should also take some time to reflect on what else you can do to help point them in the right direction on matters you normally handle. With most couples, it's natural for one spouse to take more responsibility for money management. That's fine; just make sure to talk about what's being done so that in the event that the responsible spouse dies, the surviving person knows how to jump into the driver's seat.

If you have kids (and even if you don't), you may want to give some thought to sentimental leave-behinds for your loved ones. These leave-behinds can be something like a short note telling them how much they meant to you and what you'd like them to remember about you.

The Social Security Administration can tell you how much your survivors would receive per month in the event of your death. You should factor this benefit into the amount of life insurance that you calculate in Table 16-1. For example, suppose your annual after-tax income is $25,000 and Social Security provides a survivors benefit of $10,000 annually. Therefore, for the purposes of Table 16-1, you should determine the amount of life insurance needed to replace $15,000 annually ($25,000 – $10,000), not $25,000.

Comparing term life insurance to cash value life insurance

I'm going to tell you how you can save hours of time and thousands of dollars. Ready? *Buy term life insurance.* (An exception is if you have a high net worth — several million bucks or more — in which case you may want to *consider* other options. See the estate-planning section in Chapter 17.) If you've already figured out how much life insurance to purchase and this is all the advice you need, you can jump to the "Buying term insurance" section that follows.

If you want the details behind my recommendation for term insurance, the following information is for you. Or maybe you've heard (and have already fallen prey to) the sales pitches from life insurance agents, most of whom love selling cash value life insurance because of its huge commissions.

Despite the variety of names that life insurance marketing departments have cooked up for policies, life insurance comes in two basic flavors:

- ✔ **Term insurance:** This insurance is pure life insurance. You pay an annual premium for which you receive a particular amount of life insurance coverage. If you, the insured person, pass away, your beneficiaries collect; otherwise, the premium is gone, but you're grateful to be alive!

- ✔ **Cash value insurance:** All other life insurance policies (whole, universal, variable, and so on) combine life insurance with a supposed savings feature. Not only do your premiums pay for life insurance, but some of your dollars are also credited to an account that grows in value over time, assuming you keep paying your premiums. On the surface, this type of insurance sounds potentially attractive. People don't like to feel that their premium dollars are getting tossed away.

But cash value insurance has a big catch. For the same amount of coverage (for example, for $100,000 of life insurance benefits), cash value policies cost you about eight times (800 percent) more than comparable term policies.

Insurance salespeople know the buttons to push to interest you in buying the wrong kind of life insurance. In the following sections, I give you some of the typical arguments they make for purchasing cash value polices, followed by my perspective on each one.

"Cash value policies are all paid up after X years. You don't want to be paying life insurance premiums for the rest of your life, do you?"

Agents who pitch cash value life insurance present projections that imply that after the first ten or so years of paying your premiums, you don't need to pay more premiums to keep the life insurance in force. The only reason you may be able to stop paying premiums is because you poured a lot of extra money into the policy in the early years. Remember that cash value life insurance costs about eight times as much as term insurance.

Imagine that you're currently paying $500 a year for auto insurance and that an insurance company comes along and offers you a policy for $4,000 per year. The representative tells you that after ten years, you can stop paying and still keep your same coverage. I'm sure you wouldn't fall for this sales tactic, but many people do when they buy cash value life insurance.

You also need to be wary of the projections, because they often include unrealistic and lofty assumptions about the investment return that your cash balance can earn. When you stop paying into a cash value policy, the cost of each year's life insurance is deducted from the remaining cash value. If the rate of return on the cash balance is not sufficient to pay the insurance cost, the cash balance declines, and eventually you receive notices saying that your policy needs more funding to keep the life insurance in force.

"You won't be able to afford term insurance when you're older."

As you get older, the cost of term insurance increases because the risk of dying rises. But life insurance is not something you need all your life! It's typically bought in a person's younger years when financial commitments and obligations outweigh financial assets. Twenty or thirty years later, the reverse should be true — if you use the principles in this book!

When you retire, you don't need life insurance to protect your employment income, because there isn't any to protect! You may need life insurance when you're raising a family and/or you have a substantial mortgage to pay off, but by the time you retire, the kids should be out on their own (you hope!), and the mortgage should be paid down.

In the meantime, term insurance saves you a tremendous amount of money. For most people, it takes 20 to 30 years for the premium they're paying on a term insurance policy to finally catch up to (equal) the premium they've been paying all along on a comparable amount of cash value life insurance.

"You can borrow against the cash value at a low interest rate."

Such a deal! It's your money in the policy, remember? If you deposited money in a savings or money-market account, how would you like to pay for the privilege of borrowing your own money back? Borrowing on your cash value policy is potentially dangerous: You increase the chances that the policy will lapse — leaving you with nothing to show for your premiums.

"Your cash value grows tax-deferred."

Ah, a glimmer of truth at last. The cash value portion of your policy grows without taxation until you withdraw it, but if you want tax-deferral of your investment balances, you should first take advantage of funding 401(k)s, 403(b)s, SEP-IRAs, and other tax-advantaged retirement accounts. Such accounts give you an immediate tax deduction for your current contributions in addition to growth without taxation until withdrawal.

The money you pay into a cash value life policy gives you no upfront tax deductions. If you exhaust the tax-deductible plans, consider a Roth IRA and then variable annuities, which provide access to better investment options and tax-deferred compounding of your investment dollars. Roth IRAs have the added bonus of tax-free withdrawal of your investment earnings. (See Chapter 11 for details on retirement accounts.)

Life insurance tends to be a mediocre investment at best. The insurance company generally quotes you an interest rate for the first year; after that, the company changes the rate annually. If you don't like the future interest rates, you can be penalized for quitting the policy. Would you ever invest your money in a bank account that quoted an interest rate for the first year and then penalized you for moving your money within the next seven to ten years?

"Cash value policies are forced savings."

Many agents argue that a cash value plan is better than nothing — at least it's forcing you to save. This line of thinking is silly because so many people drop cash value life insurance policies after just a few years of paying into them. You can accomplish "forced savings" without using life insurance. Any of the retirement savings accounts mentioned in Chapter 11 can be set up for automatic monthly transfers. Employers offering such a plan can deduct contributions from your paycheck — and they don't take a commission! You can also set up monthly electronic transfers from your bank checking account to contribute to mutual funds (see Chapter 10).

"Life insurance is not part of your taxable estate."

If the ownership of a life insurance policy is properly structured, the death benefit is free of estate taxes. This part of the sales pitch is about the only sound reasoning that exists for buying cash value life insurance. Under current federal laws, you can pass on $5 million free of federal estate taxes. But even if you have that large of a nest egg, you have numerous other ways to reduce your taxable estate (see Chapter 17).

Making your decision

Insurance salespeople aggressively push cash value policies because of the high commissions that insurance companies pay them. Commissions on cash value life insurance range from 50 to 100 percent of your first year's premium. An insurance salesperson, therefore, can make *eight to ten times more money* (yes, you read that right) selling you a cash value policy than he can selling you term insurance.

Ultimately, when you purchase cash value life insurance, you pay the high commissions that are built into these policies. As you can see in the policy's cash value table, you don't get back any of the money that you dump into the policy if you quit the policy in the first few years. The insurance company can't afford to give you any of your money back in those early years because so much of it has been paid to the selling agent as commission. That's why these policies explicitly penalize you for withdrawing your cash balance within the first seven to ten years.

Because of the high cost of cash value policies relative to the cost of term, you're more likely to buy less life insurance coverage than you need — that's the sad part of the insurance industry's pushing of this stuff. *The vast majority of life insurance buyers need more protection than they can afford to buy with cash value coverage.*

Cash value life insurance is the most oversold insurance and financial product in the history of the financial services industry. Cash value life insurance makes sense for a small percentage of people, such as small-business owners who own a business worth at least several million dollars and don't want their heirs to be forced to sell their business to pay estate taxes in the event of their death. (See "Considering the purchase of cash value life insurance" later in this chapter.)

Purchase low-cost term insurance and do your investing separately. Life insurance is rarely a permanent need; over time, you can reduce the amount of term insurance you carry as your financial obligations lessen and you accumulate more assets.

Buying term insurance

Term insurance policies have several features from which to choose. I cover the important elements of term insurance in this section so you can make an informed decision about purchasing it.

Selecting how often your premium adjusts

Term insurance can be purchased so your premium adjusts (increases) annually or after 5, 10, 15, or 20 years. The less frequently your premium adjusts, the higher the initial premium and its incremental increases will be. (Remember, as you get older, the risk of dying increases, so the cost of your insurance goes up.)

The advantage of a premium that locks in for, say, 15 years is that you have the security of knowing how much you'll be paying annually for the next 15 years. You also don't need to go through medical evaluations as frequently to qualify for the lowest rate possible. The disadvantage of a policy with a long-term rate lock is that you pay more in the early years than you do on a policy that adjusts more frequently. In addition, you may want to change the amount of insurance you carry as your circumstances change. Thus, you may throw money away when you dump a policy with a long-term premium guarantee before its rate is set to change.

Policies that adjust the premium every five to ten years offer a happy medium between price and predictability.

Ensuring guaranteed renewability

Guaranteed renewability, which is standard practice on the better policies, assures that the policy can't be canceled because of poor health. Don't buy a life insurance policy without this feature unless you expect that your life insurance needs will disappear when the policy is up for renewal.

Deciding where to buy term insurance

A number of sound ways to obtain high-quality, low-cost term insurance are available. You may choose to buy through a local agent because you know him or prefer to buy from someone close to home. However, you should invest a few minutes of your time getting quotes from one or two of the following sources to get a sense of what's available in the insurance market. Gaining familiarity with the market can prevent an agent from selling you an overpriced, high-commission policy.

Here are some sources for high-quality, low-cost term insurance:

- **USAA:** This company sells low-cost term insurance directly to the public. Contact USAA by phone at 800-531-8722 or visit `www.usaa.com/inet/pages/insurance_life_main?wa_ref=pub_global_products_ins_life`.

- **Insurance agency quotation services:** These services provide proposals from the highest-rated, lowest-cost companies available. Like other agencies, the services receive a commission if you buy a policy from them, which you're under no obligation to do. They ask questions such as your date of birth, whether you smoke, some basic health questions, and how much coverage you want. Services that are worth considering include

  - **AccuQuote:** Phone 800-442-9899; website `www.accuquote.com`

  - **ReliaQuote:** Phone 800-940-3002; website `www.reliaquote.com`

  - **Term4Sale:** Phone 888-798-3488; website `www.term4sale.com` (this company doesn't sell life insurance but can refer you to agents who do)

See Chapter 19 for information on how to use your computer when making life insurance decisions.

Considering the purchase of cash value life insurance

Don't expect to get objective information from anyone who sells cash value life insurance. Beware of insurance salespeople masquerading under the guise of self-anointed titles, such as estate-planning specialists or financial planners.

As I discuss earlier in the chapter, purchasing cash value life insurance may make sense if you expect to have an estate-tax "problem." However, cash value life insurance is just one of many ways to reduce your estate taxes (see the section on estate planning in Chapter 17).

Among the best places to shop for cash value life insurance policies are

- ✔ **USAA:** Phone 800-531-8722; website www.usaa.com/inet/pages/insurance_life_main?wa_ref=pub_global_products_ins_life

- ✔ **Ameritas Direct:** Phone 800-555-4655; website www.ameritasdirect.com

If you want to obtain some cash value life insurance, tread carefully with local insurance agents. Most agents aren't as interested in educating as they are in selling. Besides, the best cash value policies can be obtained commission-free when you buy them from the sources in the preceding list. The money saved on commissions (which can easily be thousands of dollars) is reflected in a much higher cash value for you.

Getting rid of cash value life insurance

If you were snookered into buying a cash value life insurance policy and you want to part ways with it, go ahead and do so. *But don't cancel the coverage until you first secure new term coverage.* When you need life insurance, you don't want to have a period when you're not covered (Murphy's Law says *that's* when disaster will strike).

Ending a cash value life insurance policy has tax consequences. You generally must pay federal income tax on the amount you receive in excess of the premiums you paid over the life of the policy. Because some life insurance policies feature tax-deferred retirement savings, you may incur a 10-percent federal income tax penalty on earnings withdrawn before age 59½, just as you would with an IRA. Before withdrawing the cash balance in your life insurance policy, consider checking with the insurer or a tax advisor to clarify what the tax consequences may be.

You can avoid federal income tax early withdrawal penalties and side-step taxation on accumulated interest in a life insurance policy by doing a tax-free exchange (also known as a section 1035 exchange) into a no-load (commission-free) variable annuity. The no-load mutual-fund company through which you buy the annuity takes care of transferring your existing balance. (See Chapter 12 for more information about annuities.)

Preparing for the Unpredictable: Disability Insurance

As with life insurance, the purpose of disability insurance is to protect your income. The only difference is that with disability insurance, you're protecting the income for yourself (and perhaps also your dependents). If you're completely disabled, you still have living expenses, but you probably can't earn employment income.

I'm referring to long-term disabilities. If you strain your back while reliving your athletic glory days and you wind up in bed for a couple weeks, it likely won't be a financial disaster. But what if you were disabled in such a way that you couldn't work for several years? This section helps you figure out whether you need disability insurance, how much to get, and where to find it.

Deciding whether you need coverage

Most large employers offer disability insurance to their employees. Many small-company employees and all self-employed people are left to fend for themselves without disability coverage. Being without disability insurance is a risky proposition, especially if, like most working people, you need your employment income to live on.

If you're married and your spouse earns a large enough income that you can make do without yours, consider skipping disability coverage. The same is true if you've already accumulated enough money for your future years (in other words, you're financially independent). Keep in mind, though, that your expenses may go up if you become disabled and require specialized care.

For most people, dismissing the need for disability coverage is easy. The odds of suffering a long-term disability seem so remote — and they are. But if you suffer bad luck, disability coverage can relieve you (and possibly your family) of a major financial burden.

Most disabilities are caused by medical problems, such as arthritis, heart conditions, hypertension, and back/spine or hip/leg impairments. Some of these ailments occur with advancing age, but more than one-third of all disabilities are suffered by people under the age of 45. The vast majority of these medical problems cannot be predicted in advance, particularly those caused by random accidents.

If you think you have good disability coverage through government programs, you'd better think again:

- ✔ **Social Security disability:** Social Security pays long-term benefits only if you're not able to perform any substantial, gainful activity for more than a year or if your disability is expected to result in death. Furthermore, Social Security disability payments are quite low because they're intended to provide only for basic, subsistence-level living expenses.

- ✔ **Workers' compensation:** Workers' compensation (if you have such coverage through your employer) pays you benefits if you're injured on the job, but it doesn't pay any benefits if you get disabled away from your job. You need coverage that pays regardless of where and how you're disabled.

- ✔ **State disability programs:** Some states have disability insurance programs, but the coverage is typically bare bones. State programs are also generally not a good value because of the cost for the small amount of coverage they provide. Benefits are paid over a short period of time (rarely more than a year).

Determining how much disability insurance you need

You need enough disability coverage to provide you with sufficient income to live on until other financial resources become available. If you don't have much saved in the way of financial assets and you want to continue with the lifestyle supported by your current income if you suffer a disability, get disability coverage to replace your entire monthly take-home (after-tax) pay.

The benefits you purchase on a disability policy are quoted as the dollars per month you receive if disabled. So if your job provides you with a $3,000-per-month income after taxes, seek a policy that provides a $3,000-per-month benefit.

If you pay for your disability insurance, the benefits are tax-free (but hopefully you won't ever have to collect them). If your employer picks up the tab, your benefits are taxable, so you need a larger benefit amount.

In addition to the monthly coverage amount, you also need to select the duration for which you want a policy to pay you benefits. You need a policy that pays benefits until you reach an age at which you become financially self-sufficient. For most people, that's around age 65 to 67, when their Social Security benefits kick in. If you anticipate needing your employment income past your mid-60s, you may want to obtain disability coverage that pays you until a later age.

If you crunch some numbers (see Chapter 3) and find that you're within five to ten years of being financially independent or able to retire, five-year and ten-year disability policies are available. You may also consider such short-term policies when you're sure that someone (for example, a family member) can support you financially over the long-term.

Identifying other features you need in disability insurance

Disability insurance policies have many confusing features. Here's what to look for — and look out for — when purchasing disability insurance:

- **Definition of disability:** An *own-occupation* disability policy provides benefit payments if you can't perform the work you normally do. Some policies pay you only if you're unable to perform a job for which you are *reasonably trained.* Other policies revert to this definition after a few years of being own-occupation. Own-occupation policies are the most expensive because there's a greater chance that the insurer will have to pay you. The extra cost may not be worth it unless you're in a high-income or specialized occupation and you'd have to take a significant pay cut to do something else (and you wouldn't be happy about a reduced income and the required lifestyle changes).

- **Noncancelable and guaranteed renewable:** These features ensure that your policy can't be canceled because of your falling into poor health. With policies that require periodic physical exams, you can lose your coverage just when you're most likely to need it.

- **Waiting period:** This is the "deductible" on disability insurance — the time between the onset of your disability and the time you begin collecting benefits. As with other types of insurance, you should take the highest deductible (longest waiting period) that your financial circumstances allow. The waiting period significantly reduces the cost of the insurance and eliminates the hassle of filing a claim for a short-term disability. The minimum waiting period on most policies is 30 days. The maximum waiting period can be up to one to two years. Try a waiting period of three to six months if you have sufficient emergency reserves.

✔ **Residual benefits:** This option pays you a partial benefit if you have a disability that prevents you from working full-time.

✔ **Cost-of-living adjustments (COLAs):** This feature automatically increases your benefit payment by a set percentage annually or in accordance with changes in inflation. The advantage of a COLA is that it retains the purchasing power of your benefits. A modest COLA, such as 3 to 4 percent, is worth considering.

✔ **Future insurability:** A clause that many agents encourage you to buy, future insurability allows you to buy additional coverage regardless of health. For most people, paying for the privilege of buying more coverage later is not worth it if the income you earn today fairly reflects your likely long-term earnings (except for cost-of-living increases). You may benefit from the future insurability option if your income is artificially low now and you're confident that it will rise significantly in the future. (For example, you just got out of medical school and you're earning a low salary while being a resident.)

✔ **Insurer's financial stability:** As I discuss in Chapter 15, you should choose insurers that'll be here tomorrow to pay your claim. But don't get too hung up on the stability of the company; benefits are paid even if the insurer fails, because the state or another insurer will almost always bail out the unstable insurer.

Deciding where to buy disability insurance

The place to buy disability insurance with the best value is through your employer or professional association. Unless these groups have done a lousy job shopping for coverage, group plans generally offer a better value than disability insurance you can purchase on your own. Just make sure that the group plan meets the specifications discussed in the preceding section, especially any limitations of benefit amounts or stricter qualification terms, which are found on some group plans.

Don't trust an insurance agent to be enthusiastic about the quality of a disability policy your employer or other group is offering. Agents have a conflict of interest when they criticize these options, because they won't make a commission if you buy through a group.

If you don't have access to a group policy, check with your agent or a company you already do business with. But tread carefully when purchasing disability insurance through an agent. Some agents try to load down your policy with all sorts of extra bells and whistles to pump up the premium along with their commission.

If you buy disability insurance through an agent, consider *list billing,* where you sign up with several other people for coverage at the same time and are invoiced together for your coverage (if done through an employer, exercise care to ensure you aren't running afoul of employee benefit rules/laws set down by ERISA). It can knock up to 15 percent off an insurer's standard prices. Ask your insurance agent how list billing works.

Getting the Care You Need: Health Insurance

Almost everyone needs health insurance, but not everyone has it. Some people in the past were denied coverage or couldn't afford the coverage they were offered. Other people who could afford health insurance chose not to buy it because they believed that they were healthy and weren't going to need it. Others who opted not to buy health insurance figured that if they ever really needed healthcare, they'd get it even if they couldn't pay. To a large extent, they're right. People without health insurance generally put off getting routine care, which can lead to small problems turning into bigger and costlier ones.

Mandating health insurance: The Affordable Care Act (Obamacare)

Health insurance coverage in the United States is now generally mandatory, and if you don't have it, you can face hefty tax fines.

In March 2010, President Obama signed into law the Patient Protection and Affordable Care Act and the Health Care and Education Reconciliation Act. Together, these two laws enacted comprehensive healthcare reform in the United States.

Now, employer group health plans are subject to these rules:

✔ Plans offering dependent coverage must offer coverage to adult children up to age 26. The coverage isn't taxable to the employee or dependent.

✔ Plans must provide preventive care without cost-sharing and must cover certain child preventive care services as recommended by the government. This rule applies only to new group health plans.

- ✔ Employers must offer minimum essential coverage to full-time employees or make nondeductible payments to the government.

- ✔ Plans must remove all annual dollar limits on participants' benefit payments. They may not impose lifetime limits.

- ✔ Plans must limit cost-sharing and deductibles to levels that don't exceed those applicable to a health-savings-account-eligible, high-deductible health plan. (Such plans currently have a $1,300 individual and $2,600 family minimum deductible.)

- ✔ Plans must remove all preexisting condition exclusions on all participants.

- ✔ Plans may not have waiting periods of longer than 90 days.

You face stiff penalties for not getting coverage per the new laws in the Affordable Care Act. If you don't have a qualified health plan, you have to pay a penalty fee on your tax return. The penalty fee in 2016 is $695 per adult and $347.50 per child (up to $2,085.00) or 2.5 percent of annual income, whichever is greater. Ouch!

Higher income taxpayers are now hit with higher tax rates on their investments as well as higher Medicare tax rates to help pay for Obamacare. Taxpayers with total taxable income above $200,000 (for a single return) or $250,000 (for a joint return) from any source are subject to a 3.8 percent tax on the *lesser* of the following:

- ✔ Their net investment income (for example, interest, dividends, and capital gains)

- ✔ The amount, if any, by which their modified adjusted gross income exceeds the dollar thresholds

Taxpayers with earned income above $200,000 (for a single return) or $250,000 (for a joint return) are subject to an additional 0.9 percent Medicare tax (in other words, rising from 1.45 percent to 2.35 percent) on wages in excess of those amounts. Employers aren't required to match the payment of this incremental increase, which is applicable only to the employee.

Also, individual taxpayers seeking to claim an itemized income tax deduction for medical expenses are now only able to deduct only the portion of such expenses in excess of 10 percent of their adjusted gross income, up from the previous level of 7.5 percent of income. (This change is deferred to 2017 for those people age 65 and over.)

Opting out of Obamacare?

Soon after Obamacare began to be implemented, millions of folks (me included) who had individual health insurance policies had their policies canceled, regardless of whether they wanted to keep them, because the policies didn't meet the new guidelines. To add insult to injury, many folks found that the "replacement" policies they were forced to buy to comply with the Affordable Care Act were much more expensive because of the mandated benefits and the cost of including people with preexisting health problems in the costs for coverage.

Some were and are tempted not to replace their lost coverage. Others who had previously chosen to go without coverage were in no great hurry to buy the higher-cost plans now available. However, people without health insurance face penalties when it comes time to file their taxes.

Now, some folks reason that it may be advantageous to just pay the penalty if that ends up being cheaper than paying for a high-cost policy with bells and whistles you don't want. Anecdotal evidence suggests some folks are taking the approach "If I get sick, then I'll get insurance because people with preexisting conditions can't be turned down."

One problem with this strategy is that now you can purchase subsidized health insurance (barring special circumstances, such as the birth of a baby) only during the open enrollment period — between November 1st and January 31st. If you miss that window and get diagnosed with a serious illness, say, in July, you have to wait many months to buy coverage on the government exchanges. (You can purchase a policy outside the exchange, but banking on the ability to get insured quickly enough is risky. A major car accident or illness can happen too quickly to allow you to buy a policy. The medical bills you'd rack up almost overnight could be devastating.)

There is an exception for a so-called special enrollment period, which the federal government defines as

> "A time outside of the open enrollment period during which you and your family have a right to sign up for health coverage. In the Marketplace, you qualify for a special enrollment period 60 days following certain life events that involve a change in family status (for example, marriage or birth of a child) or loss of other health coverage. Job-based plans must provide a special enroll-ment period of 30 days."

A number of "hardship exemptions" can enable you to avoid the Obamacare tax penalty. Examples requiring documentation include the recent death of a close family member; your being unable to pay medical expenses in the previous 24 months; and your experiencing unexpected increases in necessary expenses due to caring for an ill, disabled, or aging family member, among others. Interestingly, one of the exemptions is for having your current health plan canceled and finding the replacement plans "unaffordable." And here's another: "You experienced another hardship in finding health insurance" for which you're told, "Please submit documentation if possible." This last one sounds pretty broad to me and could include issues such as not being able to see specific doctors you desire because they aren't in the plans being offered.

Choosing the best health plan

Before Medicare (the government-run insurance program for the elderly) kicks in at age 65+, odds are that you'll obtain your health insurance through your employer. Be thankful if you do. Employer-provided coverage eliminates the headache of having to shop for coverage, and it's usually cheaper than coverage you buy on your own.

Whether you have options through your employer or you have to hunt for a plan on your own, the following sections cover the major issues to consider when selecting among the health insurance offerings in the marketplace.

Major medical coverage

You need a plan that covers the *big* potential expenses: hospitalization, physician, and ancillary charges, such as X-rays and laboratory work. If you're a woman and you think that you may want to have children, make sure your plan has maternity benefits.

Choice of healthcare providers

Plans that allow you to use any healthcare provider you want are becoming less common and more expensive in most areas. Health maintenance organizations (HMOs) and preferred provider organizations (PPOs) are the main plans that restrict your choices. They keep costs down because they negotiate lower rates with selected providers.

HMOs and PPOs are more similar than they are different. The main difference is that PPOs still pay the majority of your expenses if you use a provider outside their approved list. If you use a provider outside the approved list with an HMO, you typically aren't covered at all.

If you have your heart set on particular physicians or hospitals, find out which health insurance plans they accept as payment. Ask yourself whether the extra cost of an open-choice plan is worth being able to use their services if they're not part of a restricted-choice plan. Also be aware that some plans allow you to go outside their network of providers as long as you pay a bigger portion of the incurred medical costs. If you're interested in being able to use alternative types of providers, such as acupuncturists, find out whether the plans you're considering cover these services.

Don't let stories of how hard it is to get an appointment with a doctor or other logistical hassles deter you from going with an HMO or PPO plan. These things can happen in plans with open choice, too. The idea that doctors who can't get patients on their own are the only ones who sign up with restricted-choice plans is a myth. Although HMO and PPO plans do offer fewer choices when it comes to providers, surveys show that customer satisfaction with these plans is as high as it is for plans that offer more choices.

Lifetime maximum benefits

Health insurance plans specify the maximum total benefits they'll pay over the course of time you're insured by their plan. Although a million dollars may be more money than you could ever imagine being spent on your healthcare, it's the minimum acceptable level of total benefits. With the cost of healthcare today, you can quickly blow through that if you develop major health problems. The Affordable Care Act has generally required health plans to do away with lifetime maximums. If you're shopping for a noncompliant plan, ideally choose a plan that has no maximum or that has a maximum of at least $5 million.

Deductibles and co-payments

To reduce your health insurance premiums, choose a plan with the highest deductible and co-payment you can afford. As with other insurance policies, the more you're willing to share in the payment of your claims, the less you have to pay in premiums. Most policies have annual deductible options (such as $250, $500, $1,000, and so on) as well as co-payment options, which are typically 20 percent or so.

When choosing a co-payment percentage, don't let your imagination run wild and unnecessarily scare you. A 20-percent co-payment doesn't mean that you have to come up with $20,000 for a $100,000 claim. Insurance plans generally set a maximum out-of-pocket limit on your annual co-payments (such as $1,000, $2,000, and so on); the insurer covers 100 percent of any medical expenses that go over that cap.

For insurance provided by your employer, consider plans with low out-of-pocket expenses if you know you have health problems. Because you're part of a group, the insurer won't increase your individual rates just because you're filing more claims.

Most HMO plans don't have deductible and co-payment options. Most just charge a set amount — such as $25 — for a physician's office visit.

Guaranteed renewability

The Affordable Care Act generally requires health insurers to continue your plan coverage regardless of any changes in your health. You want a health insurance plan that keeps renewing your coverage without you having to prove continued good health. If good health could be guaranteed, you wouldn't need health insurance in the first place.

Saving on taxes when spending on healthcare

If you expect to have out-of-pocket medical expenses, find out whether your employer offers a flexible spending or healthcare reimbursement account. These accounts enable you to pay for uncovered medical expenses with pretax dollars. If, for example, you're in a combined 35-percent federal and state income tax bracket, these accounts allow you to pay for necessary healthcare at a 35-percent discount. These accounts can also be used to pay for vision and dental care.

Be forewarned of the major stumbling blocks you face when saving through medical reimbursement accounts. First, you need to elect to save money from your paycheck prior to the beginning of each plan year. The only exception is at the time of a "life change," such as marriage, spouse's job change, divorce, a family member's death, or the birth of a child. You also generally need to use the money within the year you save it, because these accounts contain a "use it or lose it" feature. (Some employer plans now allow a $500 carryover; check your plan's details.)

Health savings accounts (HSAs) are another option, especially for the self-employed and people who work for smaller firms. To qualify, you must have a high-deductible (at least $1,300 for individuals; $2,600 for families) health insurance policy; then you can put money earmarked for medical expenses into an investment account that offers the tax benefits — deductible contributions and tax-deferred compounding — of a retirement account (see Chapter 4). And unlike a flexible spending account, you don't have to deplete the HSA by the end of the year: Money can compound tax-deferred inside the HSA for years. Begin to investigate an HSA through insurers offering health plans you're interested in or with the company you currently have coverage through (also see my website, www. erictyson.com, for the latest information on the best HSA plans).

You may also be able to save on taxes if you have a substantial amount of healthcare expenditures in a year. You can deduct medical and dental expenses as an itemized deduction on Schedule A to the extent that they exceed 10 percent of your adjusted gross income (7.5 percent until 2017 for those age 65 and older). Unless you're a low-income earner, you need to have substantial expenses, usually caused by an accident or major illness, to take advantage of this tax break (see Chapter 7).

Buying health insurance

Due to the Affordable Care Act (Obamacare), the way Americans buy and pay for health insurance is going through some upheaval and turmoil. In addition to traditional insurance agents, numerous states operate health insurance exchanges that offer health plans that comply with the Affordable Care Act.

You can buy many health plans through agents, and you can also buy some directly from the insurer. When health insurance is sold both ways, buying through an agent usually doesn't cost more.

If you're self-employed or you work for a small employer that doesn't offer health insurance as a benefit, get proposals from the larger and older health insurers in your area. Larger plans can negotiate better rates from providers, and older plans are more likely to be here tomorrow.

Many insurers operate in a bunch of different insurance businesses. You want those that are the biggest in the health insurance arena and are committed to that business. Nationally, Blue Cross, Blue Shield, Kaiser Permanente, Aetna, UnitedHealth, CIGNA, Assurant, and Anthem are among the older and bigger health insurers. If your coverage is canceled, you may have to search for coverage that allows an existing medical problem through www.healthcare.gov. (Find out whether your state department of insurance offers a plan for people unable to get coverage.)

Also check with professional or other associations that you belong to, because plans offered by these groups sometimes offer decent benefits at a competitive price due to the purchasing power clout that they possess. A competent independent insurance agent who specializes in health insurance can help you find insurers who are willing to offer you coverage.

Health insurance agents have a conflict of interest that's common to all financial salespeople working on commission: The higher the premium plan they sell you, the bigger the commission they earn. So an agent may try to steer you into higher-cost plans and avoid suggesting some of the strategies I discuss in the preceding section for reducing your cost of coverage. (Good agents can help guide you to the best plans that cover preexisting conditions and offer the lowest costs for your medications. Be sure to provide them with this information and compare options carefully.)

Clarifying why prices rose because of the Affordable Care Act

When millions of health insurance policy holders got their plans canceled during the years the Affordable Care Act (ACA) was implemented, many of them faced big rate hikes when shopping for a replacement policy. How can that be?

It's because of the essential health benefits that, by law, must be included in new insurance policies that take effect in 2014 and thereafter. These benefits include maternity and newborn care, mental health and substance use disorder services, prescription drugs, and pediatric services (including dental and vision care), to give a partial list. In the past, you were able to pick and choose from plans that excluded some of these services and thus were less expensive.

Plus, the ACA includes "consumer protection" provisions that have elevated prices. For example, it prohibits health insurance companies from limiting or excluding coverage related to preexisting health conditions. In order to absorb this cost and costs related to other provisions, insurance companies have raised rates substantially.

Understanding subsidies

Though the bad news is that many people faced much higher priced policies due to the ACA, the good news is that some of those folks may qualify for government subsidies that help reduce the effective price of said policies. (Of course, this money doesn't come out of thin air; it comes from the federal government and therefore taxpayers.)

Qualifying for a subsidy depends on your family income and how many children you have. Beginning in 2014, subsidies were available to qualified individuals and families whose incomes fall in the range of 138 percent to 400 percent of the poverty line (assuming they buy a policy on a government exchange). At the top of the spectrum for 2015, an individual making just under $46,680 would be eligible for a subsidy, as would a family of four earning around $95,400.

If you're self-employed and end up receiving subsidies, be careful to keep track of your earnings. If you end up making more than you thought you would in a given year, you could end up having to pay back part of your subsidy. Of course, the reverse is also true: If you make less than expected, you may receive a refund.

Coping with higher health insurance prices

In recent decades, health insurance prices have consistently increased faster than the overall rate of inflation. So far, things have worsened with the implementation of the Affordable Care Act. Here are a few tips for health insurance shoppers to make the most of their spending:

- ✔ **If your plan is/was canceled, don't just go with the plan mentioned in the cancelation letter. Shop around.** When you hear people say, "My premium doubled!" they're generally referring to the comparable plan the insurance company suggested in the cancelation letter. Try not to take the number so literally; it's the price of just one of the possible plans available to you. Call your agent and ask to see a side-by-side comparison of various plans. Check out other companies. If you're eligible for a subsidy, check out the exchanges. Chances are you'll find something a little more reasonable if you're willing to make tradeoffs in the area of deductibles and out-of-pocket expenses.

- ✔ **Be patient and do your homework.** Talk to insurers and agents. Spend some time on the computer; the ACA marketplace website is `www.healthcare.gov`. Ask friends and colleagues what they're doing. Although you do need to be mindful of enrollment deadlines, you don't want to rush into what is really a very important financial decision.

✔ **If you go with a bronze plan, consider one that is compatible with a health savings account (HSA).** A bronze plan may be best for people who are generally healthy. These have the lowest premiums. Of course, they also have the highest deductibles, which means that in the event you do get sick, you'll have to cover more of your costs out of pocket. And that is why it's important to select a bronze plan that's compatible with an HSA (not all of them are). I have always recommended HSAs as a great tax-saving strategy, and now that deductibles are so high, they make more sense than ever. After all, if you have to have a high deductible anyway, at least getting the tax break on the out-of-pocket expenses you have to pay makes sense.

✔ **Do what you can to get and stay healthy.** Chances are you'll now be paying more out of pocket for nonpreventative care, so good health should be your top priority. Of course, health insurance is needed because some conditions are unpreventable, but you can affect plenty of others with lifestyle improvements. Obviously, if you smoke, stop now; smoking is the only "preexisting condition" health insurance companies are allowed to charge you more for. But it's also important to eat healthfully, exercise, and lose weight if you need to. The healthier you are, the less you'll need to seek medical care — and the less you'll have to pay out of pocket for your care.

Dealing with medical claims headaches

If you sign up for a health plan that has deductibles and co-payments, make sure you review the benefits statements your insurer sends you. Errors often pop up on these statements and during the claims filing process. Not surprisingly, the errors are usually at your expense.

Make sure that your insurer has kept accurate track of your contributions toward meeting your plan's annual deductible and maximum out-of-pocket charges. Also, don't pay any healthcare providers who send you bills until you receive proper notification from the insurance company detailing what you are obligated to pay those providers according to the terms of your plan. Because most insurance companies have negotiated discounted fee schedules with healthcare providers, the amount that a provider bills you is often higher than the amount they're legally due as per the terms of their contract with your insurer. Your insurer's benefits statement should detail the approved and negotiated rate once the claim is processed. And don't let providers try to bully you into paying them the difference between what they billed you for and what the insurer says they are due. Providers are due only the discounted fees they agreed to with your insurer.

Haggling with your health insurer is a real pain, and it usually happens after you rack up significant medical expenses and may still not be feeling well. But if you don't stay on top of your insurer, you can end up paying thousands of dollars in overpayments. If you're overwhelmed with an avalanche of claims and benefits statements, you may want to consider using a health insurance claims processing service. You can get a referral to firms that engage in this line of work by visiting the Alliance of Claims Assistance Professionals website at www.claims.org.

Looking at retiree medical care insurance

Medicare, the government-run health insurance plan for the elderly, is a multi-part major medical plan. Enrollment in Part A (hospital expenses) is automatic. Part B, which covers physician expenses and other charges, including home healthcare coverage; Part C, supplemental Medicare coverage (sold through private insurers); and Part D, for prescription drugs (provided through private insurers), are optional. Supplemental insurance policies, also known as Medigap coverage, may be of interest to you if you want help paying for the costs that Medicare doesn't pay.

Closing Medicare's gaps

Medigap coverage generally pays the deductibles and co-payments that Medicare charges. For the first 60 days of hospitalization, you pay $1,156 total out of your own pocket. If you have an unusually long hospital stay, you pay $289 per day for the 61st through the 90th day, $578 per day for the 91st through the 150th day, and all costs beyond 150 days. Clearly, if you stay in a hospital for many months, your out-of-pocket expenses can escalate; however, the longest hospitalizations tend not to last for many months. Also note that Medicare's hospitalization benefits refresh when you're out of the hospital for 60 consecutive days.

If you're unable to pay for the deductibles and co-payments because your income is low, making a long hospital stay a financial catastrophe for you, *Medicaid* (the state-run medical insurance program for low-income people) may help pay your bills. Alternatively, Medigap insurance can help close the gap.

Check with your physician(s) to see if he charges a fee higher than the one listed on Medicare's fee schedule. If your physician does charge a higher fee, you may want to consider going to another physician if you can't afford the fee or if you want to save some money. (But don't drop your current doctor before finding another who accepts Medicare and you as a patient. Many doctors are not accepting Medicare patients.) Medicare often pays only 80 percent of the physician charges that the program allows on its fee schedule.

The biggest reason that elderly people consider long-term care insurance is that Medicare pays only for the first 100 days in a skilled nursing facility. Anything over that is your responsibility. Unfortunately, Medigap policies don't address this issue, either.

Long-term care insurance

Insurance agents who are eager to earn a hefty commission will often tell you that long-term care (LTC) insurance is the solution to your concerns about an extended stay in a nursing home. Don't get your hopes up. Policies are complicated and filled with all sorts of exclusions and limitations. On top of all that, they're expensive.

The decision to purchase LTC insurance is a trade-off. Do you want to pay thousands of dollars annually, beginning at age 60, to guard against the possibility of a long-term stay in a nursing home (or possibly to pay for in-home assistance if you qualify)? If you live into or past your mid-80s, you can end up paying $100,000 or more on an LTC policy (not to mention the lost investment earnings on these insurance premiums).

People who end up in a nursing home for years on end may come out ahead financially when buying LTC insurance. The majority of people who stay in a nursing home are there for less than a year, though, because they either pass away or move out. Medicare pays for the bulk of the cost of the first 100 days in a nursing home as long as certain conditions are satisfied. Medicare pays for all basic services (telephone, television, and private room charges excluded) for the first 20 days and then requires a co-payment of $144.50 per day for the next 80 days. First, the nursing-home stay must follow hospitalization within 30 days, and the nursing-home stay must be for the same medical condition that caused the hospitalization. When you're discharged from the nursing home, you can qualify for an additional 100-day benefit period as long as you haven't been hospitalized or in a nursing home in the 60 days prior to your readmission.

If you have relatives or a spouse who will likely care for you in the event of a major illness, you definitely should *not* waste your money on nursing-home insurance. You can also bypass this coverage if you have and don't mind using retirement assets to help pay nursing-home costs.

Even if you do deplete your assets, remember that you have a backup: Medicaid (state-provided medical insurance) can pick up the cost if you can't. However, be aware of a number of potential drawbacks to getting coverage for nursing-home stays under Medicaid:

✔ **Medicaid patients are at the bottom of the priority list.** Most nursing homes are interested in the bottom line, so the patients who bring in the least revenue — namely Medicaid patients — get the lowest priority on nursing-home waiting lists.

✔ **Some nursing homes don't take Medicaid patients.** Check with your preferred nursing homes in your area to see whether they accept Medicaid.

✔ **The states may squeeze Medicaid further.** Deciding which medical conditions warrant coverage is up to your state. With the budget noose tightening, some states are disallowing certain types of coverage (for example, mental problems for elderly people who are otherwise in good physical health).

If you're concerned about having your stash of money wiped out by an extended nursing-home stay and you have a strong desire to pass money to your family or a favorite charity, you can start giving your money away while you're still healthy. (If you're already in poor health, legal experts can strategize to preserve your assets and keep them from being used to pay nursing-home costs.)

Consider buying LTC insurance if you want to retain and protect your assets and it gives you peace of mind to know that a long-term nursing-home stay is covered. But do some comparison shopping, and make sure that you buy a policy that pays benefits for the long term. A year's worth (or even a few years' worth) of benefits won't protect your assets if your stay lasts longer. Also be sure to get a policy that adjusts the daily benefit amount for increases in the cost of living. Get a policy that covers care in your home or other settings if you don't need to be in a high-cost nursing home, and make sure that it doesn't require prior hospitalization for benefits to kick in. To keep premiums down, also consider a longer exclusion or waiting period — three to six months or a year before coverage starts.

You may also want to consider retirement communities if you're willing to live as a younger retiree in such a setting. After paying an entrance fee, you pay a monthly fee, which usually covers your rent, care, and meals. Make sure that any such facility you're considering guarantees care for life and preferably has a continuum of care levels available. Also verify that it accepts Medicaid in case you deplete your assets.

Making sense of Medicare's prescription drug program

As if there weren't enough confusing government programs, Uncle Sam created yet another that began in 2006 — the Medicare (Part D) prescription drug plan. Here are some key facts you need to know about these somewhat complicated plans, which are offered through private insurers:

✔ Plans make the most sense for those who expect to spend more than $5,000 annually on prescription drugs.

✔ If you choose not to enroll when you're first eligible and then later enroll, you'll be charged a penalty equal to 1 percent of the national average Part D premium for each month that has elapsed since you were first eligible to participate. You will pay this penalty for as long as you're in the plan.

✔ If you're on the fence about enrolling, consider starting with a low-premium plan that then gives you the right to transfer into a higher-cost and better-coverage plan without paying the late enrollment penalty.

✔ Visit www.medicare.gov for helpful information on drug plans and how to select one. For example, click on the Formulary (drug) Finder to identify specific insurer plans that cover your current medications or your anticipated future medications. AARP's website, www.aarp.org, also has plenty of information and resources to find out more about these confusing plans.

Chapter 17

Covering Your Assets

- -

In This Chapter

▶ Checking out homeowner's/renter's insurance

▶ Considering automobile insurance

▶ Understanding umbrella (excess liability) insurance

▶ Ensuring your estate is handled as you want

- -

*I*n Chapter 16, I discuss the importance of protecting your future income from disability, death, or large, unexpected medical expenses. But you also have to insure major assets that you've acquired: your home, your car, and your personal property. You need to protect these assets for two reasons:

✔ **Your assets are valuable.** If you were to suffer a loss, replacing the assets with money out of your own pocket could be a financial catastrophe.

✔ **A lawsuit can drain your finances.** Should someone be injured or killed in your home or because of your car, a lawsuit could be financially devastating.

In this chapter, I explain why, how, and for how much to insure your home, personal property, and vehicle. I also discuss excess liability insurance and how to determine where your money will go in the event of your death.

Insuring Where You Live

When you buy a home with a mortgage, most lenders require you to purchase homeowner's insurance. But even if they don't, you're wise to do so, because your home and the personal property within it are worth a great deal and would cost a bundle to replace.

As a renter, damage to the building in which you live is not your immediate financial concern, but you still have personal property you may want to insure. You also have the possibility (albeit remote) that you'll be sued by someone who's injured while in your rental.

When shopping for a homeowner's or renter's policy, consider the important features that I cover in the following sections.

Dwelling coverage: The cost to rebuild

How much would you have to spend to rebuild your home if it were completely destroyed, for example, in a fire? The cost to rebuild should be based on the size (square footage) of your home. Neither the purchase price nor the size of your mortgage should determine how much *dwelling coverage* you need.

If you're a renter, rejoice that you don't need dwelling coverage. If you're a condominium owner, find out whether the insurance the condo association bought for the entire building is sufficient.

Be sure that your homeowner's policy includes a *guaranteed replacement cost* provision. This useful feature ensures that the insurance company will rebuild the home even if the cost of construction is more than the policy coverage. If the insurance company underestimates your dwelling coverage, it has to make up the difference.

Unfortunately, insurers define guaranteed replacement cost differently. While some companies pay for the full replacement cost of the home, no matter how much it ends up costing, most insurers set limits. For example, some insurers may pay up to only 25 percent more than the dwelling coverage on your policy. Ask your insurer how it defines guaranteed replacement cost.

If you have an older property that doesn't meet current building standards, consider buying a rider (supplemental coverage to your main insurance policy) that pays for code upgrades. This rider covers the cost of rebuilding your home, in the event of a loss, to comply with current building codes that may be more stringent than the ones in place when your home was built. Ask your insurance company what your basic policy does and doesn't cover. Some companies include a certain amount (for example, 10 percent of your dwelling coverage) for code upgrades in the base policy.

Personal property coverage: For your things

On your homeowner's policy, the amount of personal property coverage is typically derived from the amount of dwelling coverage you carry. Generally, you get personal property coverage that's equal to 50 to 75 percent of the dwelling coverage. This amount is usually more than enough.

Regarding riders to cover jewelry, computers, collectibles, and other somewhat costly items that may not be fully covered by typical homeowner's policies, ask yourself whether the out-of-pocket expense from the loss of such items would constitute a financial catastrophe. Unless you have more than several thousand dollars worth of jewelry or computer equipment, skip such riders.

Some policies come with *replacement cost guarantees* that pay you the cost to replace an item. This payment can be considerably more than what the used item was worth before it was damaged or stolen. When this feature is not part of the standard policy sold by your insurer, you may want to purchase it as a rider, if available.

As a renter or condominium owner, you need to choose a dollar amount for the personal property you want covered. Tally it up instead of guessing — the total cost of replacing all your personal property may surprise you.

Make a list of your belongings — or even better, take pictures or make a video — with an estimate of what they're worth. Keep this list updated; you'll need it if you have to file a claim. Retaining receipts for major purchases may also help your case. No matter how you document your belongings, don't forget to keep the documentation somewhere besides your home — otherwise, it could be destroyed along with the rest of your house in a fire or other disaster.

Liability insurance: Coverage for when others are harmed

Liability insurance protects you financially against lawsuits that may arise if someone gets injured on your property, including wounds inflicted by the family's pernicious pup or terrible tabby. (Of course, you should keep Bruno restrained when guests visit — even your cranky in-laws.) At a minimum, get enough liability insurance to cover your financial assets — covering two times your assets is better. Buying extra coverage is inexpensive and well worth the cost.

The probability of being sued is low, but if you are sued and lose, you could end up owing big bucks. If you have substantial assets to protect, you may want to consider an umbrella, or excess liability, policy. (See "Protecting against Mega-Liability: Umbrella Insurance" later in this chapter.)

Liability protection is one of the side benefits of purchasing a renter's policy — you protect your personal property as well as insure against lawsuits. (But don't be reckless with your banana peels even if you get liability insurance!)

Flood and earthquake insurance: Protection from Mother Nature

You should purchase the broadest possible coverage when buying any type of insurance (see Chapter 15). The problem with homeowner's insurance is that it's not comprehensive enough — it doesn't typically cover losses due to earthquakes and floods. You must buy such disaster coverage separately.

If an earthquake or flood were to strike your area and destroy your home, you'd be out tens (if not hundreds) of thousands of dollars without proper coverage. Yet many people don't carry these important coverages, often as a result of some common misconceptions:

✔ **"Not in my neighborhood."** Many people mistakenly believe that earthquakes occur only in California. I wish this were true for those who live in the other 49 states, but it's not. In fact, one of the strongest earthquakes in the United States occurred in the Midwest, and known (though less active) fault lines lie along the East Coast. The cost of earthquake coverage is based on insurance companies' assessment of the risk of your area and property type. You shouldn't decide whether to buy insurance based on how small you think the risk is. The risk is already built in to the price.

An estimated 20,000 communities around the country face potential flood damage. Like earthquakes, floods are not a covered risk in standard homeowner's policies, so you need to purchase a flood insurance rider. Check with your current homeowner's insurer or with the insurers recommended in this chapter. The federal government flood insurance program (phone 888-379-9531; website www.floodsmart.gov) provides background information on flood insurance policies.

✔ **"The government will bail me out."** The vast majority of government financial assistance is obtained through low-interest loans. Loans, unfortunately, need to be repaid, and that money comes out of your pocket.

✔ **"In a major disaster, insurers would go bankrupt anyway."** This is highly unlikely given the reserves insurers are required to keep and the fact that the insurance companies *reinsure* — that is, they buy insurance to back up the policies they write. Also, state regulatory agencies facilitate the merging of faltering insurers into strong entities.

People who have little equity in their property and are willing to walk away from their property and mortgage in the event of a major quake or flood may consider not buying earthquake or flood coverage. Keep in mind that walking away damages your credit report, because you're essentially defaulting on your loan.

You may be able to pay for much of the cost of earthquake or flood insurance by raising the deductibles (discussed in the next section) on the main part of your homeowner's/renter's insurance and other insurance policies (such as auto insurance). You can more easily afford the smaller claims, not the big ones. If you think flood or earthquake insurance is expensive, compare those costs with the expenditures you would incur to completely replace your home and personal property. Buy this insurance if you live in an area that has a chance of being affected by these catastrophes. To help keep the cost of earthquake insurance down, consider taking a 10 percent deductible. Most insurers offer deductibles of 5, 10, or 20 percent of the cost to rebuild your home. Ten percent of the rebuilding cost is a good chunk of money. But losing the other 90 percent is what you want to insure against. (For most people, a 20 percent deductible is too high.)

Deductibles: Your cost with a claim

As I discuss in Chapter 15, the point of insurance is to protect against catastrophic losses, not the little losses. By taking the highest deductibles you're comfortable with, you save on insurance premiums year after year, and you don't have to go through the hassle of filing small claims.

Special discounts

You may qualify for special discounts on your policy. Companies and agents that sell homeowner's and renter's insurance don't always check to see whether you're eligible for discounts. After all, the more you spend on policy premiums, the more money they make! If your property has a security system, you're older, or you have other policies with the same insurer, you may qualify for a lower rate. Remember to ask.

Also, be aware that insurers use your credit score as a factor in setting some of your insurance rates. They do this because their studies have shown that folks who have higher credit scores tend to have fewer accidents and insurance claims. See Chapter 2 for how to assess and improve your credit reports and scores.

Buying homeowner's or renter's insurance

Each insurance company prices its homeowner's and renter's policies based on its own criteria. So the lowest-cost company for your friend's property may not be the lowest-cost company for yours. You have to shop around at several companies to find the best rates. The following list features companies that historically offer lower-cost policies for most people and have decent track records regarding customer satisfaction and the payment of claims:

- ✔ **Amica:** Although Amica does have good customer satisfaction, its prices are high in some areas. You can contact the company by calling 800-242-6422 or checking out the company's website at www.amica.com.

- ✔ **Auto-Owners:** Check your local phone directory for agents, call 517-323-1200, or visit www.auto-owners.com.

- ✔ **Erie Insurance:** This company does business primarily in the Midwest and Mid-Atlantic. Check your local phone directory for agents, call 800-458-0811 for a referral to a local agent, or visit the company's website at www.erieinsurance.com.

- ✔ **GEICO:** You can contact the company by calling 800-841-2964 or visit www.geico.com.

- ✔ **Liberty Mutual:** Check your local phone directory for agents, call 800-837-5254, or go to www.libertymutual.com.

- ✔ **Nationwide Mutual:** Check your local phone directory for agents, call 877-669-6877, or see www.nationwide.com.

- ✔ **State Farm:** Check your local phone directory for agents, call 844-803-1573, or visit www.statefarm.com.

- ✔ **USAA:** This company provides insurance for members of the military and their families. Call the company at 800-531-8722 (or visit its website at www.usaa.com) to see whether you qualify.

Don't worry that some of these companies require you to call a toll-free number for a price quote. This process saves you money, because these insurers don't have to pay commissions to local agents hawking their policies. These companies have local claims representatives to help you if and when you have a claim.

A number of the companies mentioned in the preceding list sell other types of insurance (for example, life insurance) that aren't as competitively priced. Be sure to check out the relevant sections in this part of the book for the best places to buy these other types of coverage if you need them.

Some state insurance departments conduct surveys of insurers' prices and tabulate complaints received. Look up your state's department of insurance phone number in the government section of your local phone directory or visit the National Association of Insurance Commissioners' website at www. naic.org/state_web_map.htm to find links to each state's department of insurance site.

Auto Insurance 101

Over the course of your life, you may spend tens of thousands of dollars on auto insurance. Much of the money people spend on auto insurance is not spent where it's needed most. In other cases, the money is simply wasted. Look for the following important features when searching for an auto insurance policy.

Bodily injury/property damage liability

As with homeowner's liability insurance, auto liability insurance provides insurance against lawsuits. Accidents happen, especially with a car. Make sure you have enough bodily injury liability insurance, which pays for harm done to others, to cover your assets. (Coverage of double your assets is preferable.)

If you're just beginning to accumulate assets, don't mistakenly assume that you don't need liability protection. Many states require a minimum amount — insurers should be able to fill you in on the details for your state. Also, don't forget that your future earnings, which are an asset, can be garnished in a lawsuit.

Coping with teen drivers

If you have a teenage driver in your household, you're going to be spending a lot more on auto insurance (in addition to worrying a lot more). As soon as you decide to allow your teenager to drive, you can take a number of steps to avoid spending all your take-home pay on auto insurance bills:

✔ **Make sure your teen does well in school.** Some insurers offer discounts if your child is a strong academic achiever and has successfully completed a driver's education class (which is not required).

✔ **Get price quotes from several insurers** to see how adding your teen driver to your policy affects the cost.

✔ **Have your teenager share in the costs of using the car.** If you pay all the insurance, gas, and maintenance bills, your teenager won't value the privilege of using your "free" car.

Of course, teen driving involves more than just keeping your insurance bills to a minimum. Auto accidents are the number-one cause of death for teens. For more on driving responsibly, see the sidebar later in this chapter titled "Driving safely: Overlooked auto insurance."

Property damage liability insurance covers damage done by your car to other people's cars or property. The amount of property damage liability coverage in an auto insurance policy is usually determined as a consequence of the bodily injury liability amount selected. Coverage of $50,000 is a good minimum to start with.

Uninsured or underinsured motorist liability

When you're in an accident with another motorist and she doesn't carry her own liability protection (or doesn't carry enough), *uninsured or underinsured motorist liability coverage* allows you to collect for lost wages, medical expenses, and pain and suffering incurred in the accident.

If you already have comprehensive health and long-term disability insurance, uninsured or underinsured motorist liability coverage is largely redundant. However, if you drop this coverage, you do give up the ability to sue for general pain and suffering and to insure passengers in your car who may lack adequate medical and disability coverage.

To provide a death benefit to those financially dependent on you in the event of a fatal auto accident, buy term life insurance (see Chapter 16).

Deductibles

To minimize your auto insurance premiums and eliminate the need to file small claims, take the highest deductibles you're comfortable with. (Most people should consider a $500 to $1,000 deductible.) On an auto policy, two deductibles exist: collision and comprehensive. *Collision* applies to claims arising from collisions. (Note that if you have collision coverage on your own policy, you can generally bypass collision coverage when you rent a car.) *Comprehensive* applies to other claims for damages not caused by collision (for example, a window broken by vandals).

As your car ages and loses its value, you can eventually eliminate your comprehensive and collision coverages altogether. The point at which you do this is up to you. Insurers won't pay more than the book value of your car, regardless of what it costs to repair or replace it. Remember that the purpose of insurance is to compensate you for losses that are financially catastrophic to you. For some people, this amount may be as high as $5,000 or more — others may choose $1,000 as their threshold point.

Special discounts: Auto edition

You may be eligible for special discounts on auto insurance. Don't forget to tell your agent or insurer if your car has a security alarm, air bags, or anti-lock brakes. If you're older or you have other policies or cars insured with the same insurer, you may also qualify for discounts. And make sure that you're given appropriate "good driver" discounts if you've been accident- and ticket-free in recent years.

Before you buy your next car, call insurers and ask for insurance quotes for the different models you're considering. The cost of insuring a car should factor into your decision of which car you buy, because the insurance costs represent a major portion of your car's ongoing operating expenses.

Little-stuff coverage to skip

Auto insurers have dreamed up all sorts of riders, such as towing and rental car reimbursement. On the surface, these riders appear to be inexpensive. But they're expensive given the little amount you'd collect from a claim and the hassle of filing.

Riders that waive the deductible under certain circumstances make no sense, either. The point of the deductible is to reduce your policy cost and eliminate the hassle of filing small claims.

Medical payments coverage typically pays a few thousand dollars for medical expenses. If you and your passengers carry major medical insurance coverage, this rider isn't really necessary. Besides, a few thousand dollars of medical coverage doesn't protect you against catastrophic expenses.

Buying auto insurance

You can use the homeowner's insurers list I present in the earlier section "Buying homeowner's or renter's insurance" to obtain quotes for auto insurance. In addition, you can contact Progressive by calling 800-776-4737 or visiting its website at www.progressive.com.

Driving safely: Overlooked auto insurance

Tragic events (murders, fires, hurricanes, plane crashes, and so on) are well-covered by the media, but the number of deaths that make the front pages of our newspapers pales in comparison to the more than 30,000 people who die on America's roads every year. I'm not suggesting that the national media should start reporting every automobile fatality. Even 24 hours of daily CNN coverage probably couldn't keep up with all the accidents on our roads. But the real story with auto fatalities lies not in the *who, what,* and *where* of specific accidents but in the *why*. Asking the *why* question reveals how many of them are preventable.

No matter what kind of car you drive, you can and should drive safely. Stay within the speed limits and don't drive while intoxicated or tired or in adverse weather conditions. Wear your seat belt — a U.S. Department of Transportation study found that 60 percent of auto passengers killed were not wearing their seat belts. And don't try to talk or text on your cellphone and write notes on a pad of paper attached to your dashboard while balancing your coffee cup between your legs!

You can also greatly reduce your risk of dying in an accident by driving a safe car. You don't need to spend buckets of money to get a car with desirable safety features. For a list of the safest cars along with links for more information, visit my website: www.erictyson.com.

Diversification: Investment insurance

Insurance companies don't sell policies that protect the value of your investments, but you can shield your portfolio from many of the dangers of a fickle market through diversification.

If all your money is invested in bank accounts or bonds, you're exposed to the risks of inflation, which can erode your money's purchasing power. Conversely, if the bulk of your money is invested in one high-risk stock, your financial future could go up in smoke if that stock explodes.

Chapter 9 discusses the benefits of diversification and tells you how to assemble a portfolio of investments that do well under different conditions.

Protecting against Mega-Liability: Umbrella Insurance

Umbrella insurance (which is also referred to as *excess liability insurance*) is liability insurance that's added on top of the liability protection on your home and car(s). If, for example, you have $700,000 in assets, you can buy a $1 million umbrella liability policy to add to the $300,000 liability insurance that you have on your home and car. Expect to pay a couple hundred dollars — a small cost for big protection. Each year, thousands of people suffer lawsuits of more than $1 million related to their cars and homes.

Umbrella insurance is generally sold in increments of $1 million. So how do you decide how much you need if you have a lot of assets? You should have at least enough liability insurance to protect your assets and preferably enough to cover twice the value of those assets. To purchase umbrella insurance, start by contacting your existing homeowner's or auto insurance company.

Planning Your Estate

Estate planning is the process of determining what will happen to your assets after you die. Considering your mortality in the context of insurance may seem a bit odd. But the time and cost of various estate-planning maneuvers is really nothing more than buying insurance: You're ensuring that, after you die, everything will be taken care of as you wish, and taxes will be minimized. Thinking about estate planning in this way can help you better evaluate whether certain options make sense at particular points in your life.

Depending upon your circumstances, you may eventually want to contact an attorney who specializes in estate-planning matters. However, educating yourself first about the different options is worth your time. More than a few attorneys have their own agendas about what you should do, so be careful. And most of the estate-planning strategies that you're likely to benefit from don't require hiring an attorney.

Wills, living wills, and medical powers of attorney

When you have children who are minors (dependents), a will is a necessity. The will names the guardian to whom you entrust your children if both you and your spouse die. Should you and your spouse both die without a will (called *intestate*), the state (courts and social-service agencies) decides who will raise your children. Therefore, even if you can't decide at this time who you want to raise your children, you should *at least* appoint a trusted guardian who can decide for you.

Having a will makes good sense even if you don't have kids, because it gives instructions on how to handle and distribute all your worldly possessions. If you die without a will, your state decides how to distribute your money and other property, according to state law. Therefore, your friends, distant relatives, and favorite charities will probably receive nothing. Without any living relatives, your money may go to the state government!

Without a will, your heirs are legally powerless, and the state may appoint an administrator to supervise the distribution of your assets at a fee of around 5 percent of your estate. A bond typically must also be posted at a cost of several hundred dollars.

A living will and a medical power of attorney are useful additions to a standard will. A *living will* (also known as an advanced healthcare directive) tells your doctor what, if any, life-support measures you prefer. A *medical* (or *healthcare*) *power of attorney* grants authority to someone you trust to make decisions regarding your medical care options.

The simplest and least costly way to prepare a will, a living will, and a medical power of attorney is to use the high-quality, user-friendly software packages that I recommend in Chapter 19. Be sure to give copies of these documents to the guardians and executors named in the documents. You don't need an attorney to make a legal will. Most attorneys, in fact, prepare wills and living trusts using software packages! What makes a will valid is that three people witness your signing it.

If preparing the will all by yourself seems overwhelming, you can (instead of hiring an attorney) use a paralegal typing service to help you prepare the documents. These services generally charge 50 percent or less of what an attorney charges.

Avoiding probate through living trusts

Because of the United States's quirky legal system, even if you have a will, some or all of your assets must go through a court process known as probate. *Probate* is the legal process for administering and implementing the directions in a will. Property and assets that are owned in joint tenancy or inside retirement accounts, such as IRAs or 401(k)s, generally pass to heirs without having to go through probate. However, passing through probate is necessary for most other assets.

A *living trust* effectively transfers assets into a trust. As the trustee, you control those assets, and you can revoke the trust whenever you desire. The advantage of a living trust is that upon your death, assets can pass directly to your beneficiaries without going through probate. Probate can be a lengthy, expensive hassle for your heirs — with legal fees tallying 5 percent or more of the value of the estate. In addition, your assets become a matter of public record as a result of probate.

Living trusts are likely to be of greatest value to people who meet one or more of the following criteria (the more that apply, the more value trusts have):

✔ Age 60 or older

✔ Single

✔ Assets worth more than $100,000 that must pass through probate (including real estate, nonretirement accounts, and small businesses)

✔ Real property held in other states

As with a will, you do *not* need an attorney to establish a legal and valid living trust. (See my software recommendations in Chapter 19 and consider the paralegal services that I mention in the preceding section.) Attorney fees for establishing a living trust can range from hundreds to thousands of dollars. Hiring an attorney is of greatest value to people with large estates (see the next section) who don't have the time, desire, and expertise to maximize the value derived from estate planning. Also consult with an attorney if you have nonstandard wishes to be carried out, such as special-needs beneficiaries or extra control measures you want applied to assets after incapacity or death.

Note: Living trusts keep assets out of probate but have nothing to do with minimizing estate or inheritance taxes.

Reducing estate taxes

Under current tax laws, an individual can pass $5.43 million to beneficiaries without having to pay federal estate taxes.

Whether you should be concerned about possible estate taxes depends on several issues. How much of your assets you're going to use up during your life is the first and most important issue you need to consider. This amount depends on how much your assets grow over time, as well as how rapidly you spend money. During retirement, you'll (hopefully) be using at least some of your money.

I've seen too many affluent individuals, especially in their retirements, worry about estate taxes on their assets. If your intention is to leave your money to your children, grandchildren, or a charity, why not start giving while you're still alive so you can enjoy the act? You can give $14,000 annually to each of your beneficiaries, *tax-free*. By giving away money, you reduce your estate and, therefore, the estate taxes owed on it. Any appreciation on the value of the gift between the date of the gift and your date of death is also out of your estate and not subject to estate taxes.

In addition to gifting, a number of trusts allow you to minimize estate taxes. Although it's no longer generally necessary at the federal level, you may want to establish a *bypass trust* to effectively double the estate tax limit for your state. Upon the death of the first spouse, assets held in his or her name go into the bypass trust, effectively removing those assets from the remaining spouse's taxable estate. (Speak with an estate planning attorney.)

Cash value life insurance is another estate-planning tool. Unfortunately, it's a tool that's overused or, I should say, oversold. People who sell cash value insurance — that is, insurance salespeople and others masquerading as financial planners — too often advocate life insurance as the one and only way to reduce estate taxes. Other methods for reducing estate taxes are usually superior, because they don't require wasting money on life insurance.

Small-business owners whose businesses are worth several million dollars or more may want to consider cash value life insurance under specialized circumstances. If you lack the necessary additional assets to pay expected estate taxes and you don't want your beneficiaries to be forced to sell the business, you can buy cash value life insurance to pay expected estate taxes. To find out more about how to reduce your estate (and other) taxes, visit my website at www.erictyson.com.

Part V
Where to Go for More Help

Issues to Address When Interviewing Financial Advisors

- ✔ Percentage of income from clients' fees versus commissions
- ✔ Portion of client fees for money management versus hourly planning
- ✔ Hourly fee
- ✔ Work and educational experience
- ✔ Liability insurance
- ✔ References
- ✔ Specific strategies and product recommendations

 Some financial planners put their interests ahead of yours. Find out how to spot the signs of an unscrupulous planner in the free article at www.dummies.com/extras/personalfinance.

In this part . . .

- ✔ Understand what your options are for getting financial advice and how to find a top advisor.

- ✔ Harness the power of your computer and other technology when it comes to managing your money.

- ✔ Survey the financial resources in the mass media, on radio and television, and in print.

Chapter 18

Working with Financial Planners

In This Chapter

▶ Checking out your choices for managing your finances

▶ Determining whether you need help from a financial planner

▶ Searching for a stellar financial advisor

▶ Interviewing financial planners before you hire them

*H*iring a competent and ethical financial planner or advisor to help you make and implement financial decisions can be money well spent. But if you pick a poor advisor or someone who really isn't a financial planner but rather a salesperson in disguise, your financial situation can get worse instead of better. So before I talk about the different types of help for hire, I discuss the options you have for directing the management of your personal finances.

Surveying Your Financial Management Options

Everyone has three basic choices for managing money: You can do nothing, you can do it yourself, or you can hire someone to help you. This section lays out these three options in more detail.

Doing nothing

The do-nothing (or do-little) approach has a large following (and you thought you were alone!). People who fall into this category may be leading exciting, interesting lives and are therefore too busy to attend to something as mundane as dealing with their personal finances. Or they may be leading mundane existences but are too busy fantasizing about more-appealing ways to spend their time.

The dangers of doing nothing are many. Putting off saving for retirement or ignoring your buildup of debt eventually comes back to haunt you. If you don't carry adequate insurance, accidents can be devastating. Fires, earthquakes, flooding, and hurricanes show how precarious living in paradise actually is.

If you've been following the do-nothing approach all your life, you're now officially promoted out of it! You bought this book to find out more about personal finance and make changes in your money matters, right? So take control and keep reading!

Doing it yourself

The do-it-yourselfers learn enough about financial topics to make informed decisions on their own. Doing anything yourself, of course, requires you to invest some time in learning the basic concepts and keeping up with changes. The idea that you're going to spend endless hours on your finances if you direct them yourself is a myth. The hardest part of managing money for most people is catching up on things that they should have done previously. After you get things in order, which you can easily do with this book as your companion, you shouldn't have to spend more than an hour or two working on your personal finances every few months (unless a major issue, like a real estate purchase, comes up).

Some people in the financial advisory business like to make what they do seem so complicated that they compare it to brain surgery! Their argument goes, "You wouldn't perform brain surgery on yourself, so why would you manage your money yourself?" Well, to this I say, "Personal financial management ain't brain surgery — not even close." You can manage on your own. In fact, you can do a better job than most advisors. Why? Because you're not subject to their conflicts of interest, and you care the most about your money.

Hiring financial help

Realizing that you need to hire someone to help you make and implement financial decisions can be a valuable insight. Spending a few hours and several hundred dollars to hire a competent professional can be money well spent, even if you have a modest income or assets. But you need to know what your money is buying. Financial planners or advisors make money in three ways:

- ✔ They earn commissions based on the sales of financial products.
- ✔ They charge a percentage of the assets they invest on your behalf.

> ✔ They charge by the hour (this can also be done through fixed-fee arrangements).

The following sections help you differentiate among the three main types of financial planners.

Commission-based "planners"

Commission-based planners aren't really planners, advisors, or counselors at all — they're salespeople. Many stockbrokers and insurance brokers are now called *financial consultants* or *financial service representatives* in order to glamorize the profession and obscure how they're compensated. Ditto for insurance salespeople calling themselves *estate planning specialists.*

A stockbroker referring to himself as a financial consultant is like a Honda dealer calling himself a transportation consultant. A Honda dealer is a salesperson who makes a living selling Hondas — period. He's definitely not going to tell you nice things about Ford, Chrysler, or Toyota cars — unless, of course, he happens to sell those, too. He also has no interest in educating you about potentially money-saving public-transit possibilities!

Salespeople and brokers masquerading as planners can have an enormous self-interest when they push certain products, particularly those products that pay generous commissions. Getting paid on commission tends to skew their recommendations toward certain strategies (such as buying investment or life-insurance products) and to cause them to ignore or downplay other aspects of your finances. For example, they'll gladly sell you an investment rather than persuade you to pay off your high-interest debts or save and invest through your employer's retirement plan, thereby reducing your taxes.

Table 18-1 gives you an idea of the commissions that a financial planner/salesperson can earn by selling particular financial products.

Table 18-1	Financial Product Commissions
Product	*Commission*
Life Insurance ($250,000, age 45):	
Term life	$125 to $500
Universal/whole life	$1,000 to $2,500
Disability Insurance:	
$4,000/month benefit, age 35	$400 to $1,500
Investments ($20,000):	
Mutual funds (loaded)	$800 to $1,700
Limited partnerships	$1,400 to $2,000
Annuities	$1,000 to $2,000

Percentage-of-assets-under-management advisors

A financial advisor who charges a percentage of the assets that are being managed or invested is generally a better choice than a commission-based planner. This compensation system removes the incentive to sell you products with high commissions and initiate lots of transactions (to generate more of those commissions).

The fee-based system is an improvement over product-pushers working on commission, but it has flaws, too. Suppose that you're trying to decide whether to invest in stocks, bonds, or real estate. A planner who earns his living managing your money likely won't recommend real estate because that will deplete your investment capital. The planner also won't recommend paying down your mortgage for the same reason — he'll claim that you can earn more investing your money (with his help, of course) than it'll cost you to borrow.

Fee-based planners are also only interested in managing the money of those who have already accumulated a fair amount of it — which rules out most people. Many have minimums of $250,000, $500,000, or more.

Hourly-based advisors

Your best bet for professional help with your personal finances may be an advisor who charges for his time. Because he doesn't sell any financial products, his objectivity is maintained. He doesn't perform money management, so he can help you make comprehensive financial decisions with loans, retirement planning, and the selection of good investments, including real estate, mutual funds, and small business.

Hiring someone incompetent is the primary risk you face when selecting an hourly-based planner. So be sure to check references and find out enough about finances on your own to discern between good and bad financial advice. Another risk comes from not clearly defining the work to be done and the approximate total cost of the planner's service before you begin, so consider getting these items in writing. You should also review some of the other key questions that I outline in "Interviewing Financial Advisors: Asking the Right Questions" later in this chapter.

An entirely different kind of drawback occurs when you don't follow through on your advisor's recommendations. You pay for his work but don't act on it, so you don't capture its value. If part of the reason you hired the planner in the first place was that you're too busy or not interested enough to make changes to your financial situation, look for this type of support in the services you buy from the planner.

Some planners charge a fixed fee to whip up a financial plan for you. Remember to ask how much of their time is involved in working with you so you can assess the amount you're paying per hour.

If you just need someone to act as a sounding board for ideas or to recommend a specific strategy or product, you can hire an hourly-based planner for one or two sessions of advice. You save money doing the legwork and implementation on your own. Just make sure the planner is willing to give you specific advice so you can properly implement the strategy.

Deciding Whether to Hire a Financial Planner

If you're like most people, you don't need to hire a financial planner, but you may benefit from hiring some help at certain times in your life. Good reasons for hiring a financial planner can be similar to the reasons you may have for hiring someone to clean your home or do your taxes. If you're too busy, you don't enjoy doing it, or you're terribly uncomfortable making decisions on your own, using a planner for a second opinion makes good sense. And if you shy away from numbers and bristle at the thought of long division, a good planner can help you.

How a good financial advisor can help

The following list gives you a rundown of some of the important ways a competent financial planner can assist you:

- ✔ **Identifying problems and goals:** Many otherwise intelligent people have a hard time being objective about their financial problems. They may ignore their debts or have unrealistic goals and expectations given their financial situations and behaviors. And many are so busy with other aspects of their lives that they never take the time to think about what their financial goals are. A good financial planner can give you the objective perspective you need. Surprisingly, some people are in a better financial position than they think they are in relation to their goals. Good counselors really enjoy this aspect of their jobs — good news is easier and much more fun to deliver.

- ✔ **Identifying strategies for reaching your financial goals:** Your mind may be a jumble of various plans, ideas, and concerns, along with a cobweb or two. A good planner can help you sort out your thoughts and propose alternative strategies for you to consider as you work to accomplish your financial goals.

✔ **Setting priorities:** You may be considering doing dozens of things to improve your financial situation, but making just a few key changes is likely to have the greatest value. Identifying the changes that fit your overall situation and that won't keep you awake at night is equally important. Good planners help you prioritize.

✔ **Saving research time and hassle:** Even if you know which major financial decisions are most important to you, doing the research needed to make them can be time-consuming and frustrating if you don't know where to turn for good information and advice. A good planner does research to match your needs to the best available strategies and products. A good advisor can prevent you from making a bad decision based on poor or insufficient information.

✔ **Purchasing commission-free financial products:** When you hire a planner who charges for his time, you can easily save hundreds or thousands of dollars by avoiding the cost of commissions in the financial products you buy. Purchasing commission-free is especially valuable when you buy investments and insurance.

✔ **Providing an objective voice for major decisions:** When you're trying to figure out when to retire, how much to spend on a home purchase, and where to invest your money, you're faced with some big decisions. Getting swept up in the emotions of these issues can cloud your perspective. A competent and sensitive advisor can help you cut through the confusion and provide you with sound counsel.

✔ **Helping you to just do it:** Deciding what you need to do is not enough — you have to actually do it. And although you can use a planner for advice and then make all the changes on your own, a good counselor can help you follow through with your plan. After all, part of the reason you hired the advisor in the first place may be that you're too busy or uninterested to manage your finances.

✔ **Mediating:** If you have a spouse or partner, financial decisions can produce real fireworks. Although a financial counselor isn't a therapist, a good one can be sensitive to the different needs and concerns of each party and can try to find middle ground on the financial issues you're grappling with.

✔ **Making you money and allowing you peace of mind:** The whole point of professional financial planning is to help you make the most of your money and plan for and attain your financial and personal goals. In the process, the financial planner should show you how to enhance your investment returns; reduce your spending, taxes, and insurance costs; increase your savings; improve your catastrophic-insurance coverage; and achieve your financial-independence goals.

Why advisors aren't for everyone

Finding a good financial planner isn't easy, so make sure you want to hire an advisor before you venture out in search of a competent one. You should also consider your personality type before you decide to hire help. My experience has been that some people (believe it or not) enjoy the research and number crunching. If this sounds like you, or if you're not really comfortable taking advice, you may be better off doing your own homework and creating your own plan.

If you have a specific tax or legal matter, you may be better off hiring a good professional who specializes in that specific field rather than hiring a financial planner.

Recognizing conflicts of interest

All professions have conflicts of interest. Some fields have more than others, and the financial-planning field is one of those fields. Knowing where some of the land mines are located can certainly help. Here, then, are the most common reasons that planners may not have 20/20 vision when giving financial directions.

Selling and pushing products that pay commissions

If a financial planner isn't charging you a fee for his time, you can rest assured that he's earning commissions on the products he tries to sell you and thus needs a broker's license. A person who sells financial products and then earns commissions from those products is a salesperson, *not* a financial planner. Financial planning done well involves taking an objective, holistic look at your financial situation — something brokers are neither trained nor financially motivated to do.

To make discerning a planner's agenda even harder, you can't assume that planners who charge fees for their time don't also earn commissions selling products. This compensation double dipping is common.

Selling products that provide a commission tends to skew a planner's recommendations. Products that carry commissions result in fewer of your dollars going to the investments and insurance you buy. Because a commission is earned only when a product is sold, such a product or service is inevitably more attractive in the planner's eyes than other options. For example, consider the case of a planner who sells disability insurance that you can obtain at a lower cost through your employer or a group trade association (see Chapter 16). He may overlook or criticize your most attractive option (buying through your employer) and focus on *his* most attractive option — selling you a higher-cost disability policy on which he derives a commission.

"Financial planning" in banks

Many banks have "financial representatives" and "investment specialists" sitting in their branches, waiting to pounce on bank customers with big balances. In many banks, these "financial planners" are simply brokers who are out to sell investments that pay them (and the bank) hefty sales commissions.

Customers often have no idea that these bank reps are earning commissions and that those commissions are being siphoned out of customers' investment dollars. Many customers are mistaken (partly due to the banks' and salespeople's poor disclosure) in believing that these investments, like bank savings accounts, are FDIC-insured and cannot lose value.

Another danger of trusting the recommendation of a commission-based planner is that he may steer you toward the products that have the biggest payback for him. These products are among the *worst* for you because they siphon off even more of your money up-front to pay the commission. They also tend to be among the costliest and riskiest financial products available.

Planners who are commission-greedy may also try to *churn* your investments. They encourage you to frequently buy and sell, attributing the need to changes in the economy or the companies you invested in. More trading means more commissions for the broker.

Taking a narrow view

Because of the way they earn their money, many planners are biased in favor of certain strategies and products. As a result, they typically don't keep your overall financial needs in mind. For example, if you have a problem with accumulated consumer debts, some planners may never know (or care) because they're focused on selling you an investment product. Likewise, a planner who sells a lot of life insurance tends to develop recommendations that require you to purchase it.

Not recommending saving through your employer's retirement plan

Taking advantage of saving through your employer's retirement savings plan(s) is one of your best financial options. Although this method of saving may not be as exciting as risking your money in cattle futures, it's not as dull as watching paint dry — and most important, it's tax-deductible. Some planners are reluctant to recommend taking full advantage of this option: It doesn't leave much money for the purchase of their commission-laden investment products.

Ignoring debts

Sometimes paying off outstanding loans — such as credit-card, auto, or even mortgage debts — is your best investment option. But most financial planners don't recommend this strategy because paying down debts depletes the capital with which you could otherwise buy investments — the investments that the broker may be trying to sell you to earn a commission or that the advisor would like to manage for an ongoing fee.

Not recommending real estate and small-business investments

Investing in real estate and small business, like paying off debts, takes money away from your investing elsewhere. Most planners won't help with these choices. They may even tell you tales of real-estate- and small-business-investing disasters to dissuade you.

The value of real estate can go down just like any other investment. But over the long haul, owning real estate makes good financial sense for most people. With small business, the risks are higher, but so are the potential returns. Don't let a financial planner convince you that these options are foolish — in fact, if you do your homework and know what you're doing, you can make higher rates of return investing in real estate and small business than you can in traditional securities such as stocks and bonds.

That said, certain real-estate and small-business investments can be risky, inefficient, and illiquid — so caution by an advisor informed in these fields (and that's a key point) may be helpful. See Part III to read more about your real-estate and small-business investment options.

Selling ongoing money-management services

The vast majority of financial planners who don't work on commission make their money by managing your money for an ongoing fee percentage (typically 1 to 1.5 percent of your investment annually). Although this fee removes the incentive to *churn* your account (frequently trade your investments) to run up more commissions, the service is something that you're unlikely to need. (As I explain in Part III, you can hire professional money managers for less.)

An ongoing fee percentage still creates a conflict of interest: The financial planner may tend to steer you away from beneficial financial strategies that reduce the asset pool from which he derives his percentage. Financial strategies such as maximizing contributions to your employer's retirement savings plan, paying off debts like your mortgage, investing in real estate or small business, and so on may make the most sense for you. Advisors who work on a percentage-of-assets-under-management basis may be biased against such strategies.

Selling legal services

Some planners are in the business of drawing up trusts and providing other estate-planning services for their clients. Although these and other legal documents may be right for you, legal matters are complex enough that the competence of someone who isn't a full-time legal specialist should be carefully scrutinized. And lower-cost options may be available if your situation is not complicated.

If you need help determining whether you need these legal documents, do some additional reading or consult an advisor who won't actually perform the work. If you do ultimately hire someone to perform estate-planning services for you, make sure you hire someone who specializes in estate planning and works at it full time. See Chapter 17 to find out more about estate planning.

Scaring you unnecessarily

Some planners put together nifty computer-generated projections that show you that you're going to need millions of dollars by the time you retire to maintain your standard of living or that college will cost hundreds of thousands of dollars by the time your 2-year-old is ready to enroll.

Waking up a client to the realities of his financial situation is an important and difficult job for good financial planners. But some planners take this task to an extreme, deliberately scaring you into buying what they're selling. They paint a bleak picture and imply that you can fix your problems only if you do what they say. Don't let them scare you; read this book and get your financial life in order.

Creating dependency

Many financial planners create dependency by making things seem so complicated that their clients feel as though they could never manage their finances on their own. If your advisor is reluctant to tell you how you can educate yourself about personal money management, you probably have a self-perpetuating consultant. Financial planning is hardly the only occupation guilty of this. As author George Bernard Shaw said, "All professions are conspiracies against the laity."

Finding a Good Financial Planner

Locating a good financial planner who is willing to work with the not-yet-rich-and-famous and who doesn't have conflicts of interest can feel like trying to find a needle in a haystack. Personal referrals and associations are two methods that can serve as good starting points.

Soliciting personal referrals

Getting a personal referral from a satisfied customer you trust is one of the best ways to find a good financial planner. Obtaining a referral from an accountant or attorney whose judgment you've tested can help as well. (Beware that such professionals in other fields may also do some financial planning and recommend themselves.)

The best financial planners continue to build their practices through word of mouth. Satisfied customers are a professional's best and least costly marketers. However, you should *never* take a recommendation from anyone as gospel. I don't care *who* is making the referral — even if it's your mother or the pope. You must do your homework. Ask the planner the questions I list in the upcoming section "Interviewing Financial Advisors: Asking the Right Questions." I've seen people get into real trouble because of blindly accepting someone else's recommendation. Remember that the person making the recommendation is (probably) not a financial expert and may be financially clueless.

You may get referred to a planner or broker who returns the favor by sending business to the tax, legal, or real-estate person who referred you. Hire professionals who make referrals to others based on their competence and ethics.

Seeking advisors through associations

Associations of financial planners are more than happy to refer you to planners in your area. But as I discuss earlier in this chapter, the major trade associations are composed of planners who sell products and work on commission.

Here are two solid places to start searching for good financial planners:

- ✔ **The National Association of Personal Financial Advisors:** The NAPFA (phone 888-333-6659; website www.napfa.org) is made up of fee-only planners. Its members are not supposed to earn commissions from products they sell or recommend. However, most planners in this association earn their living by providing money-management services and charging a fee that is a percentage of assets under management. And most have minimums, which can put them out of reach of the majority of people.

- ✔ **The American Institute of Certified Public Accountants:** The AICPA (phone 888-777-7077; website www.aicpa.org) is the professional association of CPAs, and it can provide names of members who have completed the Institute's Personal Financial Specialist (PFS) program.

Many of the CPAs who have completed the PFS program provide financial advice on a fee basis. Competent CPAs have the advantage of understanding the tax consequences of different choices, which are important components of any financial plan. On the other hand, it can be hard for a professional to keep current in two broad fields.

Interviewing Financial Advisors: Asking the Right Questions

Don't consider hiring a financial advisor until you read the rest of this book. If you're not educated about personal finance, how can you possibly evaluate the competence of someone you may hire to help you make important financial decisions?

I firmly believe that you are your own best financial advisor. However, I know that some people don't want to make financial decisions without getting assistance. Perhaps you're busy or simply can't stand making money decisions. You need to recognize that you have a lot at stake when you hire a financial advisor. Besides the cost of his services, which generally don't come cheap, you're placing a lot of trust in his recommendations. The more you know, the better the advisor you can hire and the fewer services you need to buy.

The following questions will help you get to the core of an advisor's competence and professional integrity. Get answers to these questions *before* you decide to hire a financial advisor.

What percentage of your income comes from clients' fees versus commissions?

Asking this question first may save you the trouble and time of asking the next nine questions. The right answer is "100 percent of my income comes from fees paid by clients." Anything less than 100 percent means that the person you're speaking to is a salesperson with a vested interest in recommending certain strategies and products.

Sadly, more than a few financial advisors don't tell the truth. In one undercover investigation, about one-third of self-proclaimed fee-only advisors turned out to be brokers who also sold investment and insurance products on a commission basis.

How can you ferret these people out? Advisors who provide investment advice and oversee at least $100 million must register with the U.S. Securities and Exchange Commission (SEC); otherwise, they generally must register with the state that they make their principal place of business. They must file Form ADV, otherwise known as the Uniform Application for Investment Adviser Registration. This lengthy document asks for the following specific information from investment advisors:

- A breakdown of where their income comes from

- Relationships and affiliations with other companies

- Education and employment history

- The types of securities the advisory firm recommends

- The advisor's fee schedule

In short, Form ADV provides — in black and white — answers to all the essential questions. With a sales pitch over the phone or marketing materials sent in the mail, a planner is much more likely to gloss over or avoid certain issues. Although some advisors fib on Form ADV, most advisors are more truthful on this form than they are in their own marketing. You can ask the advisor to send you a copy of Form ADV. You can also find out whether the advisor is registered and whether he has a track record of problems by calling the SEC at 800-732-0330 or by visiting its website at www.adviserinfo. sec.gov.

Many states require the registration of financial advisors, so you should also contact the department that oversees advisors in your state. Visit the North American Securities Administrators Association's website (www.nasaa.org) and click on the "Contact Your Regulator" link on the home page.

What portion of client fees is for money management versus hourly planning?

The answer to how the advisor is paid provides clues to whether he has an agenda to persuade you to hire him to manage your money. If you want objective and specific financial planning recommendations, give preference to advisors who derive their income from hourly fees. Many counselors and advisors call themselves "fee-based," which usually means that they make their living managing money for a percentage.

If you want a money manager, you can hire the best quite inexpensively through a mutual fund. Or, if you have substantial assets, you can hire an established money manager (refer to Chapter 10).

What is your hourly fee?

The rates for financial advisors range from as low as $75 per hour up to several hundred dollars per hour. If you shop around, you can find fine planners who charge around $100 to $150 per hour. As you compare planners, remember that what matters is the total cost that you can expect to pay for the services you're seeking.

Do you also perform tax or legal services?

Be wary of someone who claims to be an expert beyond one area. The tax, legal, and financial fields are vast in and of themselves, and they're difficult for even the best and brightest advisor to cover simultaneously.

One exception is the accountant who also performs some basic financial planning by the hour. Likewise, a good financial advisor should have a solid grounding in the basic tax and legal issues that relate to your personal finances. Large firms may have specialists available in different areas.

What work and educational experience qualifies you to be a financial planner?

This question doesn't have one right answer. Ideally, a planner should have experience in the business or financial services field. Some say to look for planners with at least five or ten years of experience. I've always wondered how planners earn a living their first five or ten years if folks won't hire them until they reach these benchmarks! A planner should also be good with numbers, speak in plain English, and have good interpersonal skills.

Education is sort of like food. Too little leaves you hungry. Too much can leave you feeling stuffed and uncomfortable. And a small amount of high quality is better than a lot of low quality.

Because investment decisions are a critical part of financial planning, take note of the fact that the most-common designations of educational training among professional money managers are MBA (master of business administration) and CFA (chartered financial analyst). And some tax advisors who work on an hourly basis have the PFS (personal financial specialist) credential.

Have you ever sold limited partnerships? Options? Futures? Commodities? Invested with Madoff?

The correct answers here are *no, no, no, no,* and *no.* If you don't know what these disasters are, refer to Chapter 9. (Bernie Madoff ran a hedge fund that was actually a Ponzi scheme.) You also need to be wary of any financial advisor who used to deal in these areas but now claims to have seen the light and reformed his ways. (Some sophisticated advisors may use some of these instruments to hedge or reduce risk, but be sure you understand what they're doing and that you and the advisor fully understand all costs and potential risks.)

Professionals with poor judgment may not repeat the same mistakes, but they're more likely to make some new ones at your expense. My experience is that even advisors who have been "reformed" are unlikely to be working by the hour. Most of them either work on commission or want to manage your money for a hefty fee.

Do you carry liability (errors and omissions) insurance?

Some counselors may be surprised by this question or think that you're a problem customer looking for a lawsuit. On the other hand, accidents happen; that's why insurance exists. So if the planner doesn't have liability insurance, he has missed one of the fundamental concepts of planning: Insure against risk. Don't make the mistake of hiring him.

You wouldn't (and shouldn't) let contractors into your home to do work without knowing that they have insurance to cover any mistakes they make. Likewise, you should insist on hiring a planner who carries protection in case he makes a major mistake for which he is liable. Make sure that he carries enough coverage given what he is helping you with.

Can you provide references from clients with needs similar to mine?

Take the time to talk to other people who have used the planner. Ask what the planner did for them, and find out what the advisor's greatest strengths and weaknesses are. You can find out a bit about the planner's track record and style. And because you want to have as productive a relationship as possible with your planner, the more you find out about him, the easier it'll be for you to hit the ground running if you hire him.

Some financial advisors offer a "complimentary" introductory consultation. If an advisor offers a free consultation to allow you to check him out and it makes you feel more comfortable about hiring him, fair enough. But be careful: Most free consultations end up being a big sales pitch for certain products or services the advisor offers.

The fact that a planner doesn't offer a free consultation may be a good sign. Counselors who are busy and who work strictly by the hour can't afford to burn an hour of their time for an in-person free session. They also need to be careful of folks seeking free advice. Such advisors usually are willing to spend some time on the phone answering background questions. They should also be able to send background materials by mail and provide references.

Will you provide specific strategies and product recommendations that I can implement on my own if I choose?

This is an important question. Some advisors may indicate that you can hire them by the hour. But then they provide only generic advice without specifics. Some planners even *double dip* — they charge an hourly fee initially to make you feel like you're not working with a salesperson, and then they try selling commission-based products. Also be aware of advisors who say that you can choose to implement their recommendations on your own and then recommend financial products that carry commissions.

How is implementation handled?

Ideally, you should find an advisor who lets you choose whether you want to hire him to help with implementation after the recommendations have been presented to you. If you know that you're going to follow through on the advice and you can do so without further discussions and questions, don't hire the planner to help you implement his recommendations.

On the other hand, if you hire the counselor because you lack the time, desire, and/or expertise to manage your financial life in the first place, building implementation into the planning work makes good sense.

Learning from Others' Mistakes

Over the many years that I've worked as a financial counselor and now fielding questions from readers, I hear too many problems that people encounter from hiring incompetent and unethical financial advisors. To avoid repeating others' mistakes, please remember the following:

- ✔ **You absolutely must do your homework before hiring any financial advisor.** Despite recommendations from others about a particular advisor, you can end up with bad advice from biased advisors.

- ✔ **Avoid or minimize conflicts of interest.** The financial planning and brokerage fields are minefields for consumers. The fundamental problem is the enormous conflict of interest that is created when "advisors" sell products that earn them sales commissions. Selling ongoing money management services creates a conflict of interest as well.

- ✔ **You are your own best advocate.** The more you know, and the more you understand that investing and other financial decisions needn't be complicated, the more you realize that you don't need to spend gobs of money (or any money at all) on financial planners and advisors. When you look in the mirror, you see the person who has your best interests at heart and is your best financial advisor.

Chapter 19

Using Technology to Manage Your Money

In This Chapter

▶ Evaluating money management software and websites

▶ Performing financial tasks via technology

*A*lthough a computer and, to a lesser extent, a smartphone may be able to assist you with your personal finances, they simply represent a couple of many tools. Computers are best for performing routine tasks (such as processing lots of bills or performing many calculations) quickly and for aiding you with research.

This chapter gives you an overview of how to use technology, software, and cyberspace with your finances. I tell you how to use this technology to pay your bills, prepare taxes, research investments, plan for retirement, trade and invest, buy insurance, and plan your estate, and I suggest the best software, websites, and apps.

Surveying Software and Websites

You can access two major repositories of personal finance information through your computer. Although the lines are blurring between these two categories, they're roughly defined as software and the Internet:

✔ *Software* refers to computer programs that are either packaged in a box or DVD case or are available to be downloaded online. Most of the mass-marketed financial software packages sell for under $100. If you've ever used a word-processing program such as Microsoft Word or a spreadsheet program such as Microsoft Excel, then you've used software. *Apps,* which you download onto a smartphone or tablet, are kind of like software. They run on your phone and tend to be less costly (albeit generally less sophisticated) than computer software.

✔ *The Internet* refers to sites that provide information and services to help you manage your financial life, including online bill-paying. Most of the financial stuff on the Internet is supplied by companies marketing their wares and, hence, is available for free. Some sites sell their content for a fee.

Adding up financial software benefits

Although the number of personal-finance software packages, apps, and websites is large and growing, quality is lagging behind quantity, especially among the free Internet sites. The best programs can

✔ Guide you to better organization and management of your personal finances

✔ Help you complete mundane tasks or complex calculations quickly and easily and provide basic advice in unfamiliar territory

✔ Make you feel in control of your financial life

Mediocre and bad software, on the other hand, can make you feel stupid or, at the very least, make you want to scream. Lousy packages usually end up in the software graveyard.

Having reviewed many of the packages available, I can assure you that if you're having a hard time with some of the programs out there (and sometimes even with the more useful programs), you're not at fault. Too many packages assume that you already know things such as your tax rate, your mortgage options, and the difference between stock and bond mutual funds. Much of what's out there is too technically oriented and isn't user-friendly. Some of it is even flawed in its financial accuracy.

A good software package, like a good tax or financial advisor, helps you better manage your finances. It simply and concisely explains financial terminology, and it helps you make decisions by offering choices and recommendations, allowing you to "play" with alternatives before following a particular course of action. With increasing regularity, financial software packages are being designed to perform more than one task or to address more than one area of personal finances. But remember that no software package covers the whole range of issues in your financial life. Later in this chapter, I recommend some of my favorite financial software and apps.

Surfing hazards online

Like the information you receive from any medium, you have to sift out
the good from the bad when you surf the Internet. If you blindly navigate
the Internet and naively think that what's out there is useful "information,"
"research," or "objective advice," you're in for a rude awakening.

Most personal-finance sites on the Internet are free, which — guess what —
means that these sites are basically advertising or are dominated and driven
by advertising. If you're looking for material written by unbiased experts
or writers, finding it on the web may seem like searching for the proverbial
needle in the haystack because the vast majority of what's online is biased
and uninformed.

Considering the source so you can recognize bias

A report on the Internet published by a leading investment-banking firm provides a list of the "coolest finance" sites. On the list is the website of a major
bank. Because it has been a long time since I was in junior high school, I'm
not quite sure what "cool" means anymore. If cool can be used to describe a
well-organized and graphically pleasing website, then I guess I can say that
the bank's site is cool.

However, if you're looking for sound information and advice, then the bank's
site is decidedly "uncool." It steers you in a financial direction that benefits
(not surprisingly) the bank and not you. For example, in the real-estate section, users are asked to plug in their gross monthly income and down payment. The information is then used to spit out the supposed amount that
users can "afford" to spend on a home. No mention is given to the other
financial goals and concerns — such as saving for retirement — that affect
one's ability to spend a particular amount of money on a home.

Consider this advice in the lending area of the site: "When you don't have
the cash on hand for important purchases, we can help you borrow what
you need. From a new car, to that vacation you've been longing for, to new
kitchen appliances, you can make these dreams real now." Click on a button
at the bottom of this screen — and presto, you're on your way to racking up
credit-card and auto debt. Why bother practicing delayed gratification, living
within your means, or buying something used if getting a loan is "easy" and
comes with "special privileges"?

Watching out for "sponsored" content

Sponsored content, a euphemism for advertising under the guise of editorial content (known in the print media as *advertorials*), is another big problem to watch out for on websites. You may find a disclaimer or note, which is often buried in small print in an obscure part of the website, saying that an article is sponsored by (in other words, paid advertising by) the "author."

A mutual-fund "education" site, for example, states that its "primary purpose is to provide viewers with an independent guide that contains information and articles they can't get anywhere else." The content of the site suggests otherwise. In the "Expert's Corner" section of the site, material is reprinted from a newsletter that advocates frequent trading in and out of mutual funds to try and guess and time market moves. Turns out that the article is "sponsored by the featured expert": In other words, it's a paid advertisement. (The track record of the newsletter's past recommendations, which isn't discussed on the site, is poor.)

Even more troubling is the increasing number of websites that fail to disclose (even cryptically) that their "content" comes from advertisers. Print publications generally have a tradition of disclosing when an article is paid advertising, but in the Wild West online, many sites fail to make this simple and vital disclosure. Mind you, I'm not saying that disclosure makes paid-for content okay — I'm simply stating that a lack of disclosure makes an already bad situation even worse.

Also, beware of websites, especially those that are "free," that are making money in a clandestine way from two sources: companies whose products they praise and affiliates to whom they direct mouse clicks/web traffic. In perusing the web, I noticed, for example, that many "free" financial websites were singing the praises of the software You Need A Budget (YNAB). I test-drove the product (which is like a slimmed-down version of Quicken or Microsoft Money), and it's a decent but not exceptional product. My research uncovered the fact that the makers of YNAB pay a whopping 35-percent commission to website affiliates who pitch and direct users to buy the product. YNAB sells for $60, so a website flogging it for them pockets $21 for each copy it sells. Does that taint a site's recommendation of YNAB? Of course it does.

Increasingly, companies are paying websites outright to simply mention and praise their products; doing so is incredibly sleazy even if it's disclosed, but to do so without disclosure is unethical. Also beware of links to recommended product and service providers to do business with — more often than not, the referring website gets paid an affiliate fee. Look for sites that post policies against receiving such referral fees from companies whose products and services they recommend. (As an example, see the disclosure I use on my own site, www.erictyson.com.)

Steering clear of biased financial-planning advice

I also suggest skipping the financial-planning advice offered by financial service companies that are out to sell you something. Such companies can't take the necessary objective, holistic view required to render useful advice.

For example, on one major investment company's website, you find a good deal of material on the firm's mutual funds. The site's college-planning advice is off the mark because it urges parents to put money in a custodial account in the child's name. Ignored is the fact that doing so will undermine your child's ability to qualify for financial aid (see Chapter 13), that your child will have control of the money at either age 18 or 21 depending upon your state, and that you're likely better off funding your employer's retirement plan. If you did that, though, you couldn't set up a college savings-plan account at the fund company.

Shunning short-term thinking

Many financial websites provide real-time stock quotes as a hook to a site that is cluttered with advertising. My experience working with individual investors is that the more short-term they think, the worse they do. And checking your portfolio during the trading day certainly promotes short-term thinking.

Another way that sites create an addictive environment for you to return to multiple times daily is to constantly provide news and other rapidly changing content. Do you really need "Breaking News" updates that gasoline prices jumped 19 cents per gallon over the past two weeks or that yet another cable show personality is having a contest with a Hollywood celebrity to see who can sign up more Twitter followers in the next week?

Also, beware of tips offered around the electronic water cooler — comment sections. As in the real world, chatting with strangers and exchanging ideas are sometimes fine. However, if you don't know the identity and competence of commenters, why would you follow their financial advice or stock tips? Getting ideas from various sources is okay, but educate yourself and do your homework before making personal financial decisions.

If you want to best manage your personal finances and find out more, remember that the old expression "You get what you pay for" contains a grain of truth. Free information on the Internet, especially information provided by companies in the financial-services industry, is largely self-serving. Stick with information providers who have proven themselves offline or who don't have anything to sell except objective information and advice.

Accomplishing Money Tasks on Your Computer, Tablet, or Smartphone

In the remainder of this chapter, I detail important personal financial tasks that your computer can assist you with. I also provide my recommendations for the best software and websites to help you accomplish these chores.

Paying your bills and tracking your money

Plenty of folks have trouble saving money and reducing their spending. Thus, it's no surprise that in the increasingly crowded universe of free websites, plenty are devoted to supposedly helping you to reduce your spending. More of these websites and apps keep springing up, but among those you may have heard of and stumbled upon are Geezeo, Mint, Mvelopes, Wally, and Yodlee. As you can already see, attracting attention online starts with having a quirky name!

I've kicked the tires and checked out these sites and frankly have mixed to negative feelings about them. The biggest problems I have with these sites are that they're loaded with advertising and/or have affiliate relationships with companies. What does this mean? The site gets paid if you click on a link to one of its recommended service providers and buy what it's selling.

I will give credit to Mint for at least admitting in black and white that it is soliciting and receiving affiliate payments when it states on its site:

> *"How can Mint be free? We give you personalized ideas on how to save money by showing you the best way to save among thousands of financial products. If you decide to make a change that saves you some cash, we sometimes earn a small fee from the bank or company you switch to."*

This, of course, creates an enormous conflict of interest and thoroughly taints any recommendation made by Mint and similar sites that profit from affiliate referrals. For starters, they have no incentive or reason to recommend companies that won't pay them an affiliate fee. And, there's little — if any — screening of companies for quality service levels that are important to you as a consumer.

Also, be forewarned that after registering you as a site user, the first thing most of these sites want you to do is connect directly to your financial institutions (banks, brokerages, investment companies) and download your investment account and spending data. If your instincts tell you this might not be a good idea, you should trust your instincts. Yes, there are security concerns, but those pale in comparison to privacy concerns and concerns about the endless pitching to you of products and services.

Another problem that I have with these websites is the incredibly simplistic calculators they offer. One that purported to help with retirement planning didn't allow users to choose a retirement age younger than 62 and had no provisions for part-time work. When it asked about your assets, it made no distinction between equity in your home and financial assets (stocks, bonds, mutual funds, and so on). Finally, if you encounter a problem using these sites, they generally offer no phone support, so you're relegated to ping-ponging emails in the hopes of getting your questions answered.

Quicken is a good software program that helps with expense tracking and bill paying. In addition to offering printed checks and electronic bill-payment, Quicken is a financial organizer. The program allows you to list your investments and other assets, along with your loans and other financial liabilities. Quicken automates the process of paying your bills, and it can track your check-writing and prepare reports that detail your spending by category so you can find the fat in your budget. (For a complete discussion on how to track your spending, see Chapter 3.)

In addition to the significant investment of time necessary to figure out how to use Quicken, another drawback is the cost of computer checks if you buy them from the software company. You can chop those costs by ordering from other companies, such as Checks Tomorrow (website www. checkstomorrow.com).

You can avoid dealing with paper checks — written or printed — by signing up for *online bill payment.* With such services, you save on checks, stamps, and envelopes. These services are available to anyone with a checking account through an increasing number of banks, credit unions, and brokerage firms, as well as through Quicken. Another option is to sign up through CheckFree's website: www.mycheckfree.com.

Planning for retirement

Good retirement-planning software and online tools can help you plan for retirement by crunching the numbers for you. But they can also teach you how particular changes — such as your investment returns, the rate of inflation, or your savings rate — can affect when and in what style you can retire. The biggest time-saving aspect of retirement-planning software and websites is that they let you more quickly play with and see the consequences of changing the assumptions.

Some of the major investment companies I profile in Part III of this book are sources for some high-quality, low-cost retirement-planning tools. Here are some good ones to consider:

✔ **T. Rowe Price's website** (www.troweprice.com) has several tools that can help you determine where you stand in terms of reaching a given retirement goal. T. Rowe Price (phone 800-225-5132) also offers some excellent workbooklets for helping you plan for retirement. Expect some marketing of T. Rowe Price's mutual funds in its booklets and software.

✔ **Vanguard's website** (www.vanguard.com) can help with figuring savings goals to reach retirement goals as well as with managing your budget and assets in retirement.

Preparing your taxes

Good, properly used tax-preparation software can save you time and money. The best programs "interview" you to gather the necessary information and select the appropriate forms based on your responses. Of course, you're still the one responsible for locating all the information needed to complete your return. More-experienced taxpayers can bypass the interview and jump directly to the forms they know they need to complete. These programs also help flag overlooked deductions and identify other tax-reducing strategies.

TurboTax and H&R Block Tax Software are among the better tax-preparation programs I've reviewed.

In addition to the federal tax packages, tax-preparation programs are available for state income taxes, too. Many state tax forms are fairly easy to complete because they're based on information from your federal form. If your state tax forms are based on your federal form, you may want to skip buying the state income-tax preparation packages and prepare your state return by hand.

If you're mainly looking for tax forms, you can get them at no charge in tax-preparation books or through the IRS's website (www.irs.gov).

Researching investments

Gone are the days of schlepping off to the library to look at investing reference manuals, buying print versions for your own use, or slogging through voice-mail hell when you call government agencies. Today you can access these and other investing resources on your computer. You can also often pay for just what you need:

- ✔ **The SEC:** The Securities and Exchange Commission (SEC) allows unlimited, free access to its documents at `www.sec.gov`. All public corporations, as well as mutual funds, file their reports with the agency. Be aware, however, that navigating this site takes patience.

- ✔ **Morningstar:** You can access Morningstar's individual stock and mutual fund reports at `www.morningstar.com`. The basic reports are free, but they're watered-down versions of the company's comprehensive software and paper products. If you want to buy Morningstar's unabridged fund reports online, you can do so for a fee.

- ✔ **Vanguard:** Although I'm leery of financial service company "educational" materials because of bias and self-serving advice, some companies do a worthy job on these materials. The investor-friendly, thrifty Vanguard Group of mutual funds has an online university on its website (`www.vanguard.com`), where investors can learn the basics of fund investing. Additionally, investors in Vanguard's funds can access up-to-date personal account information through the site.

Trading online

If you do your investing homework, trading securities online may save you money and perhaps some time. For years, discount brokers (which I discuss in Chapter 8) were heralded as the low-cost source for trading. Then, online brokers such as E*TRADE Financial (phone 800-387-2331; website `www.etrade.com`) and Scottrade (phone 800-619-7283; website `www.scottrade.com`) set a lower-cost standard. The major mutual-fund companies, such as T. Rowe Price and Vanguard, also offer competitive online services.

A number of discount brokers have built their securities brokerage business around online trading. By eliminating the overhead of branch offices and by accepting and processing trades by computer, online brokers keep their costs and brokerage charges to a minimum. Cut-rate electronic brokerage firms are for people who want to direct their own financial affairs and don't want or need to work with a personal broker. However, some of these brokers have limited products and services. For example, some don't offer many of the best mutual funds. And my own experience with reaching live people at some online brokers has been trying — I've had to wait on hold for more than ten minutes before a customer service representative answered the call.

Although online trading may save you on transaction costs, it can also encourage you to trade more than you should, resulting in higher total trading costs, lower investment returns, and higher income tax bills. Following investments on a daily basis encourages you to think short-term. Remember that the best investments are bought and held for the long haul (see Part III for more information).

Reading and searching periodicals

Many business and financial publications are online, offering investors news and financial market data. *The Wall Street Journal* provides an online, personalized edition of the paper (www.wsj.com) that allows you to tailor the content to meet your specific needs. The cost is $28.99 per month.

Leading business publications such as *Forbes* (www.forbes.com) and *BusinessWeek* (www.bloomberg.com/businessweek) put their current magazines' content on the Internet. Some publications are charging for archived articles and for some current content for nonsubscribers to their print magazine. Be careful to take what you read and hear in the mass media with many grains of salt (see Chapter 20 for more on mass media). Much of the content revolves around tweaking people's anxieties and dwelling on the latest crises and fads.

My website (www.erictyson.com) includes analysis of current news and highlights and summarizes the best content from many sources and sites, including leading newsletters.

Investing through automated investment managers: Robo advisors

Increasing numbers of websites offer an automated investing service. These sites purport to help you choose an overall investment mix (asset allocation) and then divvy that money up, typically among exchange-traded funds. Over time, the allocations can be tweaked or adjusted based on some predetermined formulas.

For this largely automated service, so-called robo advisors like Betterment and WealthFront generally charge around 0.25 percent to 0.5 percent per year of the assets they are managing. I believe that you can educate yourself enough about investing in funds that paying an ongoing fee for such services isn't worth it.

Buying life insurance

If loved ones are financially dependent on you, you probably know you need life insurance. But add together the dread of life-insurance salespeople and a fear of death, and you have a recipe for procrastination. Although your computer can't stave off the Grim Reaper, it can help you find a quality, low-cost policy that can be more than 80 percent less costly than the most expensive options, all without having you deal with high-pressure sales tactics.

The best way to shop for term life insurance online is through one of the quotation services I discuss in Chapter 16. At each of these sites, you fill in your date of birth, whether you smoke, how much coverage you'd like, and for how long you'd like to lock in the initial premium. When you're done filling in this information, a new web page pops up with a list of low-cost quotes (based on assumed good health) from highly rated (for financial stability) insurance companies.

Invariably, the quotes are ranked by how cheap they are. Although cost is certainly an important factor, many of these services don't do as good of a job explaining other important factors to consider when doing your comparison shopping. For example, the services sometimes don't cover the projected and maximum rates after the initial term has expired. Be sure to ask about these other future rates before you agree to a specific policy.

If you decide to buy a policy from one of the online agencies, you can fill out an online application form. The quotation agency will then mail you a detailed description of the policy and insurer, along with your completed application. In addition to having to deal with snail mail, you'll also have to deal with a *medical technician,* who will drop by your home to check on your health status . . . at least until some computer genius figures out a way for you to give blood and urine samples online!

Preparing legal documents

Just as you can prepare a tax return with the advice of a software program, you can also prepare common legal documents. This type of software may save you from the often difficult task of finding a competent and affordable attorney.

Using legal software is generally preferable to using fill-in-the-blank documents. Software has the built-in virtues of directing and limiting your choices and preventing you from making common mistakes. Quality software also incorporates the knowledge and insights of the legal eagles who developed the software. And it can save you money.

If your situation isn't unusual, legal software may work well for you. As to the legality of documents that you create with legal software, remember that a will, for example, is made legal and valid by your witnesses; the fact that an attorney prepares the document is *not* what makes it legal.

An excellent package for preparing your own will is Quicken WillMaker Plus, which is published by Nolo, a name synonymous with high quality and user-friendliness in the legal publishing world. In addition to allowing you to prepare wills, WillMaker can also help you prepare a living will and medical power of attorney document. The software also allows you to create a living trust that serves to keep property out of probate in the event of your death (see Chapter 17). Like wills, living trusts are fairly standard legal documents that you can properly create with the guidance of a top-notch software package. The package advises you to seek professional guidance for your situation, if necessary.

Chapter 20

On Air and in Print

*W*e have too many options for finding radio and television news, websites, newspapers, magazines, and books that talk about money and purport to help you get rich. Tuning out poor resources and focusing on the best ones are the real challenges.

Because you probably don't consider yourself a financial expert, more often than not you won't know who to believe and listen to. I help you solve that problem in this chapter.

Observing the Mass Media

For better and for worse, America's mass media has a profound influence on our culture. On the good side, news is widely disseminated these days. So if a product is recalled or a dangerous virus breaks out in your area, you'll probably hear about it, perhaps more than you want to, through the media or from tuned-in family members! The downsides of the mass media are plenty, though.

Alarming or informing?

In case you didn't already know, you've recently lived through the second Great Depression. During the "financial crisis" of 2008–09, we heard over and over and over again how it was the worst economy and worst economic crisis since the Great Depression. Endless parallels were drawn between the Great Depression of the 1930s and the recently slumping economy.

For sure, we suffered a significant recession (economic downturn). But some in the news media (and pundit class) went overboard in suggesting we were in the midst of another depression. During the Great Depression of the 1930s, the unemployment rate hit 25 percent and remained in double digits for years on end. Half of all homes ended up in foreclosure during that period. Although job losses and home foreclosures mounted during the recent recession, they were nowhere near the Great Depression levels. The recessions of the late 1970s and early 1980s were actually worse because of the pain and hardship caused by the 10+ percent inflation rate and interest rates of that period. The unemployment rate was also above 10 percent in the early 1980s recession.

The U.S. stock market suffered a steep decline during the recent recession and, in fact, the percentage decline in the widely followed Dow Jones Industrial Average was the worst since the 1930s. Interestingly, the severity of the 2008–09 stock market decline was likely exacerbated by all the talk and fear of another Depression. Various research polls taken during late 2008 found that more than 6 in 10 Americans believed we were about to enter another Great Depression. Those who panicked and bailed out when the Dow sagged below 6,500 in early 2009 learned another hard lesson when the market surged back, as it always inevitably does after a significant sell-off. (To date, the Dow has nearly tripled in value since that market bottom in '09).

Some news producers, in their quest for ratings and advertising dollars, try to be alarming to keep you tuned in and coming back for their "breaking news" updates. The more you watch, the more unnerved you get over short-term, especially negative, events.

Teaching questionable values

Daily doses of American mass media, including all the advertising that comes with them, essentially communicate the following messages:

- Your worth as a person is directly related to your physical appearance (including the quality of clothing and jewelry you wear) and your material possessions — cars, homes, electronics, and other gadgets.

- The more money you make, the more "successful" you clearly are.

- The more famous you are (especially as a movie or sports star), the more you're worth listening to and admiring.

- Don't bother concerning yourself with the consequences before engaging in negative behavior.

- Delaying gratification and making sacrifices are for boring losers.

Continually inundating yourself with poor messages can cause you to behave in a way that undermines your long-term happiness and financial success. Don't support (by watching, listening, or reading) forms of media that don't reflect your values and morals.

Worshipping prognosticating pundits

Quoting and interviewing experts are perhaps the only things that the media loves more than hyping short-term news events. What's the economy going to do next quarter? What's stock XYZ going to do next month? What's the stock market going to do in the next few hours? No, I'm not kidding about that last one — the stock market cable channel CNBC regularly interviews floor traders from the New York Stock Exchange during the trading day to get their opinions about what the market will do in the hours just before closing!

Prognosticating pundits keep many people tuned in because their advice is constantly changing (and is therefore entertaining and anxiety-producing), and they lead investors to believe that investments can be maneuvered in advance to outfox future financial market moves. Common sense suggests, though, that no one has a working crystal ball, and if he did, he certainly wouldn't share such insights with the mass media for free. (For more on experts who purport to predict the future, see Chapter 8.)

Rating Radio and Television Financial Programs

Over the years, money issues have received increased coverage through the major media of television and radio. Some topics gain more coverage in radio and TV because they help draw more advertising dollars (which follow what people are watching). When you turn on the radio or TV, you don't pay a fee to tune in to a particular channel (with pay cable channels being an exception). Advertising doesn't necessarily prevent a medium from delivering coverage that is objective and in your best interests, but it sure doesn't help foster this type of coverage either.

For example, can you imagine a financial radio or TV correspondent saying the following?

> *"We've decided to stop providing financial market updates every five minutes because we've found it causes some investors to become addicted to tracking the short-term movements in the markets and to lose sight of the bigger picture. We don't want to encourage people to make knee-jerk reactions to short-term events."*

Sound-bite-itis is another problem with both of these media. Producers and network executives believe that if you go into too much detail, viewers and listeners will change the channel.

Finding the Best Websites

Yes, the Internet has changed the world, but certainly not always for the better and not always in such a big way. Consider the way we shop. You can buy things online that you couldn't in the past. Purchasing items online broadens the avenues through which you can spend money. I see a big downside here: Overspending is easier to do when you surf the Internet a lot.

Some of the best websites allow you to more efficiently access information that may help you make important investing decisions. However, this doesn't mean that your computer allows you to compete at the same level as professional money managers. The best pros work at their craft full-time and have far more expertise and experience than the rest of us. Some nonprofessionals have been fooled into believing that investing online makes them better investors. My experience has been that people who spend time online every day dealing with investments tend to trade and react more to short-term events and have a harder time keeping the bigger picture and their long-term goals and needs in focus.

If you know where to look, you can more easily access some types of information. However, you often find a lot of garbage online — just as you do on other advertiser-dominated media like TV and radio. In Chapter 19, I explain how to safely navigate online to find the best of what's out there.

Navigating Newspapers and Magazines

Compared with radio and TV, print publications generally offer lengthier discussions of topics. And in the more financially focused publications, the editors who work on articles generally have more background in the topics they write about. Even within the better publications, I find a wide variety of quality. So don't instantly believe what you read, even if you read a piece in a publication you like. Here's how to get the most from financial periodicals:

✔ **Read some back issues.** Go to your local library (or visit the publication's website) and peruse some issues that are at least one to two years old. Although reading old issues may seem silly and pointless, it actually can be enlightening. You can begin to get a taste of a publication's style, priorities, and philosophies as well as how its prior advice has worked out.

✔ **Look for solid information and perspective.** Headlines reveal a lot about how a publication perceives its role. Publications with cover stories such as "10 hot stocks to buy now!" and "Funds that will double your money in the next three years!" are probably best avoided. Look for articles that seek to educate with accuracy, not predict.

✔ **Note bylines.** As you read a given publication over time, you should begin to make note of the different writers. After you get to know who the better writers are, you can skip over the ones you don't care for and spend your limited free time reading the best.

✔ **Don't react without planning.** Here's a common example of how *not* to use information and advice you glean from publications: I had a client who had some cash he wanted to invest. He would read an article about investing in real-estate investment trusts and then go out the next week and buy several of them. Then he'd see a mention of some technology stock funds and invest in some of those. Eventually his portfolio was a mess of investments that reflected the history of what he had read rather than an orchestrated, well-thought-out investment portfolio.

Betting on Books

Reading a good book is one of my favorite ways to get a crash course on a given financial topic. Good books can go into depth on a topic in a way that simply isn't possible with other resources. Books also aren't cluttered with advertising and the conflicts inherent therein.

As with the other types of resources I discuss in this chapter, you definitely have to choose carefully — plenty of mediocrity and garbage is out there.

Understanding the book publishing business

Book publishers are businesses first. And like most businesses, their business practices vary. Some have a reputation for care and quality; others just want to push a product out the door with maximum hype and minimum effort.

For instance, you may think that book publishers check out an author before they sign him to write an entire book. Well, you may be surprised to find out that some publishers don't do their homework. What most publishers care about first is the marketability of a particular book and author. Some authors are marketable because of their well-earned reputation for sound advice. Others are marketable because of stellar promotional campaigns built on smoke and mirrors. Even more troubling is that few publishers require advice guides to be technically reviewed for accuracy by an expert in the field other than the author, who sometimes is not an expert. You, the reader, are expected to be your own technical reviewer. But do you have the expertise to do that? (Don't worry; this book has been checked for accuracy.)

As an author and financial counselor, I know that financial ideas and strategies can differ considerably. Different is not necessarily wrong. When a technical reviewer looks at my text and makes a comment or suggestion, I take a second look. I may even see things in a new way. If I were the only expert to see my book before publication, I wouldn't benefit from this second expert opinion. How do you know whether a book has been technically reviewed? Check the credits page or the author's acknowledgments.

Authors write books for many reasons other than to teach and educate. The most common reason financial book authors write books is to further their own business interests. That's not the best thing for you when you're trying to educate yourself and better manage your own finances. For example, some investment newsletter sellers write investment books. Rather than teach you how to make good investments, the authors make the investment world sound complicated so you feel the need to subscribe to their ongoing newsletters.

Books at the head of their class

In addition to books that I've recommended at various places throughout this book, here's a list of some of my other favorite financial titles (please also see the book summaries I provide on my website, www.erictyson.com):

- ✔ *A Random Walk Down Wall Street* by Burton G. Malkiel (Norton)
- ✔ *Built to Last: Successful Habits of Visionary Companies* by Jim Collins and Jerry I. Porras (HarperCollins)
- ✔ *Good to Great: Why Some Companies Make the Leap . . . and Others Don't* by Jim Collins (HarperCollins)
- ✔ *Paying for College without Going Broke* by Kalman A. Chany (Princeton Review)
- ✔ Nolo's legal titles
- ✔ And, not surprisingly, my *For Dummies* books on investing, mutual funds, home buying, house selling, mortgages, real estate investing, and small business (all published by Wiley)

Part VI
The Part of Tens

Check out 20 keys to personal financial success on the Cheat Sheet at www.dummies.com/extras/personalfinance.

In this part . . .

✔ Get advice on how to deal with major life changes.

✔ Discover how to minimize and prevent identity theft.

Chapter 21

Survival Guide for Ten Life Changes

In This Chapter

▶ Handling the financial challenges that arise during life changes

▶ Minimizing money worries so you can focus on what matters most

Some of life's changes come unexpectedly, like earthquakes. Others you can see coming when they're still far off, like a big storm moving in off the horizon. Whether a life change is predictable or not, your ability to navigate successfully through its challenges and adjust to new circumstances depends largely on your degree of preparedness.

Perhaps you find my comparison of life changes to natural disasters to be a bit negative. After all, some of the changes I discuss in this chapter should be occasions for joy. But understand that what one defines as a "disaster" has everything to do with preparedness. To the person who has stored no emergency rations in her basement, the big snowstorm that traps her in her home can lead to problems. But to the prepared person with plenty of food and water, that same storm may mean a vacation from work and some relaxing time off in the midst of a winter wonderland.

First, here are some general tips that apply to all types of life changes:

✔ **Stay in financial shape.** An athlete is best able to withstand physical adversities during competition by prior training and eating well. Likewise, the sounder your finances are to begin with, the better you'll be able to deal with life changes.

✔ **Changes require change.** Even if your financial house is in order, a major life change — starting a family, buying a home, starting a business, divorcing, retiring — should prompt you to review your personal financial strategies. Life changes affect your income, spending, insurance needs, and ability to take financial risk.

✔ **Don't procrastinate.** With a major life change on the horizon, procrastination can be costly. You (and your family) may overspend and accumulate high-cost debts, lack proper insurance coverage, or take other unnecessary risks. Early preparation can save you from these pitfalls.

✔ **Manage stress and your emotions.** Life changes often are accompanied by stress and other emotional upheavals. Don't make snap decisions during these changes. Take the time to become fully informed and recognize and acknowledge your feelings. Educating yourself is key. You may want to hire experts to help (see Chapter 18), but don't abdicate decisions and responsibilities to advisors — the advisors may not have your best interests at heart or fully appreciate your needs.

Here, then, are the major changes you may have to deal with at some point in your life. I wish you more of the good changes than the bad.

Starting Out: Your First Job

If you just graduated from college or some other program, or you're otherwise entering the workforce, your increased income and reduction in educational expenses are probably a welcome relief. You'd think, then, that more young adults would be able to avoid financial trouble and challenges. But they face these challenges largely because of poor financial habits picked up at home or from the world at large. Here's how to get on the path to financial success:

✔ **Don't use consumer credit.** The use and abuse of consumer credit can cause long-term financial pain and hardship. To get off on the right financial foot, young workers need to shun the habit of making purchases on credit cards that they can't pay for in full when the bill arrives. Here's the simple solution for running up outstanding credit-card balances: Don't carry a credit card. If you need the convenience of making purchases with a piece of plastic, get a debit card (see Chapter 5).

✔ **Get in the habit of saving and investing.** Ideally, your savings should be directed into retirement accounts that offer tax benefits unless you want to accumulate down-payment money for a home or small-business purchase (see Chapter 4). Thinking about a home purchase or retirement is usually not in the active thought patterns of first-time job seekers. I'm often asked, "At what age should a person start saving?" To me, that's similar to asking at what age you should start brushing your teeth. Well, when you have teeth to brush! So I say you should start saving and investing money from your first paycheck. Try saving 5 percent of every paycheck and then eventually increase your saving to 10 percent. If you're having trouble saving money, track your spending and make cutbacks as needed (refer to Chapters 3 and 6).

✔ **Get insured.** When you're young and healthy, imagining yourself feeling otherwise is hard. Many twenty-somethings give little thought to the potential for healthcare expenses. But because accidents and unexpected illnesses can strike at any age, forgoing coverage can be financially devastating. When you're in your first full-time job with more-limited benefits, buying disability coverage, which replaces income lost due to a long-term disability, is also wise. And as you begin to build your assets, consider making out a will so your assets go where you want them to in the event of your untimely passing.

✔ **Continue your education.** After you get out in the workforce, you (like many other people) may realize how little you learned in formal schooling that can actually be used in the real world and, conversely, how much you need to learn that school never taught you. Read, learn, and continue to grow. Continuing education can help you advance in your career and enjoy the world around you.

Changing Jobs or Careers

During your adult life, you'll almost surely change jobs — perhaps several times a decade. I hope that most of the time you'll be changing by your own choice. But let's face it: Job security is not what it used to be. Downsizing has impacted even the most talented workers, and more industries are subjected to global competition.

Always be prepared for a job change. No matter how happy you are in your current job, knowing that your world won't fall apart if you're not working tomorrow can give you an added sense of security and encourage openness to possibility. Whether you're changing your job by choice or necessity, the following financial maneuvers can help ease the transition:

✔ **Structure your finances to afford an income dip.** Spending less than you earn always makes good financial sense, but if you're approaching a possible job change, spending less is even more important, particularly if you're entering a new field or starting your own company and you expect a short-term income dip. Many people view a lifestyle of thriftiness as restrictive, but ultimately those thrifty habits can give you more freedom to do what you want to do. Be sure to keep an emergency reserve fund (see Chapter 8).

If you lose your job, batten down the hatches. You normally get little advance warning when you lose your job through no choice of your own. It doesn't mean, however, that you can't do anything financially. Evaluating and slashing your current level of spending may be necessary. Everything should be fair game, from how much you spend on housing to how often you eat out to where you do your grocery shopping. Avoid at all costs the temptation to maintain your level of spending by accumulating consumer debt.

✔ **Evaluate the total financial picture when relocating.** At some point in your career, you may have the option of relocating. But don't call the moving company until you understand the financial consequences of such a move. You can't simply compare salaries and benefits between the two jobs. You also need to compare the cost of living between the two areas: housing, commuting, state income and property taxes, food, utilities, and all the other major expenditure categories that I cover in Chapter 3.

✔ **Track your job search expenses for tax purposes.** If you're seeking a new job in your current (or recently current) field of work, your job search expenses may be tax-deductible, even if you don't get a specific job you desire. Remember, however, that if you're moving into a new career, your job search expenses are not tax-deductible.

Getting Married

Ready to tie the knot with the one you love? Congratulations — I hope that you'll have a long, healthy, and happy life together. In addition to the emotional and moral commitments that you and your spouse will make to one another, you're probably going to be merging many of your financial decisions and resources. Even if you're largely in agreement about your financial goals and strategies, managing as two is far different than managing as one. Here's how to prepare:

✔ **Take a compatibility test.** Many couples never talk about their goals and plans before marriage, and failing to do so breaks up many marriages. Finances are just one of numerous issues you should discuss. Ensuring that you know what you're getting yourself into is a good way to minimize your chances for heartache. Ministers, priests, and rabbis sometimes offer premarital counseling to help bring issues and differences to the surface.

✔ **Discuss and set joint goals.** After you're married, you and your spouse should set aside time once a year, or every few years, to discuss personal and financial goals for the years ahead. When you talk about where you want to go, you help ensure that you're both rowing your financial boat in unison.

✔ **Decide whether to keep finances separate or manage them jointly.** Philosophically, I like the idea of pooling your finances better. After all, marriage is a partnership. In some marriages, however, spouses may choose to keep some money separate so they don't feel the scrutiny of a spouse with different spending preferences. Spouses who have been through divorce may choose to keep the assets they bring into the new marriage separate in order to protect their money in the event of another divorce. As long as you're jointly accomplishing what you need to financially, some separation of money is okay. But for the health of your marriage, don't hide money, transactions (unless it's a gift for your spouse), or debts from one another, and if you're the higher-income spouse, don't assume power and control over your joint income.

✔ **Coordinate and maximize employer benefits.** If one or both of you have access to a package of employee benefits through an employer, understand how best to make use of those benefits. Coordinating and using the best that each package has to offer is like getting a pay raise. If you both have access to health insurance, compare which of you has better benefits. Likewise, one of you may have a better retirement savings plan — one that matches and offers superior investment options. Unless you can afford to save the maximum through both your plans, saving more in the better plan will increase your combined assets. (*Note:* If you're concerned about what will happen if you save more in one of your retirement plans and then you divorce, in most states, the money is considered part of your joint assets to be divided equally.)

✔ **Discuss life and disability insurance needs.** If you and your spouse can make do without each other's income, you may not need any income-protecting insurance. However, if you both depend on each other's incomes, or if one of you depends fully or partly on the other's income, you may each need long-term disability and term life insurance policies (refer to Chapter 16).

✔ **Update your wills.** When you marry, you should make or update your wills. Having a will is potentially more valuable when you're married, especially if you want to leave money to others in addition to your spouse, or if you have children for whom you need to name a guardian. See Chapter 17 for more on wills.

✔ **Reconsider beneficiaries on investment and life insurance.** With retirement accounts and life insurance policies, you name beneficiaries to whom the money or value in those accounts will go in the event of your passing. When you marry, you'll probably want to rethink your beneficiaries.

Buying a Home

Most Americans eventually buy a home. You don't need to own a home to be a financial success, but home ownership certainly offers financial rewards. Over the course of your adult life, the real estate you own is likely going to appreciate in value. Additionally, you'll pay off your mortgage someday, which will greatly reduce your housing costs. If you're thinking about buying a home, take these steps:

✔ **Get your overall finances in order.** Before buying, analyze your current budget, your ability to afford debt, and your future financial goals. Make sure your expected housing expenses allow you to save properly for retirement and other long- or short-term objectives. Don't buy a home based on what lenders are willing to lend.

✔ **Determine whether now's the time.** Buying a house when you don't see yourself staying put three to five years rarely makes financial sense. Buying and selling a home gobbles up a good deal of money in transaction costs — you'll be lucky to recoup all those costs even within a five-year period. Also, if your income is likely to drop or you have other pressing goals, such as starting a business, you may want to wait to buy.

For more about buying a home, be sure to read Chapter 14.

Having Children

If you think that being a responsible adult, holding down a job, paying your bills on time, and preparing for your financial future are tough, wait 'til you add kids to the mix. Most parents find that with children in the family, their already precious free time and money become much scarcer. The sooner you discover how to manage your time and money, the better able you'll be to have a sane, happy, and financially successful life as a parent. Here are some key things to do both before and after you begin your family:

✔ **Set your priorities.** As with many other financial decisions, starting or expanding a family requires that you plan ahead. Set your priorities and structure your finances and living situation accordingly. Is having a bigger home in a particular community important, or would you rather feel less pressure to work hard, giving you more time to spend with your family? Keep in mind that a less hectic work life not only gives you more free time but also often reduces your cost of living by decreasing meals out, dry-cleaning costs, day-care expenses, and so on.

✔ **Take a hard look at your budget.** Having kids requires you to increase your spending. At a minimum, expenditures for food and clothing will increase. But you're also likely to spend more on housing, insurance, day care, and education. On top of that, if you want to play an active role in raising your children, working at some full-time jobs may not be possible. So while you consider the added expenses, you may also need to factor in a decrease in income.

No simple rules exist for estimating how kids will affect your household's income and expenses. On the income side, figure out how much you want to cut back on work. On the expense side, government statistics show that the average household with school-age children spends about 20 percent more than a household without children. Going through your budget category by category and estimating how kids will change your spending is a more scientific approach. (You can use the worksheets in Chapter 3.)

✔ **Boost insurance coverage *before* getting pregnant.** Make sure you have health insurance in place if you're going to try to get pregnant. Even though the Affordable Care Act mandated maternity benefits in all health plans, if you lack coverage and then get pregnant, you won't be able to enroll outside of the small portion of the year for open enrollment. With disability insurance, pregnancy is considered a preexisting condition, so women should secure this coverage before getting pregnant. And most families-to-be should buy life insurance. Buying life insurance *after* the bundle of joy comes home from the hospital is a risky proposition — if one of the parents develops a health problem, he or she may be denied coverage. You should also consider buying life insurance for a stay-at-home parent. Even though the stay-at-home parent is not bringing in income, if he or she were to pass away, hiring assistance could cripple the family budget.

✔ **Check maternity leave with your employers.** Many of the larger employers offer some maternity leave for women and, in rare but thankfully increasing cases, for men. Some employers offer paid leaves, while others may offer unpaid leaves. Understand the options and the financial ramifications before you consider the leave and, ideally, before you get pregnant. Also, check laws within your state for mandated maternity and paternity leave.

✔ **Update your will.** If you have a will, update it; if you don't have a will, make one now. With children in the picture, you need to name a guardian who will be responsible for raising your children should you and your spouse both pass away.

✔ **Enroll the baby in your health plan.** After you welcome your baby into this world, enroll him or her in your health insurance plan. Most insurers give you about a month or so to enroll.

✔ **Understand child-care tax benefits.** For every one of your children with an official Social Security number, you get a $3,800 deduction on your income taxes (for tax year 2012). So if you're in the 25 percent federal tax bracket, each child saves you $950 in federal taxes. On top of that, you may be eligible for a $1,000 tax credit for each child under the age of 17. That should certainly motivate you to apply for your kid's Social Security number!

If you and your spouse both work and you have children under the age of 13, you can also claim a tax credit for child-care expenses. Or you may work for an employer who offers a flexible benefit or spending plan. These plans allow you to put away up to $5,000 per year on a pretax basis for child-care expenses. For many parents, especially those in higher income tax brackets, these plans can save a lot in taxes. Keep in mind, however, that if you use one of these plans, you can't claim the child-care tax credit. Also, if you don't deplete the account every tax year, you forfeit any money left over.

✔ **Skip saving in custodial accounts.** One common concern is how to sock away enough money to pay for the ever-rising cost of a college education. If you start saving money in your child's name in a so-called custodial account, however, you may harm your child's future ability to qualify for financial aid and miss out on the tax benefits that come with investing elsewhere (see Chapter 13).

✔ **Don't indulge the children.** Toys, art classes, music lessons, travel sports and associated lessons, field trips, and the like can rack up big bills, especially if you don't control your spending. Some parents fail to set guidelines or limits when spending on children's programs. Others mindlessly follow the examples set by the families of their children's peers. Introspective parents have told me that they feel some insecurity about providing the best for their children. The parents (and kids) who seem the happiest and most financially successful are the ones who clearly distinguish between material luxuries and family necessities.

As children get older and become indoctrinated into the world of shopping, all sorts of other purchases come into play. Consider giving your kids a weekly allowance and letting them discover how to spend and manage it. And when they're old enough, having your kids get a part-time job can help teach financial responsibility.

Starting a Small Business

Many people aspire to be their own bosses, but far fewer people actually leave their jobs in order to achieve that dream. Giving up the apparent security of a job with benefits and a built-in network of co-workers is difficult for most people, both psychologically and financially. Starting a small business is not for everyone, but don't let inertia stand in your way. Here are some tips to help get you started and increase your chances for long-term success:

✔ **Prepare to ditch your job.** To maximize your ability to save money, live as Spartan a lifestyle as you can while you're employed; you'll develop thrifty habits that'll help you weather the reduced income and increased expenditure period that comes with most small-business start-ups. You may also want to consider easing into your small business by working at it part-time in the beginning, with or without cutting back on your normal job.

✔ **Develop a business plan.** If you research and think through your business idea, not only will you reduce the likelihood of your business's failing and increase its success if it thrives, but you'll also feel more comfortable taking the entrepreneurial plunge. A good business plan describes in detail the business idea, the marketplace you'll compete in, your marketing plans, and expected revenue and expenses.

✔ **Replace your insurance coverage.** Before you finally leave your job, get proper insurance. With health insurance, employers allow you to continue your existing coverage (at your own expense) for 18 months. Individuals with existing health problems are legally entitled to purchase an individual policy at the same price that a healthy individual pays. With disability insurance, secure coverage before you leave your job so you have income to qualify for coverage. If you have life insurance through your employer, obtain new individual coverage as soon as you know you're going to leave your job. (See Chapter 16 for details.)

✔ **Establish a retirement savings plan.** After your business starts making a profit, consider establishing a retirement savings plan such as a SEP-IRA. As I explain in Chapter 11, such plans allow you to shelter up to 20 percent of your business income from federal and state taxation.

Caring for Aging Parents

For many, there comes a time when they reverse roles with their parents and become the caregivers. As your parents age, they may need help with a variety of issues and living tasks. Although you probably won't have the time or ability to perform all these functions yourself, you may end up coordinating some service providers who will. Here are key issues to consider when caring for aging parents:

✔ **Get help where possible.** In most communities, a variety of nonprofit organizations offer information and counseling to families who are caring for elderly parents. Numerous for-profit agencies can help with everything from simple cleaning and cooking, to health checks and medication monitoring, to assisted living and health advocacy. You may be able to find your way to such resources through your state's department of insurance, as well as through recommendations from local hospitals and doctors. You'll especially want to get assistance and information if your parents need some sort of home care, nursing home care, or assisted living arrangement.

✔ **Get involved in their health care.** Your aging parents may already have a lot on their minds, or they simply may not be able to coordinate and manage all the healthcare providers who are giving them medications and advice. Try, as best as you can, to be their advocate. Speak with their doctors so you can understand their current medical condition, the need for various medications, and how to help coordinate caregivers. Visit home care providers and nursing homes, and speak with prospective care providers.

✔ **Understand tax breaks.** If you're financially supporting your parents, you may be eligible for a number of tax credits and deductions for elder care. Some employers' flexible benefit plans allow you to put away money on a pretax basis to pay for the care of your parents. Also explore the dependent care tax credit, which you can take on your federal income tax Form 1040. And if you provide half or more of the support costs for your parents, you may be able to claim them as dependents on your tax return.

✔ **Discuss getting the estate in order.** Parents don't like thinking about their demise, and they may feel awkward discussing this issue with their children. But opening a dialogue between you and your folks about such issues can be healthy in many ways. Not only does discussing wills, living wills, living trusts, and estate planning strategies (see Chapter 17) make you aware of your folks' situation, but it can also improve their plans to both their benefit and yours.

✔ **Take some time off.** Caring for an aging parent, particularly one who is having health problems, can be time-consuming and emotionally draining. Do your parents and yourself a favor by using some vacation time to help get things in order.

Divorcing

In most marriages that are destined to split up, both parties usually recognize early warning signs. Sometimes, however, one spouse may surprise the other with an unexpected request for divorce. Whether the divorce is planned or unexpected, here are some important considerations when getting a divorce:

✔ **Question the divorce.** Some say that divorcing in America is too easy, and I tend to agree. Although some couples are indeed better off parting ways, others give up too easily, thinking that the grass is greener elsewhere, only to later discover that all lawns have weeds and crabgrass. Just as with lawns that aren't watered and fertilized, relationships can wither without nurturing.

Money and disagreements over money are certainly contributing factors in marital unhappiness. Try talking things over, perhaps with a marital counselor.

✔ **Separate your emotions from the financial issues.** Feelings of revenge may be common in some divorces, but they'll probably only help ensure that the attorneys get rich as you and your spouse butt heads. If you really want a divorce, work at doing it efficiently and harmoniously so you can get on with your lives and have more of your money to work with.

✔ **Detail resources and priorities.** Draw up a list of all the assets and liabilities that you and your spouse have. Make sure you list all the financial facts, including investment account records and statements. After you know the whole picture, begin to think about what is and isn't important to you financially and otherwise.

✔ **Educate yourself about personal finance and legal issues.** Divorce sometimes forces nonfinancially oriented spouses to get a crash course in personal finance at a difficult emotional time. This book can help educate you financially. Visit a bookstore and pick up a good legal guide or two about divorce.

✔ **Choose advisors carefully.** Odds are that you'll retain the services of one or more specialists to assist you with the myriad issues, negotiations, and concerns of your divorce. Legal, tax, and financial advisors can help, but make sure you recognize their limitations and conflicts of interest. The more complicated things become and the more you haggle with your spouse, the more attorneys, unfortunately, benefit financially. Don't use your divorce attorney for financial or tax advice — your lawyer probably knows no more than you do in these areas. Also, realize that you don't need an attorney to get divorced. A variety of books and kits can help you. As for choosing tax and financial advisors, if you think you need that type of help, see Chapters 7 and 18 for advice on how to find good advisors.

✔ **Analyze your spending.** Some divorcees find themselves financially squeezed in the early years following a divorce because two people living together in the same property can generally do so less expensively than two people living separately. Analyzing your spending needs pre-divorce can help you adjust to a new budget and negotiate a fairer settlement with your spouse.

✔ **Review needed changes to your insurance.** If you're covered under your spouse's employer's insurance plan, make sure you get this coverage replaced (see Chapter 16). If you or your children will still be financially dependent on your spouse post-divorce, make sure the divorce agreement mandates life insurance coverage. You should also revise your will (see Chapter 17).

✔ **Revamp your retirement plan.** With changes to your income, expenses, assets, liabilities, and future needs, your retirement plan will surely need a post-divorce overhaul. Refer to Chapter 4 for a reorientation.

Receiving a Windfall

Whether through inheritance, stock options, small-business success, or lottery winnings, you may receive a financial windfall at some point in your life. Like many people who are totally unprepared psychologically and organizationally for their sudden good fortune, you may find that a flood of money can create more problems than it solves. Here are a few tips to help you make the most of your financial windfall:

✔ **Educate yourself.** If you've never had to deal with significant wealth, I don't expect you to know how to handle it. Don't pressure yourself to invest it as soon as possible. Leaving the money where it is or stashing it in one of the higher-yielding money-market funds I recommend in Chapter 12 is far better than jumping into investments that you don't understand and haven't researched.

✔ **Beware of the sharks.** You may begin to wonder whether someone has posted your net worth, address, and home telephone number in the local newspaper and on the Internet. Brokers and financial advisors may flood you with marketing materials, telephone solicitations, and lunch date requests. These folks pursue you for a reason: They want to convert your money into their income either by selling you investments and other financial products or by managing your money. Stay away from the sharks, educate yourself, and take charge of your own financial moves. Decide on your own terms whom to hire, and then seek them out.

✔ **Recognize the emotional side of coming into a lot of money.** One of the side effects of accumulating wealth quickly is that you may have feelings of guilt or otherwise be unhappy, especially if you expected money to solve your problems. If you didn't invest in your relationship with your parents and, after their passing, you regret how you interacted with them, getting a big inheritance from your folks may make you feel bad. If you poured endless hours into a business venture that finally paid off, all that money in your investment accounts may leave you with a hollow feeling if you're divorced and you lost friends by neglecting your relationships.

✔ **Pay down debts.** People generally borrow money to buy things that they otherwise can't buy in one fell swoop. Paying off your debts is one of the simplest and best investments you can make when you come into wealth.

✔ **Diversify.** If you want to protect your wealth, don't keep it all in one pot. Mutual funds and exchange-traded funds (see Chapter 10) are ideally diversified, professionally managed investment vehicles to consider. And if you want your money to continue growing, consider the wealth-building investments — stocks, real estate, and small-business options — that I discuss in Part III of this book.

✔ **Make use of the opportunity.** Most people work for a paycheck for many decades so they can pay a never-ending stream of monthly bills. Although I'm not advocating a hedonistic lifestyle, why not take some extra time to travel, spend time with your family, and enjoy the hobbies you've long been putting off? How about trying a new career that you may find more fulfilling and that may make the world a better place? And what about donating some to your favorite charities?

Retiring

If you've spent the bulk of your adult life working, retiring can be a challenging transition. Most Americans have an idealized vision of how wonderful retirement will be — no more irritating bosses and pressure of work deadlines; unlimited time to travel, play, and lead the good life. Sounds good, huh? Well, the reality for most Americans is different, especially for those who don't plan ahead (financially and otherwise). Here are some tips to help you through retirement:

✔ **Plan both financially and personally.** Planning your activities is even more important than planning financially. If the focus during your working years is solely on your career and saving money, you may lack interests, friends, and the ability to know how to spend money when you retire.

✔ **Take stock of your resources.** Many people worry and wonder whether they have sufficient assets for cutting back on work or retiring completely, yet they don't crunch any numbers to see where they stand. Ignorance may cause you to misunderstand how little or how much you really have for retirement when compared to what you need. See Chapters 4 and 11 for help with retirement planning and investing.

✔ **Reevaluate your insurance needs.** When you have sufficient assets to retire, you don't need to retain insurance to protect your employment income any longer. On the other hand, as your assets grow over the years, you may be underinsured with regards to liability insurance (refer to Chapter 17).

✔ **Evaluate healthcare/living options.** Medical expenses in your retirement years (particularly the cost of nursing home care) can be daunting. Which course of action you take — supplemental insurance, buying into a retirement community, or not doing anything — depends on your financial and personal situation. Early preparation increases your options; if you wait until you have major health problems, it may be too late to choose specific paths. (See Chapter 16 for more details on healthcare options.)

✔ **Decide what to do with your retirement plan money.** If you have money in a retirement savings plan, your employer may offer you the option of leaving the money in the plan rather than rolling it over into your own retirement account. Brokers and financial advisors clearly prefer that you do the latter because it means more money for them, but it can also give you many more (and perhaps better) investment choices to consider. Read Part III of this book to find out about investing and evaluating the quality of your employer's retirement plan investment options.

✔ **Pick a pension option.** Selecting a *pension option* (a plan that pays a monthly benefit during retirement) is similar to choosing a good investment — each pension option carries different risks, benefits, and tax consequences. Pensions are structured by actuaries, who base pension options on reasonable life expectancies. The younger you are when you start collecting your pension, the less you get per month. Check to see whether the amount of your monthly pension stops increasing past a certain age. You obviously don't want to delay access to your pension benefits past that age, because you won't receive a reward for waiting any longer and you'll collect the benefit for fewer months.

If you know you have a health problem that shortens your life expectancy, you may benefit from drawing your pension sooner. If you plan to continue working in some capacity and earning a decent income after retiring, waiting for higher pension benefits when you're in a lower tax bracket is probably wise.

At one end of the spectrum, you have the risky single life option, which pays benefits until you pass away and then provides no benefits for your spouse thereafter. This option maximizes your monthly take while you're alive. Consider this option only if your spouse can do without this income. The least risky option, and thus least financially rewarding while the pensioner is still living, is the *100-percent joint and survivor option,* which pays your survivor the same amount that you received while still alive. The other joint and survivor options fall somewhere between these two extremes and generally make sense for most couples who desire decent pensions early in retirement but want a reasonable amount to continue in the event that the pensioner dies first. The 75-percent joint and survivor option is a popular choice, because it closely matches the lower expense needs of the lone surviving spouse at 75 percent of the expenses of the couple, and it provides higher payments than the 100-percent joint and survivor option while both spouses are alive.

✔ **Get your estate in order.** Confronting your mortality is never fun, but when you're considering retirement or you're already retired, getting your estate in order makes all the more sense. Find out about wills and trusts that may benefit you and your heirs. You may also want to consider giving monetary gifts now if you have more than you need.

Chapter 22

Ten Tactics to Thwart Identity Theft and Fraud

In This Chapter

▶ Protecting your personal information

▶ Paying attention to activity in your accounts and credit history

*H*ucksters and thieves are often several steps ahead of law enforcement. Eventually, some of the bad guys get caught, but many don't, and those who do get nabbed often go back to their unsavory ways after penalties and some jail time. They may even be in your neighborhood or on your local Little League board. (For an enlightening read, check out Dr. Martha Stout's book *The Sociopath Next Door* [Three Rivers Press].)

Years ago when I lived on the West Coast, I got a call from my bank informing me that it had just discovered "concerning activity" on the joint checking account I held with my wife. Specifically, what had happened was that a man with a bogus ID in my name had gone into five different Bank of America branches on the same day and withdrawn $80 from our checking account at each one. After some detective work, I discovered that someone had pilfered our personal banking information at my wife's employer's payroll office. Fortunately, the bank made good on the money that it had allowed to be withdrawn by my impostor.

I had been the victim of identity theft. In my situation, the crook had accessed one of my accounts; in other cases, the criminal activity may develop with someone opening an account (such as a credit card) using someone's stolen personal information. Victims of identity theft can suffer trashed credit reports, reduced ability to qualify for loans and even jobs (with employers who check credit reports), out-of-pocket costs and losses, and dozens of hours of time to clean up the mess and clear their credit record and name.

Unfortunately, identity theft is hardly the only way to be taken to the cleaners by crooks. All sorts of scamsters hatch schemes to separate you from your money. Please follow the ten tips in this chapter to keep yourself from falling prey and unnecessarily losing money.

Save Phone Discussions for Friends Only

Never, ever give out personal information over the phone, especially when you aren't the one who initiated the call. Suppose you get a call and the person on the other end of the line claims to be with a company you conduct business with (such as your credit-card company or bank). Ask for the caller's name and number and call back the company's main number (which you look up) to be sure he is indeed with that company and has a legitimate business reason for contacting you.

With caller ID on your phone line, you may be able to see what number a call is originating from, but more often than not, calls from business-registered phone numbers come up as "unavailable." A major red flag: calling back the number that comes through on caller ID and discovering that the number is bogus (a nonworking number).

Never Respond to Emails Soliciting Information

You may have seen or heard about official-looking emails sent from companies you know of and may do business with asking you to promptly visit their website to correct some sort of billing or account problem. Crooks can generate a return/sender email address that looks like it comes from a known institution but really does not. This unscrupulous practice is known as *phishing,* and if you bite at the bait, visit the site, and provide the requested personal information, your reward is likely to be some sort of future identity-theft problem and possibly a computer virus.

To find out more about how to protect yourself from phishing scams, visit the website of the Anti-Phishing Working Group (APWG) at www. antiphishing.org.

Review Your Monthly Financial Statements

Although financial institutions such as banks may call you if they notice unusual activity on one of your accounts, some people discover problematic account activity by simply reviewing their monthly credit-card, checking-account, and other statements.

Do you need to balance bank account statements to the penny? No, you don't. I haven't for years (decades actually), and I don't have the time or patience for such minutiae. The key is to review the line items on your statement to be sure that all the transactions were yours and are correct.

Secure All Receipts

When you make a purchase, be sure to keep track of and secure receipts, especially those that contain your personal financial or account information. You can keep these in an envelope in your home, for example. Then cross-check them against your monthly statement.

When you no longer need to retain your receipts, be sure to dispose of them in a way that prevents a thief, who may get into your garbage, from being able to decipher the information on them. Rip up the receipts or, if you feel so inclined, buy a small paper shredder for your home and/or small business.

Close Unnecessary Credit Accounts

Open your wallet and remove all the pieces of plastic within it that enable you to charge purchases. The more credit cards and credit lines you have, the more likely you are to have problems with identity theft and fraud and the more likely you are to overspend and carry debt balances. Also, reduce preapproved credit offers by contacting 888-5OPTOUT (888-567-8688) or visiting www.optoutprescreen.com.

Unless you maintain a card for small-business transactions, you really "need" only one piece of plastic with a VISA or MasterCard logo. Give preference to a debit card if you have a history of accumulating credit-card-debt balances.

Regularly Review Your Credit Reports

You may also be tipped off to shenanigans going on in your name when you review your credit report. Some identity-theft victims have found out about credit accounts opened in their name by reviewing their credit reports.

Because you're entitled to a free credit report from each of the three major credit agencies every year, I recommend reviewing your reports at least that often. The reports generally contain the same information, so you can request and review one agency report every four months, which enables you to keep a closer eye on your reports and still obtain them without cost. (Be sure to use the free site www.annualcreditreport.com.)

I don't generally recommend spending the $100 or so annually for a so-called credit monitoring service that updates you when something happens on your credit reports. If you're concerned about someone illegally applying for credit in your name, know that another option for you to stay on top of things is to "freeze" your personal credit reports and scores (see the next section).

Freeze Your Credit Reports

To address the growing problem of identity theft, all states have credit freeze laws, which enable consumers to prevent access to their personal credit reports. Typically for a nominal fee, consumers can freeze their credit information.

In some states, only identity-theft victims may freeze their reports. The individual whose credit report is frozen is the only person who may grant access to the frozen credit report.

Keep Personal Info Off Your Checks

Don't place personal information on checks. Information that is useful to identity thieves — and that you should not put on your checks — includes your credit-card number, driver's license number, Social Security number, and so on. I also encourage you to leave your home address off your preprinted checks when you order them. Otherwise, every Tom, Dick, and Jane whose hands your check passes through knows exactly where you live.

When writing a check to a merchant, question the need for adding personal information to the check (in fact, in numerous states, requesting and placing credit-card numbers on checks is against the law). Remember that your credit card doesn't advertise your home address and other financial account data, so there's no need to publicize it to the world on your checks.

Protect Your Computer and Files

Especially if you keep personal and financial data on your computer, consider the following safeguards to protect your computer and the confidential information on it:

- ✔ Install a firewall.
- ✔ Use virus protection software.
- ✔ Password-protect access to your programs and files.

Protect Your Mail

Some identity thieves have collected personal information by simply helping themselves to mail in home mailboxes. Stealing mail is easy, especially if your mail is delivered to a curbside box.

Consider using a locked mailbox or a post office box to protect your incoming mail from theft. Consider having your investment and other important statements sent to you via email, or simply access them online and eliminate mail delivery of the paper copies.

Be careful with your outgoing mail as well, such as bills with checks attached. Minimize your outgoing mail and save yourself hassles by signing up for automatic bill payment for as many bills as possible. Drop the rest of your outgoing mail in a secure U.S. postal box, such as those you find at the post office.

Glossary

adjustable-rate mortgage (ARM): A mortgage whose interest rate and monthly payments vary throughout its life. ARMs typically start with an artificially low interest rate that gradually rises over time. The interest rate is determined by a formula: margin (which is a fixed number) plus index (which varies). Generally speaking, if the overall level of interest rates drops, as measured by a variety of different indexes, the interest rate of your ARM generally follows suit. Similarly, if interest rates rise, so does your mortgage's interest rate and monthly payment. Caps limit the amount that the interest rate can fluctuate. Before you agree to an ARM, be certain that you can afford its highest possible payments.

adjusted cost basis: For capital gains tax purposes, the adjusted cost basis is how the IRS determines your profit or loss when you sell an asset such as a home or a security. For an investment such as a mutual fund or stock, your cost basis is what you originally invested plus any reinvested money and any trading or transaction fees. For a home, you arrive at the adjusted cost basis by adding the original purchase price to the cost of any capital improvements (expenditures that increase your property's value and life expectancy).

adjusted gross income (AGI): The sum of your taxable income (such as wages, salaries, and tips) and taxable interest less allowable adjustments (such as retirement account contributions and moving expenses). AGI is calculated before subtracting your personal exemptions and itemized deductions, which are used to derive your taxable income.

after-tax contributions: Some retirement plans (such as Roth IRAs) allow you to contribute money that has already been taxed. Such contributions are known as after-tax contributions.

alternative minimum tax (AMT): The name given to a sort of shadow tax system that may cause you to pay a higher amount in federal income taxes than you otherwise would. The AMT was designed to prevent higher income earners from lowering their tax bills too much through large deductions.

annual percentage rate (APR): The figure that states the total yearly cost of a loan as expressed by the actual rate of interest paid. The APR includes the base interest rate and any other add-on loan fees and costs. The APR is thus inevitably higher than the rate of interest that the lender quotes.

annuity: An investment that is a contract backed by an insurance company. An annuity is frequently purchased for retirement purposes. Its main benefit is that it allows your money to compound and grow without taxation until withdrawal. Selling annuities is a lucrative source of income for insurance agents and financial planners who work on commission, so don't buy an annuity until you're sure it makes sense for your situation.

asset allocation: When you invest your money, you need to decide how to proportion (allocate) it between risky, growth-oriented investments (such as stocks), whose values fluctuate, and more stable, income-producing investments (like bonds). How soon you'll need the money and how tolerant you are of risk are two important determinants when deciding how to allocate your money.

audit: An IRS examination of your financial records, generally at the IRS offices, to substantiate your tax return. IRS audits are generally feared to be among life's worst experiences.

bank prime rate: See *prime rate.*

bankruptcy: Legal action that puts a halt to creditors' attempts to collect unpaid debts from you. Of use to people who have a high proportion of consumer debt to annual income (25 percent or greater).

bear market: A period (such as the early 2000s and late 2000s) when the stock market experiences a strong downward swing. It is often accompanied by (and sometimes precedes) an economic recession. Imagine a bear in hibernation, because this is what happens in a bear market: Investors hibernate, and the market falters. During a bear market, the value of stocks can decrease significantly. The market usually has to drop at least 20 percent from its peak before it is considered a bear market.

beneficiaries: The people to whom you want to leave your assets (or in the case of life insurance or a pension plan, benefits) in the event of your death. You denote beneficiaries for each of your retirement accounts.

blue-chip stock: The stock of the largest and most consistently profitable corporations. This term comes from poker, where the most valuable chips are blue. This list is unofficial and changes.

bond: A loan investors make to a corporation or government. Bonds generally pay a set amount of interest on a regular basis. They're an appropriate investment vehicle for conservative investors who don't feel comfortable with the risk involved in investing in stocks and who want to receive a steady income. All bonds have a maturity date when the bond issuer must pay back the bond at *par* (full) value to the bondholders (lenders). Bonds should not be your primary long-term investment vehicle, because they produce little real growth on your original investment after inflation is factored in.

bond rating: See *Standard & Poor's (S&P) ratings* and *Moody's ratings*.

bond yield: A yield is quoted as an annual percentage rate of return that a bond will produce based on its current value if it makes its promised interest payments. How much a bond will yield to an investor depends on three important factors: the stated interest rate paid by the bond, changes in the creditworthiness of the bond's issuer, and the maturity date of the bond. The better the rating a bond receives, the less risk involved and, thus, the lower the yield. As far as the maturity date is concerned, the longer you loan your money, the higher the risk (because it's more likely that rates will fluctuate) and the higher your yield generally will be.

broker: A person who acts as an intermediary for the purchase or sale of investments. When you buy a house, insurance, or stock, you're most likely to do so through a broker. Most brokers are paid on commission, which creates a conflict of interest with their clients: The more the broker sells, the more he makes. Some insurance companies let you buy their policies directly, and many mutual-fund families bypass stockbrokers. If you're going to work with a broker, a discount broker can help you save on commissions.

bull market: A period (such as most of the 1990s and mid-2000s in the United States) when the stock market moves higher, usually accompanied and driven by a growing economy and increasing corporate profits.

callable bond: A bond for which the lender can decide to pay the holder earlier than the previously agreed-upon final maturity date. If interest rates are relatively high when a bond is issued, lenders may prefer to issue callable bonds because they have the flexibility to call back these bonds and issue new, lower-interest-rate bonds if interest rates decline. Callable bonds are risky for investors, because if interest rates decrease, the bond holder will get his investment money returned early and may have to reinvest his money at a lower interest rate.

capital gain: The profit from selling your stock at a higher price than the price for which it was purchased. For example, if you buy 50 shares of Rocky and Bullwinkle stock at $20 per share and two years later you sell your shares when the price rises to $25 per share, your profit or capital gain is $5 per share, or $250. If you hold this stock outside of a tax-sheltered retirement account, you'll owe federal tax on this profit when you sell the stock. Many states also levy such a tax.

capital gains distribution: Taxable distribution by a mutual fund or real-estate investment trust (REIT) created by securities that are sold within the fund or REIT at a profit. These distributions may be either short-term (assets held a year or less) or long-term (assets held for more than one year).

cash value insurance: A type of life insurance that's extremely popular with insurance salespeople because it commands a high commission. In a cash value policy, you buy life insurance coverage but also get a savings-type account. Unless you're looking for ways to limit your taxable estate (if you're extremely wealthy, for example), avoid cash value insurance. The investment returns tend to be mediocre, and your contributions aren't tax-deductible.

certificate of deposit (CD): A specific-term loan that you make to your banker. The maturity date for CDs ranges from a month up to several years. The interest paid on CDs is fully taxable, thus making CDs inappropriate for higher tax-bracket investors investing outside tax-sheltered retirement accounts.

closed-end mutual fund: A mutual fund for which the exact number of shares that are going to be issued to investors is decided upfront. After all the shares are sold, an investor seeking to invest in the closed-end fund can only do so by purchasing shares from an existing investor. Shares of closed-end funds trade on the major stock exchanges and therefore sell at either a discount, if the sellers exceed the buyers, or at a premium, if demand exceeds supply.

COBRA (Consolidated Omnibus Budget Reconciliation Act): Name of the federal legislation that requires health insurers and larger employers to continue to offer health insurance, at the employee's expense, for 18 months after coverage would otherwise end — for example, when an employee is laid off.

commercial paper: A short-term debt or IOU issued by larger, stable companies to help make their businesses grow and prosper. Credit-worthy companies can sell this debt security directly to large investors and thus bypass borrowing money from bankers. Money-market funds invest in soon-to-mature commercial paper.

commission: The percentage of the selling price of a house, stock, bond, or other investment that's paid to agents and brokers. Because most agents and brokers are paid by commission, understanding how the commission can influence their behavior and recommendations is important for investors and home buyers. Agents and brokers make money only when you make a purchase, and they make more money when you make a bigger purchase. Choose an agent carefully and take your agent's advice with a grain of salt, because this conflict of interest can often set an agent's visions and goals at odds with your own.

commodity: A raw material (gold, wheat, sugar, or gasoline, for example) traded on the futures market.

common stock: Shares in a company that don't offer a guaranteed amount of dividend to investors; the amount of dividend distributions, if any, is at the discretion of company management. Although common-stock investors may or may not make money through dividends, they hope that the stock price will appreciate as the company expands its operations and increases its profits. Common stock tends to offer you a better return (profit) than other investments, such as bonds or preferred stock. However, if the company falters, you may lose some or all of your original investment.

comparable market analysis (CMA): A written analysis of similar houses currently being offered for sale and those that have recently sold. Real estate agents usually complete CMAs.

consumer debt: Debt on consumer items that depreciate in value over time. Credit card balances and auto loans are examples of consumer debt. This type of debt is bad for your financial health because it carries a high interest rate and encourages you to live beyond your means.

Consumer Price Index (CPI): The Consumer Price Index reports price changes, on a monthly basis, in the cost of living for such items as food, housing, transportation, healthcare, entertainment, clothing, and other miscellaneous expenses. The CPI is used to adjust government benefits, such as Social Security, and is used by many employers to determine cost-of-living increases in wages and pensions. An increase in prices is also known as inflation.

co-payment: The percentage of your medical bill that your health plan requires you to pay out of your own pocket with each medical visit or treatment, often even after you satisfy your annual deductible. A typical co-payment is 20 percent.

credit report: A report that details your credit history. It's the main report that a lender uses to determine whether to give you a loan. You may now obtain free copies of your credit reports annually.

debit card: Although they may look like credit cards, debit cards are different in one important way: When you use a debit card, the cost of the purchase is deducted from your checking account. Thus, a debit card gives you the convenience of a credit card without the danger of building up a mountain of consumer debt.

deductible: You may be thinking that this is a new product from the Keebler elves. Unfortunately, a deductible is actually much more mundane. With insurance, the deductible is the amount you pay when you file a claim. For example, say that your car sustains $800 of damage. If your deductible is $500, the insurance covers $300, and you pay $500 out of your own pocket for the repairs. The higher the deductible, the lower your insurance premiums and the less paperwork you expose yourself to when filing claims (because small losses that are less than the deductible don't require filing a claim). Take the highest deductibles that you can afford when selecting insurance.

deduction: An expense you may subtract from your income to lower your taxable income. Examples include mortgage interest and property taxes (itemized deductions), and most retirement account contributions.

derivative: An investment instrument whose value is derived from other securities. For example, the value of an option to buy Disney stock is derived from the price of Disney's stock.

disability insurance: Disability insurance replaces a portion of your employment income in the unlikely event that you suffer a disability that keeps you from working.

discount broker: Unlike a full-service broker, a discount broker generally offers no investment advice and has employees who work on salary rather than on commission. In addition to trading individual securities, most discount brokerage firms also offer no-load (commission-free) mutual-fund-trading networks.

diversification: If you put all your money into one type of investment, you're potentially setting yourself up for a big shock. If that investment collapses, so does your investment world. By spreading (diversifying) your money among different investments — bonds, U.S. stocks, international stocks, real estate, and so on — you ensure yourself a better chance of investing success and fewer sleepless nights.

dividend: The dividend is the income paid to investors holding an investment. With stock, the dividend is a portion of a company's profits paid to its shareholders. For example, if a company has an annual dividend of $2 per share and you own 100 shares, your total dividend is $200. Usually, established and slower-growing companies pay dividends, while smaller and faster-growing companies reinvest their profits for growth. For assets held outside retirement accounts, dividends (except from tax-free money-market and tax-free bond funds) are taxable.

dollar cost averaging (DCA): The process of regularly investing money. You can do it with a lump sum of money you may have awaiting investment or through regular payroll earnings.

Dow Jones Industrial Average (DJIA): A widely followed stock market index comprised of 30 large, actively traded U.S. company stocks. Senior editors at *The Wall Street Journal* select the stocks in the DJIA.

down payment: The part of the purchase price for a house that the buyer pays in cash upfront and does not finance with a mortgage. The larger the down payment, the smaller the mortgage amount and often the lower the interest rate. You can usually get access to the best mortgage programs with a down payment of at least 20 percent of the home's purchase price.

earthquake insurance: Although the West Coast is often associated with earthquakes, other areas are also quake prone. An earthquake insurance rider (which usually comes with a deductible of 5 to 15 percent of the cost to rebuild the home) on a homeowner's policy pays to repair or rebuild your home if it is damaged in an earthquake. If you live in an area with earthquake risk, consider earthquake insurance coverage!

Emerging Markets Index: The Emerging Markets Index, which is published by Morgan Stanley, tracks stock markets in developing countries. The main reason for investing in emerging markets is that these economies typically experience a higher rate of economic growth than developed markets. However, the potential for higher returns is coupled with greater risk.

equity: In the real-estate world, this term refers to the difference between the market value of your home and what you owe on it. For example, if your home is worth $250,000, and you have an outstanding mortgage of $190,000, your equity is $60,000. Equity is also a synonym for stock.

estate: The value, at the time of your death, of your assets minus your loans and liabilities.

estate planning: The process of deciding where and how your assets will be transferred when you die and structuring your assets during your lifetime so as to minimize likely estate taxes.

exchange-traded fund (ETF): These funds are similar to mutual funds except that they trade on a major stock exchange and thus can be bought and sold throughout the trading day.

Federal National Mortgage Association (FNMA): The FNMA (or Fannie Mae) is one of the best-known institutions in the secondary mortgage market.

Fannie Mae buys mortgages from banks and other mortgage-lending institutions and, in turn, sells them to investors. These loan investments are considered safe because Fannie Mae buys mortgages only from companies that conform to its stringent mortgage regulations, and Fannie Mae guarantees the repayment of principal and interest on the loans that it sells. FNMA, although it is a public company, also has an implicit federal government guarantee that was demonstrated in late 2008 during the financial crisis.

financial assets: A property or investment (such as investment real estate or a stock, mutual fund, or bond) that is held primarily as an investment to generate a positive return over time.

financial liabilities: Your outstanding loans and debts. To determine your net worth, subtract your financial liabilities from your financial assets.

financial planners (or advisors): A motley crew that professes an ability to direct your financial future. Financial planners come with varying backgrounds and degrees: MBAs, Certified Financial Planners, and Certified Public Accountants, to name a few. A useful way to distinguish among this mixed bag of nuts is to determine whether the planners are commission-, fee-, or hourly-based.

fixed-rate mortgage: The granddaddy of all mortgages. You lock into an interest rate (for example, 5 percent), and it never changes during the life (term) of your 15- or 30-year mortgage. Your mortgage payment and interest rate will be the same amount each and every month. If you become a cursing, frothing maniac when you miss your morning coffee or someone is five minutes late, then this mortgage may be for you!

flood insurance: If there's a remote chance that your area may flood, having flood insurance, which reimburses rebuilding your home and replacing its contents in the event of a flood, is wise.

401(k) plan: A type of retirement savings plan offered by many for-profit companies to their employees. Your contributions compound without taxation over time and are usually exempt (yes!) from federal and state income taxes until withdrawal.

403(b) plan: Similar to a 401(k) plan but for employees of nonprofit organizations.

full-service broker: A broker who gives advice and charges a high commission relative to discount brokers. Because the brokers work on commission, they have a significant conflict of interest: namely, to advocate strategies that will benefit them financially.

futures: An obligation to buy or sell a commodity or security on a specific day for a preset price. When used by most individual investors, futures represent a short-term gamble on the short-term direction of the price of a commodity. Companies and farmers use futures contracts to hedge their risks of changing prices.

guaranteed-investment contracts (GICs): Insurance company investments that appeal to skittish investors. GICs generally tell you one year in advance what your interest rate will be for the coming year. Thus, you don't have to worry about fluctuations and losses in your investment value. On the other hand, GICs offer you little upside, because the interest rate is comparable to what you may get on a short-term bank certificate of deposit.

home equity: See *equity.*

home-equity loan: Technical jargon for what used to be called a second mortgage. With this type of loan, you borrow against the equity in your house. If used wisely, a home-equity loan can help pay off high-interest consumer debt or be tapped for other short-term needs (such as a remodeling project). In contrast with consumer debt, mortgage debt usually has a lower interest rate and is tax-deductible.

homeowner's insurance: Dwelling coverage that covers the cost of rebuilding your house in the event of fire or other calamity. The liability insurance portion of this policy protects you against lawsuits associated with your property. Another essential element of homeowner's insurance is the personal property coverage, which pays to replace your damaged or stolen worldly possessions.

index: 1) A security market index, such as the Standard & Poor's 500 Index, is a statistical composite that tracks the price level and performance of a basket of many securities, typically within a specific investment asset class. Indexes exist for various stock and bond markets and are typically set at a round number, such as 100, at a particular point in time. See also *Dow Jones Industrial Average* and *Russell 2000.* 2) The index can also refer to the measure of the overall level of interest rates that a lender uses as a reference to calculate the specific interest rate on an adjustable-rate loan. The index plus the margin is the formula for determining the interest rate on an adjustable-rate mortgage.

Individual Retirement Account (IRA): A retirement account into which anyone with sufficient employment income or alimony may contribute up to $5,500 per year ($6,500 if age 50 or older). Based on your eligibility for other employer-based retirement programs and which type of IRA you select (regular/traditional or Roth), your contributions may be tax-deductible.

inflation: The technical term for a general rise in prices in the economy. Inflation usually occurs when too much money is in circulation and not enough goods and services are available to spend it on. As a result of this excess money, prices rise. A link is present between inflation and interest rates: If interest rates don't keep up with inflation, no one will invest in bonds issued by the government or corporations. When the interest rates on bonds are high, it usually reflects a high rate of expected inflation that will eat away at your return.

initial public offering (IPO): The first time a company offers stock to the investing public. An IPO typically occurs when a company wants to expand more rapidly and seeks additional money to support its growth. A number of studies have demonstrated that buying into IPOs in which the general public can participate produces subpar investment returns. A high level of IPO activity may indicate a cresting stock market, as companies and their investment bankers rush to cash in on a "pricey" marketplace. (IPO could stand for *It's Probably Overpriced.*)

interest rate: The rate lenders charge you to use their money. The higher the interest rate, the higher the risk entailed in the loan. With bonds of a given maturity, a higher rate of interest means a lower quality of bond — one that's less likely to return your money.

international stock markets: Stock markets outside of the United States account for a significant portion of the world stock market capitalization (value). Some specific stock indices track international markets (see ***Morgan Stanley EAFE index*** and ***Emerging Markets Index***). International investing offers one way for you to diversify your portfolio and reduce your risk. Some of the foreign countries with major stock exchanges outside the United States include Japan, Britain, France, Germany, and Canada.

junk bond: A bond rated Ba (Moody's) or BB (Standard & Poor's) or lower. Historically, these bonds have had a 1 to 2 percent chance of default, which is not exactly "junky." Of course, the higher risk is accompanied by a higher interest rate.

Keogh plan: A tax-deductible retirement savings plan available to self-employed individuals. Certain Keoghs allow you to put up to 20 percent of your self-employment income into the account.

leverage: Financial leverage affords its users a disproportionate amount of financial power relative to the amount of their own cash invested. In some circumstances, you can borrow up to 50 percent of a stock price and use all funds (both yours and those that you borrow) to make a purchase. You repay this so-called margin loan when you sell the stock. If the stock price rises, you make money on what you invested plus what you borrowed. Although this money sounds attractive, remember that leverage cuts both ways — when prices decline, you lose money not only on your investment but also on the money you borrowed.

limited partnership (LP): A private partnership, which is designed to limit the legal liability of the investors who participate, is often promoted in a way that promises high returns, but it generally limits one thing: your investment return. Why? Because it's burdened with high commissions and management fees. Another problem is that it's typically not liquid for many years.

load mutual fund: A mutual fund that includes a sales load, which is the commission paid to brokers who sell commission-based mutual funds. The commission typically ranges from 4 to 8.5 percent. This commission is deducted from your investment money, so it reduces your returns.

marginal tax rate: The rate of income tax you pay on the last dollars you earn over the course of a year. Why the complicated distinction? Because not all income is treated equally: You pay less tax on your first dollars of your annual earnings and more tax on the last dollars of your annual income. Knowing your marginal tax rate is helpful because it can help you analyze the tax implications of important personal financial decisions.

market capitalization: The value of all the outstanding stock of a company. Market capitalization is the quoted price per share of a stock multiplied by the number of shares outstanding. Thus, if Rocky and Bullwinkle Corporation has 100 million shares of outstanding stock and the quoted price per share is $20, the company has a market capitalization of $2 billion (100 million × $20).

Moody's ratings: Moody's rating service measures and rates the credit (default) risks of various bonds. Moody's investigates the financial condition of a bond issuer. Its ratings use the following grading system, which is expressed from highest to lowest: Aaa, Aa, A, Baa, Ba, B, Caa, Ca, C. Higher ratings imply a lower risk but also mean that the interest rate will be lower.

Morgan Stanley EAFE (Europe, Australia, Far East) index: The Morgan Stanley EAFE index tracks the performance of the more established countries' stock markets in Europe and Asia. This index is important for international-minded investors who want to follow the performance of overseas stock investments.

mortgage-backed bond (GNMAs and FNMAs): The Government National Mortgage Association (GNMA, or Ginnie Mae) specializes in mortgage-backed securities. It passes the interest and principal payments of borrowers to investors. When a homeowner makes a mortgage payment, GNMA deducts a small service charge and forwards the mortgage payments to its investors.

The payments are guaranteed in case a borrower fails to pay his mortgage. The Federal National Mortgage Association (FNMA or Fannie Mae) is a publicly owned, government-sponsored corporation that purchases mortgages from lenders and resells them to investors. FNMA mainly deals with mortgages backed by the Federal Housing Administration.

mortgage broker: Mortgage brokers buy mortgages wholesale from lenders and then mark the mortgages up (typically from 0.5 to 1 percent) and sell them to borrowers. A good mortgage broker is most helpful for people who don't want to shop around on their own for a mortgage or people who have blemishes on their credit reports.

mortgage life insurance: Mortgage life insurance guarantees that the lender will receive its money in the event that you meet an untimely demise. Many people may try to convince you that you need this insurance to protect your dependents and loved ones. Mortgage life insurance is relatively expensive given the cost of the coverage provided. If you need life insurance, buy low-cost, high-quality term life insurance instead.

municipal bond: A loan for public projects, such as highways, parks, or cultural centers, that an investor makes to cities, towns, and states. The tax-exempt status of their interest is what makes municipal bonds special: They're exempt from federal taxes and, if you reside in the state where the bond is issued, state taxes. Because of that tax exclusion, municipal bonds are generally issued with interest rates that are lower than taxable corporate bonds of comparable credit quality. Municipal bonds are most appropriate for people in high tax brackets who invest money outside of tax-sheltered retirement accounts.

mutual fund: A portfolio of stocks, bonds, or other securities that is owned by numerous investors and managed by an investment company. See also *no-load mutual fund.*

National Association of Securities Dealers Automated Quotation (NASDAQ) system: An electronic network that allows brokers to trade from their offices all over the country. With NASDAQ, brokers buy and sell shares using constantly updated prices that appear on their computer screens.

negative amortization: Negative amortization occurs when your outstanding mortgage balance increases despite the fact that you're making the required monthly payments. Negative amortization occurs with adjustable-rate mortgages that cap the increase in your monthly payment but do not cap the interest rate. Therefore, your monthly payments don't cover all the interest that you actually owe. Avoid loans with this "feature."

net asset value (NAV): The dollar value of one share of a mutual fund. For a no-load fund, the market price is its NAV. For a load fund, the NAV is the "buy" price minus the commission.

New York Stock Exchange (NYSE): The largest stock exchange in the world in terms of total volume and value of shares traded. It lists companies that tend to be among the oldest, largest, and best-known companies.

no-load mutual fund: A mutual fund that doesn't come with a commission payment attached to it. Some funds claim to be no-load but simply hide their sales commissions as an ongoing sales charge; you can avoid these funds by educating yourself and reading the prospectuses carefully.

open-end mutual fund: A mutual fund that issues as many shares as investors demand. These open-end funds do not generally limit the number of investors or amount of money in the fund. Some open-end funds have been known to close to new investors, but investors with existing shares can often still buy more shares from the company.

option: The right to buy or sell a specific security (such as a stock) for a preset price during a specified period of time. Options differ from futures in that with an option, you pay a premium fee up-front and you can either exercise the option or let it expire. If the option expires worthless, you lose 100 percent of your original investment. The use of options is best left to companies as hedging tools. Investment managers may use options to reduce the risk in their investment portfolio. As with futures, when most individual investors buy an option, they're doing so as a short-term gamble, not as an investment.

pension: Pensions (also known as defined benefit plans) are a benefit offered by some employers. These plans generally pay you a monthly retirement income based on your years of service and former pay with the employer.

performance: You traditionally judge an investment's performance by looking at the historic rate of return. The longer the period over which these numbers are tallied, the more useful they are. Considered alone, these numbers are practically meaningless. You must also note how well a fund has performed in comparison to competitors with the same investment objectives. Beware of advertisements that tout the high returns of a mutual fund, because they may not be looking at risk-adjusted performance, or they may be promoting performance over a short time period. Keep in mind that high return statistics are usually coupled with high risk and that this year's star may turn out to be next year's crashing meteor.

precertification: A condition for health insurance benefit coverage that requires a patient to get approval before being admitted to a hospital for non-emergency care.

preferred stock: Preferred stock dividends must be paid before any dividends are paid to the common stock shareholders. Although preferred stock reduces your risk as an investor (because of the more secure dividend and greater likelihood of getting your money back if the company fails), it also often limits your reward if the company expands and increases its profits.

price/earnings (P/E) ratio: The current price of a stock divided by the current (or sometimes the projected) earnings per share of the issuing company. This ratio is a widely used stock analysis statistic that helps an investor get an idea of how cheap or expensive a stock price is. In general, a relatively high P/E ratio indicates that investors feel that the company's earnings are likely to grow quickly.

prime rate: The rate of interest that major banks charge their most credit-worthy corporate customers. Why should you care? Well, because the interest rates on various loans you may be interested in are often based on the prime rate. And, guess what — you pay a higher interest rate than those big corporations!

principal: No, I'm not talking about the big boss from elementary school who struck fear into the hearts of most 8-year-olds. The principal is the amount you borrow for a loan. If you borrow $100,000, your principal is $100,000. Principal can also refer to the amount you originally placed in an investment.

prospectus: Individual companies and mutual funds are required by the Securities and Exchange Commission to issue a prospectus. For a company, the prospectus is a legal document presenting a detailed analysis of that company's financial history, its products and services, its management's background and experience, and the risks of investing in the company. A mutual-fund prospectus tells you about the fund's investment objectives, costs, risk, and performance history.

real estate investment trust (REIT): Real estate investment trusts are like a mutual fund of real estate investments. Such trusts invest in a collection of properties (from shopping centers to apartment buildings). REITs trade on the major stock exchanges. If you want to invest in real estate while avoiding the hassles inherent in owning property, real estate investment trusts may be the right choice for you.

refinance: Refinance, or refi, is a fancy word for taking out a new mortgage loan (usually at a lower interest rate) to pay off an existing mortgage (generally at a higher interest rate). Refinancing is not automatic, nor is it guaranteed. Refinancing can also be a hassle and expensive. Weigh the costs and benefits of refinancing carefully before proceeding.

return on investment: The percentage of profit you make on an investment. If you put $1,000 into an investment and then one year later it's worth $1,100, you make a profit of $100. Your return on investment is the profit ($100) divided by the initial investment ($1,000) — in this case, 10 percent.

reverse mortgage: A reverse mortgage enables elderly homeowners, typically those who are low on cash, to tap into their home's equity without selling their home or moving from it. Specifically, a lending institution makes a check out to you each month, and you can use the check as you want. This money is really a loan against the value of your home, so it's tax-free when you receive it. The downside of these loans is that they deplete your equity in your estate, the fees and interest rates tend to be on the high side, and some require repayment within a certain number of years.

Russell 2000: An index that tracks the returns of 2,000 small-company U.S. stocks. Small-company stocks tend to be more volatile than large-company stocks. If you invest in small-company stocks or stock funds, this index is an appropriate benchmark to compare your stock's performance to.

Securities and Exchange Commission (SEC): The federal agency that administers U.S. securities laws and regulates and monitors investment companies, brokers, and financial advisors.

simplified employee pension individual retirement account (SEP-IRA): Like other retirement plans, a SEP-IRA allows your money to compound over the years without the parasitic effect of taxes. SEP-IRAs are relatively easy to set up, and they allow self-employed people to make annual contributions on a pretax basis.

Social Security: If you're retired or disabled, Social Security is a government safety net that can provide you with some income. The program is based on the idea that government is responsible for the social welfare of its citizens. Whether you agree with this notion or not, part of your paycheck goes to Social Security, and when you retire, you receive money from the program.

Standard & Poor's 500 Index: An index that measures the performance of 500 large-company U.S. stocks that account for about 80 percent of the total market value of all stocks traded in the United States. If you invest in larger-company stocks or stock funds, the S&P 500 Index is an appropriate benchmark to compare the performance of your investments to.

Standard & Poor's (S&P) ratings: Standard & Poor's rating service is one of two services that measure and rate the risks in buying a bond. The S&P ratings use the following grading system, listed from highest to lowest: AAA, AA, A, BBB, BB, B, CCC, CC, C. See also *Moody's ratings.*

stock: Shares of ownership in a company. When a company goes public, it issues shares of stock to the public (see also *initial public offering*). Many, but not all, stocks pay dividends — a distribution of a portion of the company's profits. In addition to dividends, you make money investing in stock via appreciation in the price of the stock, which normally results from growth in revenues and corporate profits. You can invest in stock by purchasing individual shares or by investing in a stock mutual fund that offers a diversified package of stocks.

term life insurance: If people are dependent on your income for their living expenses, you may need this insurance. Term life insurance functions simply: You determine how much protection you would like and then pay an annual premium based on that amount. Premium rates vary by age, health, and whether you smoke. Although much less touted by insurance salespeople than cash value insurance, it's the best life insurance out there for the vast majority of people.

Treasury bill: IOUs from the federal government that mature within a year. The other types of loans that investors can make to the federal government are Treasury notes, which mature within one to ten years, and Treasury bonds, which mature in more than ten years. The interest that these federal government bonds pay is free of state taxes, but it's federally taxable.

underwriting: The process an insurance company uses to evaluate a person's likelihood of filing a claim on a particular type of insurance policy. If significant problems are discovered, an insurer will often propose much higher rates or refuse to sell the insurance coverage.

will: A legal document that ensures that your wishes regarding your assets and the care of your minor children are heeded when you die.

zero-coupon bond: A bond that doesn't pay explicit interest during the term of the loan. Zero-coupon bonds are purchased at a discounted price relative to the principal value paid at maturity. Thus, the interest is implicit in the discount. These bonds do not offer a tax break, because the investor must pay taxes on the implicit interest that is paid when the bond matures.

Index

About the Author

Eric Tyson first became interested in money more than three decades ago. After his father was laid off during a recession and received some retirement money from his employer, Eric worked with his dad to make investing decisions with the money. A couple of years later, Eric won his high school's science fair with a project on what influences the stock market. Dr. Martin Zweig, who provided some guidance, awarded Eric a one-year subscription to the *Zweig Forecast,* a famous investment newsletter. Of course, Eric's mom and dad share some credit with Martin for Eric's victory.

After toiling away for a number of years as a management consultant to Fortune 500 financial-service firms, Eric finally figured out how to pursue his dream. He took his inside knowledge of the banking, investment, and insurance industries and committed himself to making personal financial management accessible to all.

Today, Eric is an internationally acclaimed and best-selling personal finance book author, syndicated columnist, and speaker. He has worked with and taught people from all financial situations, so he knows the financial concerns and questions of real folks just like you. Despite being handicapped by an MBA from the Stanford Graduate School of Business and a BS in Economics and Biology from Yale University, Eric remains a master of "keeping it simple."

An accomplished personal finance writer, his "Investor's Guide" syndicated column, distributed by King Features, is read by millions nationally, and he is an award-winning columnist. He is the author of five national best-selling financial books in the *For Dummies* series, on personal finance, investing, mutual funds, home buying (coauthor), and small business (coauthor). A prior edition of this book was awarded the Benjamin Franklin Award for best business book of the year.

Eric's work has been featured and quoted in hundreds of local and national publications, including *Newsweek, The Wall Street Journal,* the *Los Angeles Times,* the *Chicago Tribune, Forbes, Kiplinger's Personal Finance* magazine, *Parenting, Money, Family Money,* and *Bottom Line/Personal;* on NBC's *Today Show,* ABC, CNBC, FOX News, PBS *Nightly Business Report,* CNN, and on CBS national radio, NPR's *Sound Money,* Bloomberg Business Radio, and Business Radio Network.

Eric's website is www.erictyson.com.

Dedication

This book is hereby and irrevocably dedicated to my family and friends, as well as to my counseling clients and customers, who ultimately have taught me everything that I know about how to explain financial terms and strategies so that all of us may benefit.

Author's Acknowledgments

Being an entrepreneur involves endless challenges, and without the support and input of my good friends and mentors Peter Mazonson, Jim Collins, and my best friend and wife, Judy, I couldn't have accomplished what I have.

I hold many people accountable for my perverse and maniacal interest in figuring out the financial services industry and money matters, but most of the blame falls on my loving parents, Charles and Paulina, who taught me most of what I know that's been of use in the real world.

I'd also like to thank Michael Bloom, Chris Dominguez, Maggie McCall, David Ish, Paul Kozak, Chris Treadway, Sally St. Lawrence, K.T. Rabin, Will Hearst III, Ray Brown, Susan Wolf, Rich Caramella, Lisa Baker, Renn Vera, Maureen Taylor, Jerry Jacob, Robert Crum, Duc Nguyen, Maria Carmicino, and all the good folks at King Features for believing in and supporting my writing and teaching.

Many thanks to all the people who provided insightful comments on this edition and previous editions of this book, especially Bill Urban, Barton Francis, Mike van den Akker, Gretchen Morgenson, Craig Litman, Gerri Detweiler, Mark White, Alan Bush, Nancy Coolidge, and Chris Jensen.

And thanks to all the wonderful people at my publisher on the front line and behind the scenes, especially Stacy Kennedy and Vicki Adang.

Publisher's Acknowledgments

Acquisitions Editor: Stacy Kennedy

Development Editor: Victoria M. Adang

Copy Editor: Megan Knoll

Technical Editor: Kathleen Hartman, CFA, CFP

Production Editor: Shaik Siddique

Cover Image: ©DNY59/iStockphoto.com